T0212061

Computer Communications and Networks

Editor
A.J. Sammes
Centre for Forensic Computing
Cranfield University
Shrivenham Campus
Swindon, UK

The **Computer Communications and Networks** series is a range of textbooks, monographs and handbooks. It sets out to provide students, researchers, and non-specialists alike with a sure grounding in current knowledge, together with comprehensible access to the latest developments in computer communications and networking.

Emphasis is placed on clear and explanatory styles that support a tutorial approach, so that even the most complex of topics is presented in a lucid and intelligible manner.

More information about this series at http://www.springer.com/series/4198

Zaigham Mahmood
Editor

Continued Rise of the Cloud

Advances and Trends in Cloud Computing

 Springer

Editor
Zaigham Mahmood
University of Derby
United Kingdom

North West University
South Africa

ISSN 1617-7975
ISBN 978-1-4471-7252-9   ISBN 978-1-4471-6452-4 (eBook)
DOI 10.1007/978-1-4471-6452-4
Springer London Heidelberg New York Dordrecht

Springer is part of Springer Science+Business Media (www.springer.com)

To
Eyaad Imran Rashid Khan:
Happy 1ˢᵗ Birthday

Preface

Overview

Cloud Computing is an attractive paradigm that allows consumers to self-provision cloud-based resources, application services, development platforms, and virtualized infrastructures. The benefits associated with the cloud paradigm are enormous, and although there still are numerous inherent issues, the newness is disappearing and the hype is turning into reality. With time, cloud consumers are becoming more knowledgeable and beginning to dictate what they require. Cloud providers are learning from experiences of the past few years and beginning to provide what consumers actually need. Robust new technologies and methodologies are appearing and existing technologies are becoming mature and useable. Standards organizations are developing the necessary controls and beginning to enforce them for the benefit of all. Other agencies and cloud-related industries are also appearing to provide specialist services to support cloud providers as well as cloud consumers.

Alongside this, researchers and practitioners are coming up with strategies to resolve any issues that previously existed. New areas being investigated include: cloud security, interoperability, service level agreements, identity and access management, cloud governance, big data, data analytics, and cloud applications in other subject areas and different walks of life. New frameworks and methodologies are being developed and further refined for construction, deployment, and delivery of cloud services and environments to ensure that: the software developed is scalable and suitable for virtualized distributed environments; the deployment of platforms is secure and exhibits the in-built characteristic of multi-tenancy; and the new breed of security threats that now exist due to the shared trust boundaries are, at least, minimized.

This book, *Continued Rise of the Cloud: Advances and Trends in Cloud Computing,* aims to capture the state of the art and present discussion and guidance on the current advances and trends in the emerging cloud paradigm. In this text, 36 researchers and practitioners from around the world have presented latest research developments, current trends, state of the art reports, case studies, and suggestions for further development of the cloud computing paradigm.

Objectives

The aim of this text is to present the current research and future trends in the development and use of methodologies, frameworks, and the latest technologies relating to Cloud Computing. The key objectives include:

- Capturing the state of the art in cloud technologies, infrastructures, service delivery and deployment models
- Analyzing the relevant theoretical frameworks, practical approaches and methodologies currently in use
- Discussing the latest advances, current trends and future directions in the cloud computing paradigm
- Providing guidance and best practices for development of cloud-based services and infrastructures
- In general, advancing the understanding of the emerging new methodologies relevant to the cloud paradigm

Organization

There are 15 chapters in *Continued Rise of the Cloud: Advances and Trends in Cloud Computing*. These are organized in five parts, as follows:

- Part I: *Access Control Mechanisms and Cloud Security*. This section has a focus on security and access control mechanisms for cloud environments. There are three chapters. The first chapter looks into the security issues of GPU clouds. The other two contributions present access control strategies focusing on taxonomy, classification, impact and implications of such mechanisms.
- Part II: *Standards, Brokerage Services and Certification*. This comprises three chapters. The first chapter evaluates standards for Open Cloud environment whereas the second contribution analyzes the role of brokerage services in Inter-Cloud environments. The third chapter in this section discusses the role of certification for cloud adoption especially for small-to-medium sized enterprises.
- Part III: *Frameworks for ERP, Big Data and Interoperability*: There are three chapters in this part that focus on frameworks and strategies. The first chapter presents an evaluation of cloud ERP. The second contribution suggests a framework for the implementation of Big Data Science. The final chapter also presents a framework for Cloud Interoperability based on compliance and conformance.
- Part IV: *Management, Governance and Capability Assessment*. This section presents contributions on cloud governance. The first chapter surveys the existing elasticity management solutions. The second chapter presents a discussion on cloud management vs cloud governance. The last contribution of this part presents a framework for the development of a cloud service capability assessment model.
- Part V: *Applications in Education and Other Scenarios*. This is the last section of the book, comprising three chapters. The first two contributions present

cloud applications in higher education: the first chapter focusing on the use of knowledge-as-a-service in the provision of education and the other focusing on cloud-based e-learning for students with disabilities. The final contribution presents application scenarios suitable for cloud adoption.

Target Audiences

The current volume is a reference text aimed to support a number of potential audiences, including the following:

- *Enterprise architects, business analysts and software developers* who wish to adopt the newer approaches to developing and deploying cloud-based services and infrastructures.
- *IT infrastructure managers and business leaders* who need to have a clear understanding and knowledge of the current advances and trends relating to the newer methodologies and frameworks in the context of cloud paradigm.
- *Students and lecturers* of cloud computing who have an interest in further enhancing the knowledge of the cloud related technologies, mechanisms and frameworks.
- *Researchers* in this field who need to have the up to date knowledge of the current practice, mechanisms and frameworks relevant to the cloud paradigm to further develop the same.

Acknowledgements

The editor acknowledges the help and support of the following colleagues during the review and editing phases of this text:

- Dr. Asiq Anjum, University of Derby, Derby, UK
- Josip Lorincz, FESB-Split, University of Split, Croatia
- Prof. Saswati Mukherjee, Anna University, Chennai, India
- Dr. Mahmood Shah, University of Central Lancashire, Preston, UK
- Amro Najjar, École Nationale Supérieure des Mines de Saint Étienne, France
- Dr. S. Parthasarathy, Thiagarajar College of Engineering, Madurai, India
- Dr. Pethuru Raj, IBM Cloud Center of Excellence, Bangalore, India
- Dr. Muthu Ramachandran, Leeds Metropolitan University, Leeds, UK
- Dr. Lucio Agostinho Rocha, State University of Campinas, Brazil
- Dr. Saqib Saeed, Bahria University, Islamabad, Pakistan
- Aleksandar Milić, University of Belgrade, Serbia,
- Dr. Fareeha Zafar, GC University, Lahore, Pakistan

I would also like to thank the contributors to this book: 36 authors and co-authors, from academia as well as industry from around the world, who collectively submitted 15 chapters. Without their efforts in developing quality contributions, conforming to the guidelines and meeting often the strict deadlines, this text would not have been possible.

Grateful thanks are also due to the members of my family—Rehana, Zoya, Imran, Hanya and Ozair—for their continued support and encouragement.

Contents

Contributors

Alain Abran Department of Software Engineering and Information Technology, ETS—University of Quebec, Montreal, Canada

Alain April Department of Software Engineering and Information Technology, ETS—University of Quebec, Montreal, Canada

Rahul Bandopadhyaya InfosysLabs, Infosys Limited, Bangalore, Karnataka, India

Olivier Boissier École Nationale Supérieure des Mines de Saint Etienne, FAYOL-EMSE, LSTI, Saint-Etienne, France

Noel Carroll Department of Marketing and Management, University of Limerick, Limerick, Ireland

T. Chandrakumar Department of Computer Applications, Thiagarajar College of Engineering, Madurai, India

Alexandros Chrysikos School of Computing, University of Huddersfield, Huddersfiel, UK

José Carlos Martins Delgado Department of Computer Science and Engineering, Instituto Superior Técnico, Universidade de Lisboa, Porto Salvo, Portugal

Alea M. Fairchild Hogeschool Universiteit Brussel, Brussels, Belgium

Teodor-Florin Fortis Faculty of Mathematics and Informatics, West University of Timisoara, Timisoara, Romania
Research Institute e-Austria Timisoara, Timisoara, Romania

Yumna Ghazi School of Electrical Engineering and Computer Science (SEECS), National University of Sciences and Technology (NUST), Islamabad, Pakistan

Christophe Gravier Université Jean Monnet, Saint-Etienne, France

Umme Habiba School of Electrical Engineering and Computer Science (SEECS), National University of Sciences and Technology (NUST), Islamabad, Pakistan

Markus Helfert School of Computing, Dublin City University, Glasnevin, Ireland

Ayesha Kanwal School of Electrical Engineering and Computer Science (SEECS), National University of Sciences and Technology (NUST), Islamabad, Pakistan

Shyamala Loganathan Department of Information Science and Technology, CEG, Anna University, Chennai, India

Flavio Lombardi Springer Research Group, Maths and Physics Department, University of Roma Tre, Rome, Italy

Theo Lynn Irish Centre of Cloud Computing and Commerce (IC4), School of Business, Dublin City University, Glasnevin, Ireland

Abhishek Majumder Department of Computer Science & Engineering, Tripura University, Suryamaninagar, Tripura West, Tripura, India

Rahat Masood School of Electrical Engineering and Computer Science (SEECS), National University of Sciences and Technology (NUST), Islamabad, Pakistan

Aleksandar Milić Faculty of Organizational Sciences, University of Belgrade, Belgrade, Serbia

Miloš Milutinović Faculty of Organizational Sciences, University of Belgrade, Belgrade, Serbia

Rafia Mumtaz School of Electrical Engineering and Computer Science (SEECS), National University of Sciences and Technology (NUST), Islamabad, Pakistan

Saswati Mukherjee Department of Information Science and Technology, CEG, Anna University, Chennai, India

Victor Ion Munteanu Faculty of Mathematics and Informatics, West University of Timisoara, Timisoara, Romania
Research Institute e-Austria Timisoara, Timisoara, Romania

Vinay Rangaraju Nagavara InfosysLabs, Infosys Limited, Bangalore, Karnataka, India

Amro Najjar École Nationale Supérieure des Mines de Saint Etienne, FAYOL-EMSE, LSTI, Saint-Etienne, France

Suyel Namasudra Department of Computer Science & Engineering, Tripura University, Suryamaninagar, Tripura West, Tripura, India

Samir Nath Department of Computer Science & Engineering, Tripura University, Suryamaninagar, Tripura West, Tripura, India

S. Parthasarathy Department of Computer Applications, Thiagarajar College of Engineering, Madurai, India

Roberto Di Pietro Springer Research Group, Maths and Physics Department, University of Roma Tre, Rome, Italy

Xavier Serpaggi École Nationale Supérieure des Mines de Saint Etienne, FAYOL-EMSE, LSTI, Saint-Etienne, France

Muhammad Awais Shibli School of Electrical Engineering and Computer Science (SEECS), National University of Sciences and Technology (NUST), Islamabad, Pakistan

G M Siddesh Department of Information Science & Engineering, M S Ramaiah Institute of Technology, Bangalore, Karnataka, India

Konstantin Simić Faculty of Organizational Sciences, University of Belgrade, Belgrade, Serbia

K G Srinivasa Department of Computer Science & Engineering, M S Ramaiah Institute of Technology, Bangalore, Karnataka, India

Luis Eduardo Bautista Villalpando Department of Electronic Systems, Autonomous University of Aguascalientes, Aguascalientes, AGS, Mexico
Department of Software Engineering and Information Technology, ETS—University of Quebec, Montreal, Canada

Rupert Ward School of Computing, University of Huddersfield, Huddersfiel, UK

About the Editor

Zaigham Mahmood Professor Zaigham Mahmood is a published author of nine books, four of which are dedicated to Electronic Government and the other five focus on the subject of Cloud Computing including: 1) *Cloud Computing: Concepts, Technology & Architecture;* 2) *Cloud Computing: Methods and Practical Approaches;* 3) *Software Engineering Frameworks for the Cloud Computing Paradigm;* 4) *Cloud Computing for Enterprise Architectures;* and 5) this current volume. Additionally, he is developing three new books to appear later in 2014. He has also published more than 100 articles and book chapters and organized numerous conference tracks and workshops.

Professor Mahmood is the Editor-in-Chief of *Journal of E-Government Studies and Best Practices* as well as the Series Editor-in-Chief of the IGI book series on *E-Government and Digital Divide*. He is a Senior Technology Consultant at Debesis Education UK and Associate Lecturer (Research) at the University of Derby UK. He further holds positions as a Foreign Professor at NUST and IIUI Universities in Islamabad Pakistan and Professor Extraordinaire at the North West University Potchefstroom South Africa. Professor Mahmood is also a certified cloud computing instructor and a regular speaker at international conferences devoted to Cloud Computing and E-Government. His specialized areas of research include distributed computing, project management, and e-government.

Professor Mahmood can be reached at *z.mahmood@debesis.co.uk.*

Part I
Access Control Mechanisms and Cloud Security

Chapter 1
Towards a GPU Cloud: Benefits and Security Issues

Flavio Lombardi and Roberto Di Pietro

Abstract Graphics processing unit (GPU)-based clouds are gaining momentum, and GPU computing resources are starting to be offered as a cloud service, either as parallel computing power or accessible as a part of a leased virtual machine (VM). For this reason, the GPU cloud is one of the most promising cloud evolutions. However, the present cloud offerings do not effectively exploit GPU computing resources, which could well improve the performance and security of distributed computing systems. In fact, heterogeneous many-core hardware and especially GPUs, offer a potentially massive increase in computing power. They are also very power efficient, enabling significant price/performance improvements over traditional central processing units (CPUs). Unfortunately, and more importantly, GPU clouds do not guarantee an adequate level of security with respect to access control and isolation. There is no effective control on how parallel code (a.k.a. kernels) is actually executed on a GPU. In fact, the present GPU device drivers are entirely based on proprietary code and are optimized for performance rather than security. As a result, GPU architectures and hardware (HW)/software (SW) implementations are not yet considered to be mature enough for a GPU cloud. In particular, the level of security offered by this novel approach has yet to be fully investigated, as there is a limited security-related research that specifically targets GPU architectures. This chapter describes how GPU-as-a-Service can be exposed to misuse and to potential denial of service (DoS) and information leakage. It also shows how GPUs can be used as a security and integrity monitoring tool by the cloud, for instance, to provide timely integrity checking of VM code and data, allowing scalable management of the security of complex cloud computing infrastructures. Some further relevant security concerns are discussed in this chapter, including GPU service availability, access transparency and control.

Keywords Graphics processing unit · GPU · Isolation · Many-core architecture · Multithreading · Privacy · Security

F. Lombardi (✉) · R. Di Pietro
Springer Research Group, Maths and Physics Department,
University of Roma Tre, Rome, Italy
e-mail: lombardi@mat.uniroma3.it

R. Di Pietro
e-mail: dipietro@mat.uniroma3.it

Z. Mahmood (ed.), *Continued Rise of the Cloud,* Computer Communications
and Networks, DOI 10.1007/978-1-4471-6452-4_1,
© Springer-Verlag London 2014

1.1 Introduction

The most powerful computer clusters in the world are based on many-core central processing units (CPUs) and graphics processing units (GPUs) [38]. As an example, the supercomputer Tianhe-2 at the National Supercomputing Center in Guangzhou is among the world's top five fastest supercomputers, and it is based on Intel Xeon Phi processors to achieve 33.86 petaflops processing.

Cloud providers such as Amazon, SoftLayers and Zillians are also starting to offer access to GPU computing resources as transparently available computing power or as a part of a leased VM [36]. This allows each single GPU to be shared across different customers (i.e. GPU-as-a-Service). Heterogeneous many-core hardware (and GPUs in particular) has the potential to increase the available parallel computing power and efficiency, enabling significant price/performance improvements. Unfortunately, these new resources lack an adequate level of security with respect to access control and isolation, given that there is no effective control on how parallel code (a.k.a. kernels) is actually executed on a GPU. One of the main reasons is that GPU device drivers are based on proprietary code and focus on performance rather than security. As a consequence, GPU architectures and hardware (HW)/software (SW) implementations have been targeted by a number of attacks in the past [19]. However, just a few research papers specifically cover such complex architectures [8].

As one of the broader aims of cloud computing is to make *supercomputing* available to the masses; GPUs and in particular pay-per-use general purpose (GP) GPU computing is the next step in cloud evolution. GPGPU computing allows deploying massively parallel computing on regular commodity off-the-shelf (COTS) HW where the GPU can be used as a "streaming coprocessor". However, a GPU cloud can also enable Graphics-as-a-Service, as an example for dumb/cheap game consoles that offload computation to the "game" cloud to reduce HW costs and most importantly, to prevent game piracy. Further, dumb desktop terminals can completely offload both traditional and graphics computation to the GPU cloud. This will allow both a cost reduction and increased control/monitoring of employee and user activity.

Some of the reasons why companies should consider GPU cloud computing solutions include:

- Reduction in costs associated with delivering parallel computing intensive services for scientific and big data analysis tasks.
- Increased efficiency in power and space consumption, allows hosting a larger number of cores even on premise.
- Increased scalability of computing power, allowing enterprises to satisfactorily meet the timing needs of complex (possibly real-time) computations.

In the reminder of this chapter, we introduce the characteristics and benefits associated with a GPU cloud and discuss the technological background in Sect. 1.2. Then we survey existing work on many-core security in Sect. 1.3. GPU contribution to Ccloud security is discussed in Sect. 1.4 followed by GPU cloud issues and challenges in Sect. 1.5. The chapter provides an outlook on the future trends and related issues in Sect. 1.6 followed by Sect. 1.7 that highlights research directions. Final considerations and perspectives are given in the concluding section.

1.2 Technology Background

Present GPUs are classified as many-core since they feature a large number (100s to 1,000s) of computing cores that often run a single GPU kernel code at a time (executed in parallel by a subset of the available cores). This is the main rationale behind the need in GPU computing to allow as much concurrency as possible among different host processes using the GPU. In fact, if the number of running threads is smaller than the number of available cores, the exceeding capacity is wasted. Examples of this trend are Compute Unified Device Architecture (CUDA) stream and dynamic parallelism. Another relevant trend is that many-core SW architectures aim at rendering thread management as seamless and programming friendly as possible. This is also represented by SW approaches such as CUDA, OpenCL, JavaCL, Pocl and Aparapi. In the following sections, we briefly review specific GPU technologies and programming languages and highlight advantages and disadvantages of each of them. First, the present-day state-of-the-art HW technologies are surveyed. Then, we discuss the SW layers that allow accessing such resources from programs written in standard languages such as C and Java.

1.2.1 GPU HW Technologies

GPU HW manufacturers have come up with increasingly powerful GPU HW in the last few years. NVIDIA, being the first to enter the GPU market, features the most scientific-oriented HW that is now in the mainstream of scientific computing. AMD (previously ATI) is a leader in gaming GPUs that feature large number of flexible cores. Intel is the latest manufacturer to enter this expanding market. However, Intel is investing a large amount of resources to recover the gap by introducing novel integrated CPU + GPU architectures and high-end many-core accelerators such as the Xeon-Phi.

A survey of the most relevant technologies can be depicted as follows:

- NVIDIA KEPLER, FERMI, TESLA: They are the first and most widespread GPGPU computing platforms. They are also the first platforms to be offered as a service in the Ccloud, whether Pprivate, Ppublic or Hhybrid.
- AMD RADEON: This is the main NVIDIA competitor. While extremely popular for gaming, the support for GPGPU in AMD GPUs was introduced later than NVIDIAs. AMD is, however, the first CPU/GPU designer to have produced a hybrid CPU/GPU architecture, namely APU, standing for accelerated processing unit. This is the reason why AMD is presently the innovation leader in heterogeneous computing.

- Intel (HD4000 +): Intel was the last big firm to enter the GPGPU market. At present, its low-end GPUs offer worse performance than AMD and NVIDIA counterparts. However, standard support, low power consumption and Intel investments and marketing could improve widespread acceptance of these GPU platforms.
- Intel Xeon Phi. This is the high-end Intel accelerated coprocessor based on Intel Many Integrated Core Architecture (MIC), i.e. a multiprocessor computer architecture offering a many-core architecture based on simplified x86 technology. The cores of Intel MIC are based on a modified version of P54C design used in the original Pentium. The basis of the Intel MIC architecture is to leverage x86 legacy by creating an x86-compatible multiprocessor architecture that can utilize existing parallelization SW tools. MIC is based on a very wide (512 bits) single instruction multiple data (SIMD) x86 architecture, with a coherent multiprocessor cache connected to the memory via a ring bus.
- Single-chip cloud computer (SCCC): (SCCC) : This is an Intel research project, implementing x86 architecture on a multicore processor with a design mimicking a cloud computing computer data centre on a single chip with multiple independent cores. First SCCC is a 1 GHz, 48 Pentium-based cores per chip. The chip has two 24-dual-core tiles connected using a mesh network.

Some of the HW features mentioned above are common to all present many-core architectures. In particular, a hierarchical memory layout is usually adopted allowing:

- Fast access low-latency "register" memory feeding cores
- Some, slightly slower but shared memory areas where data can be passed to sibling GPU cores
- Some, much slower but globally shared memory where data can be shared with all other cores and/or with the CPU

Unfortunately, the terms that are used by different manufacturers to indicate such memory layers are often contradictory. The main reason is that each producer wants his own HW/SW stack to prevail over the other ones and as such he differentiates his offering on the model/SW side, as we will see in the following, starting with the SW side.

1.2.2 GPU SW Technologies

GPU HW technology required a leap forward of accompanying SW. Most relevant architectures are briefly introduced as follows:

- NVIDIA CUDA [28]: Apart from being the HW platform, CUDA is the name NVIDIA gave to the supporting SW development platform and programming language (CUDA C/C + + /FORTRAN). In this context, CUDA provides several facilities aimed at simplifying access to NVIDIA GPUs (CUDA is only compatible with NVIDIA GPUs). In particular, CUDA is composed of three parts: the device driver, the runtime and the compilation toolchain (i.e. compiler, debugger and other tools). The device driver handles the low-level interaction with the GPU (e.g. task scheduling); the runtime handles the requests coming from CUDA applications (e.g. dynamic memory allocation) and routes such requests to the device driver. The compilation toolchain allows compiling CUDA applications from source code into intermediate and executable binary code. A CUDA application is composed of host code (running on the CPU) and one or more kernels (running on the GPU). Kernels are special functions that are executed in parallel by N different CUDA threads (each thread running on a GPU core). The number of CUDA threads that executes a kernel for a given call can be specified at launch time. It is possible to group threads together in one or more blocks, depending on the specific task that has to be performed.

- OpenCL [17]: This is a standard parallel computing language specification (supporting C and C + +) proposed by Khronos group (composed of Apple, AMD, NVIDIA, Intel, etc.) and now quite mature at Version 1.2 (soon to be followed by Version 2.0). OpenCL code can run on AMD, Intel and NVIDIA GPUs as well as on CPU supporting the MMX instruction set (the vast majority of x86 CPUs). This renders the code more portable on heterogeneous clouds and cloud nodes albeit at the expense of a slight performance loss over similar CUDA code.

- AMD HSA [2]: (HSA is the AMD heterogeneous systems architecture) : AMD's latest approach to ease parallel computing on heterogeneous CPU + GPU platforms with the aim to optimize performance. This SW platform is still very young. It is at the heart of Playstation 4 and Xbox. One game consoles that feature 8 + CPU cores and 100s of GPU cores cooperatively operating over large data sets.

- JavaCL [5]: A Java language front end to OpenCL code. The main purpose of JavaCL is to allow calling kernel code from inside Java code. The approach allows leveraging fast kernel code, but it requires complex interactions with the Java virtual machine (JVM) that have to be handled by programmers.

- Aparapi [10]: Another Java language front end to OpenCL code. Aparapi abstracts away kernel code implementation and management. Aparapi allows seamless porting of legacy Java code, yet it presently affects performance. In fact, kernel code is generated automatically from Java code. This eases GPU code writing but does not allow low-level code optimizations.

- POCL [31]: Portable computing language (POCL) is an open-source portable version of the OpenCL language. Its goal is to become an efficient open-source implementation of the OpenCL 1.2 (and soon OpenCL 2.0) standard. In addition to producing a portable open-source OpenCL implementation, another major goal of this project is improving performance portability of OpenCL programs with compiler optimizations, reducing the need for target-dependent manual optimizations. At the core of POCL is the kernel compiler that consists of a set of low-level virtual machine (LLVM) passes used to statically transform kernels into work group functions with multiple work items, even in the presence of work group barriers. These functions are suitable for parallelization in multiple ways (e.g. SIMD, very long instruction words [VLIWs], superscalar).

The next section offers an overview of how these technologies have been used so far.

1.3 Related Work

Multicore and many-core computing has been the subject of much research in recent years [4, 22, 37]. Apart from multicore CPUs, specialized GPUs featuring hundreds of cores have been used for performance and security in cloud computing. So far various attempts to make use of advanced many-core HW for distributed computing have been proposed [17]. In particular, many cloud vendors such as Amazon, Nimbix, Peer1Hosting, Penguin computing and SoftLayer have begun offering GPU resources as cloud services in the form of:

- GPU cloud—shared VM with GPU offered to multiple tenants
- Hosted GPUs—VM and GPU in the cloud not concurrently shared with other tenants
- Hosted reality server—vertical software as a service (SaaS) offering for outsourced rendering/gaming
- High-performance computing (HPC)—hosting of scientific applications (e.g. data mining, numerical analysis) on distributed VMs with GPUs

All the above GPU resource-sharing approaches potentially leak data from one user to another, given that few attentions have been devoted to security aspects in the GPU design but performance was to be maximized.

Information leakage is a serious problem that affects a large variety of different scenarios. Many side-channel attacks on cache timing have been proposed in the literature [25]. Such attacks are relevant as they exploit the vulnerabilities of the underlying HW/SW architecture. In particular, Osvik et al. [29] managed to infer information about the internal state of a cipher by exploiting time-based side channels on the x86 CPU caches. It is worth noting that CPU caches are quite different from GPU-shared memory considered here because GPU-shared memory is addressable by the programmer [42], whilst CPU cache memory is not. In the GPU environment, the adversary does not need to exploit time-based side channels to infer information about the shared memory since the adversary can just read it. In fact, time-based attacks are much more common on the CPU than the GPU because timing facilities in the CPU are much more precise than the coarse-grained timing HW currently available on GPUs. As a result, exploiting time-based side channels of GPU cache memories does not seem feasible at present as it would require a much larger effort.

Rebeiro and Mukhopadhay [33] analyse a category of side-channel attacks known as profiled cache-timing attacks and develop a methodology that allows an adversary (capable of a limited number of side-channel measurements) to choose the best attack strategy. Kang and Moskowitz [14] propose a HW solution to minimize the capacity of covert timing channel across different levels of trust in multilevel security systems. Gorantla et al. [12] devise a technique to compromise the security provided by these HW components. As noted earlier, timing side-channels are very difficult to achieve, as reliable timing is quite hard to achieve on present GPU platforms. As regards security and isolation, they are not considered as important as performance. In fact, the trend towards increased resource sharing among cores is represented by Gupta et al. [13] that encourage resource sharing inside future multicores for performance, fault tolerance and customized processing. The vision suggests reducing isolation among cores for the sake of performance and reliability. However, this opens up new interesting information leakage opportunities. Oz et al. [30] propose and evaluate a new reliability metric called the thread vulnerability factor (TVF) that depends on thread code but also on the codes of sibling threads. Their evaluation shows that TVF values tend to increase as the number of cores increases, which means the system becomes more vulnerable as the core count rises. A preliminary work by Barenghi et al. [3] investigated side-channel attacks to GPUs using both power consumption and electromagnetic (EM) radiations. The proposed approach can be useful for GPU manufacturers to protect data against physical attacks. However, for attacks on work, the adversary does not need either physical access to the machine or root privileges. Protecting from an adversary with superuser (or root) administration privileges is extremely difficult, as shown in [23].

For what concerns malware-related leaks, trusted platform modules (TPM) [15] and remote attestation can provide an acceptable level of security by leveraging secure boot. However, vulnerabilities can also stem from perfectly "legal" code that accesses other parties' data, exploiting vulnerabilities inherently tied to the platform. Moreover, malicious HW such as Trojan circuitry can bypass SW TPM mechanisms and access sensitive information over the bus. In [7], an architecture is proposed based on an external guardian core that is required to approve each memory request. Even though the induced performance overhead is very high (60 %), their work is particularly interesting, as actual cooperation from the HW (i.e. from its manufacturers) would be beneficial for information leakage detection and prevention.

Unfortunately, due to the widespread commercial strategy to hide implementation details from competitors, manufacturers are reluctant on publishing the internals of their solutions. Documentation is mostly generic, marketing oriented and incomplete, which hinders the analysis of the information leakage problem on GPUs. As such, in the literature most of the available architectural information over existing HW is due to black-box analysis. In particular, Wong et al. [40] developed a micro-benchmark suite to measure architectural characteristics of CUDA GPUs. The analysis showed various undisclosed characteristics of the processing elements and the memory hierarchies and exposed undocumented features that affect both program performance and program correctness. CUBAR [4] used a similar approach to discover some of the undisclosed CUDA details. In particular, CUBAR showed that CUDA features a Harvard architecture on a von Neumann unified memory. Further, since the closed-source driver adopts the (deprecated) security through obscurity paradigm, inferring information from PCIe bus is possible as partially shown in [16]. The main contributions on GPU security in the literature are mainly related to the integrity of the platform and to the exploitation of driver vulnerabilities. GPU thread synchronization issues are introduced and discussed by Feng [9], whereas reliability of multicore computing is discussed in [37]. The analysis in these papers is aimed towards correctness, reliability and performance. We presently focus on actual GPU thread behaviour and related consequences on data access. In addition, vulnerabilities have been discovered in the past in the NVIDIA GPU driver [18, 19]. The device driver is a key component of the CUDA system and has kernel level access (via the NVIDIA kernel module). Therefore, vulnerabilities in the CUDA system can have nasty effects on the whole system and can lead to even further information leakage, due to root access capabilities. A limitation of the current GPU architecture is related to the fact that the operating system (OS) is completely excluded from the management of computations that have to be performed on the device. The first attempts in overcoming the limits of present GPU platforms aim at giving the OS kernel the ability to control the marshalling of the GPU tasks [35]. This way, the GPU can be seen as an independent computing system where the OS role is played by the GPU device driver; as a consequence, host-based memory protection mechanisms are actually ineffective to protect GPU memory.

1.4   GPUs for Cloud Security

The cloud can largely benefit from GPU computing both for data and computation (code) integrity. Another area where data parallel computing can help is that of improved privacy guarantees. GPU parallel computing power has especially been used for the following security-related tasks:

- Accelerated on-the-fly encryption and decryption if GPU cores are properly leveraged as in [1].
- Fast GPU signature scanning for malware detection, as reported by Pungila [32].
- Real-time integrity checking mechanisms for vital system components, especially through transparent virtualization as in [21, 22, 39].
- Data privacy protection techniques that are aimed to protect the privacy of the users whose data are stored in the cloud.

Among all the workloads that can benefit from the parallel computing power of GPUs, those based on the anonymity concept are relevant. In particular, in order to show one of the concrete contributions of GPU techniques for security, we will explore the GPU k-anonymity concept more in detail. In simple terms, k-anonymity-based techniques divide the data in clusters of k or more elements and substitute the elements in each k-cluster with a unique synthetic one, commonly the mean of the elements. The majority of the techniques that ensure k-anonymity have a computational time equal to O (n^2); so, they are quite slow as the number of elements increases. For this reason, GPU usage could be very helpful. Two sorts of fusion of these techniques with the use of parallel computing are proposed by Hong [41] who modified the k-means algorithm, parallelizing it using CUDA. Further, You Li [20] introduces an algorithm that analyses the k-anonymity approach and it is suitable for extracting tuples with the same values.

Table 1.1 Security issues of different CUDA compute capabilities

CC	Novelty with respect to previous version	Potential leakage due to
1.0	Original architecture	Memory isolation
1.1	Atomic operations on global memory	Memory isolation
1.2	Atomic operations on shared memory, 64-bit words, *warp*-vote functions	Memory isolation
1.3	Double precision floating point	Memory isolation
2.0	64-bit addressing, unified virtual addressing, GPUDirect [27]	Memory isolation, GPUDirect
2.1	Performance improvements	Memory isolation, GPUDirect
3.0	Enhanced stream parallelism and resource sharing	Memory isolation, GPUDirect
3.1	Dynamic parallelism, Hyper-Q	Memory isolation, GPUDirect, Hyper-Q isolation

Using GPUs can potentially be highly effective at accelerating the clustering operations of k-anonymity-based techniques; as with GPUs many security tools have been parallelized, improving their performance. However, as for other problems, GPUs can improve performance only linearly with respect to the number of computing cores. So, any GPU implementation approach would aim at maximizing parallelism within an algorithm in order to maximize the core usage. Apart from being a security tool for themselves, GPU resources are targeted by attacks, similar to other physical resources or even more, given they are novel technology and lack maturity, as we will show in the following section.

1.5   Security for Cloud GPUs

Notwithstanding the benefits that (GP) GPU cloud computing offers, there are numerous issues and challenges for organizations embracing this new paradigm. A number of major challenges can be summarized as follows:

- GPU data management (transferring and CPU-bus bottleneck)
- GPU process control and monitoring
- GPU information leakage and visualization security
- GPU service reliability and availability (and DoSes)

GPU cloud computing has a number of security issues, especially as regards isolation, denial of service (DoS) and information leakage, as summarized in Table 1.1 (see [8]). As regards information leakage in particular, co-location issues are particularly relevant, since, as shown by Ristenpart [34], it is possible to extract information from a target VM on the same physical machine. A number of issues with respect to GPU cloud include the following:

- Concerns over security with respect to information and data residing on a shared device such as a GPU.
- Concerns over availability and resources and performance guarantees of services.
- Concerns over data transmission to and from GPUs.

In particular, as depicted in Table 1.1, the CUDA platform has been affected by various information leakage issues over time. As a matter of fact, the strategy adopted by information technology (IT) companies to preserve trade secrets consists in not revealing details about the internals of their products. Although this is considered the best strategy from a commercial point of view, for what concerns security, this approach usually leads to unexpected breaches [26]. Despite this serious drawback, the security-through-obscurity approach has been embraced by the graphics technology companies as well. Many implementation details about GPU architectures are not publicly available. Once a program invokes a GPU function/subroutine, it partially loses control over its data. In particular, uncertainty increases when data are transferred to the GPU. If we only consider the public information about the architecture, it is unclear whether any of the security mechanisms that are usually enforced in the OS are maintained inside the GPU. The only implementation details available via official sources just focus on performance. For instance, NVIDIA describes in detail which are the suggested access patterns to global memory in order to achieve the highest throughput. In contrast, important implementation details about security features are simply omitted. For instance, there is no official information about the internals of CUDA memory management: it is undefined or uncertain whether memory is zeroed after releasing it.

Despite GPU success and pervasiveness, a thorough analysis of the GPU environment from a security point of view is missing. In fact, GPU and CPU architectures are quite different; therefore, they are subject to much different threats. Running a task on a GPU requires three main steps:

- A host application (i.e. a regular application running on the CPU) requests the execution of a kernel (i.e. a code to be run in parallel on the GPU).
- The host application copies the input data from host memory onto the GPU memory.
- The host application launches the kernel and gets back the results.

Data movements from the host application to the GPU are usually performed via the GPU proprietary device driver; once data enter the GPU, the device driver takes control over data. Therefore, the isolation between different kernels is mainly a responsibility of the GPU device driver. Since GPU memory stores a copy of the process-specific data, a flaw in the isolation mechanisms on the GPU would undermine the isolation mechanisms of the OS, causing information leakage vulnerability.

Any kind of information leakage from security-sensitive applications (e.g. encryption algorithms) would seriously hurt the success of the shared GPU computing model, where the term shared GPU indicates all those scenarios where the GPU resource is actually shared among different users, whether it is on a local server, on a cluster machine or on a GPU cloud [11]. The security implications on both GPU computing clusters and on remote GPU-as-a-Service offerings, such as those by companies like SoftLayers and Amazon, can be dramatic.

Due to its sensitiveness, we would expect the existence of secure and robust memory protection mechanisms on the GPU. Unfortunately, current GPU device drivers are aimed at performance rather than security and isolation. As a consequence, GPU architectures are not robust enough when it comes to security [19] and the adoption of GPUs effectively introduces new threats that require specific considerations. Further, in view of the GPU virtualization approach offered by the upcoming hypervisors (e.g. NVIDIA GRID [6]), information leakage risks will eventually increase.

Our working hypothesis as for the strategy adopted by GPU manufacturers is that they lean to trade-off security with performance. Indeed, one of the main objectives of the GPGPU framework is to speed-up computations in HPC. In such a scenario, the memory initialization after each kernel invocation could introduce a non-negligible overhead [44].

To make things worse, NVIDIA implemented memory isolation between different *cudaContexts* within its closed source driver. Such a choice can introduce vulnerabilities, as explained in the following example. Suppose that a host process Pi needs to perform some computation on a generic data structure S. The computation on S needs to be offloaded to the GPU for performance reasons. Hence, Pi allocates some host memory M_i to store S, then it reserves memory on the device M_j and copies M_i to M_j using GPU runtime primitives. From this moment onwards, the access control on M_j is not managed by the host OS and CPU. It becomes exclusive responsibility of the GPU driver, i.e. the driver takes the place of the OS. Due to their importance, the isolation mechanisms provided by an OS are usually subjected to a thorough review. The same is not true for GPU drivers. Hence, this architecture raises questions such as whether it is possible for a process Pj to circumvent the GPU virtual memory manager (VMM) and obtain unauthorized access to the GPU memory of process Pi.

Providing memory isolation in a GPU is probably far more complex than in traditional CPU architectures. In fact, CUDA threads may access data from multiple memory spaces during their execution. Although this separation allows improving the performance of the application, it also increases the complexity of access control mechanisms and makes it prone to security breaches. Multiple memory transfer across the data transmission bus for the global, constant and texture memory spaces is costly. As such, they are made persistent across kernel launches by the same application. This implies that the NVIDIA driver stores application-related *state information* in its data structures. As a matter of fact, in case of interleaved execution of CUDA kernels belonging to different host processes, the driver should prevent process Pj to perform unauthorized access to memory locations reserved to any process Pi. Indeed, this mechanism has a severe flaw and could leak information.

A solution that preserves isolation in memory spaces like global memory, that in recent boards reaches the size of several gigabytes, could be unsuitable for more constrained resources like shared memory or registers. Indeed, both shared memory and registers have peculiarities that raise the level of complexity for the memory isolation process. As an example, the shared memory is like a cache memory with the novel feature that it is directly usable by the developers. This is in contrast with more traditional architectures such as x86, where SW is usually cache oblivious. For what concerns registers, a feature that could taint memory isolation is that registers can be used to access global memory as well; in fact, a modern GPU feature (named *register spilling*) allows mapping a large number of kernel variables onto a small number of registers. When the GPU runs out of HW registers, it can transparently leverage global memory instead [8].

Even when making use of perfectly standard GPU code, information leakage flaws can be produced; the leakages can be induced by stressing the existing GPU memory allocation and de-allocation primitives that lead to exploiting three critical vulnerabilities. As for the first vulnerability, it is possible to induce information leakage on GPU shared memory. Further, an information leakage vulnerability based on GPU global memory, and another one based on GPU register spilling over global memory are possible. The impact of one of these leakages on a publicly available GPU implementation of a cryptographic protocol (e.g. the AES standard [24]) can be devastating. In particular, through the global memory vulnerability it is possible, for a non-legitimate user, to access both the plain text and the encryption key. However, countermeasures and alternative approaches can be devised to fix the highlighted vulnerabilities. In general, from the SW point of view, GPU code writers are required to pay particular attention to zeroing memory as much as possible at the end of kernel execution. Unfortunately, this is troublesome for a number of reasons:

- Most of the programmers do not have fine control over kernel code (e.g. if the kernel is the outcome of high-level programming environments such as JavaCL, JCUDA, OpenCL, etc).
- The parallel kernel programmer usually aims at/is asked to write the fastest possible code without devoting time to address security/isolation issues that might hamper performance.

As such, the best results can be obtained if security enhancements are performed at the driver/HW level. From the GPU platform point of view, the suggestions comprise:

- Memory management unit (MMU) memory protection mechanisms. The memory protection mechanisms have to be devised to prevent concurrent kernels from reading other kernels' memory.
- Monitoring and access control. GPU drivers should be modified in order to allow the OS to monitor usage and to control access to GPU resources; by doing so, anomalous resource usage and suspicious access patterns could be detected and/or prevented.

Some relevant contribution to GPU security is presented in [8], measuring the overhead those information-leakage-preventing approaches would have on a real GPU. In the following section, possible mitigations are discussed for specific information leakages due to the GPU memory architecture.

1.5.1 Shared Memory

As for the shared memory leakage, there is a vulnerability window that goes from kernel completion to host process completion. As such, the shared memory attack is ineffective once the host process terminates. A possible fix makes use of a memory-zeroing mechanism that is better executed inside the kernel. This is a sensible solution since shared memory is an on-chip area that cannot be directly addressed or copied by the host thread.

1.5.2 Global Memory

As regards the unauthorized access to global memory through GPU primitives, this can cause an information leakage. The natural fix would consist of zeroing memory before it is given to the requesting process. This way, when information is deleted the malicious process/party is unable to access such information. This approach should naturally be implemented inside the GPU runtime. In fact, in the memory-zeroing approach, threads run in parallel, each one zeroing its serial memory area. However, in general, zeroing does worsen performance in GPU [43], as these techniques force additional memory copies between a host and a device memory. Introducing an additional mechanism to perform smart memory zeroing would require an overall redesign of the graphics double data rate (GDDR) approach and as such it will most probably increase RAM cost. HW-based fast zeroing would probably be the most feasible and convenient solution. However, the inner details about low-level memory implementation for GPU cards are only known by their designers.

As regards the selective deletion of sensitive data, selectively zeroing specific memory areas is feasible in theory and it would potentially reduce unnecessary memory transfers between GPU and CPU, since most data would not have to be transferred again. A "smart" solution would probably be the addition of language extensions (source code tags) to mark the variables/memory areas that have to be zeroed due to the presence of sensitive data. On the one hand, this would require language/compiler modifications while, on the other hand, it would save some costly data transfers. However, this approach implies some caveats, as sensitive data when in transit between CPU and GPU cross various memory areas that are still potentially accessible. As such, for performance sake, sensitive areas should be as contiguous as possible.

1.5.3 Register Memory

When register usage exceeds HW capacity at runtime, register data content is spilled over global memory. Register allocation is handled at the lower level of the SW stack; hence, the leak is probably due to an implementation bug regarding the memory isolation modules. Therefore, fixing this information leakage at the application level is quite difficult. A much simpler workaround would be to implement the fix at the GPU driver level that, given the closed-source nature of the driver, at present only GPU designers can provide. In particular, the driver should prevent registers from spilling to locations in global memory that are reserved for host threads; second, the data content of the spilled registers has to be reset to zero when they are released.

1.5.4   GPU Reliability and Availability

A GPU cloud also introduces problems related to effective performance guarantees among competing GPU sessions. With respect to latter, a relevant issue with present GPUs is the possibility of causing a DoS by leveraging purely standard GPU code (kernel code). In fact, present implementations of both HW and SW do not consider pre-emption or at least use it as a last resort. As such ad hoc GPU code can be used to spawn a very large number of threads that take forever to complete and/or strongly interact with the host with large data exchanges. This can surely render the GPU unresponsive but can also render the CPU itself unresponsive, given that data transfers to the GPU also involve the CPU. It is possible to set a time-out in the driver to detect when the GPU becomes unresponsive. However, if the CPU is also heavily involved in the data exchange, the GPU time-out becomes ineffective as the CPU itself will get stuck, thus generating a complete system DoS.

As seen earlier, the GPU SW/HW platform has to further evolve over the years to become securer and easier to deal with. This latter point is one of the most important results, which has to be achieved, as will be discussed in the following section.

1.6   Visionary Thoughts for Practitioners

One of the trends for the future of GPU cloud is undoubtedly the ease of fruition of resources and services. This is one of the reasons for the increasing popularity of heterogeneous computing in IT and in the future clouds. In particular, a number of new technologies and approaches will pave the way for revolutionary advances in the use of GPU cloud:

- Heterogeneous Systems Architecture (HSA is one of the most promising trends in system architectures. HSA systems will have a large number of different processor cores, connected together and operating as peers, most probably offered as computing resources in clouds. The APU approach integrating GPU and CPU cores on the same die was not enough. In fact, GPGPU computing is complex to SW developers as CPU and GPUs have different memory addressing. As such a CPU program has to copy the data back and forth from the GPU memory. This wastes time and renders it difficult to make use of both CPU and GPU code on the same data concurrently. This also implies that the GPU cannot seamlessly access the same data structures the CPU is working on. In fact, CPU data structures make use of pointers; essentially, memory addresses that refer to other pieces of data. These structures cannot simply be copied into GPU memory, because CPU pointers refer to locations in CPU memory. Since GPU memory is separate, these locations have no meaning when referred to in CPU addressing. In order to fully leverage heterogeneous computing, full and fast shared access to memory has to be guaranteed. The HSA approach can be extended to other accelerators/coprocessors/heterogeneous cores.

- NVIDIA GPUDirect [27] provides the following features:
  - Accelerated communication with network and storage devices. Network and GPU device drivers can share "pinned" (page-locked) buffers, eliminating the need to make a redundant copy in CUDA host memory.
  - Peer-to-peer transfers between GPUs to high-speed direct memory access (DMA) transfers to copy data between the memories of two GPUs on the same system/PCIe bus.
  - Peer-to-peer memory access to optimize communication between GPUs using NUMA-style access to memory on other GPUs from within CUDA kernels.
  - Remote DMA (RDMA) collaboration among different GPUs requires fast and seamless transfer of possibly large amounts of data among different GPUs on the same physical machine or on the network towards remote GPUs.
- Heterogeneous uniform memory access (HUMA) will be introduced, as an example on future AMD Jaguar APUs and NVIDIA Maxwell GPUs. With HUMA, a cache-coherent system, the CPU and GPU share a single memory space. The GPU can directly access CPU memory addresses, allowing full sharing consistent view of in-memory data by GPU and CPU cores. Cache coherency renders the HW more complex, as SW errors only affect performance and not functionality and correctness. GPU cloud can enormously benefit from HUMA. In fact, the support for virtual addressing will render the distributed system approach feasible inside the cloud, provided that the OS will support it in the host. In fact, with HUMA, GPUs and CPUs use the same virtual addressing.
- Kernel launch parameters also depend on the available number of cores and their capabilities. Automatic parallelism (AP) renders the GPU as an active part of the choice and allows it to self-adjust and scale the number of concurrent threads of a single kernel.

The above technological/architectural trends and advances will increase scalability and shared access to GPU resources in the cloud. This will allow other components, such as ARM CPUs, cryptographic accelerators and field programmable gate arrays FPGAs, to cooperatively work on a large amount of data. As an example, future AMD Kaveri APUs will embed a small ARM core for creation of secure execution environments on the main CPU. This will allow clouds to seamlessly host complex heterogeneous serial/parallel algorithm implementations that would use specialized HW over cloud nodes. However, increasing the self-configurability and the shared-ness of GPU platforms in the cloud further exposes them to SW bugs, access and manipulation by malicious users and malware. In particular, the following ones are relevant:

- Shared access to memory and data structures will exacerbate the problems of concurrent programming to levels never reached before.

- Shared access to memory and to other resources (network card, bus) will render DoS attacks much easier to be launched and effective.
- Self-configuration will introduce new bugs and issues that are difficult to spot and debug.

Apart from specific technological points seen above, the research community will have to investigate, evaluate and deploy GPU approaches pervasively in order to overcome present limitations, as will be discussed in the following section.

1.7 Future Research Directions

Future GPU cloud trends indicate the provisioning of improved sharing of data among heterogeneous cores. This will give rise on the one hand to a potential performance increase, however difficult to achieve. On the other hand, this trend will increase the number of potential GPU isolation issues. As such, GPU-aware virtualization [36] and guaranteed core isolation will require further attention as well as integrity protection approaches that call for further investigation.

Among the future research direction that will deserve particular attention in the near future:

- *Convergence*: GPU cloud computing can be massively scalable and powerful, however, present differences both in HW architecture and SW driver behaviour do not enable to write long living portable code (one-code-to-rule-them-all) to perform adequately well in different scenarios. Novel approaches are needed for code portability and self-configuration/optimization. It is true that the last compilation step is performed on the fly, but novel, more effective, language-based approaches are needed to fully take advantage of the available computing cores and memory hierarchy.
- *Scalability*: Parallel computing resources scale quite well on a single host. However, distributed GPU computing is still in its infancy due to the current limitations in data sharing across remote GPUs. HUMA and RDMA, together with message passing interface (MPI), system services interface (SSI) and/or Hadoop-like approaches, will have to be investigated and combined in the future to allow larger general-purpose tasks to be offloaded to GPU cloud distributed computing. Even though specialized scientific computing solutions exist, they are high-cost specialized solutions that rarely scale to GPU as a service level.
- *Advanced core sharing*: Effective approaches to correctly share GPU resources among different tenants have to be devised and evaluated for GPU cloud to be successful. Present GPU sharing approaches exclusively/selectively associate the GPU with a given tenant or VM. The used approach is not secure as isolation is not natively supported by GPUs. GPU virtualization is the way forward, but it has to be supported at the HW and driver level. To this end, having the GPU driver integrated into advanced OS isolation mechanisms might help. As a matter of fact, novel open-source support for GPGPU computing over NVIDIA, AMD

and Intel GPUs is slowly maturing. Homogenizing the SW architecture under the OS supervision would help adopting advanced isolation approaches that would allow good performance over heterogeneous computing cores.

Let us now point the reader to some rules of the thumb or guidelines to follow when approaching a GPU cloud solution.

1.7.1 The Way Forward

Given the large savings and computing agility that GPU cloud environments offer, large enterprises are starting to experiment with heterogeneous multicore cloud computing into their existing IT systems and resources. For the newcomers aiming to consider leveraging to GPU cloud, the following best practices can be seen as a way forward:

- *Learn from others' mistakes*—adopting the practices that have been successful elsewhere
- *Evaluate technology internally*—start deploying on premise as much as possible
- *Avoid vendor lock in*—aim towards open standards as they eventually lead to reduced migration costs as the technology evolves
- *Ensure autonomy*—minimizing the development and maintenance activities
- *Ensure security of data*—noting that this is a major concern on any public/hybrid cloud

Following the above suggestions helps enterprises and users to reduce/limit the risks involved with adopting such new approaches and technologies. Provided the GPU cloud issues and caveats are taken into consideration, the benefits of using them are worth the effort, as summarized in the concluding section.

1.8 Conclusion

As shown above, a GPU cloud allows on-demand access to a large shared pool of powerful parallel computing resources. It helps providers in reducing costs and management responsibilities, and it allows increasing business agility. For these reasons, it will become even more a popular paradigm and increasingly more companies will shift toward GPU cloud computing. The advantages are clear and significant. Nevertheless, as in any new paradigm, there are also challenges and inherent issues. These ones relate to effective usage, scalability, data governance, process monitoring, infrastructure reliability, information security, data integrity and business continuity. The way forward for an enterprise is to plan a strategy for integrating existing resources into GPU cloud offerings, to have appropriate internal knowledge to correctly align the IT resources with applications, to follow best practices suggested by other organizations and strategically think in terms to moving towards distributed heterogeneous computing. Once, this is done, the enterprise is well on its way to fully benefit from the GPU cloud environment and gain the benefits that such novel cloud technologies offer.

As a final remark, it is very likely that GPU cloud computing will be the *next big thing* for cloud users and stakeholders.

References

1. Agosta G, Barenghi A, Santis FD, Biagio AD, Pelosi G (2009) Fast disk encryption through GPGPU acceleration. In: Proceedings of the 2009 international conference on parallel and distributed computing, applications and technologies. Washington, DC, IEEE Computer Society, pp 102–109
2. AMD (2012) HSA—what is heterogeneous system architecture. http://developer.amd.com/resources/heterogeneous-computing/what-is-heterogeneous-system-architecture-hsa/. Accessed 06 May 2014
3. Barenghi A, Pelosi G, Teglia Y (2011) Information leakage discovery techniques to enhance secure chip design. In: Ardagna C, Zhou J (eds) Information security theory and practice. Security and privacy of mobile devices in wireless communication, vol 6633. Springer, Berlin, pp 128–143
4. Black N, Rodzik J (2010) My other computer is your GPU: System-centric CUDA threat modeling with CUBAR. http://dank.qemfd.net/dankwiki/images/d/d2/Cubar2010.pdf. Accessed 12 May 2014
5. Chafik O (2011) JavaCL OpenCL bindings for Java. http://code.google.com/p/javacl/. Accessed 06 May 2014
6. Citrix (2013) NVIDIA. NVIDIA Grid
7. Das A, Memik G, Zambreno J, Choudhary A (2010) Detecting/preventing information leakage on the memory bus due to malicious hardware. In: Proceedings of the conference on design, automation and test in Europe. European Design and Automation Association, pp 861–866
8. Di Pietro R, Lombardi F, Villani A (2013) CUDA leaks: information leakage in GPU architectures. arXiv:1305.7383
9. Feng W-C, Xiao S (2010) To GPU synchronize or not GPU synchronize? In: Proceedings of 2010 IEEE international symposium on circuits and systems (ISCAS), pp 3801–3804
10. Frost G (2011) Aparapi a parallel API. Tratto da https://code.google.com/p/aparapi/. Accessed 06 May 2014
11. Georgescu S, Chow P (2011) GPU accelerated CAE using open solvers and the cloud. SIGARCH Comput Archit News 39(4):14–19
12. Gorantla S, Kadloor S, Kiyavash N, Coleman T, Moskowitz IS, Kang MH (2012) Characterizing the efficacy of the (NRL) network pump in mitigating covert timing channels. Inf Forensics Secur IEEE Trans 7(1):64–75
13. Gupta S, Feng S, Ansari A, Mahlke S (2010) Erasing core boundaries for robust and configurable performance. In: 43rd annual IEEE/ACM international symposium on Microarchitecture (MICRO), Atlanta, Georgia, pp 325–336
14. Kang MH, Moskowitz IS (1993) A pump for rapid, reliable, secure communication. In: Proceedings of the 1st ACM conference on computer and communication security, fairfax, 3–5 Nov 1993, pp 119–129
15. Kanuparthi A, Zahran M, Karri R (2012) Architecture support for dynamic integrity checking. Inf Forensics Secur IEEE Trans 7(1):321–332
16. Kato S, McThrow M, Maltzahn C, Brandt S (2012) Gdev: First-class GPU resource management in the operating system. In: Proceedings of the 2012 USENIX conference on Annual Technical Conference (USENIX ATC'12). USENIX Association, Berkeley, CA, USA, p 37

17. Kim J, Kim H, Lee JH, Lee J (2011) Achieving a single compute device image in OpenCL for multiple GPUs. In: Proceedings of the 16th ACM symposium on principles and practice of parallel programming. New York, NY, USA, ACM, pp 277–288
18. Larabel M (2011) NVIDIA 295.40 closes high-risk security flaw. http://www.phoronix.com/scan.php?page=news_item&px=MTA4NTk. Accessed 06 May 2014
19. Larabel M (2012) NVIDIA root access. http://www.phoronix.com/scan.php?page=news_item&px=MTE1MTk. Accessed 06 May 2014
20. Li Y, Zhao K, Chu X, Liu J (2010) Speeding up K-means algorithm by GPUs. In: 10th IEEE international conference on computer and information technology (CIT '10), Bradford, UK
21. Lombardi F, Di Pietro R (2009) KvmSec: a security extension for Linux kernel virtual machines. In: Proceedings of the 2009 ACM symposium on applied computing. New York, NY, USA, ACM, pp 2029–2034
22. Lombardi F, Di Pietro R (2010) CUDACS: securing the cloud with CUDA-enabled secure virtualization. In: Proceedings of the 12th international conference on Information and communications security. Berlin, Heidelberg, Springer-Verlag, pp 92–106
23. Lombardi F, Di Pietro R (2011) Secure virtualization for cloud computing. J Netw Comput Appl 34(4):1113–1122
24. Mei C, Jiang H, Jenness J (2010) CUDA-based AES parallelization with fine-tuned GPU memory utilization. In: 2010 IEEE international symposium on parallel distributed processing, workshops and Phd forum (IPDPSW), pp 1–7
25. Menichelli F, Menicocci R, Olivieri M, Trifiletti A (2008) High-level side-channel attack modeling and simulation for security-critical systems on chips. IEEE Trans Dependable Secur Comput 5(3):164–176
26. Mercuri RT, Neumann PG (2003) Security by obscurity. Commun ACM 46(11):160–166
27. NVIDIA GPUDirect Cuda Toolkit Documentation. http://docs.nvidia.com/cuda/gpudirect-rdma/index.htm. Accessed 12 May 2014
28. NVIDIA (2013) CUDA developers guide. http://docs.nvidia.com/cuda. Accessed 12 May 2014
29. Osvik D, Shamir A, Tromer E (2006) Cache attacks and countermeasures: the case of AES. In: Pointcheval D (ed) Topics in cryptology CT-RSA 2006, vol 3860. Springer, Berlin, pp 1–20
30. Oz I, Topcuoglu HR, Kandemir M, Tosun O (2012) Thread vulnerability in parallel applications. J Parallel Distrib Comput 72(10):1171–1185
31. POCL (2011) POCL—portable computing language. http://pocl.sourceforge.net/. Accessed 06 May 2014
32. Pungila C, Negru V (2012). A highly-efficient memory-compression approach for GPU-accelerated virus signature matching. In: Gollmann D, Freiling FC (eds) Information security. Springer, Berlin, pp 354–369
33. Rebeiro C, Mukhopadhay D (2012) Boosting profiled cache timing attacks with A priori analysis. Inf Forensics Secur IEEE Trans 7(6):1900–1905
34. Ristenpart T (2009) Hey, you, get off of my cloud: exploring information leakage in third-party compute Clouds. In: Proceedings of the 16th ACM conference on computer and communications security, CCS '09, New York, NY, pp 199–212
35. Rossbach CJ, Currey J, Silberstein M, Ray B, Witchel E (2011) PTask: operating system abstractions to manage GPUs as compute devices. In: Proceedings of the twenty-third ACM symposium on operating systems principles. New York, NY, USA, ACM, pp 233–248
36. Sengupta D, Belapure R, Schwan K (2013) Multi-tenancy on GPGPU-based servers. In: Proceedings of the 7th international workshop on virtualization technologies in distributed computing. New York, NY, USA, ACM, pp 3–10
37. Shye A, Blomstedt J, Moseley T, Reddi VJ, Connors DA (2009) PLR: a software approach to transient fault tolerance for multicore architectures. IEEE Trans Dependable Secur Comput 6(2):135–148
38. Tsai T-C, Hsieh C-W, Chou C-Y, Cheng Y-F, Kuo S-H (2012) NCHC's Formosa V GPU cluster enters the TOP500 ranking. In: Proceedings of the 2012 IEEE 4th international conference on cloud computing technology and science (CloudCom). Washington, DC, USA, IEEE Computer Society, pp 622–624

39. Wang Z, Wu C, Grace M, Jiang X (2012) Isolating commodity hosted hypervisors with Hyper-Lock. In: Proceedings of the 7th ACM European conference on computer systems. New York, NY, USA, ACM, pp 127–140

40. Wong H, Papadopoulou M-M, Sadooghi-Alvandi M, Moshovos A (2010) Demystifying GPU microarchitecture through microbenchmarking. In: IEEE international symposium on performance analysis of systems software (ISPASS), pp 235–246

41. Wu J, Hong B (2011) An efficient k-means algorithm on CUDA. In: 25th IEEE international symposium on parallel and distributed processing workshops and PhD forum (IPDPSW '11), Anchorage, Alaska, pp 1740–1749

42. Xu W, Zhang H, Jiao S, Wang D, Song F, Liu Z (2012) Optimizing sparse matrix vector multiplication using cache blocking method on Fermi GPU. In: Proceedings of the 2012 13th ACIS international conference on software engineering, artificial intelligence, networking and parallel/distributed computing. Washington, DC, USA, IEEE Computer Society, pp 231–235

43. Yang X, Blackburn SM, Frampton D, Sartor JB, McKinley KS (2011) Why nothing matters: the impact of zeroing. SIGPLAN Not 46(10):307–324

44. Yang Y, Xiang P, Kong J, Mantor M, Zhou H (2012) A unified optimizing compiler framework for different GPGPU architectures. ACM Trans Archit Code Optim 9(2):1–33

Chapter 2
Taxonomy and Classification of Access Control Models for Cloud Environments

Abhishek Majumder, Suyel Namasudra and Samir Nath

Abstract Cloud computing is an emerging and highly attractive technology due to its inherent efficiency, cost-effectiveness, flexibility, scalability and pay-per-use characteristics. But alongside these advantages, many new problems have also surfaced and some of these issues have become a cause of grave concern. One of the existing problems that have become critical in the cloud environment is the issue of access control and security. Access control refers to a policy that authenticates a user and permits the authorized user to access data and other resources of cloud-based systems. In access control, there are several restrictions and rules that need to be followed by the users before they can access any kind of data or resource from the cloud-based servers. In this context, there are many access control models suggested by researchers that currently exist. In this chapter, a brief discussion of the various access control models has been presented. Moreover, the taxonomy of access control schemes has also been introduced. Finally, based on the analysis of the mechanisms adapted therein, the access control models are classified into different classes of the proposed taxonomy.

Keywords Access control models · Taxonomy · Classification · Cloud environment · Identity-based · Non identity-based · Centralized · Collaborative

2.1 Introduction

Cloud computing is an emerging computing paradigm that relies on sharing of resources rather than having local servers or personal devices to handle applications and data. Cloud computing is a synonym for distributed computing over a network.

A. Majumder (✉) · S. Namasudra · S. Nath
Department of Computer Science & Engineering, Tripura University, Suryamaninagar,
Tripura West, Tripura, India
e-mail: abhi2012@gmail.com

S. Namasudra
e-mail: suyelnamasudra@gmail.com

S. Nath
e-mail: nathsamcse@gmail.com

Z. Mahmood (ed.), *Continued Rise of the Cloud,* Computer Communications and Networks, DOI 10.1007/978-1-4471-6452-4_2,
© Springer-Verlag London 2014

The term *cloud* in cloud computing can be defined as a combination of hardware, networks, storage, services and interfaces to deliver aspects of computing *resources*. A cloud-based service includes the delivery of software, infrastructure and storage over the Internet, based on user requirements and demands. These services are provided *on demand*, as and when *consumers* require.

Cloud computing is a rapidly developing area in information technology (IT). In fact, it has revolutionized the software industry. Because of the current growth of IT and database (db) system, there is an increased need for confidentiality and privacy protection. Access control has been considered as a major issue in the information security community. Through access control, the system restricts unauthorized users to access resources and guarantees confidentiality and integrity of its resources and valid consumers. But traditional access control models (ACMs) primarily consider static authorization decisions based on the subject's permissions on target objects.

The goal of cloud computing is to realize "the network as a high-performance computer". It allows the users to have all their data in the cloud and get all kinds of services from the cloud using their Internet terminal equipment. In this way, all users become capable of running processes and storing data in the cloud. There are three requirements for cloud services:

- Cloud service provider (CSP) must be able to specify access control policies for users to access data and other resources.
- An organization must be able to enforce more access control policies on its user requests for resources of the organization. When an organization wants to use a cloud service, it must map its policies on access control policies of the CSP. This mapping of policies may be violated. Therefore, an organization can prevent violation of its policies by enforcing more policies on access requests.
- Data owner (DO) must be able to offer cloud services to consumer.

Cloud services are accessed using some kind of network, e.g. Internet. But the Internet has many security issues because of its vulnerabilities to hackers and other threats. Therefore, cloud services will face a larger number of security issues. Many security policies and technologies for web services are already available. These techniques can have significant impact on resolving security issues of cloud service.

Of all the security issues, access control is an important issue. Traditional ACMs cannot be applied directly in cloud environment because of their static nature. A large amount of resource, huge number of dynamic users, dynamic and flexible constructions are some important characteristics of cloud services which should be considered in ACMsaccess control models for cloud computing. Each autonomous domain in a cloud system has its own security policy. So it is important that the access control be flexible enough to have these multiple policies in multiple domains. Many access control scheme for cloud computing have already been proposed. In this chapter, a detailed discussion on various access control schemes has been presented. Moreover, the taxonomy of these ACMs has been proposed.

The organization of the chapter is as follows. Section 2.2 provides an overview of the concept of access control and the necessity of access control models ACMs. Section 2.3 provides an in-depth analysis of the various existing ACMs. In Sect. 2.4, the importance of taxonomy of ACMs has been discussed and Sect. 2.5 introduces the taxonomy of ACMs. Finally, the chapter concludes with Sect. 2.6.

2.2 Access Control

Access control [19] is generally a mechanism or procedure that allows, denies or restricts user access to a system. It is the process of deciding who can use specific system, resources and applications. An ACM is defined as a set of criteria a system administrator utilizes to define the system user's right. This ensures that only authorized users can access the data, and it also monitors and records all attempts made to access a system. It is a very important component of cloud security.

Nowadays, a large number of distributed open systems are being developed. These systems are like virtual organizations. The relationship between users and resources is dynamic. In these systems, users and DOs are not in the same security domain. Users are normally identified by their attributes or characteristics and not by their predefined identities. In such cases, the traditional ACMs are not very much suitable and therefore many access control schemes have been developed. All ACMs rely on authentication of the user by the site at the time of request. Sometimes they are labelled as authentication-based access control.

ACM provides security to the resources or data by controlling access to the resources and the system itself. However, access control is more than just controlling which users can access a computing or a network resource. In addition, access control manages users, files and other resources. It controls user's privileges to files or resources or data. In ACM, various steps like identification, authentication, authorization and accountability are performed before a user actually accesses the resources or the original objects.

2.2.1 Issues and Challenges

Access control is a useful mechanism, but it has a number of issues that need to be addressed:

- DO must always be online for providing access right (AR) and authorization certificate.
- When a user makes a request for accessing data, the CSP must check the whole system for providing data, therefore the searching cost gradually increases.
- Because of searching the whole system for providing data, accessing time becomes higher.
- When a user wants to access data from an outside server, the user faces a lot of problems because he/she must be registered outside his/her domain.
- Data loss is a very serious problem in cloud computing while accessing data. If the vendor closes due to financial or legal problems, there will be a loss of data for the customers. The customers would not be able to access those data.

- Granularity (fine grained) is one of the most important issues in cloud computing while accessing data.
- When data are on a cloud, anyone can access it from any location. Access control algorithms should differentiate between a sensitive data and a common data, otherwise anyone can access sensitive data.
- There is a high possibility that the data can be stolen by a malicious user.
- The customer does not know where the data are located in cloud server. The vendor does not reveal where all the data are stored. Data may be located anywhere in the world, which may create legal problems over the access of the data.

2.3   Access Control Models

This section presents a detailed discussion and analysis of different ACMs.

2.3.1   Mandatory Access Control Model

Mandatory access control (MAC) model [2] can be defined as a means of restricting access to objects based on the sensitivity of the information contained in it and the authorization of subjects. Whenever a subject attempts to access an object, an authorization rule enforced by the administrator examines the security attributes and decides whether the access to the object can be given. MAC is the most important ACM amongst the available ACMs. It takes a hierarchical procedure to control access of resources or data. MAC focuses on controlling disclosure of information by assigning security levels to objects and subjects, limiting access across security levels and consolidating all classification and access controls into the system. It is relatively straightforward and is considered as a good model for commercial systems that operate in hostile environments where the risk of attack is very high. In MAC, the policy set-up and management are performed in a secured network and are limited to system administrators. It is a type of access control where the central administrator controls all the tasks. The administrator defines the usage and access policy, which cannot be modified by the user. The policy defines who can have access to which data or resources. MAC can be used in the military security [8] for preserving information confidentiality.

The main advantage of MAC is its simplicity. It also provides higher security because only a system administrator can access or alter controls. Moreover, MAC facilitates the use of multilevel security [8]. The disadvantage of MAC is that the central administrator is the single point of failure. It does not ensure fine-grained least privilege, dynamic separation of duty and validation of trusted components. Moreover, in MAC, users need permission from the central administrator for each and every activity. MAC model is difficult and expensive to implement due to its reliance on trusted components and the necessity for applications.

2.3.2 Discretionary Access Control Model

Discretionary access control (DAC) restricts access of objects within the group of users to which they belong. A user or subject, who is given a discretionary access to a resource, is capable of passing the access to another subject. This model adopts the concept of object ownership. Here, the owner of the object is authorized to grant its access permissions to other subjects. In DAC [2], separate rules for each or a group of user are defined. Access to system resource is controlled by the operating system [31].

DAC allows each user or a group of user to access the user's or the group's data. It is a type of access control in which a user has complete control over all the programs the user owns and executes. The user can also give permission to other user to use the user-owned files or program. DAC is a default access control mechanism for almost all operating systems. It is very flexible and widely used in commercial and government sectors. In DAC, an access control list (ACL) is maintained. ACL is a tabular representation of subjects mapped to their individual ARs over the objects. It is effective but not much time efficient, with less number of subjects. In DAC, the system knows who the user of a process is but does not know what rights the user has over the objects of the system. Therefore, for creation and maintenance of ACL, the system either performs a right lookup on each object access or somehow maintains the active ARs of the subject. Because of this right management issue, modification of multi-object rights for individual users becomes difficult.

The main advantage of this model is that a user can give their ARs to another user belonging to same group. DAC focuses on fine-grained access control of objects through the access control matrices [21] and object-level permission modes. The main problem is that ACL does not scale well on systems with large numbers of subjects and objects. Maintenance of the system and verification of security principles are extremely difficult in DAC because the users control ARs of their own objects. Lack of constraints on copying of information from one file to another makes it difficult to maintain safety polices.

2.3.3 Attribute-Based Access Control Model

In attribute-based access control (ABAC) [2], the access control decisions are taken based on the attribute of the requestor, the service, the resources and the environment. Here, access is granted on the basis of attributes that the user could prove to have such as date of birth or social security number (SSN). But setting these attributes is very difficult. The ABAC system is composed of three parties, namely DO, data consumers, cloud server and third-party auditor, if necessary. To access the data files, shared by DO, data consumers or users can download the data files of their interest from the cloud server. After downloading, consumers decrypt the file. Neither the DO nor the user will be online all the time. They come online if necessary. The ABAC provides policy for sensitive data. It allows an organization to maintain its autonomy while collaborating efficiently. The ABAC is composed of four entities:

Fig. 2.1 Health-care scenario

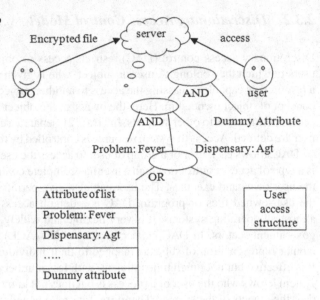

- Requestor: It sends request to the cloud and invokes action on the service
- Service: In this section, software and hardware provide services
- Resource: Resources are shared among the cloud services. When a user sends a request for a particular data or resource which is not present in that cloud service, the resource will be gathered from another service
- Environment: It contains information that might be useful for taking the access decision such as date and time

Each data file can be associated with a set of attributes which are meaningful in the area of interest [19]. The access structure of each user is defined as a unique logical expression of these attributes to reflect the scope of user AR over data files. As the logical expression can represent any desired data file set, fine graininess of data access control is achieved [41]. To enforce this access structure, a public key component for each attribute is defined. Data files are encrypted using a public key component corresponding to their attributes. User secret keys are defined to reflect their access structures so that a user can easily decrypt a cipher text if and only if the data file attributes satisfy the user's access structure.

If this mechanism is deployed alone, there will be heavy computational overhead. Specifically, problem will arise when a user wants to revoke from the server, which requires the DO to re-encrypt all the data files accessible to the leaving user. To resolve this problem and make the mechanism suitable for cloud computing, proxy re-encryption is combined with key policy-attribute-based encryption. This enables the DO to delegate most of the computation-intensive operations to cloud servers without disclosing the file contents. Here, data confidentiality is achieved because cloud servers cannot read the plain text of the DO.

Figure 2.1 presents a scenario of a health-care centre. For each data file, the DO assigns a set of meaningful attributes. Different data file can have a common set of attributes. Cloud servers keep an attributes history list (AHL) which keeps the version evolution history of each attribute. There are proxy re-encryption [1] keys. In the ABAC, there is a dummy attribute (Att_D). The main duty of the Att_D is key management. The Att_D is required in every data file's attribute set and will never be updated in future. The access structure of each user is implemented by an access tree. For key management, the root node must be an AND gate, and one child of that root node is a leaf node which is associated with the Att_D. The Att_D is not attached to any other node.

The ABAC allows fine grandness of data access without disclosing the data contents in a cloud server. But the ABAC does not provide data confidentiality and scalability simultaneously.

2.3.4 Role-Based Access Control Model

The role-based access control (RBAC) [14] determines the user access to the system by the job role. The role of a user is assigned based on the latest privileges concept. It is defined by the minimum amount of permissions and functionalities that are necessary for the job to be done. Permissions can be added or deleted if the role changes. Access control decisions are often determined by the individual roles users play as part of an organization. This includes the specification of duties, responsibilities and qualifications. For example, the roles in a bank include user, loan officer and accountant. Roles can also be applied to military system. Analyst, situation analyst and traffic analyst are common roles in a tactical system. The RBAC is based on access control decisions which allow user to access data within the organization. ARs are grouped by role name and access to resources is restricted to users who have been authorized to assume the associated role. The users cannot pass access permissions to the other users. For example, if an RBAC system is used in a hospital, each person who is allowed to access the hospital's network has a predefined role (doctors, nurse, lab technician, etc). RBAC is used in many applications [3, 13, 22] such as mobile application and naming and grouping of a large db. All roles are group of transactions. A transaction can be thought of as a transformation procedure [10] plus a set of associated data items. Each role has an associated set of individual members. The RBAC provides a many-to-many relationships between individual users and ARs.

Figure 2.2 shows the relationship between individual users, roles/groups or transformation procedures and system objects. The RBAC can be described in terms of sets and relations. These sets and relationships are as follows:

- For each subject an active role is assigned which is currently used by the subject. It is denoted as:
  AR (s = subject) = [the active role for subject s].
- Each subject may be authorized to perform one or more roles. It is denoted as
  RA (s = subject) = [authorized roles for subject s].

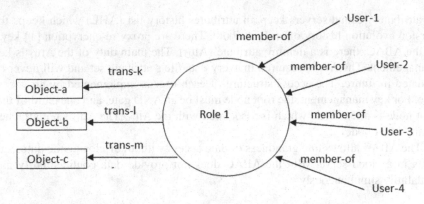

Fig. 2.2 How to assign a role for a particular user

- Each role may be authorized to perform one or more transactions.
  TA (r = role) = [transaction authorized for one role].
- Subjects may execute transactions. The execution operation will be performed if a subject can execute transaction at the current time otherwise execution operation will not be performed.
  exec (s = subject, t = tran) = [true if and only if subject s can execute transaction t].

In RBAC, for accessing the data or communicating with the cloud server, the users should give their identity and then must satisfy the following three basic rules:

- Role assignment: A subject can execute a transaction only if the subject has selected or been assigned a role, i.e. $\forall$s = subject, t = tran, (exec (s, t) $\Longrightarrow$ AR(s) $\neq$ Null).
- Role authorization: A subject's role must be authorized for the subject, i.e. $\forall$s: subject (AR (s) $\subseteq$ RA (s)). With the previous rule, this rule ensures that users can take one role for which they are authorized.
- Transaction authorization: A subject can execute a transaction only if the transaction is authorized for the subject's active role, i.e. $\forall$s = subject, t = tran, (exec (s, t) $\Longrightarrow$ t $\in$ TA(AR (s))).

With the rule of role assignment and role authorization, transaction authorization ensures that the users can execute only a transaction for which they are authorized. Because the condition is "only if", the transaction authorization rule allows additional restriction on a transaction [14]. That is, the rule does not guarantee a transaction to be executed just because it is in TA (AR (s)). This would require a fourth rule to enforce control over the modes. Fourth rule is:

- $\forall$ s: subject, t: tran, o: object, (exec(s, t) $\Longrightarrow$ access(AR(s), t, o, x)), where x is a mode of operation like read, write, append, etc.

RBAC is a non-DAC mechanism which allows and promotes central administration of an organizational-specific security policy [28]. That means administrative task consists of granting and revoking membership to the set of specified roles within the

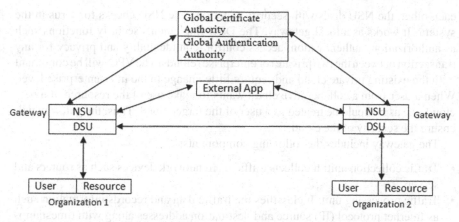

Fig. 2.3 The VPC gateway connections

system. For example, when a new user enters the organization, administration simply grants membership to an existing role. When a user's function changes within the organization, the user membership to the user's existing roles can be easily deleted and new roles can be granted. At last, when the user leaves the organization all memberships to all roles are deleted. The main problems arise on RBAC when it is extended across administrative domain of the organization.

2.3.5 Gateway-Based Access Control Model

The gateway-based access control (GBAC) [38] enables the users in a private cloud to access resources of other collaborative private clouds transparently, dynamically and anonymously. The GBAC is mainly based on a gateway. For each and every organization, there is a gateway which is responsible for converting the user's original data into Security Assertion Markup Language (SAML). Then this SAML goes to the target organization. Here, the gateway plays a vital role for communication of data. It enables a secure connection between the two private clouds. In order to complete a task, several enterprises will form a collaborative cloud so that they can share data. As a collaborative cloud is task oriented, the users involved in that task make a virtual team. The team members are dynamic and anonymous to the peer clouds. They may use a third party to communicate with each other because the peer cloud may not have the same platform for communication.

Figure 2.3 shows a gateway connection of a virtual private cloud (VPC). In a VPC [30], a user in one cloud is able to access the resources in a peer cloud. As shown in Fig. 2.3, there are two layers. The first and the second layers are used to implement inter-enterprise and intra-enterprise securities, respectively. In inter-enterprise layer, there are two units, namely the network security unit (NSU) and the data security unit (DSU). When two organizations want to communicate with each other, the NSU deals with security function. The NSU checks for virus in the system. It works as a local gateway. The DSU implements security functions such as authorization, authentication, access control, confidentiality and privacy for any transaction between the two private (or enterprise) clouds. The VPC will be compliant with the existing private cloud and require little change to the inter-enterprise layer. When a user from a collaborative cloud wants to make use of the resource of a peer cloud, the user should be treated as a user of the target cloud. Thus, the gateway will ensure the security of the cloud.

The gateway includes the following components:

- Traffic collection unit: It collects traffic from network devices such as routers and servers.
- Traffic processing unit: It classifies the traffic data and records information such as Internet protocol (IP) source and destination addresses along with timestamps in a db.
- NSU: It comprises firewall, intrusion detection system (IDS) and virus scanner, etc., which handles security function as local legacy gateway. When a threat is identified, it notifies the response unit.
- DSU: It uses the db in traffic processing unit along with the rules from policy management unit to analyse network traffic. When a threat is identified, it notifies the response unit.
- Policy management unit: It provides predefined rules for the behaviour of analysis unit to identify the network.
- Response unit: When threats are detected, it notifies the alarm reporting and security configuration management who in turn will react accordingly.

In GBAC, there is a unit called management organization unit (MOU) [39]. MOU may be installed in each computer of the enterprise in order to reduce the burden of the security gateway and to reduce the risk of information leakage. In GBAC, the users can access three types of resources:

- Access to inter-cloud resources: In an enterprise, any user can be verified using the legacy authentication mechanism. If a gateway is assigned for a special user of the enterprise, the user and the gateway can be authenticated [42] via the enterprise's internal mechanism. As shown in Fig. 2.4, when a user wants to access the resource of a collaborative enterprise, the user sends a request to the local authenticator A1, containing the user's authentication information. The user notifies the local gateway to send its credential to the local authenticator A1. After the local authenticator A1 verifies its authenticity, it sends the request to the gateway G1. The gateway G1 translates the request into an SAML format [32], replaces the requestor with an authorized identity, and signs on the translated request. Then it sends the request to the target gateway G2. The target gateway G2 verifies the request based on the signature of the sending gateway G1 and translates the "standard" request format into its own request format. G2 sends the request to its own authenticator A2. After A2 authenticates the request, the user can access the resource of service.

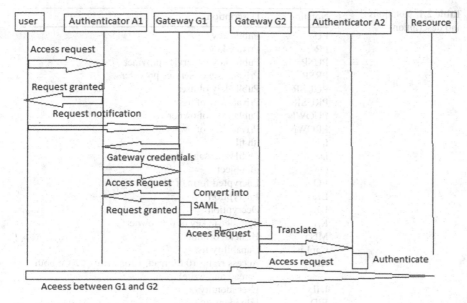

Fig. 2.4 A one-way inter-cloud access

- Access to intra-cloud resources: In GBAC, the gateway is considered as a special user of the enterprise and can be authenticated by the enterprise's internal mechanism. So they can achieve mutual authentication [25]. There is no need to change the internal access mechanism of an enterprise because all the internal resources are transparent to the enterprise members. The gateway can represent any user within its enterprise to send and receive data in proper security [17, 20].
- Access to external resources: Access to external resources means gathering of some extra data or information via a third party. When two users want to communicate with each other via a third-party platform, the virtual cloud should build its own protection.

In GBAC, the resources are converted into SAML format, so it is difficult to be accessed by an unauthorized user. GBAC is a one-way ACM. In GBAC, access from one organization to another cannot proceed in a bi-directional manner.

2.3.6   Novel Data Access Control Model

Novel data access control (NDAC) [15] is an ACM that ensures secured and confidential data communication between user and cloud server. The model consists of three participants: DO, CSP and user. Table 2.1 shows all the notations and their description used in this section to explain the scheme.

Table 2.1 Notations and description

Notation	Description
PU	Public key
PR	Private key
PUSP	Public key of service provider
PRSP	Private key of service provider
PUUSR	Public key of user
PRUSR	Private key of user
PUOWN	Public key of owner
PROWN	Private key of owner
f_i	ith file
D_i	ith file message digest
O_i	ith object
EO_i	Encrypted form of ith object
EK	Encryption
DK	Decryption
K_O	Symmetric key of data owner
MD5	Hash algorithm
CapList	Capability list
AR	Access rights (0 for read, 1 for write or 2 for both read and write)
UID	User identity
FID	File identity
K_S	Secret session key
ND_i	New message digest for ith file
DS_i	ith dataset
N_1, N_2+1	Random generated number

NDAC is composed of three phases, namely file storage, user authorization and file access phase. These phases use different algorithms for storage, access and authorization purposes [15], as outlined subsequently.

- File storage: In this phase, the DO outsources the encrypted data files and capability list to the CSP. The CSP decrypts and stores the data item in the cloud server. The phase consists of the following steps:
  - Step1: Let data be outsourced ($f_1, f_2, \ldots f_n$). The DO initially computes the hash value for each file, i.e. $D_i \leftarrow MD5 (f_i)$, encrypts f_i and D_i with a secret key K_0, i.e. $O_i \leftarrow Ek_0(f_i, D_i)$. Since f_i and D_i are encrypted, the security between the user and the DO increases. To update the capability list, the DO computes the CapList $\leftarrow (UID_{USR}, FID, AR)$ and sends {$EK_{PUSP}(UID_{DO}, EK_{PROWN}(O_i, CapList))$} to the CSP.
  - Step2: After receiving the message, the CSP decrypts it by CSP's private key and store UID_{DO}, O_i and CapList in the cloud server.
- User authentication: In this phase, the DO authorizes a user to access some of the user's data that are managed at the cloud and the user becomes a valid data consumer [29]. The user sends a registration request to the DO after encrypting it by the DO's public key. The DO decrypts the message using the DO's private key and checks the user request. Then the DO adds the user into the user's capability list and sends the updated capability list to the CSP after encrypting it by the public keys of the CSP. The CSP now decrypts the message and checks the timestamp. If

Fig. 2.5 Secured data
exchange between the CSP
and user using the D-H key
exchange

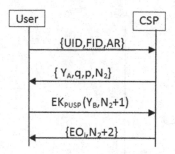

it is correct, the CSP decrypts the CapList using the DO's public key and updates
the CapList. The DO encrypts the key parameters using the user's public key and
sends the message $\{EK_{PUUSR}\ (N_1+1, \text{TimeStamp}, K_0, MD5)\}$ to the user. The
user decrypts the message and checks N_1+1 and timestamps. If it is correct, the
user stores K_0 and MD5.

- File access: In this phase, the data exchange between user and CSP is done using
  the modified Diffie–Hellman (D-H) key exchange algorithm. For accessing the
  file, the user encrypts a data access request by the CSPs public key and sends it to
  the CSP. On receiving the request, the CSP first decrypts the message using the
  CSP's private key and checks timestamp. If it is correct, the CSP authenticates
  the user through comparing UID_{DO}, UID_{USR}, FID and AR, else stops the whole
  procedure. The CSP generates a private value Y_A and other D-H parameters and
  encrypts them using public key of user (Fig. 2.5). Then it sends the encrypted
  message to the user. The user decrypts the message using the user's private key
  and calculates user's private value Y_B. The user encrypts Y_B using the CSP's
  public key and sends it to the CSP. The CSP decrypts the message and checks
  whether N_2+1 is correct. If it is correct, the CSP calculates the shared session
  key K_S and then encrypts the data using K_s, i.e. $EO_i \leftarrow EK_S(O_i)$ and sends $\{EO_i,$
  $N_2+2\}$ to the user.

The main difficulty with the NDAC is that the DO should be always online when a
user wishes to access the data. But this model provides data confidentiality, secured
data access and resists various attacks. It removes the problem of two major attacks
namely the replay attack [26] and the man in the middle attack.

2.3.6.1 Replay Attack

In the replay attack, when two parties communicate with each other, the attacker
simply copies one user's profile and replaces it by the attacker's own profile. In the
cloud environment, the two users are the cloud service user and CSP. The details of
this attack in the cloud environment are described below:

- Step 1: The attacker sends an access request to the CSP, i.e. request (UID, FID, AR)
  to CSP.

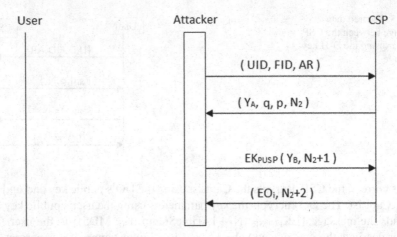

User   Attacker   CSP

(UID, FID, AR)

(Y_A, q, p, N_2)

EK_{PUSP} (Y_B, N_2+1)

(EO_i, N_2+2)

Fig. 2.6 Replay attack

- Step 2: The CSP checks the validity of request and chooses private key (X_A), timestamp (N_2) and parameter (p, q) and computes Y_A, then sends (Y_A, p, q, N_2) to the attacker.
- Step 3: After receiving the message, the attacker generates the attacker's private key (Y_B) and computes a secret key (K_s), then encrypts it using the CSP's public key and sends it to the CSP, i.e, $EK_{PUSP}(Y_B, N_2+1)$ to CSP.
- Step 4: Now the CSP decrypts the message and checks N_2+1, computes a secret key K_s and re-encrypts the user's data using K_s to get EO_i and sends it (EO_i, N_2+1) to the attacker.
- Step 5: At last, the attacker decrypts the user's message using K_s and K_o, i.e. the attacker successfully reads the user's data. Figure 2.6 shows how a replay attack occurs in a cloud server.

The NDAC withstands the replay attack by introducing timestamp, N_1 and N_2. For user authorization, timestamp and N_1 have been used in the message between the user and DO and also between the DO and CSP. Timestamp and N_1 assure freshness in user authorization. On the other hand, timestamp and N_2 are used at the time of data exchange between the user and cloud server to ensure the validity of the data request.

2.3.6.2 Man in the Middle Attack

In this case, the attacker resides between the two users. When the users exchange a message, the attacker can intercept those packets. But the user cannot detect the attacker during message transfer. The steps of this attack in the cloud environment are described as follows:

- Step 1: The user sends an access request to the CSP.
- Step 2: The CSP checks the validity, chooses a private key (X_A), timestamp (N_2) and parameter (p, q) and computes Y_B using the modified D-H key exchange

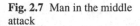

Fig. 2.7 Man in the middle attack

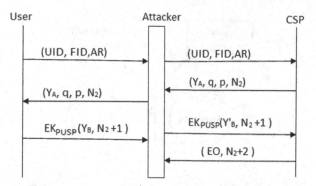

(MDKE) protocol. Then, it sends (Y_A, p, q, N_2) to the user. The attacker intercepts the message and stores it in the attacker's own db.

- Step 3: After receiving the message, the user generates the user's private key X_B, a secret key K_s, and computes Y_B using (MDKE). It encrypts (Y_B, N_2+1) using the public key of the CSP and sends the encrypted message, i.e. $EK_{PUSP}(Y_B, N_2+1)$ to the CSP. But at that time, the attacker intercepts this message and deletes it. And generates the attacker's own private key, then computes Y_{B1} same as the user. After that it encrypts the message using the CSP's public key and sends it to the CSP.
- Step 4: The CSP decrypts the message and checks N_2+1. It computes the secret key using MDKE and re-encrypts the data by the secret key. After putting timestamp, the message is sent to the attacker. Now the attacker simply decrypts the user's message and successfully reads the user's data. Figure 2.7 shows how man in the middle attack occurs in the cloud environment.

To counter the problem of man in the middle attack, the NDAC uses public key encryption. The CSP uses the public key of the user to encrypt Y_A, q and p. On the other hand, the user uses the public key of the CSP to encrypt Y_B. Therefore, anybody except the intended user will not know Y_A, Y_B, q and p. Thus, the man in the middle attack cannot be undertaken.

2.3.7 Usage Control-Based Access Model

Usage control-based access (UCON) [11] can easily implement the security strategy of DAC, MAC and RBAC. UCON inherits all the merits of the traditional access control technologies. Usage control based on authorizations, obligations and conditions ([ABCs] UCON$_{ABCs}$) [24] is the most integrated model. UCON provides a very superior decision-making ability and is a better choice to be used as a cloud service ACM. UCON is just a conceptual model and no exact specification is given, so still much work is needed for establishing ACM based on UCON. Figure 2.8 shows a basic structure of the UCON model. The UCON model consists of six parts: subject, rights, objects, authorization, obligation and conditions.

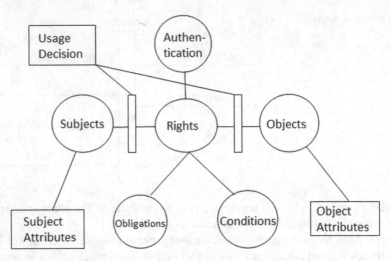

Fig. 2.8 The UCON model

- Subject and subject attribute: A subject is an entity which has some rights marked as S. The subject may be the user group, the user or it can also be a computer terminal. The subject attribute identifies the main capabilities and features of a subject [4]. The common subject attributes include identity, user group, role, membership and capacity list.
- Object and object attribute: Object is an entity which accepts the visit of a subject. Object may be information, document and record used in a workflow system. The object attribute identifies the important information of an object. It includes security level, relations, type, ACLs and so on.
- Rights: Rights are the set of actions that the subject can perform on an object. The set also specifies some conditions and restriction on request from the subject.
- Authorization: Authorization is the decision-making factor. Authorization is an important part in the UCON model. It is based on a subject's attributes, an object's attributes as well as the right to request. Implementation of authorization may lead to some changes to the subject attribute or object attribute value. It will also have an impact on the decision-making process of the user's visit to the server.
- Obligation: Obligation is the function that must be implemented before visiting or during visiting of a user to a cloud server. The obligation that should be fulfilled will not statically be set by the system administrator in advance, and it is dynamically selected according to the subject attributes and object attribute. The implementation of obligation may also update the variable attributes of the entities.
- Condition: Condition is the decision-making factor. Condition assesses current hardware environment or system limitations to decide whether the user request will be granted or not. Condition assessment does not change any subject attributes or object attributes.

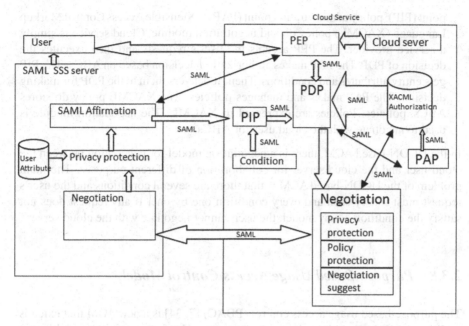

Fig. 2.9 The Nego-UCON$_{ABC}$ model

In UCON, negotiation module is applied for increasing flexibility. When the access request mismatches with the access rules, instead of refusing access directly, the model allows the user to get a second access choice through negotiation in some condition. So the user can get another chance to access the object through the change of parameters and attributes in the negotiation process. Authorization of the UCON model is based on the entity's attributes and access policies, but sometimes these attributes and policies are sensitive and need to be protected. The protection of these sensitive attributes and policies has to be considered in negotiation. Figure 2.9 shows the Nego-UCON$_{ABC}$ model. The UCON basically consists of three platforms, namely cloud user, SAML server and cloud service. These platforms are used for user-friendly communication or negotiation with the cloud server:

- Cloud user: The cloud user is the initiator in service request. When the user attributes are insufficient or condition parameters are inconsistent, the user request will not be executed.
- SAML server: The SAML server mainly consists of three modules: SAML assertion module, sensitive attributes protection module and negotiation module. The SAML assertion module is responsible for assertions and responses to assertion requests. The sensitive attributes protection module is used to protect the user's sensitive attributes. The negotiation module is responsible for the negotiation of the user with the cloud server for attributes, obligations and conditions.
- Cloud service: Cloud service includes seven modules, namely cloud service, policy enforcement point (PEP), policy decision point (PDP), policy information

point (PIP), policy administration point (PAP), eXtensible Access Control Markup Language (XACML) policy db and negotiation module. Cloud service is simply a service provider. The PEP accepts the user's requests and then executes the decision of PDP. The PDP makes authorization decision based on ABCs. The PIP gets entity attributes and conditions. Then, it delivers them to the PDP for making decision. The PAP makes and manages policies. The XACML policy db stores ABCs' policies. Policies are expressed in XACML. The negotiation module is used to negotiate with the cloud user for ABCs.

In the UCON-based ACM, there is a negotiation model for negotiation between the cloud user and the cloud server for collaboration of different purposes. The main problem of the UCON-based ACM is that there are several conditions and the user's request must satisfy each and every condition one by one. If any request does not satisfy the condition of any model, the user cannot negotiate with the cloud server.

2.3.8   Purpose-Based Usage Access Control Model

The purpose-based usage access control (PBAC) [7, 34] is a new ACM that extends traditional ACM to multiple cloud environments. The feature of this model is that it allows the checking of access purpose (AP) against the intended purpose for the data item. A purpose describes the reasons for data collection and data access. A set of purposes P is organized in a tree structure known as purpose tree (PT), where each node represents a purpose in P and each edge represents a hierarchical relation between the two purposes. This access model directly dictates how data items should be controlled. Purpose plays a central role in privacy protection in the cloud server. The system has to make the access decision directly based on the AP.

To access a specific data item, the purpose should be matched with the intended purpose of the data item that is already assigned in the cloud server. Intended purposes are purposes associated with data and are used to regulate data access. An intended purpose consists [34] of two components: allowed intended purposes (AIPs) and prohibited intended purposes (PIPs). Intended purposes can be viewed as a brief summary of privacy policies for data. An access decision is made based on the relationship between the AP and the intended purpose of data. That is, access is granted if the AP is entailed by the AIPs and not entailed by the PIPs. If the access request is not granted, it can be said that the AP is not compliant with the intended purpose. Users are also required to state their APs along with the data access request. System validates the stated APs by ensuring that the users are allowed to access data for the purposes. The AP authorizations are granted to the users based on the AP of the data, obligations and conditions.

Let PT be a Purpose Tree and P be the set of all purposes in PT. Pu is the set of intended purposes, i.e. Pu = (AIP, PIP) and AP is an access purpose defined over PT. So it can be written as, AIP $\in$ P and PIP $\in$ P. AP is compliant with Pu, i.e. AP $\Rightarrow_{PT}$ Pu, if the following two conditions are satisfied:

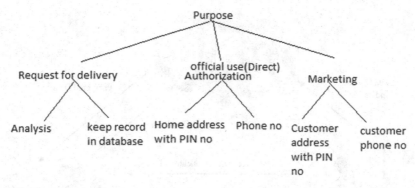

Fig. 2.10 The purpose tree structure

1. AP $\notin$ PIP
2. AP $\in$ AIP

Otherwise, AP is not compliant with Pu, which is denoted by AP $\not\Rightarrow_{PT}$Pu.

In the PBAC [9], AP is authorized to the user through the subjects. As discussed above, let PT be a Purpose Tree, Pu be an intended purpose in PT and S be the set of subjects in the system (Fig. 2.10). An AP is authorized to a specific set of users by 2 tuples (s, pu), where s $\in$ S and pu $\in$ Pu. Here both the AP and the subjects may be organized in hierarchies. Suppose Pu = ({General Purpose}, {Marketing}). If AP = phone number, then AP $\not\Rightarrow_{PT}$ Pu since in the hierarchy structure phone number is not under marketing and phone number $\in$ PIP and phone number $\notin$ AIP. However, if AP = Official use, then AP $\Rightarrow_{PT}$ Pu, as official use $\notin$ PIP and official use $\in$ AIP.

The purpose-based ACM is suitable for hierarchical data [33]. The main advantage of this model is that it can be used to control the data in a dynamic environment. The problem with this model is that it describes only authorization but is silent on the rest of the steps necessary for ensuring secured access of data.

2.3.9 *Capability-Based Access Control Model*

Capability-based access control (CBAC) [16] is an ACM where the DO is able to create, modify or delete an appropriate capability from the capability list (CapList) of a user.

The CBAC is composed of a DO, many data consumers called as the users and a CSP. As shown in Fig. 2.11, the DO encrypts the data using the DO's private key and places the data on the CSP. The CSP stores the encrypted [35] data files that the user wants to access. When the DO receives the data access request from the user and it sends the required keys and a certificate to the user. The user then presents the certificate to the CSP and gets the encrypted data from the CSP. The DO comes online when a new user is to be registered or when the CapList is to be updated at the CSP. But the CSP is always online. The DO can also execute a binary application code at

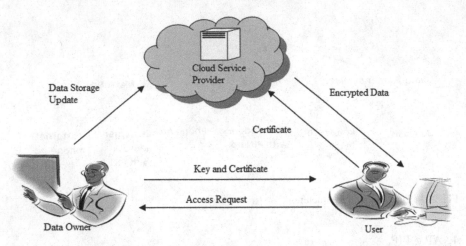

Fig. 2.11 Secure data access between the user and CSP

the CSP for managing the DO's data files. Communication between the CSP and the user or between the user and the DO [12, 40] is made secured using the cryptographic primitives like secure socket layer (SSL)/transport layer security (TLS) [37].

In this model, the DO encrypts the outsourced data with a symmetric key, which is shared only with the user. On the other hand, for the purpose of secured communication [40] between the CSP and user, a symmetric key is generated using a modified D-H key exchange protocol. It relieves the CSP from key management burden that is needed in the public key cryptography. The model guarantees secured access to the outsourced data and at the same time it relieves the DO from worrying about every data access request made by the user, except the initial one. Hence, the DO will not be a bottleneck and the efficiency of this model increases.

As shown in Fig. 2.12, every data or data request is maintained by the service provider who actually stores the data file. It maintains a CapList containing the user id, object id and AR. On the other hand, an object table is also maintained to map objects to their base address. For example, the DO can be a university teacher who posts the students' grades into the cloud, and the user can be any university student registered in the same course who views his/her grades from the cloud. The DO computes a message digest using MD5 [36]. In the CBAC, a 128-bit MD5 hash value is used for data integrity. This model ensures data confidentiality and integrity between the DO and the users.

On receiving the request from the user, the DO adds an entry into the CapList if it is a valid request. For simplicity, the DO has a separate procedure for verifying the genuineness of the client request. The DO now sends the CapList and an encrypted message intended for the user with all the key parameters needed by the user for decrypting the data files to the CSP. After receiving the data files and CapLists from the DO, the CSP stores the information in its storage and sends a registration reply to the user using over-encryption, i.e. encrypting twice using EK$_{PUUSR}$. The notation PUUSR is defined in Table 2.1. This scheme does not allow the CSP to see the

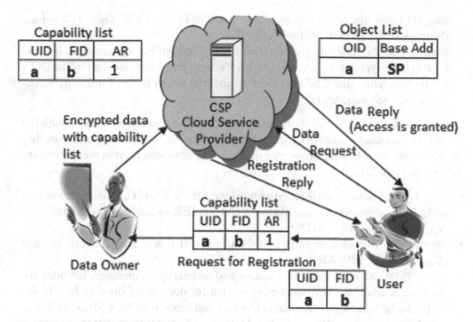

Fig. 2.12 The education scenario

original data file. Here, the data files are only visible to the user and the DO. For sending the data files and CapList, the following steps are executed by the DO:

- Step 1: The DO groups the data as files (f_i) and generates message digest D_i of each file using MD5, i.e. $D_i ß MD5(f_i)$. Now the DO encrypts D_i and f_i by its own symmetric key (K_o) and generates an object list O_i, i.e. $O_i ß EK_o(f_i, D_i)$. The DO re-encrypts the whole encrypted message by the CSP's public key and obtains EO_i, i.e. $EO_i ß EK_{PUSP}(EK_{PROWN}(O_i))$. The notations PUSP and PROWN are described in Table 2.1.
- Step 2: The DO now updates the DO's CapList with the user id, file id and AR, i.e. capListß (UID, FID, and AR, respectively).
- Step 3: After updating the CapList, the DO first encrypts this list by the DO's own private key and re-encrypt this encrypted list by the CSP's public key, i.e. $EK_{PUSP}(EK_{PROWN}(CapList))$.
- Step 4: At last the DO sends the encrypted data items that means object list and encrypted CapList to the CSP, i.e. Send (EO_i, $EK_{PUSP}(EK_{PROWN}(CapList))$).

After receiving the data files and CapList from the DO, the CSP stores it in its own db. For storing these items, the CSP executes the following steps:

- Step 1: Upon receiving the data items and CapList from the DO, the CSP stores the data items and CapList in separate arrays, i.e. StorageArray[ ] ß(EO_i) and StorageArray[ ] ß(CapList).
- Step 2: The CSP first decrypts StorageArray[ ] by the CSP's own private key and decrypts this decrypted array again by the DO's public key. It stores the encrypted

files (O_i) and updates the object table list (OBT), i.e. O_ißDK$_{PRSP}$ (DK$_{PUOWN}$ (StorageArray[ ])) and ObjTableß(O_i, SP$_i$).

- Step 3: The CSP also updates the CSP's own CapList. For updating the list, the CSP first decrypts StorageArray[ ] by CSP's own private key and then by the DO's public key. Thus, the CSP gets the CapList and stores it, i.e. CapListßDK$_{PRSP}$ (DK$_{PUOWN}$ (StorageArray[ ])).

When a new user is to be added, the user needs to send a registration request with the UID, FID, timestamp and ARs required for the data file to the DO. For registering the new user, the following steps are executed. The notations used in these steps are defined in Table 2.1.

- Step 1: User sends a registration request with the UID, FID, Nonce, timestamp and ARs required for the data file to the DO, i.e. (EK$_{PUOWN}$ (EK$_{PRUSR}$ (UID, FID, N_1, TimeStamp, AR))) to DO.
- Step 2: The DO adds an entry into the CapList if it is a valid request, i.e. add (CapList (UID, FID, AR)).
- Step 3: The DO now sends the CapList and an encrypted message, intended for the user, with all the key parameters needed for decrypting the data files to the CSP. The DO encrypts the updated CapList and sends it to the CSP i.e. (EK$_{PUSP}$ (CapList, (EK$_{PROWN}$ (EK$_{PUUSR}$ (K$_O$, MD5, N_1+1, TimeStamp))))) to the CSP.
- Step 4: The CSP updates the copy of the CapList and sends the message to the user, which is intended for the user, i.e. (EK$_{PUUSR}$ (EK$_{PROWN}$ (EK$_{PUUSR}$ (K$_O$, MD5, N_1+1, TimeStamp)))) to the user.
- Step 5: At last, the user decrypts the message and knows the symmetric key and hash functions used by the owner. Thus, the new user gets registered.

After the completion of the registration request, the user can access the data from the cloud server using secured data exchange algorithm, i.e. the D-H key exchange algorithm. The main advantage of this model is efficient data access, i.e. the DO need not always be online. This ACM is flexible in the sense that it can create, add and delete capabilities as and when required. Other advantages are data confidentiality, authentication and integrity.

2.3.10   Towards Temporal Access Control Model

Towards temporal access control (TTAC) [43] has drawn a great amount of interest as it gives emphasis on the issue of security. The model has been proposed to fulfil the needs of practical cloud applications in which each outsourced resource or data can be associated with an access policy on a set of temporal attributes. Each user can also be assigned [5] a license with several privileges based on the comparative attributes. To enforce the valid matches between access policies and user's privileges, a proxy-based re-encryption mechanism [1] with respect to the current time has been introduced.

Fig. 2.13 The simple scenario of the TTAC

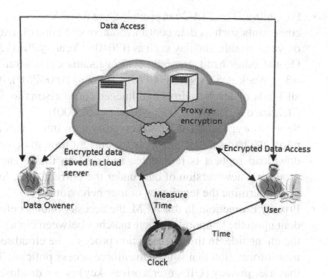

In the cloud-based data storage service, the TTAC mentions three different entities: DO, cloud server and users (Fig. 2.13). To ensure the data access to be compliant with the assigned policy, fine-grained access control has been introduced into the storage service. This access model is extended with the concept of encryption technique. At first, the DO makes use of a temporal access policy P to encrypt data before storing it in the cloud. On receiving an access request from a user, the cloud service checks whether the corresponding temporal constraints can be satisfied in P with respect to the current time t_c. Then, it converts the data into another cipher text (C_{tc}) using re-encryption method and sends this cipher text to the user. At last, the authorized user can use the user's private key (SK) with access privilege (L) to decrypt C_{tc}. In order to implement temporal access control, a clock server is set-up that always provides exactly the same current time by communicating with the user and the CSP.

In this model, the following notations are used:

- A is the set of attributes, $A = \{A_1.....A_m\}$.
- $A_k(t_i, t_j)$ is the range constraint of attribute A_k on (t_i, t_j).
- P is the access control policy expressed as a Boolean function and generated by grammar P = A_K (ti, tj) | P AND P|P OR P.
- L is the access privilege assigned into the user's licence and it is generated by L = $\{A_k(t_a, t_b)\}$ where $A_k \in A$.

This scheme follows the principle of secured temporal control [6]. Let $A_K \in A$ be a range-based temporal attribute and (P, L) be a constraint–privilege pair with A_K, where $A_k [t_i, t_j] \in P$ and $A_k [t_a, t_b] \in L$. Given a current time t_c, secure temporal control requires that the access is granted if and only if $t_c \in [t_i, t_j]$ and $t_c \in [t_a, t_b]$. This model provides some user benefits [23] for accessing the cloud data. The benefits are as follows:

- Flexibility: The TTAC can provide more flexible access control based on temporal constraints such as date control and periodic control. Day control means control on year, month, and day such as $((2010 \leq \text{Year} \leq 2011) \text{ AND } (4 \leq \text{Month} \leq 7))$. On the other hand, periodic control means control on week and hour such as $((3 \leq \text{Week} \leq 5) \text{ AND } (8{:}00\text{PM} \leq \text{Hour} \leq 10{:}00\text{PM}))$. Also this model supports all kinds of level controls and integer comparisons for example $((3 \leq \text{Security Clearance} \leq 5) \text{ OR } (2,000 \leq \text{Salary} \leq 5,000))$.
- Supervisory: The TTAC-based cryptosystem introduces a proxy-based re-encryption mechanism that can apply the current time to determine whether the user's download request is reasonable and rely on the re-encryption technologies to produce a new version of data under the current time. Such a proxy service can also determine the legitimacy of user behaviours.
- Privacy Protection: In this ACM, the access policies enforced are entirely dependent upon the temporal attribute matches between cipher texts and private keys in the client side. In the re-encryption process, the cloud servers do not require any user information that is used to enforce access policies. This mechanism ensures that user privacy (UID, user's private key) is not disclosed to cloud servers.

This scheme helps the DO to achieve temporal data access control on the file stored in the cloud server.

2.3.11 Organization-Based Access Control

Organization-based access control (OrBAC) [27] defines the security policy only for abstract entities by assigning permissions, prohibitions, recommendations and obligations. In OrBAC [18], eight entities are used for accessing the cloud data:

- Subject: Subject means users or active entities to whom rights are assigned.
- Objects: Files, emails, printed form, etc., are objects. They are mainly non-active entities.
- Organization: It represents the structure or group of active users or entities, where each user or subject plays certain roles.
- Role: It is used to structure the relationship between individuals and organizations when the individual user wants to access the data from the cloud server.
- Action: Actions such as $<<$ select $>>$, $<<$ open file ()$>>$, $<<$ send $>>$ etc. are used to access the data.
- View: A set of objects that satisfy a common property. In a cloud, the view administrative records cover all administrative records of a user.
- Activity: Activity performs the action that has a common goal. Such as "consult", "edit", "pass", etc.
- Context: Context is used to express the situation such as normal or emergency. Context can also consider the temporal access history.

OrBAC does not provide the relationship between trust and reputation for service quality within the cloud. This model takes into consideration the management of trust in the cloud environment via the function of a trusted third party (TTP) and parameter confidence indicators.

2.4 The Need for Classification

All ACMs have their own merits and demerits. An ACM that performs the best in one scenario may not perform well in the other scenario. So while designing a system, proper selection of an ACM is very important. Classification of the ACMs will help the system designers to understand the properties of an ACM. Thus, it will lead to proper selection of the ACM for a system. A detailed discussion on the taxonomy of ACM has been presented in Sect. 2.5.

If there are small numbers of users in a cloud, the identity-based ACM can be applied, as each user can be defined with a unique name and role. But if the number of users is large, it will be quite difficult to assign a name for each and every user. In that scenario, the non-identity-based ACM can be used by the CSP. Sometimes large number of users wants to access data for some special purpose, then the CSP can use the tree-based non-identity ACM for accessing data. Otherwise the CSP can use one of the ACMs among the non-tree-based non-identity ACMs.

If the CSP wishes to assign different rule for different user and the number of users are small, the CSP can use centralized ACM for each user. If the rules for a group of users are same, the CSP can use the group-based ACM. On the other hand, if all the users are under the same cloud, centralized ACM can be used. If in the considered system there are multiple collaborating clouds, the CSP can use collaborative ACM.

It is, therefore, clear that for selection of an appropriate ACM by the CSP, classification of ACMs plays a vital role.

2.5 Taxonomy of ACM

This section presents the classification of ACMs. The ACM can be classified in two ways. First one is based on the process of identification of the user in the cloud. The second one is based on the management of access control.

Based on the process of identification of the user, the ACM can be classified into two types: identity based and non-identity based (Fig. 2.14). In the identity-based ACM, the users and resources are identified by a unique name or role. Identification may be done directly or through roles. These ACMs are effective in unchangeable system, i.e. users are fixed or predefined. The identity -based ACM is mainly used when there are small numbers of users in a cloud server. In the non-identity-based ACM, there are no unique names or roles for the users and resources. The DO defines the access policies and encrypts the data under the policies before putting them in the cloud server. They do not rely on the cloud server to do the access control. When the DO puts cipher text in the cloud server, all the legal user can use the cipher text. The identity-based ACM can further be divided into two classes: tree-based ACM

Fig. 2.14 Classification based
on identity and non-identity

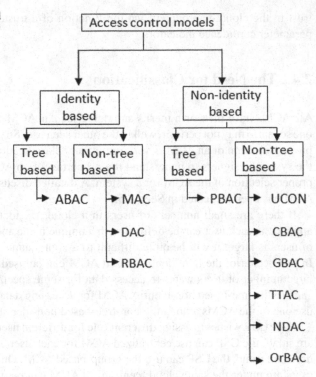

and non-tree-based ACM. In the tree-based approach, each user is assigned an access structure that is usually defined as an access tree over data attributes or files. The user secret key is defined to reflect the access structure so that the user is able to decrypt a cipher text if and only if the data attributes satisfy the user's access structure. On the other hand, in a non-tree-based approach, no such tree is maintained for accessing the data.

In the non-identity- based ACM, there are two types of ACMs namely tree-based and non-tree-based ACMs. In the tree-based ACM, a PT is made based on the requirement of the user, i.e. what the user wants to access from the cloud server. There are different PTs for different purposes. On the other hand, in a non-tree-based model such kind of tree is not maintained.

Attribute-based access control (ABAC) is a tree-based identity ACM. As discussed in Sect. 2.3.3, there are unique roles or names for each and every user and resource. Each user is assigned an access structure which is usually defined as an access tree over data attributes. User secret key is defined to reflect the access structure so that the user is able to decrypt a cipher text if and only if the data attributes satisfy the user's access structure. Because of all these reasons, the ABAC is a tree-based identity ACM. On the other hand, MAC, DAC, and RBAC are non-tree-based identity ACM. In MAC, DAC and RBAC, there is a unique role or name for each and every user or resource. But no tree is maintained for accessing the file. In MAC, the administrator defines the usage and access policy, which cannot be modified by the user. The policy also defines who can have access to which data or resources. As discussed in Sect. 2.3.2, the DAC is a model where separate rules for each or a group of user are defined. Access to the system resource is controlled by the operating system. In the DAC, the user can also give the permission to the other user to use the user's own files or programs. The RAC determines the user access to the system based on the job role. The role of a user is assigned based on the latest privileges concept. The role is defined with the minimum amount of permissions and functionalities. Permissions can be added or deleted if the role changes. In the RBAC, there are separate ARs for individual user. So MAC, DAC and RBAC do not maintain any tree for access control and thus comes under the category of non-tree-based identity ACM.

On the other hand, the PBAC, UCON, CBAC, GBAC, TTAC, NDAC and Or-BAC are non-identity-based ACMs. In these models, there are no such unique roles or names for each and every user. The PBAC allows the checking of AP against the intended purpose for the data item. A set of purposes P is organized in a tree structure, which is known as PT, where each node represents a purpose in P and each edge represents a hierarchical relation between the two purposes. This access model directly dictates how the data items should be controlled, i.e. purpose plays a central role in protecting privacy in the cloud server. So the PABC is considered as a tree-based non-identity ACM. On the other side, the UCON provides very superior decision-making ability and does not use any tree. As discussed earlier, CBAC is an ACM where the DO is able to create, modify or delete an appropriate capability from the CapList for a user to access a data file. In GBAC, for each and every organization, there is a gateway which is responsible to convert the user's original data into SAML. Then, this SAML goes to the target organization. The TTAC gives an efficient temporal access control encryption scheme for cloud services with the help of cryptographic integer comparisons and a proxy-based re-encryption mechanism. In the TTAC, each user can be assigned a license with several privileges based on the comparative attributes. To enforce a valid match between access policies and user's privileges, a proxy-based re-encryption mechanism with respect to the current time has been introduced. The NDAC provides data communication between the user and cloud server. This scheme implements data storage, user authentication, data access and integrity checking. The OrBAC defines the security policy only for abstract entities. Therefore, in UCON, CBAC, GBAC, TTAC, NDAC and OrBAC, there is no tree for accessing data file, and these ACMs are considered as non-tree-based non-identity ACM.

There is another way of classification which is shown in Fig. 2.15. This classification is mainly based on centralized and collaborative approach. In a centralized ACM, there is a central administrator which can control all the tasks of a user. The central administrator controls the whole system or cloud server. In a centralized ACM, a user cannot do anything of the user's wish. Actually, in centralized ACM, all the rules and obligations are assigned by the authority.

On the other hand, in collaborative ACM there is collaboration between two or more cloud organizations. Here, collaboration is mainly maintained by the gateway of each and every cloud organization. A collaborative cloud is a cloud community that consists of private enterprise clouds. It includes virtual computing resources

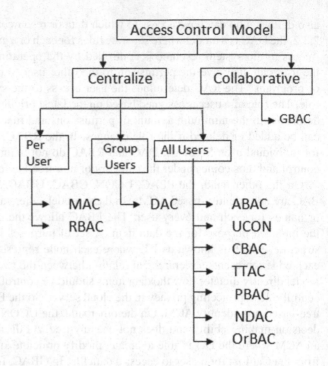

dedicated to a particular collaborative activity and is subjected to information-sharing policies. The users in each private cloud are able to access the resources of other private clouds to which it is collaborating in a controlled manner. The users in different clouds may exchange information via the third-party platforms. A collaborative cloud is task oriented and provides high-access relationship among private clouds.

Centralized ACM is divided into three categories, namely per user based (PUB), group user based (GUB) and all user based (AUB). In PUB, the ACM administrator assigns rules and obligations for each and every user. Here, the user cannot do anything against the rules of the central administrator. The administrator can allow different rules and obligation for different users. Same rules and obligations can be assigned for different users or all users. In GUB, there are rules and obligations assigned for a group of users. All users belonging to the group use same rule for accessing any kind of data or resources. There are different rules for different groups. A user who belongs to one group cannot use the rules of another group. In AUB, the administrator assigns common rules and obligations for all the users of that server. All the users of that server should follow those rules for accessing data or file or any kind of resources from that cloud server.

MAC and RBAC are considered as the PUB-centralized ACM. In MAC and RBAC, the administrator assigns access rules for individual user. Here, in these schemes, the central administrator controls the whole system. The user cannot do anything by the user's wish. The user must follow the rules which have been assigned by the central administrator. So, both MAC and RBAC are considered as the PUB-centralized ACM. The DAC is considered as the GUB-centralized access model.

In the DAC, the central administrator assigns AR for a group of users. The user can give the user's AR to another user who belongs to the same group. So the DAC is a GUB-centralized ACM. ABAC, UCON, CBAC, TTAC, PBAC, NDAC and OrBAC are considered as the AUB-centralized ACM. In these models, there is a common rule for each and every user. The CSP assigns ARs for all users in the system.

On the other hand, the GBAC is a collaborative ACM. The GBAC represents virtual cloud for collaborative clouds based on the gateway. There is collaboration between two or more private cloud environments. In order to complete a task, several enterprises will form a collaborative cloud so that they can share data. There is a gateway for each and every private cloud. Here, the gateway plays a vital role for communication of data. Gateway converts the user original data into an SAML. Then, this SAML goes to target organization.

2.6 Conclusion

Nowadays, cloud computing has become very popular due to its cost-effectiveness and flexibility. However, there are also various issues in the cloud computing paradigm such as data security, data access, performance as well as energy-related issues and fault tolerance. Among them, the problem of data access has been discussed in this chapter. A detailed discussion and analysis of ACMs in cloud environment has been presented. Taxonomies of ACMs have also been proposed. The ACMs have been classified in different ways e.g. identity based and non-identity based and centralized and collaborative. The identity-based and non-identity-based approaches are further subdivided into sub-categories, e.g. tree-based and non-tree-based approaches. The centralized approach is classified into three types: PUB, GUB and AUB approach. All the models discussed in this chapter have some advantages and some limitations also. Classification of ACMs is helpful for understanding the characteristics of the access models. New ACMs can be developed in future for faster user access to the data. Moreover, there is a huge scope of work to improve confidentiality, security and scalability of ACMaccess control models in the cloud environment.

References

1. Ateniese G, Fu K, Green M, Hohenberger S (2006) Improved proxy re-encryption schemes with applications to secure distributed storage. ACM T Inf Sys Secur 9(1):1–30
2. Ausanka-Crues R (2006) Methods for access control: advances and limitations. http://www.cs.hmc.edu/mike/public_html/courses/security/s06/projects/ryan.pdf. Accessed 9 Oct 2013
3. Baldwin RW (1990) Naming and grouping privileges to simplify security management in large databases. In: Proceedings of the IEEE computer society symposium on research in security and privacy, pp 116–132, Oakland, USA, May 1990
4. Bell DE, Padula LJL (March 1976) Secure computer system: unified exposition and multics interpretation (Mitre Corporation). http://www.dtic.mil/dtic/tr/fulltext/u2/a023588.pdf. Accessed 7 Oct 2013

5. Bertino E, Bonatti PA, Ferrari E (2001) TRBAC: a temporal role-based access control model. ACM T Inf Syst Secur 4(3):191–233
6. Bertino E, Carminati B, Ferrari E (2002) A temporal key management scheme for secure broadcasting of XML documents. In: Proceedings of 9th ACM conference on computer and communications security, pp 31–40, Washington, DC, USA, Nov 2002
7. Bertino E, Byun JW, Li N (2005) Privacy-preserving database systems. In: Aldini A, Gorrieri R, Martinelli F (eds) Foundations of security analysis and design III. Springer, Berlin, pp 178–206
8. Bishop M (2002) Computer security: art and science, Addison-Wesley, Boston
9. Byun J W, Bertino E, Li Ninghui (2005) Purpose based access control of complex data for privacy protection. In: Proceedings of 10th ACM symposium on access control models and technologies, pp 102–110, Stockholm, Sweden, June 2005
10. Clark DD, Wilson DR (1987) A comparison of commercial and military computer security policies. In: Proceedings of IEEE symposium on computer security and privacy, pp 184–194, Oakland, USA, April 1987
11. Danwei C, Xiuli H, Xunyi R (2009) Access control of cloud service based on UCON. Proceedings of CloudCom, pp 559–564, Beijing, China, Dec 2009
12. Fabry RS (1974) Capability-based addressing. Commun ACM 17(7):403–412
13. Federal Information Processing Standards (1994) Security requirements for cryptographic modules. http://www.itl.nist.gov/fipspubs/fip140-1.htm. Accessed 6 Oct 2013
14. Ferraiolo DF, Kuhn DR (1992) Role-based access controls. In: Proceedings of the 15th national computer security conference, pp 554–563, Baltimore, USA, Oct 1992
15. Gao X, Jiang Z, Jiang R (2012) A novel data access scheme in cloud computing. In: Proceedings of the 2nd international conference on computer and information applications, pp 124–127, Taiyuan, Chaina, Dec 2012
16. Hota C, Sankar S, Rajarajan M, Nair SK (2011) Capability-based cryptographic data access control in cloud computing. Int J Adv Netw Appl 3(03):1152–1161
17. Jiyi W, Qianli S, Jianlin Z, Qi X (2011) Cloud computing: cloud security to trusted cloud. Adv Mater Res 186:596–600
18. Kalam AAE, Baida RE, Balbiani P, Benferhat S (2003) Organization based access control. In: Proceedings of the 4th IEEE international workshop on policies for distributed systems and networks, pp 120–131, Lake Como, Italy, June 2003
19. Khan AR (2012) Access control in cloud computing environment. ARPN J Eng Appl Sci 7(5):1819–6608
20. Khan KM, Malluhi Q (2010) Establishing trust in cloud computing. IT Prof 12(5):20–27
21. Lampson BW (1971), Protection. In: Proceedings of 5th Princeton symposium on information science and systems, pp 437–443, Princeton University, USA, March 1971 (reprinted in Oper Syst Rev 8(1):18–24, Jan 1974)
22. Mayfield T, Roskos JE, Welke SR, Boone JM (1991) Integrity in automated information systems (Institute for Defence Analysis). http://www.csirt.org/color_%20books/C-TR-79-91.pdf. Accessed 4 Oct 2013
23. Park J, Sandhu R (2002) Towards usage control models: beyond traditional access control. In: Proceedings of the 7th ACM symposium on access control models and technologies, pp. 57–64, Monterey, USA, June 2002
24. Park J, Sandhu R (2004) The UCONABC usage control model. ACM T Inf Syst Secur 7(1): 128–174
25. Popovic K, Hocenski Z (2010) Cloud computing security issues and challenges. In: Proceedings of the 33rd international convention on information and communication technology, electronics and microelectronics, pp 344–349, Opatija, Croatia, May 2010
26. Pries R, Yu W, Fu X, Zhao W (2008) A new replay attack against anonymous communication networks. In: Proc IEEE international conference on communication, pp 1578–1582, Beijing, China, May 2008
27. Saidi MB, Elkalam AA, Marzouk A (2012) TOrBAC: a trust organization based access control model for cloud computing systems. Int J Soft Comput Eng 2(4):122–130

28. Sandhu R, Ferraiolo D, Kuhn R (2000) The NIST model for role based access control: toward a unified standard. In: Proceedings of the 5th ACM workshop on role based access control, pp 47–63, Berlin, Germany, July 2000

29. Sanka S, Hota C, Rajarajan M (2010) Secure data access in cloud computing. In: Proceeding 4th international conference on internet multimedia systems architectures and applications, pp 1–6, Bangalore, India, Dec 2010

30. Sasaki T, Nakae M, Ogawa R (2010) Content oriented virtual domains for secure information sharing across organizations. In: Proceedings of the ACM workshop on cloud computing security, pp 7–12, Chicago, USA, 2010

31. Singh P, Singh S (2013) A new advance efficient RBAC to enhance the security in cloud computing. Int J Adv Res Comput Sci Softw Eng 3(6):1136–1142

32. Somorovsky J, Mayer A, Schwenk J, Kampmann M, Jensen M (2012) On breaking SAML: be whoever you want to be. In: Proceedings of the 21st USENIX conference on security symposium, pp 21–21, Bellevue, WA, Aug 2012

33. Sun L, Li Y (2006) DTD level authorization in XML documents with usage control. Int J Comput Sci Netw Secur 6(11):244–250

34. Sun L, Wang H (2010) A purpose based usage access control model. Int J Comput Inf Eng 4(1):44–51

35. Vimercati SDC, Foresti S, Jajodia S, Paraboschi S, Samarati P (2007a) Over-encryption: management of access control evolution on outsourced data. In: Proceedings of the 33rd international conference on very large databases, pp 123–134, Vienna, Austria, Sept 2007

36. Vimercati SDC, Foresti S, Jajodia S, Paraboschi S, Samarati P (2007b) A data outsourcing architecture combining cryptography and access control. In: Proceedings of the ACM workshop on computer security architecture, pp 63–69, Alexandria, USA, Oct 2007

37. Wang W, Li Z, Owens R, Bhargava B (2009) Secure and efficient access to outsourced data. In: Proceedings of the ACM cloud computing security workshop, pp 55–65, Chicago, USA, Nov 2009

38. Wu Y, Suhendra V, Guo H (2012) A gateway-based access control scheme for collaborative clouds. In: Wagner A (ed) Seventh International Conference on Internet Monitoring and Protection, Stuttgart, Germany, June 2012. Red Hook, Curran Associates, pp. 54–60

39. Xu J, Yan J, He L, Su P, Feng D (2010) CloudSEC: a cloud architecture for composing collaborative security services. In: Proceedings of the IEEE International Conference on Cloud Computing Technology and Science, pp 703–711, Indiana, USA, Dec 2010

40. Youseff L, Butrico M, Da Silva D (2008) Toward a unified ontology of cloud computing. In: Proceedings of the grid computing environments workshop, pp 1–10, Austin, USA, Nov 2008

41. Yu S, Wang C, Ren K, Lou W (2010) Achieving secure, scalable, and fine-grained data access control in cloud computing. Proceedings of the IEEE INFOCOM, pp 1–9, San Diego, USA, March 2010

42. Zargar ST, Hassan T, Joshi JBD (2011) DCDIDP: a distributed, collaborative, and data-driven intrusion detection and prevention framework for cloud computing environments. In: Proceedings of the 7th international conference on collaborative computing: networking, applications and worksharing (collaborateCom), pp 332–341, Orlando, USA, Oct 2011

43. Zhu Y, Hu H, Ahn GJ, Huang D (2012) Towards temporal access control in cloud computing. In: Proceedings of IEEE INFOCOM, pp 2576–2580, Orlando, USA, March 2012

Chapter 3
Access Control As a Service in Cloud: Challenges, Impact and Strategies

Muhammad Awais Shibli, Rahat Masood, Umme Habiba, Ayesha Kanwal, Yumna Ghazi and Rafia Mumtaz

Abstract The evolution of service-oriented architecture has given birth to the promising cloud technology, which enables the outsourcing of existing hardware and software information technology (IT) infrastructure via the Internet. Since the cloud offers services to a variety of organizations under the same umbrella, it raises security issues including unauthorized access to resources and misuse of data stored in third-party platform. The fact that the cloud supports multiple tenants is the cause for the biggest concern among organizations: how to prevent malicious users from accessing and manipulating data they have no right to access. In this regard, various access control techniques have been proposed, which concentrate on certain authorization issues like the ease of privilege assignment or the resolution of policy conflicts, while ignoring other important weaknesses such as the lack of interoperability and management issues which arise in the dynamic cloud environment. To cover all these challenges, access control as a service (ACaaS), which stems from its significantly more popular parent, security as a service (SECaaS), is considered a viable solution for mediating cloud service consumers' access to sensitive data. In this chapter, we assist the cloud community in understanding the various issues associated with providing authorization services in the cloud that may be technical, such as privilege escalation and separation of duties, or managerial, such as the steep requirement of time and money for this purpose. ACaaS is the comprehensive

M. A. Shibli (✉) · R. Masood · U. Habiba · A. Kanwal · Y. Ghazi · R. Mumtaz
School of Electrical Engineering and Computer Science (SEECS), National University
of Sciences and Technology (NUST), Sector H-12, Islamabad—44000, Pakistan
e-mail: awais.shibli@seecs.edu.pk

R. Masood
e-mail: rahat.masood@seecs.edu.pk

U. Habiba
e-mail: 11msccsuhabiba@seecs.edu.pk

A. Kanwal
e-mail: 11msccsakanwal@seecs.edu.pk

Y. Ghazi
e-mail: 09bicseyghazi@seecs.edu.pk

R. Mumtaz
e-mail: rafia.mumtaz@seecs.edu.pk

Z. Mahmood (ed.), *Continued Rise of the Cloud,* Computer Communications
and Networks, DOI 10.1007/978-1-4471-6452-4_3,
© Springer-Verlag London 2014

solution to some of the issues highlighted previously. We have also discussed the significance and impact of ACaaS, along with the strategies reported in the literature for providing a secure access to the applications hosted on the cloud. We then holistically cover the authorization requirements of the cloud environment, specifically for software as a service (SaaS) model, evaluating the extant relevant solutions based on certain defined factors from the National Institute of Standards and Technology (NIST)-. The outcome of our research is that an ideal ACaaS should be extensive and holistic, which encompasses all the requisite security and managerial features and provides an efficient and reliable access control mechanism to the cloud consumers that complies with international standards.

Keywords Access control as a service · Authorization · Cloud security · Security as a service · Software as a service

3.1 Introduction

Cloud, being a distributed environment, comprises large groups of servers with dedicated connections that are used to distribute the data-processing tasks among them. Cloud computing promises many benefits to the information technology (IT) industry such as unlimited storage and processing power, along with the services that are meant to be available, scalable and flexible [47, 66]. Cloud services typically offer five basic and essential characteristics, namely *on-demand self-service*, *broad network access*, *resource pooling*, *rapid elasticity* and *measured service* [66]. These features make cloud computing diverse from the traditional computing methodologies. Since the cloud paradigm is based on *pay-as-you-go* model, it allows the organizations to outsource their data and IT services at economical rates [66]. In addition, its service-oriented architecture (SOA) helps in providing opportunities for creating, organizing and reusing the existing components. Cloud is capable of offering anything as a service such as software as a service (SaaS), platform as a service (PaaS), infrastructure as a service (IaaS) [66, 95], database as a service (DbaaS), security as a service (SECaaS) [20], identity as a service (IDaaS) and satiates numerous needs of the IT using the virtualization techniques.

Regardless of the evident advantages of cloud, the security of the services and resources stored in there is highly questionable, thus requiring further exploration and alleviation of significant cloud security issues to help ensure its rapid adoption. The emergence of its various service models, like SaaS, PaaS and IaaS, has introduced new security challenges for cloud service consumers (CSCs) [48, 95]. Security of this paradigm is a troubling concern not only for the cloud consumers but also for the service providers. It has many open security issues such as secure data management, risk from malicious insiders, data segregation, authentication and authorization [48, 79, 95]. In order to resolve these security issues, cloud computing has been revolutionized with the new delivery model of security as a service [20].

The motivation behind the proposition of SECaaS is to facilitate CSCs and cloud service providers (CSPs) with different security solutions delivered over the Internet or providing them more control over the security features of their data and applications. SECaaS supports different security services to service consumers including mainly *access management services, identity management services, identity federation services, email security services, data encryption* and *intrusion detection services* [20]. The SECaaS can be applied at SaaS, PaaS or IaaS layers for protection of customer's assets at cloud platform. At the SaaS level, the security services are provided to protect the data and applications running at cloud. At the PaaS level, the security features protect the data, applications, as well as the underlying operating system (OS). Moreover, the SECaaS layer on top of the IaaS supports the protection of application data, OS and the underlying virtual environment [25].

Among the aforementioned categories of SECaaS, identity and access management [55] is generally considered one of the thorniest issues in cloud security. However, we are particularly accentuating access management owing to its significance in ensuring the security of data and services in cloud. Once the business organizations bypass their enterprise IT barriers to adopt the benefits of cloud, the management of user identities and access control becomes the most complex and critical hurdle [79, 95]. It is one key area where the CSPs are still playing to catch up to the mainframe computing world. Therefore, an effective access control mechanism is required that formulates policies and rules for defining the access level for each service consumer. Generally, access is considered as an all-or-nothing proposition, which means that after successful authentication to the cloud, the service consumers have the autonomy to do a lot of inadvertent harm to start and stop a virtual server or wreak havoc inside the entire cloud environment [45]. Therefore, cloud providers are required to ensure segregated and virtualized networks for each CSC within a particular environment. Many third-party security software, such as *Reflex Systems vTrust* [81, 82] ensure more granularities, where the CSCs may execute their applications but not change the configuration or shut down the virtual server itself. Granular-level access control improves the management of service consumers across multiple environments. It is critical to ensure that the CSCs can only access the files they are authorized for and offers the management to keep an eye over the entire activities performed over the network. In addition, the sensitivity level of applications also varies depending upon their operation and data usage, so the CSCs need to have the capability to incorporate required access control model accordingly.

In this chapter, we primarily focus on access control as a service (ACaaS) for cloud, which provides the required access control services (ACSs) to data owners (DOs) and CSPs without involving them in any aspect of the implementation. To be precise, the ACaaS aims to ensure the segregation and confidentiality of the data contents in a multi-tenant cloud environment. Moreover, the ACaaS facilitates the CSPs and CSCs by ensuring the ease of the user profile management, defining a common policy format for its translation and defining an efficient, cost-effective mechanism for access control. In this chapter, we describe various SECaaS issues specifically related to the ACaaS for cloud. In addition, and equally importantly, we elaborate the access control challenges, their impact and corresponding strategies reported in the literature. Further, we have identified open issues and potential research directions

Fig. 3.1 Cloud security issues

in the area of ACaaS, after performing an extensive literature survey of industrial and research-based access control for cloud solutions. The identified unattended issues serve as potential problems that need to be addressed by cloud community, thus helping the CSCs to protect their data on cloud.

3.2 Cloud Computing Challenges and Security Issues

Cloud computing security is still in its infancy, which means that it still requires further investigation and mitigation of prevailing security issues to help ensure its mass adoption [8, 79]. These issues include secure data management, risk from malicious insiders, data segregation, authentication and authorization, confidentiality, integrity and availability of personal and business critical information stored at cloud [17, 95]. Figure 3.1 depicts many cloud computing challenges and security concerns that need to be addressed. Enumerated subsequently are some of the most critical problems faced by the CSCs today.

3.2.1 Confidentiality

Privacy is one of the main concerns in the cloud environment, which is ensured by maintaining the confidentiality of data and information [47, 97]. Confidentiality is somewhat related to authentication and aims to prevent unauthorized disclosure of the protected data. Since cloud is ubiquitous, it can be accessed through various devices and applications, causing an increase in the number of access points, which consequently adds to the threat of unauthorized disclosure [110]. On the other hand, delegation of complete access control rights to the CSP, whose trustworthiness is rather uncertain, adds to the risk of data compromise. Therefore, some methods must be introduced to maintain the confidentiality of the data stored at the cloud, such as encryption; however, encryption brings about critical issues of its own, such as key management problems and querying the encrypted information, etc. [8, 51]. The common modes of encryption are the implementation of algorithms such as data encryption standard (DES) and advanced encryption standard (AES) [35].

3.2.2   Data Integrity

Data integrity is a key component of information security, which means that information will be protected against illegal modification, fabrication and deletion [88, 95]. It is a serious issue in the multi-tenant cloud environment for which authorization mechanisms are applied [75]. Authorization specifies and enforces the access rights for every authenticated user. However, due to the increase in access points and system entities, it is crucial to be ensured that only authorized entities are allowed to access the protected data [75]. Another common method used for ensuring the integrity is to use digital signatures. The corporate methods used for hashing and digital signatures include digital signature algorithm (DSA), algorithm by Rivest, Shamir and Adleman (RSA) [32], SHA1 and SHA2 [92]. However, similar to encryption, digital signatures also have issues of their own. Various attacks can be launched against the digital signature schemes including the meet-in-the-middle attack [74], adaptive chosen attacks [33], key-only attacks, known message attacks and forger [41, 77, 84].

3.2.3   Data Locality

Cloud computing allows service consumers to use its applications and resources for the processing of their business critical data and related requests. However, CSCs are completely unaware of the data storage location, which typically raises privacy, security and transparency concerns [47, 95, 97]. Since information disclosure laws and policies vary from country to country, the locality of data storage is of utmost importance for organizations having stringent privacy policies. For instance, few countries including Europe and America have data privacy and disclosure laws to ensure that certain type of sensitive data cannot leave the country territory [13, 25]. Thus, the lack of transparency and data control are the key barriers towards the adoption of cloud computing services.

3.2.4   Trust

Trust in a cloud environment is dependent upon the selection of deployment model, as control of data, applications and information are externalized and delegated out of the owner's firm control [54]. Trust between the CSP and the CSC is one of the main issues that cloud computing is dealing with. In addition to this, cloud hides the data storage and maintenance details from its service consumer, which raises many transparency and trust-related issues [3, 76], as discussed above. Selection of CSP with fully trusted and appropriate services is one of the challenging issues in multi-tenant and heterogeneous cloud environment, as trust is a subjective and context-sensitive term [89]. Similarly, the trust level may increase or decrease with new experiences, and new knowledge, or external opinion causes an overriding influence over the old values of trust. Therefore, in order to establish trust between consumer and CSP, an agreement is signed between the service consumers and CSPs, technically known as service-level agreement (SLA) [30]. This document merely contains the list of cloud services that the service provider is offering and willing to perform [50, 97]. SLAs do not have a standard format; therefore, they cannot be regarded as an effective mechanism to ensure the relationship of trust between CSP and CSC.

3.2.5   Virtualization

Virtualization is among the key components of cloud infrastructure with many security risks [47, 62]. In a typical scenario, one physical machine may host multiple instances at a time. Virtualization is intended to ensure that each virtual machine (VM) instance is running in isolation; however, this required isolation is not met completely. Control and administration of these guest and host OS is another substantial challenge [30]. Vulnerabilities have been identified in almost all of the virtualization software that can be misused by malicious users. For instance, one of the most well-known virtualization solution, VM monitor (VMM), fails to ensure perfect isolation. The VMMs are required to be 'root secure', preventing the guest OS interference in the host OS [52]. Many other design and implementation vulnerabilities due to increased code size and use of unpatched old images are also vulnerable to zero-day attacks, VM escape attack, and VM checkpoint attack [47]. Furthermore, malicious hypervisors such as BLUEPILL rootkit [85], Vitriol [11] and SubVir are installed on the fly, which give attacker the host privileges to modify and control VMs [38]. These vulnerabilities may allow the insiders to bypass certain security boundaries, escalate privileges and remote code execution.

3.2.6   Compliance and Audit

Organizations face new challenges as they move from traditional enterprise solutions to cloud. Management, delivery and communication of compliance with a multitude of regulations across various authorities are among the major cloud security challenges [65]. Both the CSCs and CSPs are required to understand the similarities and differences in the standing compliance and audit standards and practices. Issues dealing with evaluating as to how cloud computing affects compliance with the internal security policies as well as various regulatory and legislative requirements need to be addressed. The CSPs with services compliant with the international security standards, such as Payment Card Industry-Data Security Standard (PCI DSS) [75], Sarbanes-Oxley Act (SOX) [102], Health Insurance Portability and Accountability Act (HIPAA) [7], Federal Information Security Management Act (FISMA) and ISO 270001 [44], are considered more reliable, trustworthy and secure [1].

3.2.7 Identity and Access Control

Identity and access management are a definite cause of concern for CSPs and CSCs [83, 95]. Various traditional rules may no longer apply in virtual cloud environments; however, identity and access management models are the basis of reliable and secure availability of cloud services to consumers. When identity and access control solutions are implemented outside the local boundary of organization, the management and applicability of these mechanisms become more complex and challenging. Leveraging the existing enterprise directory services such as lightweight directory access protocol (LDAP) in cloud environment typically fails to provide access control, since they offer no support for the management of access control from the CSC's end points. In addition, some organizations provide manual provisioning and de-provisioning of users and applications in the cloud, which adds to the administrative burden of IT staff. On the other hand, malicious insiders may exploit the weaknesses within the data security model and gain unauthorized access to the protected information using various attack mechanisms. These attacks mainly include cross-site scripting, Structured Query Language (SQL) injection, cookie manipulation [14], taking advantage of the known vulnerabilities that are unpatched, zero-day attacks and more specifically data encryption and availability issues as far as cloud computing is concerned.

3.2.8 Digital Forensics

Digital forensics is an emerging field that helps law enforcement with digital evidence collection, inspection, exploration and reporting, at minimal operational cost and investigation complexity [16]. Digital forensics in cloud brings to light new technical and legal challenges, since the detection and collection of evidences in remote, flexible, scalable and third-party controlled cloud environment is different from the conventional digital forensic tasks. In addition, tools for cloud-based digital forensics are not available, thus investigators are restricted to use the traditional tools like Guidance EnCase or AccessData Forensic Toolkit (FTK) [30]. Even though the objectives of cloud forensic investigator are similar to the conventional investigators, however, due to the generally untrustworthy nature of cloud environment, the issues in cloud forensics are multiplied such as distributed information, large data stores and lack of physical access.

3.2.9 Other Security Issues

In addition to the above-mentioned issues, there are many other security and privacy challenges which have been familiarized after the emergence of new cloud concepts that mainly include cloud federation, insourcing and outsourcing of dynamic resources [38, 47, 62, 97]. These advance-level security challenges can be categorized into five main classes, including safety standards, network, access control, cloud infrastructure and data categories. The safety class deals with standard bodies and authorities where the lack of safety standards, compliance risks, lack of auditing [37], lack of legal aspects (SLA) and lack of trust between CSPs and cloud consumers are the focused challenging issues [46, 34]. The network category issues are considered to be the most challenging since cloud computing is more prone to network-related attacks compared to the traditional computing paradigms [105]. This category deals with proper installation of network firewalls, network security configurations, Internet protocol vulnerabilities, and Internet dependence security issues [96, 106].

Access control category focuses on account and service hijacking issue, which includes fraud, phishing and other attacks to steal the sensitive credentials of cloud consumers [62]. Malicious insiders, unreliable authentication mechanisms, privileged user's access and browser security have been identified as the major issues of this category [103]. Insecure interfaces of application programming interfaces (APIs) are the most focused challenging issues under the cloud infrastructure category, which cover various vulnerabilities in the set of APIs provided by the cloud providers to their consumers to access services. Quality of service, sharing technical flaws, reliability of suppliers, security misconfiguration, multi-tenancy, server location and backup are the other major security issues in cloud infrastructure category. Furthermore, data redundancy [46], data loss and leakage [12], data location [46], data recovery [63], data privacy [15], data protection [15] and data availability [15, 64] have been identified as the key issues in different scenarios where data have to be properly encrypted, transmitted, secured, controlled and available in the time of need.

3.3 Security As a Service

In the cloud paradigm, sensitive data are held by the third-party service providers in remote, unknown locations, which highlights the requirement of the primary security of data and applications. In this regard, the SECaaS delivery model refers to providing different security services to the cloud consumers, with the aim to protect critical assets stored in cloud [20]. This service delivery model offers various benefits to the cloud consumers by providing the basic protection to business critical data and applications. One of the major benefits includes the availability of greater security expertise and advanced features as compared to the traditional security mechanisms within the local boundary of an organization. SECaaS can be applied to any of the SaaS, PaaS and IaaS level to protect the data, or the security features can be subscribed as on-demand services for protection of data in local organization [43].

The major purpose of this delivery model is to reduce the cost of hiring the security experts and analysts [2, 20]. It also reduces the complexity and workload of housing and managing the security solutions and underlying resources. All the security-related administrative tasks are outsourced, which saves cost and time, hence

Fig. 3.2 Security as a service

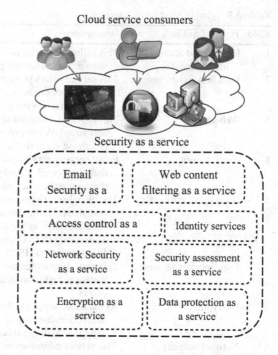

allowing the organization to devote more time to its core functionalities. This model provides a special type of environment where the CSCs have a greater control over their data and applications, and the additional security features mitigate the risk of any intrusion and illegal access [43]. Another major advantage of SECaaS is a web interface that allows in-house administration of some tasks as well as a view of the security environment and ongoing activities [2]. This service delivery model includes different security mechanisms as a service, e.g. 'email security as a service (ESECaaS)', 'identity and access control as a service' (ACaaS) and 'web security as a service', as depicted in Fig. 3.2.

One of the SECaaS types is ESECaaS, which is a well-defined utility for securing customer's emails in cloud as well as in enterprises [21]. This service type provides on-demand email SECaaS to cloud consumers by incorporating the existing solutions on a more abstract level rather than instituting new methods of email security. This email security is provided by two main methods: fully outsourced and enterprise augmentation methodologies [21]. In the fully outsourced methodology, the entire inbox and interfaces are outsourced to the cloud platform. An email user interface is provided by the cloud provider for all the organization's end users. The CSP is responsible for circumventing the different threats, e.g. email spam, malware and virus propagation and phishing attacks. In the second method, the on premise emails and interfaces are secured through additional security features subscribed as on-demand cloud services.

Another important type of SECaaS is 'Identity and access management-as-a-service' also known as 'ACaaS', where the identity management and access control

Table 3.1 Types of security as a service

S.No	Types of SECaaS	Description
1	Identity and access management	This includes people, processes and systems that are used to manage access to enterprise resources by assuring the identity
2	Data loss and prevention	This service offers protection of data, usually by running as some sort of client on desktops/servers and running rules around what can be done
3	Web security	This provides an added layer of protection on top of things like anti-virus (AV) to prevent malware from entering the enterprise via activities such as web browsing
4	Email security	Email security service provides control over inbound and outbound email, thereby protecting the organization from phishing and malicious attacks
5	Security assessment	Traditional security assessments for infrastructure and compliance audits are defined and supported by multiple standards such as the National Institute of Standards and Technology (NIST) and International Organization for Standardization (ISO)
6	Intrusion management	This service provides intrusion management processes for pattern recognition to detect and react to statistically unusual events
7	Encryption	As the name suggests, this service consists of encryption and decryption, hashing, digital signatures, certificate generation and renewal, key exchange
8	Network security	This service addresses security controls at the network in aggregate or specifically addressed at the individual network of each resource

solutions are provided as on-demand services to the cloud consumers [22]. Different identity management solutions for securely maintaining, creating and managing the digital information of organization's end users are available as cloud services. Similarly, access management mechanisms, including attribute-based access control (ABAC), role-based access control (RBAC), task-based access control and usage-based access control, are provided to consumers for assuring the authorized access to data and applications. This service is provided by CSPs by adopting either of the two methods. According to the first method, the entire application is outsourced to cloud platform where the identity and access management of data and application are provided by the cloud provider. Whereas in the second method, the enterprise rents in the on-demand identity and ACSs and adds these solutions as extra security features to the application running on local systems [22]. These services assure the identity of application's users by proper verification mechanisms and then granting the correct level of access to the resource.

'Web security as a service', as shown in Table 3.1, is another significant type of SECaaS where different key components of web security are provided as on-demand services to consumers that mainly include web malware scanning, uniform resource locator (URL) filtering, central access control policy set and vulnerability intelligence [23]. The web SECaaS is responsible for providing the cloud-based dynamic services to protect the end users and their devices without requiring static approaches of security and is provided by adopting three different methods. The simplest method of web SECaaS is to directly forward the web traffic to the cloud platform, where content filtering and different anti-virus (AV) services are used to protect the web content. The second method involves the use of a security gateway that is deployed by the enterprise in its local domain to cache the static web content. The gateway is managed through using the management and reporting interfaces provided by the cloud provider. All the web traffic is forwarded to the malware protection, vulnerability assessment and web filtering services of CSP. Third approach is the use of security agents which protect the remote users by pushing the web traffic to the content filtering services of cloud provider [23].

As discussed previously, there are various categories of SECaaS [20], where each category stands alone and can be provided as an independent service through cloud, much to the benefit of the service consumers. In addition, each category has its own definite set of functions such as intrusion management that specifically deals with the detection and prevention of unusual patterns and events, whereas the network security is responsible for governing the network security controls only. Of all the aforementioned categories, identity and access management is an important one and due to many open authorization issues, this chapter mainly focuses on access management for cloud.

3.4   Access Control As a Service

In the cloud environment, when the users move their applications, traditional controls are no longer effective enough to protect sensitive data as they are is residing on untrusted networks (de-parameterization) [36]. Various access control systems have been developed so far, however, all of those systems are suitable only for distributed computing environments, where a set of service consumers and services are known beforehand [53]. In addition, conventional access control models do not ensure the security and confidentiality of data and resources at cloud. In most of the cases, CSC and their requested resource belong to different security domains. All these factors render traditional access control models ineffective for cloud. Moreover, as every cloud has unique security policies; therefore, cloud requires a flexible access control mechanism applicable to various kinds of environments.

The ACaaS is a cloud-based approach that aims to ensure the ease of the authentication and authorization of CSCs while they access various cloud services and resources [67]. In the ACaaS, the management and evaluation of access control decisions are externalized and handled by some trusted third-party service provider. The ACaaS operates on application layer and provides an authorization store that is managed and accessed either through code or through a managerial gateway. After the one-time configuration, the CSCs access the applications via ACaaS using an authentication token bundled with authorization claims [67]. Instead of implementing the application-specific access control mechanisms, one can choose the ACaaS to organize the authentication and much of the authorization of their service consumers.

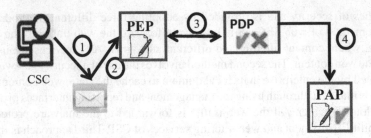

Fig. 3.3 Workflow of policy decision point

The ACaaS not only facilitates fast and easy application development but also allows its customers to access and acquire multiple services and resources with reduced or single sign-on authentications.

The ACaaS is required to be developed in a way that it offers compatibility with the well-known programming languages and runtime environments along with the support for international standards such as OpenID, OAuth, WS-Trust [4], etc. In addition, ACaaS must be compatible with most of the modern web platforms such as Python, Java,.NET, Ruby and PHP. Some real-time implementations of ACaaS are also available in the market: *Azure Platform AppFabric* ACS [68], *Junos Pulse Access Control Service* Ver. 4.4 [49] just to name few. An ACaaS comprises policy decision point (PDP), policy enforcement point (PEP), policy administrator point (PAP) and policy information point (PIP) [108] components. Each of these components can be developed and managed by the service consumer or they may use the ones provided by the ACaaS provider (trusted third party). To be precise, the ACS provider ensures the segregation and confidentiality of the data contents, even if it gets together with CSCs and CSPs.

3.4.1 Components of Access Control As a Service

3.4.1.1 Policy Decision Point

The PDP is responsible for the retrieval of access control policies from the PAP module into the main memory and evaluating the CSC requests against those policies [57, 80], as shown in Fig. 3.3. The typical response that a web resource access request might have is either permit or deny. After evaluating the policy, if the decision made by the PDP is as desired, then it responds with a permit token; otherwise, it denies the authorization request. In case of no matching policy or error, the PDP generates a response declaring *not applicable* or *indeterminate*, respectively. Hence, the PDP essentially answers to 'yes' or 'no' questions. In a common use case scenario, (1) the CSC requests for a cloud resource, (2) the PEP captures the access request, and (3) forwards it to the PDP module, (4) the PDP consults its policy stores (PAP and PIP) and responds with the authorization decision as either permit or deny.

Fig. 3.4 Workflow of policy enforcement point

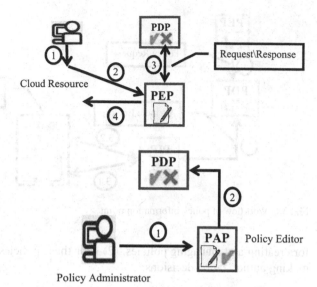

Cloud Resource

Request\Response

PEP

Fig. 3.5 Workflow of policy administration point

Policy Administrator

Policy Editor

3.4.1.2 Policy Enforcement Point

The PEP is the most trusted component in the authorization architecture, responsible for the enforcement of the decisions made by the PDP, as depicted in Fig. 3.4. PEP is the logical entity that implements policy-based management and controls the access to secure cloud applications and resources [57, 80].

It can be embedded within the web service or placed as an interceptor in front of it and describes the service consumer's attributes to other entities on the system. However, regardless of its placement, the PEP protects a resource in many different ways. In a common use case scenario, (1) whenever the CSC attempts to access a resource on cloud, (2) the PEP intercepts the resource access request and translates it into any of the policy language such as *eXtensible Access Control Markup Language* (XACML) that is understandable by the PDP, (3) it then forwards the access request to the PDP for policy evaluation, (4) after evaluation the PEP enforces its decision, which is either permit or deny.

3.4.1.3 Policy Administration Point

The PAP is responsible for authoring, managing and debugging the access control policies [57, 80]. The PAPs are required to have user-friendly graphical user interfaces (GUIs) with editors having complete language support to define and administer polices, as per the user requirements. The web service accession request of service consumers to a protected resource, as shown in policies created are used by the PDP to evaluate and decide whether to permit or deny. Common use-case scenario is presented in Fig. 3.5, where (1) policy administrator interacts with the PAP module

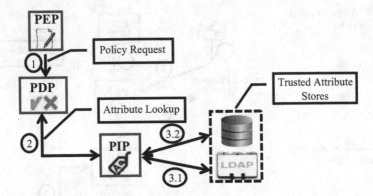

Fig. 3.6 Workflow of policy information point

for creating and managing policies, (2) later these policies are used by the PDP for making authorization decisions.

3.4.1.4 Policy Information Point

The PIP refers to an attribute store that works in conjunction with the PDP to perform the policy evaluation [57, 80] as shown in Fig. 3.6. When the CSC attempts to access the protected cloud resource, (1) the PEP intercepts that request, generates a resource access request and sends it to the PDP, (2) all the required attributes for policy evaluation are queried from the PIP, (3) the PIP further requests its attribute stores (LDAP or SQL database) for attribute aggregation and answers back with the attributes required for decision making.

A complete overview of the ACaaS is portrayed in Fig. 3.7, where the CSCs' request for cloud applications and their service acquisitioning requests are intercepted by the PEP that consults the PDP for access decision. The PDP, after consulting the PIP and PAP, responds with either deny or permit. The cloud-based ACaaS must be flexible and reliable to satisfy the user requirements and dynamic nature of the cloud.

3.5 Access Control Challenges in the Cloud

The risk of security breach in cloud-hosted applications is rather high due to the immature, shared and distributed nature of the paradigm. Many enterprises and cloud consumers have critical data to be stored in the cloud, which makes the access control an essential requirement to be catered by the cloud providers. Many traditional access control solutions and mechanisms are inadequate in dynamic environment due to which cloud authorization is facing several challenges and issues. Major challenges that are faced by access control in the cloud are discussed in the following sections.

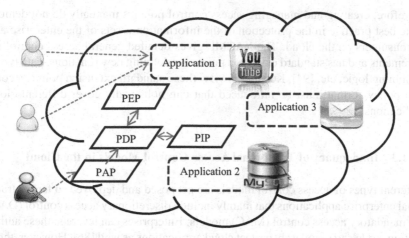

Fig. 3.7 Access control in cloud

3.5.1   Access Control Challenges with Respect to Management

There are various challenges and issues of access control models with respect to their management in distributed cloud platform. Few of these access control challenges are discussed subsequently.

3.5.1.1   Management of User Profile and Access Control Policies

In a cloud computing environment, maintaining and creating the user profiles and access control policies are more challenging because the information may come from different sources—using different processes, naming conventions and technologies—and may need to be transmitted securely between organizations over a hostile Internet. Moreover, there are typically too many technical rules to manage, and these rules do not match the understanding of human administrators. Furthermore, these technical rules needs to be updated frequently to maintain them correct after each time system change, and it is hard to establish that the level of confidence/assurance of the technical policy enforcement matches the intent of the human administrator. As a consequence, it is critical to carefully plan the tools and processes to make the access policies updating process manageable through automation.

3.5.1.2   Developing Common Policy Format

In order to avoid interoperability and compatibility issues between policies specified by the cloud providers and cloud consumers, commonly used policy specification format is required. According to the OASIS XACML [94], managing the policy configuration at each point of policy enforcement is quite expensive and unreliable [93].

Therefore, creating and managing access control policies manually do not demonstrate best practice in the protection of the information assets of the enterprise and its consumers on the cloud. The XACML gives detailed general access control requirements and has standard extension points for defining new functions, data types, combining logic, etc. [94]. Keeping in view these standard extension points, a common policy format must be introduced that can holistically cover different cloud applications.

3.5.1.3 Inadequacy of Traditional Access Control Models in the Cloud

Different types of access control models are proposed and deployed so far for traditional enterprise applications that mainly include discretionary access control (DAC) and mandatory access control (MAC) models. Enterprises can leverage these authorization models to seamlessly protect cloud applications as well [86]. However, these access control models have some specific parameters that are suitable only for particular scenarios to provide restricted access of data. To make authorized access to resources on cloud, the access control policies must be formulated in a way that they can handle the dynamic nature of the cloud environment. Some of the cloud services do not call for strict authorization rules and are accessed after confirmation of few user attributes. Other services require the verification of several factors, considering the additional constraints before permitting access to the cloud-based data. Therefore, an access control model having static and specific features is not suitable for the variety of applications and services hosted on the cloud.

3.5.1.4 Time Consuming and Expensive for Organizations

If organizations start making access control policies for their data and applications, it would consume a lot of their time and money. Reason for this insufficiency is that most organizations do not hire security experts, they ask their network administrators to create and execute policies. Most of these administrators do not have sufficient knowledge on security and they leave loopholes and ambiguity in specifying the security policies. If security professionals are hired, it may lead to over-budgeting for small organizations. In addition, those security professionals first need to understand company infrastructure before creating policies, which is a time-consuming task.

3.5.1.5 Translation of Security Policies into Deployment Environment

Another authorization challenge is the translation of access control policies into security implementation, which is more time consuming, repetitive, pricey, and error prone. If organizations try to implement security policies within their applications that would easily amount to the bulk of security costs as traditional users are managed into and out of the access control lists (ACLs) for various access control models.

3.5.1.6   Selection of Suitable Access Control Model for the Cloud

The cloud security alliance (CSA) specifies some challenges in selecting or reviewing the adequacy of access control solutions for the cloud services [18, 60]. According to the CSA, it is very difficult to determine the suitability of an access control model for different types of services and applications hosted on the cloud. Also, these organizations do not find suitable format for specification of policies and user information. These problems need to be catered by providing the liberty to select any model that suits the security requirement of organization.

3.5.1.7   Complex Management and Implementation of Access Control Models

All the data and applications of cloud consumers are distributed on different locations which introduce complexity in applicability and management of access control models. The location of data in the cloud is distributed and unknown to the consumers, which makes it difficult to analyse the access control vulnerabilities and threats at these locations. These authorization threats are invisible to the cloud consumer which introduces complexity in implementation and management of a unified access control model that can reliably secure the distributed data on various locations in the cloud.

3.5.1.8   Performance of Access Control Models in the Cloud

Cloud computing technology contains tens of thousands of physical servers and VMs. These VMs and servers are constantly added and detached, depending upon the number of consumers and their required computing resources. In this regard, traditional access control models are not adequate to handle the access control of such a large-scale resources. The speed and performance of these models decreases if these are implemented in the cloud. There is a need to introduce new access control models that can meet the high-performance requirements of the cloud environment and handle the large-scale resources.

3.5.1.9   Dynamic Provisioning and De-provisioning of Users

Traditional access control models are not effective in the cloud environment because dynamic provisioning between the consumers and cloud providers needs more flexible models to be implemented. In a multi-tenant environment, the consumers are added at runtime to use the different cloud resources and removed at any time dynamically. Traditional access control models are static in nature and cannot provide dynamic addition and removal of consumers from ACLs. There is no functionality to manage the delegation and revocation of access privileges at the runtime as new consumers are added to access the resources.

3.5.1.10 Application-Specific Access Control Requirements

The sensitivity level of applications also varies depending upon their operation and data usage, so the cloud consumers must have the capability to incorporate the required level of access control model accordingly. Similarly, as the cloud is offering services to various users—individual user, application, corporate user of organization—their access levels must be differentiated in order to have controlled data access. These problems need to be catered by providing flexible and more efficient access control models as compared to the traditional models.

3.5.2 Access Control Challenges with Respect to Security

There are several security attacks and threats that introduce challenging issues in adoption and implementation of the access control mechanisms in the cloud environment. Some of these threats are described subsequently.

3.5.2.1 Elevation of Privileges

Elevation of privilege is a threat in which a user is logged in to the system as a normal user having low-level privileges [29, 71]. After the successful login, the user tries to obtain the root privileges or high-level access to the system. In the cloud scenario, the elevation in privilege helps the attacker to access the VMs and stored data of consumers. In a multi-tenant environment, this threat affects more than one consumer's resources and the attacker can obtain unauthorized access to many VMs at a time.

3.5.2.2 Disclosure of Confidential Data

In the disclosure of confidential data, the attacker accesses the sensitive data due to the failure of access control operation [71]. This is the attack on confidentiality of data stored at different locations. In the cloud scenario, this threat allows the attacker to illegally access the critical data of consumers stored at distributed locations [29]. Confidential data can be illegally accessed either due to the failure of access control mechanism provided by the cloud providers or due to the absence of efficient mechanisms.

3.5.2.3 Data Tempering

Data tempering is the threat in which the user accesses the stored data and makes modifications according to requirements and kind of attack [29, 71]. This is the attack on integrity of data stored due to failure of access control operations and functions. In the cloud scenario, the data tempering causes unauthorized access to the consumer's data in physical servers or VMs at the cloud platform. This attack mostly targets the infrastructure layer services where complete VM is hijacked and required modifications are made to the data.

3.5.2.4 Unauthorized Access to Configuration Stores

This type of unauthorized access makes an attacker able to modify the sensitive configuration files as well as the binding settings of system. This is the attack on integrity and confidentiality of configuration files due to the either failure of access control operations or absence of proper access control mechanism. This attack targets the system and configuration files of the cloud services at the SaaS, PaaS or IaaS layer.

3.5.2.5 Unauthorized Access to the Administrator Interfaces

Unauthorized access to the administrator interfaces makes an attacker to access the administrator settings and modify them according to the type of privileges required to the system. In this type of attack, the attacker exploits different vulnerabilities in web interfaces of cloud providers using which the services are provided to the consumers.

3.5.2.6 Retrieval of Plain Text Configuration Secrets

Retrieval of plain text configuration secrets makes an attacker to successfully access the configuration files and their secrets [71]. The attacker can retrieve sensitive information from these files like the strings having database connection URL and path. This retrieved information about the consumer's database leads to unauthorized access to sensitive data stored in the cloud.

3.6 Literature Review and Analysis

Despite the various advantages of the cloud computing, there are still challenging issues which are preventing different organizations from migrating their critical data and applications onto the cloud. In order to assure adequate data security in the cloud, the implementation and deployment of efficient and reliable access control mechanisms are required. Various access control techniques have been introduced for assuring the effective access management of data and applications on cloud. However, in order to highlight the key challenges that the cloud consumers can face for adequate protection of their data, there is a need to perform a comprehensive analysis of various famous access control techniques. In this regard, we have performed a detailed and in-depth critical analysis of access control techniques according to the NIST- defined assessment features, including mainly *separation of duty, ease of privilege assignment, least privilege, policy conflicts, configuration flexibility, policy repository and retrieval, policy distribution* and *horizontal scope* [42].

In the following subsections, we present a detailed analysis of the various cloud-based access control techniques against the above-mentioned NIST- defined access control features. Furthermore, the merits and demerits of each presented technique are provided from the ACaaS perspective. Our analysis intends to help all the stakeholders (CSCs and CSPs) in taking a knowledgeable decision while making a choice for the cloud-based access control models.

3.6.1   API Access Control in Cloud Using the RBAC Model

Sirisha et al. [91] proposed the secure access control APIs for the cloud. This technique uses the RBAC model involving two stages, the user attribute authentication and then role validation. This technique assumes that the user is already authenticated with some authentication mechanism, and all its attributes and roles are managed in some database. Once the user is authenticated, its attribute will be verified from a database, and a specific role against its attribute will be assigned to it. Therefore, the user can only access those services that are allowed for assigned role. Same is the case in the second stage of access control; there is a database of permissions corresponding to different roles. After identifying the roles, the permissions are checked in the database against that role and accordingly, the access is granted or denied.

The proposed access control technique implements the RBAC in which all the permissions to an object are associated with the roles of the subjects. The management for assigning and revoking the roles and permissions is simple, thus providing the feature of ease of privilege assignments. The RBAC and ABAC mechanisms are implemented at API level where the management of attributes, e.g. subjects, roles and resources require little modifications to deploy in different scenarios which escalate the configuration flexibility. The attribute-validation and role-validation modules use the underlying local database, hence supporting the policy distribution and retrieval features. There is no support to the *policy conflicts* and least privilege features in the proposed API access control in the cloud. The RBAC and ABAC models are implemented at the application layer through which the cloud consumers can access the cloud services. This API-level access control is platform independent and can be incorporated in any environment that escalates the horizontal scope. The assignment, revocation and management of roles are performed by the '*role validation mechanism*' module. Similarly, the assignment and revocation of objects and their attributes are performed by the '*Attribute validation mechanism*" module, due to which the proposed technique supports the separation of duty.

3.6.2   Ensuring Access Control in the Cloud-Provisioned Health-Care Systems

Narayanan et al. [73] have proposed a solution to ensure authorized access in cloud-based health-care systems. In the RBAC, the roles and tasks are not separated so the combination of these two parameters, task–role-based access control (TRBAC), has been adopted for these systems. Authors have analyzed some access control requirements for electronic health-care system. Tenant, user, task, information resource, business role, permission, session and work flow are the factors to be considered for access control mechanisms. Classification of tasks is done on the basis of active and passive access control and inheritable and noninheritable tasks.

The proposed access control for health-care systems provides both static and dynamic separation of duty at task definition and task instance levels. The static separation of duty is supported by prohibiting the assignment of two or more mutual tasks to the same role at the same time. Similarly, the dynamic separation of duty is performed at the time of the task instance creation level. At that time, the dynamic separation of duty prohibits the concurrent execution of two or more tasks by the same role in work flow. In the proposed TRBAC model, the tasks are classified into passive and active access controls. In order to add a task from the passive access control to active access control, the user assignments, role hierarchy, permissions assignment and constraints, all are modified. This affects the usability and performance of the access control systems and thus fails to support the ease of privilege assignments feature. The proposed system has local policy repository due to which it supports local distribution and retrieval of access control policies. Least privilege is achieved through task instances. The access permissions are granted when the task is initiated and the access control permissions are revoked when the task is completed. The task instance is created for each user and the user gets to see only certain information. However, the proposed system does not support any mechanism to resolve the policy conflicts between two or more rules. The proposed system parameters, e.g. roles hierarchy and tasks classification need to be modified for environments that demand multiple factors for access decision, reducing system's configuration flexibility.

3.6.3   Multi-Tenancy-Based Access Control in the Cloud

Due to multi-tenancy in cloud computing, duty separation between the CSP and tenant is a main concern. The solution proposed by Li et al. [61] is a multi-tenancy-based access control (MTACM) model for application security in the public cloud. The main idea of the MTACM is to classify the subjects and objects in the traditional access control mechanisms into two granule levels. One was tenant granule level and the other was application granule level. First level was managed or controlled by the CSP to implement the compartmentalization of different tenants, while the second was controlled by the tenants to control the access to their applications.

In the MTACM, the separation of duty between the CSP and consumers is supported by classifying the subjects and objects into two granular levels, as described previously. Furthermore, the tenant rules are defined to provide separation of duty at the tenant granular level by prohibiting the assignment of two or more same management subjects to one tenant. The five core modules OpenSSL module, Identification and Authentication module, Audit module, Access control module and Management module adhere to the platform dependency as all of these are implemented on Nginx module, hence limiting the *scope* of the MTACM. The overhead of adding, creating and removing the objects rules, subject rules and security policies is distributed between the cloud providers and cloud consumers, thus providing the ease of privilege assignments feature and improving the performance of the MTACM system. The access control module implements the DAC and MAC mechanisms and uses its local policy repository for storage of access control rules. Furthermore, the MAC model of the MTACM assures the assignment of only those *privileges* to the tenant's subjects, which are necessary to complete the tasks. However, the MTACM system does not mention any procedure to avoid the policy conflicts which may arise because of the access decisions of multiple rules. The DAC and MAC mechanisms are implemented at the API level; however, the dependency of access control module on top of Nginx requires complex modifications for different environments that lower the configuration flexibility.

3.6.4   SaaS Access Control Research Based on Usage-Based Access Control

Junli Zhu et al. [109] have highlighted the access control problem faced by the cloud consumers, which is mandatory for protecting the user's sensitive information in the SaaS model. Traditional access control models like attribute-based, role-based or fine-grained access models are not sufficient for protecting the private data of users in the cloud. This system presents a unified access control model which is designed for preventing the user's critical data from unauthorized and illegitimate access. Trust management and digital rights management have been identified as the important security problems faced by today's business world and the IT organizations. In this system, the usage-based access control (UCON) post-obligation model has been implemented that can guarantee the fine-grained and secure access control on the customer's private data. Attributes mutability and continuity of attributes are the two significant properties of the UCON model. Authorization and obligations are the major components of the model. Types of authorization mainly include PreA, where authorization is performed before granting any access, and OnA, where authorization is executed during the usage. Similarly, PreB are some mandatory requirements that should be satisfied before granting access. OnB are those requirements that needed to be satisfied during the execution of access control.

In the proposed UCON model, the PreA, PreB, PostB and OnB are managed and maintained separately by distributed modules and PEPs due to which the model adheres to the separation of duty feature. The UCON PreA, PreB, PostB and OnB model checks for the user privileges and makes an authorization decision before the usage of specific resource is allowed to the customer. During the use of that resource, the model facilitates the continuous checking of required obligations as well as encounter policies for the user privileges, thus supporting the least privilege feature. The proposed access control model is platform independent and can be implemented for wide range of SaaS applications in the cloud, therefore supporting the horizontal scope. In order to alter the defined privileges of a user, all the associated PreA, PreB, PostB and OnB policies are needed to be modified, which affects the speed and performance of access control model; therefore, making the process of *privileges assignment* more difficult. However, the model does not support any mechanism for policy distribution as well as policy repository and retrieval. Similarly, there is no procedure that can make authorization decisions when there is any conflict between two or more rules, thus lacking the policy conflicts support. The model is implemented for any SaaS layer application, thus supporting the configuration flexibility.

3.6.5 Policy Enforcement Framework for Cloud Data Management

Hamlen et al. [39] have identified different security and privacy concerns of the user's data, which are the major hindrances to the adoption of the cloud technology by the IT and business world. In order to provide secure and robust cloud services, there is a need for highly flexible and distributed policy framework that can ensure the integrity and privacy of customer's data on the cloud platform. In this technique, authors have proposed a flexible policy enforcement framework for data management on cloud which includes two types of access control models, i.e. the rule-based access control and context-based access control model. In this framework, three significant dimensions are considered for policies, namely data type, computation and policy requirements. Major modules of the proposed framework include policy-reasoning module, data-processing task rewriting module, preprocessing module and post-processing module. Different policy types that include policies for data sharing and traditional access control mechanisms have been catered by the proposed framework.

In the proposed framework, preprocessing and post-processing modules separately manage the policies regarding the different users, their attributes and data-processing tasks thus adhere to the separation of duty principle. The model provides the multiple groups' principle, which can resolve the conflicts of data access rules between two or more consumers by adding the mutually exclusive users into a separate group; therefore, it supports the policy conflicts' feature. The inclusion and exclusion of enforcement mechanisms into the binary code of the job require complex modifications for every new data management policy, which limits the configuration flexibility of the model. Moreover, there is no mechanism to support the least privilege principle in the model. The preprocessing and post-processing modules are responsible for generating and storing the formulated data management policies, hence providing the local repository for policy storage and retrieval. The aspect-oriented in-lined reference monitors (IRMs) and aspect-oriented programming (AOP) are responsible for creating and formulating the platform-independent data access control policies, thus increasing the horizontal scope of the model. Policy reasoning module maps the access control policies to a specific set of tasks, and it defines the user privileges automatically, hence introducing the ease of privilege assignments' feature in the model.

3.6.6 The Privacy-Aware Access Control System Using A-RBAC in a Private Cloud

There are three parties involved in offering cloud services to consumers: DO, CSP (CSP) and user. Capability-based access control system along with cryptographic techniques is proposed for cloud platform by Mon et al. [72]. Capability list consists of user ID (UID), file ID (FID) and their corresponding access rights. Values for access rights are assigned as 0 for read, 1 for write, and 2 for both read and write. The DO computes the MD5 hash of data files and encrypts it with the DO's private key and public key of the CSP. The CSP stores these encrypted data files and capability lists for users, but the contents of data files are not revealed to them. Diffie–Hellman algorithm is used to generate the symmetric keys that are shared between the CSP and the user for the purpose of secure communication. New user first performs the registration by the DO sending UID, FID, nonce, timestamp and the required access rights. The DO sends the capability list, intended encrypted content and corresponding decryption keys to the CSP after the user verification. The CSP updates the capability list accordingly and also sends registration confirmation to the newly added user. After that, the user directly requests the CSP for data access and gets encrypted response which is then decrypted to get the session key and hash value.

Least privilege is followed for this technique by assigning access rights for the basic unit of data file. Duties are clearly defined for cloud consumers with the specification of access rights in capability access list. Users can only perform the functions specified by the DOs in their corresponding list following the separation of duty. Policy conflicts are not managed in this proposed system. The capability list contains the static entities of users and their corresponding allowable objects that are not well suited for dynamic environment like cloud. It does not consider the multiple factors for access decision, which is the major requirement for distributed environment results in limiting its configuration flexibility. Double encryption is used in the proposed technique to provide strong cryptographic strength through which keys management, configuration and their distribution to a large number of consumers become overhead. It will make the system inflexible to be adopted in different computing platforms and environments, thus limiting its *scope*. The access control policies for the private cloud are stored at the local databases of data provider and the user's logs, whereas the privacy preference specifications are managed at the DO's end, thus offering local as well as federated policy repository and retrieval feature. The system specifies policy by defining permissions in the capability list with

UID and FID that will somehow simplify the policy creation process and therefore introducing the ease of privilege assignments' feature.

3.6.7 Secure Access Mechanism for Cloud Storage

Harnik et al. [40] also propose the capability-based access control mechanism to address the access control requirements for cloud storage. Proposed access control model offers the extensive delegation mechanism by appending original capability with reduced delegated capability. Identity field is introduced in the capability that performs user authentication and eliminates the identification overhead at the enforcement point. The proposed mechanism also offers features like scalability, chains of services, user-to-user access delegation, improved performance, availability, revocation, interoperability, and pre-resource audit ability.

In the proposed capability-based access control model, the propagation of end user access rights all the way down in hierarchical manner is incorporated via the chain of services mechanism. This chain of services mechanism ensures the least privilege principle by propagating the end-client access token to only the required users according to their capabilities. The authentication component is responsible for authenticating a client and provides it with a token for its identity. After the authentication, the client is directed towards the authorization component that generates a token having the capability of the user, thus ensuring the separation of the duty principle in the model. However, the model does not incorporate any mechanism for resolving the *conflicts* between two or more access control policies. The access control manager of the proposed design is flexible enough to implement a diverse range of access control models that can include capability based, attribute based or role based, allowing compatibility with any of the underlying platforms and environments, thus escalating the horizontal scope. The data centers in the proposed model are high coupled with the storage layer and replication manager; therefore, adding any new module or deploying the existing solution in the new scenario introduces complex interoperability issues making the configuration flexibility low. The identity manager and access manager use their separate databases for storage of policies and user's capabilities-related data, thus offering local policy repository and retrieval. The replica manager updates the entire user's capabilities information across the distributed data centers; however, the large number of replicas makes the update process complex and the *privilege assignments* more difficult.

3.6.8 Provenance-Based Access Control in Cloud Environments

Adam Bates et al. [10] stated the granular access control to be the most challenging and promising security issue for data storage in cloud computing. Relevant policies for migration of data across the boundaries and scattered policies of organizations have been identified as the major reasons for this issue. In this article, an access control model has been introduced, which is based on provenance and its use in critical applications. Provenance provides all the information about different actions and processes taken on specific data and is used to mitigate these access control challenges in the cloud. The system achieves the three main goals which include distribution of provenance in the dynamic cloud environment, assessment of remote data objects and provenance-based access control model where provenance is also a significant component along with the basic objects, subjects and rights for access control. The system also includes the additional provenance database and policy database modules other than the core PEPand PDP.

The proposed access control mechanism supports least privilege where the consumers are permitted to use only those data objects which are mandatory to perform certain actions in accordance with their data provenance policies. However, there is no specific procedure or rules defined for assuring the separation of duty principle, which is necessary to limit the access of subjects for eliminating the security breaches. If some conflicts appear between two or more policies, the provenance records in the provenance database are used to immediately revoke the subject's privileges on that data object, hence providing support to the policy conflict feature in the model. The access control policies are not integrated into the OS; however, transferring from one policy to another is not an easy task even at the API level due to the large number of provenance records associated with each single data object. Therefore, the configuration flexibility is lower in this provenance-based access control model. The provenance database is responsible for storage of provenance information, and the policy database manages the storage of security policies, thus incorporating the policy repository and retrieval feature locally. The core components of the cloud provenance authority, which mainly include the PEP, PDP, provenance database and policy database, can easily be deployed in any environment independent of the underlying infrastructure; therefore, supporting high horizontal scope. However, the presented provenance-based system does not specify any mechanism for ensuring ease of privilege assignment feature.

3.6.9 Access Control of Cloud Services Based on Usage-Based Access Control

Danwei et al. [27] describe a cloud service security solution. The presented solution is based on the UCON and negotiation module. The article gives a brief introduction to the cloud computing and service models, followed by the high-level design and architecture of Nego-UCON$_{ABC}$ authorization module for cloud environment. In the Nego-UCON$_{ABC}$, access control decisions are based on attributes, obligations and conditions. Digital certificates are used to declare the entity's attributes assigned by the issuer. Obligations are stored in policy database as rules using the XACML, whereas conditions are formulated from the operating environment and stored in the policy database using the XACML. The negotiation module is specifically designed to resolve the issues related to inadequacy of the user attributes and inconsistency in condition parameters. The Nego module helps ensure the flexibility of access control model and is comprised of Security Assertion Markup Language (SAML) server and cloud service module.

In this system, the negotiation module handles the issues regarding the conflicts between access request and access rules. It allows the user to get a second access choice by changing certain parameters and attributes instead of refusing the access directly. Therefore, it offers support to policy conflicts. Configuration flexibility is another important feature that is offered through its negotiation module that assists the change in attribute and conditions according to the user requirement. The Nego-UCON$_{ABC}$ offers local repositories for policy storage and retrieval, thus improving the efficiency as well as the cost of access control. Since the proposed system is based on the UCON model and maintains separate databases for the storage of policies regarding services, negotiations and attributes, thus adhering to the separation of duty principle. Furthermore, the presented solution defines a clear access control mechanism for privileges assignment, offering support to the ease of privilege assignment as well. The system uses local repositories for policy storage and retrieval, thus helping in efficient policy distribution and applicability. Presented system does not specify any mechanism for ensuring the least privilege principle. Horizontal scope is another critical feature that the proposed system does not incorporate in its design and architecture.

3.6.10 Access Control As a Service for Public Cloud Storage

Zhang et al. [108] presented an ACS for the public cloud storage, where authorization decision is subject to the DO's decision or PDP (PDP) and PEP modules. This article aims to address the problem of flexible access control in service and data outsourcing scenarios to protect the sensitive data of the owners. In order to implement the designed service, an attribute-full proxy re-encryption (AF-PRE) scheme is offered as a core component of the proposed solution. The key features of the presented solution include realization of simple key management, capacity to compose the attributes along with the anticipated combination of authorization and encryption with appropriate separation. In order to give the proof of concept, authors performed security analysis of their system. They further claim that their scheme for executing queries on the encrypted data can be efficiently integrated with the presented solution.

In the presented AF-PRE scheme, the access control expressions are often generated from the attributes that advance to establish a privilege value. This value is then sent to the PDP delegation module to assist in the decision-making process and ensures the least privilege principle. In case of policy conflicts between the ACSs, the AF-PRE scheme ensures the confidentiality of data contents and provides certain mechanisms to prevent *policy conflicts*. The presented scheme offers a clear separation of policy and mechanism such as attribute-based encryption for outsourced situations, thus offering support to configuration flexibility. The ACS for the public cloud storage is under the control of the DO, and the PDP (PDP) and PEP can be securely delegated, thus offering local as well as federated policy repository and retrieval feature. In addition, the authors highlight separation of duty as the most significant feature of their scheme that offers support to separation methodology in cloud scenarios. Horizontal scope is another critical feature that this scheme offers via its AF-PRE mode; access control policies are publicized by re-encryption keys and privilege values and are generated independently from encryption operation. Authorization update is the dedicated module that handles the change in privileges and ensures the ease of privilege assignments. Policy distribution is offered through the policy translator module that computes a new privilege value, updates its PriV table and sends it to the PDP delegation module that performs the replacing operation.

3.6.11 Usage Control in the Cloud Systems

Lazouskiet al. [58] present an advanced authorization framework based on the usage control (UCON) model and the OASIS XACML standard to control the usage of cloud resources. The presented framework is capable of handling the issue of long-lasting accesses by interrupting the ongoing usage of previously assigned resources when the object's access rights are revoked by the owner. Proposed framework's prototype is implemented and integrated with the OpenNebula toolkit (ONE) that provides ACLs and usage quotas. OpenNebula is a widespread framework for the management of cloud services and resources. System performance tests are also carried out on the prototype to validate the effectiveness of the proposed system. The ONE front end and the authorization service (AS) are hosted in the VM with Ubuntu 10.04 and Java 3.6 support. However, the prototype requires improvements in terms of security and management of various other long-lasting cloud resources and services.

The presented framework addresses the issue of unauthorized accesses by interrupting the accesses that are in progress when the corresponding access rights do not hold any more. In addition, the designed ACS continuously checks for the policy enforcement, so guarantees the least privilege principle. If there is some conflict between the policies or if the decision process recognizes the policy violation, resources are immediately released and the access rights are revoked, offering support to policy conflict feature. The prototype of the authorization system is developed and that API is then integrated with the OpenNebula, thus ensuring configuration flexibility. Proposed scheme provides a GUI and ACS for the *retrieval* of user attributes required for the UCON authorization system. The PIP contacts the attribute managers (AMs) to acquire the required attributes that are *stored* in its local repository. The system offers horizontal scope through its AS module that may execute on other machines instead of the one that is enforcing the access control decision. The AM module is responsible for the handling of the policy distribution among various components of the ACSs. However, this framework does not specify any mechanism to ensure the separation of duty. Similarly, the ease of privilege assignment is also not incorporated in the design and architecture of the presented framework.

3.6.12   OpenPMF SCaaS: Authorization As a Service for Cloud and Service-Oriented Architecture Applications

Lang [56] presents the concept of portable security and compliance policy automation for cloud applications. Proposed system aims to provide protection to the cloud applications and mashups in a seamless manner. Further, this system intends to improve and simplify the secure software development life cycle for cloud applications. The presented system comprises two main components, the policy automation and technical policy generation. The policy automation aspect includes policy configuration, technical policy generation, application authorization management, and incident reporting. The policy configuration is offered as a pay-per-use cloud service to the various application development tools. On the other hand, the technical policy generation, enforcement and monitoring module is implanted into cloud application development and runtime platforms. The article also discusses a reference implementation called OpenPMF Security & Compliance as a Service (SCaaS) which is based on ObjectSecurity OpenPMF, Intalio BPMS and Promia Raven.

The SCaaS enforces the security policies to ensure that only authorized users may invoke secure cloud services and applications following the least privilege principle. The SCaaS policy feed services are used by multiple cloud tenants, thus, to avoid the policy conflicts that may arise due to the generation of multiple conflicting technical policy rules for shared resources, proposed scheme makes the use of the model-driven security (MDS) concepts. The process of policy update is asynchronous and is performed at application start-up or whenever the security rules change (without the need to restart the protected end system). This greatly enhances performance and robustness and ensures configuration flexibility principle. Policies are either generated within cloud using hosted MDS and PaaS development tools or uploaded from local MDS and development tools, thus offering local repository for policy storage and retrieval. Furthermore, the separation of duty principle is ensured through the policy modeling module that divides the tasks among various modules to guarantee the security and compliance requirements. The SCaaS is developed to support the diverse cloud environment where the MDS is installed across multiple development tool (e.g. Eclipse, Intalio BPMS) and aims to protect the applications on various runtime application platforms (e.g. various web application servers, JavaEE, DDS, CORBA/CCM), hence supports horizontal scope. In OpenPMF, the OpenPMF runtime policy repository is responsible for the distribution of policy to the various Open-PMF PDP/PEPon each protected application runtime platform. However, the presented ScaaS does not specify any mechanism for ensuring the ease of privilege assignment feature.

3.6.13   Secure Data Access in Cloud Computing

Privacy-aware access control system (ARBAC) is proposed for cloud that is composed of two models: RBAC and ABAC [87]. It provides secure access to personal identifiable information (PII). The system consists of the DOs, data users, cloud providers and privacy managers. The DOs use VM instances to host their data according to organizational permissions and specify the privacy preferences of data. Users access the cloud-based services and data according to the defined access rights and policies. Cloud providers perform different operations and management tasks on servers according to the rules specified by the DOs. The privacy manager is the essential component of the system responsible for the specification of privacy policies based on the user and data classification levels. In the proposed ARBAC system, the user requests to access data and provides corresponding subject, resource and environment attributes that are required for the service. The CSP verifies the given attributes according to the defined privacy policy in order to return the response of either permit or deny.

Since the ARBAC is the composition of RBAC and ABAC, the least privilege is supported by granting permissions according to specified attributes and role parameters in policy. Management of attributes (subject, resource and environment) in different scenarios requires detailed configuration modifications, resulting in low configuration flexibility. Access control policies are *stored and retrieved* from a local repository; and prior to enforcement, these policies are evaluated against the attributes defined for subject, resource, environment and user roles, which improves the system reliability. Separation of duty is achieved in a way that each subject and resource is associated with particular attributes based on which job functions and access rights are defined. The user and data classification levels are defined according to which privacy preferences, access policies and privileges are formulated. Hence, it offers support to ease the privilege assignment principle. Incorporation of additional parameter like environment attributes (that can manage the system-related properties and characteristics) helps in increasing horizontal scope of the system across different platforms and applications. However, the paper does not specify any mechanism for the *distribution* of generated policies. Similarly, the policy conflicts avoiding procedure is not mentioned in the proposed ARBAC system, which may occur due to the difference in access decision of multiple policies.

3.6.14   Distributed Access Control Architecture for Cloud Computing Software Control in the Cloud Systems

Almutairi et al. [5] has presented a technique for data storage and distributed access control in the cloud paradigm. This technique uses the attribute-based encryption scheme and key distribution centers that assign keys to the users on the basis of attribute groups. An access policy will be assigned to each DO that contains a list of attributes and public keys to encrypt the data against those attributes. A secure SSL channel was used to transfer the data on to the cloud. When a user wants to access some data, it requests the data from cloud and the cloud will give required information in an encrypted form. Access policies are in the form of trees, wherein the attributes act as leaf nodes and the Boolean functions act as internal nodes. This scheme also provides user revocation feature in which the revoked user will not able to use or see the data of providers.

The proposed architecture uses the RBAC model, where the least privilege principle is ensured by limiting the user access privileges according to the assigned roles. Considering the collaborative nature of the cloud, the authors offer a specification for semantic and contextual constraints that ensures adequate protection of services and resources, thus ensuring adherence to the configuration flexibility principle as well. This technique offers clear separation between the specification of semantic, such as separation of duty and contextual (such as temporal or environmental constraints included in an access request) constraints, to ensure the security of cloud services and resources, especially for mobile services. The design of the proposed architecture is generic enough to support other access control policies (such as DAC and MAC), increasing the horizontal scope of the system. The distributed access control architecture includes support for both federated and loosely coupled collaboration models that enhances the *policy storage and retrieval* capabilities of the system. Access control module (ACM) is composed of PDP, PEP and policy repository and deals with the distribution of policy at various layers. In order to avoid and resolve the policy conflicts in the cloud, some verification models and tools are required; however, the authors mention it as their future work. In the same way, the authors do not specify any mechanism to ensure the ease of privilege assignment's feature.

3.6.15 RBAC-Based Access Control for SaaS Systems

Software as a service (SaaS) eradicates the need for installation and execution of a software or application on the customers' own machine, thus facilitating maintenance and support. Considering the features like multi-tenancy and configuration, the existing access control (AC) methods when applied to the SaaS systems may raise problems like role name conflicts, cross-level management and the isomerism of tenants' access control. Therefore, the author proposes the S-RBAC [59] model that combines the best features of RBAC and ABAC model to solve the AC problems in the SaaS system. Proposed solution comprises certain components where each component separately handles some related set of responsibilities to ensure consistency and proper authentication, and permission management likewise limits the access rights of users and administrators.

The S-RBAC model includes the RBAC features also, thus, offering support to the least privilege principle, where resource's access rights are evaluated according to the assigned roles. The access filter server (AFS) is responsible for filtering the resource access requests, via filter configuration and the capability list generated by the ACS, enhanceing the configuration flexibility principle. General permission-role constraints (GPRCs) module of the proposed system ensures separation of duty principle where user roles are assigned after dividing the different skills and different interests to different kinds of people in order to prevent or reduce the chance of fraud and cut down the loss made by mistakes. The S-RBAC model enhances the horizontal scope of the system since it offers scalability and supports the heterogeneous access control requirement of tenants. The user–role constraint (URC) module of the presented system helps to ensure the ease of privilege assignments, where the authorization rules are specified between the users and roles in a tenant to avoid assigning the exclusive roles to the same user. Furthermore, the tenant administrator is responsible for the description and distribution of roles and permissions among the tenants. The proposed model presents a solution to address the role name conflicts, however, policy conflicts are not considered in the proposed solution. Similarly, policy repository and retrieval mechanisms are not specified in the proposed solution.

3.6.16   Fine-Grained Data ACS with User Accountability in Cloud Computing

Attribute-based encryption (ABE) was proposed in [60], which aims to ensure fine-grained access control and resolves the issues related to user accountability and real-time revocation. There are two kinds of ABE: key policy ABE (KP-ABE) and cipher text policy (CP-ABE). In KP-ABE, the access policy and the user's private key are bounded together, which helps to determine the files the user is authorized to access. On the other hand, in CP-ABE, the access policy is defined within the cipher text where each file and user key has different attributes; here, the relationship is between the user key and its attributes. In the proposed model, the broadcast encryption has been performed by the DO on the user group by selecting a random number. The encrypted data are then uploaded on the cloud.

In the current system, the least privilege principle is followed by defining the access structure for each user. If the user access structure matches with the requested file attributes, then access is granted to the data hosted on the cloud. Separation of duty is followed in a way that jobs are defined for all the system entities: DO, cloud provider, consumer and third-party auditor. Cloud provider can keep the encrypted data files, users can access them if their access structure is matched with the file attributes specified by the DO. Access control policies are generated and stored in a local policy repository for quick retrieval; furthermore, each policy is associated with a user rather than with each file to be accessed. Policy specification module of this system requires defining the access structure for each user, which may introduce large overhead in terms of mathematical operations and algorithms and thus does not provide ease in privilege assignment. Policy conflicts are not managed by this system, which may occur due to the difference between decisions of two or more access control policies. In addition, these systems require great amount of time to execute the mathematical operations and algorithms along with minimal support for different execution environments, therefore, failing to deliver horizontal scope. The system is not flexible enough because it requires the management of complex operations which decrease its applicability in different environments that result in low configuration flexibility. Similarly, the proposed system does not include the mechanisms for policy distribution.

3.6.17   Achieving Secure, Scalable and Fine-Grained Data Access Control in Cloud computing

Hierarchical attribute-based encryption (combining hierarchical identity-based encryption [HIBE] and cipher text policy-based attribute-based encryption (CP ABE)) on cloud has also been proposed for access control [107]. Hierarchical structure has been given in which there are root master (RM) and domain masters (DMs). RM corresponds to the private key generator and generates and distributes keys and other important parameters. DM is like the attribute authority in the CP ABE and the DM in the HIBE, which handles the delegation of keys to DM and their distribution to users at the next level. Unique identifier has been assigned to each DM and attribute, ID and attributes have been assigned to the users. Each user's position has been defined by the user's own ID and public key of DM administrating the user.

The proposed system follows the least privilege principle with the help of access structure assigned to the users. This access structure defines the set of access rights corresponding to each data file. Separation of duty is satisfied in such a way that job functions are assigned for each system entity and the system does not allow them to execute tasks that are not permissible for them. Complexity and overhead for policy specification increases with the number of attributes and steps required to execute mathematical operations. Inclusion of new feature within system requires tedious tasks that introduces overhead and lowers the ease of privilege assignment. Scope of the proposed system is limited to specific application environments due to the operational complexity of its mathematical functions, thus offering no support to horizontal scope. For efficient user revocation, a two-step algorithm is proposed to update the keys for the remaining users. However, the addition of any other property for access control introduces a large number of processes and operations that involve complex interoperability issues making the overall system's configuration flexibility low. There is no mechanism available in the system to handle the policy conflicts for access decision between two or more policies. In addition, the access control components such as PAP and PDP, PEP for policy storage and distribution are not specified in the design and architecture of the proposed system.

3.6.18   Cloud Police: Taking Access Control Out of the Network

Popa et al. [78] proposed a hypervisor-based access control technique, named 'cloud police', for cloud paradigm. Several security policies such as tenant isolation, inter-tenant communication, fair sharing among tenants, rate-limiting tenants and locally initiated connections for intra-cloud-based environment are identified. Based on these policies, a policy model is defined that uses predicate logic, wherein several rules in the form of 'if-then' action condition separated by comparison operator are used.

The proposed hypervisor-based access control technique offers configuration flexibility for supporting policies in multi-tenant environments, network-independence to decouple the access control from the network, and scalability to handle hundreds of thousands servers and users. In the proposed distributed solution, policy repository and retrieval is handled in a distributed way where the hypervisors are required to be aware of the policies of their hosted VMs only and not the policies of any other group or the group membership. This model does not require a policy management service from the cloud provider but requires an additional API in both the hypervisor and the VMs. The use of API help ensures the horizontal scope of the proposed system. In the cloud police, the cloud provider is responsible for the distribution of the group policy to the hypervisor at the VM start-up and updates it to all the group members when the policy changes. The authors of the proposed technique do not explicitly talk about any system module that aims to ensure the *conflict resolution* between policies. Moreover, this framework does not specify any mechanism to ensure *separation of duties*. Similarly, the ease of privilege assignment is also not incorporated in the design and architecture of the cloud police. The principle of least privilege is also of great importance; however, it is not included in the proposed technique.

3.6.19 Towards a Multi-Tenancy Authorization System for Cloud Services

Calero et al. [18] discuss multi-tenancy authorization system suitable for middleware services in the PaaS layer of cloud. The authorization system proposed in this article provides access control to the information of different cloud services using the cloud infrastructure. This authorization system is able to support collaboration agreements between different cloud providers also known as federation. The system supports RBAC model where the users are assigned to given roles having a set of privileges associated with that role. Additionally, hierarchical role-based access control (HRBAC) is also incorporated within the authorization model, which enables hierarchies of roles within a system. For cloud environment, this model could be best explained by Fig. 3.14. The cloud services belonging to distinct businesses can use a different information model having information related to users, privileges, roles, and resources.

The proposed system is based on the RBAC and HRBAC in which the roles are assigned to the subjects, and each subject is given access rights on only required objects according to its role, thus following the least privilege principle. Similarly, the RBAC and HRBAC access mechanisms follow the separation of duty principle by prohibiting the assignment of two or more mutual tasks to the same role at the same time. The proposed authorization model supports the HRBAC and path-based object hierarchies and provides access control decisions on API level, which increases

Table 3.2 Analysis of cloud-based access control systems

Cloud Authorization Systems	SoD	HS	EPA	PD	LP	PC	CF	PR &R
API AC in cloud using the RBAC [91]	✓	✓	✓	✓	×	×	✓	✓
Ensuring AC in cloud provisioned systems [73]	✓	×	×	✓	✓	×	×	✓
Multi-tenancy based AC in cloud [61]	✓	×	✓	✓	✓	×	×	✓
Toward a MT Authz system for cloud [18]	✓	✓	×	✓	✓	×	✓	✓
SaaS AC research based on UCON [109]	✓	✓	×	✓	×	×	✓	✓
PEF for cloud data management [39]	✓	✓	✓	✓	×	✓	×	✓
PA-ACS ARBAC in private cloud [72]	✓	×	✓	✓	✓	×	×	✓
Secure access mech. for cloud storage [39]	✓	✓	×	✓	✓	×	×	✓
Towards secure Prov.-based AC in cloud [10]	×	✓	×	✓	✓	✓	×	✓
AC of cloud service based on UCON [27]	✓	×	✓	✓	×	✓	✓	✓
AC as a service for public cloud storage [108]	✓	×	✓	✓	×	✓	✓	✓
Usage control in cloud systems [58]	×	✓	×	✓	✓	✓	✓	✓
Openpmf SCaaS: AaaS for cloud [56]	✓	✓	×	✓	✓	✓	✓	✓
Secure data access in cloud computing [87]	✓	✓	✓	×	✓	×	✓	✓
A distributed AC for CC software [5]	✓	✓	×	✓	✓	×	✓	✓
RBAC-based AC for SaaS systems [59]	✓	×	✓	✓	✓	×	✓	×
Fine-grained ACS & accountability in CC [60]	✓	×	×	×	✓	×	×	✓
Achieving secure & FGD-AC in CC [107]	✓	×	✓	×	✓	×	×	×
Cloud police: AC out of the network [78]	×	✓	×	✓	×	×	✓	✓

CF Configuration flexibility, *EPA* Ease of privilege assignment, *HS* Horizontal space, *LP* Least priviledge, *PC* Policy conflict, *PD* Policy distribution, *PR&R* policy repository and retrieval, *SoD* Separation of duties

the *scope* across different federated cloud environments. In the HRBAC model, the roles are defined as the specialized categories of generic roles, and all the privileges of the high-level roles are delegated to the derived roles. This process continues throughout the hierarchy, thus making the process of *privilege assignment* easier. The proposed system has a knowledge base module which is responsible for the storage of access control policies, authorization statements and trust relationships; therefore, it supports the local policy repository and retrieval. The system does not specify any mechanism to resolve the policy conflicts between multiple users and tenants in distributed cloud environments. The proposed multi-tenancy access control is implemented at the API level having the simple configurations for wide range of applications that require little modifications in defined hierarchies and roles, therefore supporting high level of configuration flexibility.

3.6.20 Synopsis

The aforementioned cloud-based access control systems have been evaluated against the NIST- defined assessment criterion and its summary is presented in Table 3.2, highlighting their capabilities and limitations. We have analyzed various cloud-based access control models on the basis of the NIST-defined security metrics. Our analysis reveals that most of the access control models do not offer support to all the essential security features, hence forfeiting an effective access control system for the cloud. None of the access control models heuristically covers all the essential features; moreover, they lack compliance to international standards as well. There is a need for an extensive and holistic access control system in the form of a framework to cover these required features and provide an efficient and reliable access control mechanism to cloud consumers. The cloud-based ACaaS is supposed to address the management and security challenges highlighted in Sect. 3.5 such as the formation of common policy format, translation of policies into deployment environments, etc. However, our analysis shows that none of the analyzed system caters to these imperious access management challenges completely, therefore requiring further research and development in this area.

3.7 Industrial Survey and Opportunities

Nowadays, various organizations are focusing on providing the ACaaS which will be based on the centralized policy decisions regardless of the location of individual customers. In this regard, *Ping Identity* is providing on-demand authorization solutions to its customers and supports portability and extensibility beyond the enterprise boundaries [99, 100]. First, the SAML assertions are generated, which include some additional attributes from the external identity management systems. These SAML assertions are used for authorization decisions of different applications and its users. One of the major services is *PingFederate*, which provides cloud identity connector for authorizing different users to their accounts and their data and applications [101], e.g. for Facebook, Twitter and LinkedIn, etc.

The *SETECS* is an information security company that implements and advertises three main technologies and products, which include corporate security, secure mobile transactions, and secure medical applications [90]. The core SETECS products are based on strong cryptographic algorithms, compliant to all relevant standards and certified by the NIST and US Government. The role-based authorization service is provided by the SETECS, and it is compliant with the standards of the XACML profiles. The authorization solution uses three major protocols for providing the core functionalities, which mainly include PAP, PDP and PEP.

Trusted Integration is another well-known vendor that provides authorization solutions. Their *FedRAMP Security Authorization Solution* offers standardized approach to security evaluation, authorization, and real-time monitoring for cloud services and resources [104]. It intends to meet the diverse requirements of CSP. FedRAMP's ASs aim to reduce the cost and time required for the implementation and execution of the cloud-based services while ensuring that the delivered services implicate adequate information security protection [26]. Their authorization solution applies to almost all the service deployment models, for instance, IaaS, PaaS and SaaS with security controls responsibility that is shared between the organizations and the CSP.

Dell-Quest's Access Management System controls user and group access to cloud services and resources throughout the Windows enterprise and network attached storage (NAS) devices in order to meet the security and compliance requirements, control operational costs and optimize infrastructure performance [28]. It gives logical suggestions as to who should 'own' which data resources, bringing accountability and visibility from a single console into resources that are actively used. Its key benefits include data intelligence, access insight, data control, compliance accountability and access.

The Microsoft's Identity and Access Solution allows its customers to control access to organizational data and resources while offering a seamless end-user authentication experience [69, 70]. It allows the management and federation of identities across multiple organizations and CSPs to give employees appropriate access to the resources they require. It ensures secure and always available remote access capabilities of the resources that can be reached from anywhere but only to the legitimate users with appropriate permissions.

The Axiomatics is another major vendor that offers solution for cloud-based access control management. ABAC service from Axiomatics is based on XACML 3.0 and is specifically designed for federated cloud environments [9]. It defines a hierarchical authorization structure that is capable of resolving and delegating the complex access management tasks to the appropriate system entity. There are numerous other solutions available in industry including Cloudera's *Sentry,* which is an open source, fine-grained access control for *Apache Hive* and *Cloudera Impala* [24], IBM's *Software Value Plus* (SVP) *Authorization* [98], Cloud access's *Access Management System* [19, 55] and Amazon's *Identity and Access Management* (IAM) [6]. The prominent features of these access control solutions are shown in Table 3.3.

All of these above discussed vendors facilitate the cloud consumers with access control solutions; however, their products are not open source and cannot be purchased. Cloud consumers are not able to obtain the required details and modify the existing solutions according to their requirements and preferences. Furthermore, these third-party solutions are designed to provide access control for specific applications and are not sufficient for a wide range of applications deployed at the SaaS, PaaS and IaaS layer cloud services. Similarly, most of these solutions do not offer support to all the essential access control features and the ones that offer support to all of them have their own certain weakness. For instance, the '*Ping Identity's* access control solution' adheres separation of duty and least privilege features, whereas the '*Axiomatics's* ABAC model' offers horizontal scope and ensures the ease of privilege assignment. There is a need to propose more flexible and extensible access control solutions which can holistically cover all the essential features of the access control models.

3.8 New Horizons—Open Issues and Directions of Work in ACaaS

The ACaaS is a rather recent concept of offering ASs in cloud, which is steadily gaining traction in the market. Ideally, ACSs should incorporate all the managerial and technical aspects perfectly to provide the best possible solution. Even though the research in this domain is moving towards the increasingly mature solutions, there are still a large number of critical issues that have gone unattended.

Table 3.3 Access control industrial solutions

Industrial solution	Significant features
Ping Identity	Cloud identity connector
	SAML assertions for communication
SETECS	Corporate security
	Secure mobile transactions
	Secure medical applications
Trusted Integration	Real-time monitoring for cloud services and resources
	Security evaluation
Dell-Quest's Access Management System	Supports Windows enterprise and network attached storage (NAS) devices
	Accountability and visibility of resources
	Data intelligence and control
Microsoft's Identity and Access Solution	Seamless end-user authentication experience
Axiomatics	Support for federated cloud environments
	Dynamic access rights delegation
	Attribute-based access control with XACML 3.0
Cloudera's Sentry	Fine-grained access control
	Multi-tenant administration
	Regulatory compliance with HIPAA, SOX and PCI
Cloud access's Access Management System	Single sign-on (SSO) between multiple network applications
	Provides self service capabilities
Amazon's Identity and Access Management (IAM)	Supports identity federation
	Fine-grained access control to Amazon Web Service resources

One glaring issue that needs to be addressed is the lack of a common policy format that would alleviate the inherent interoperability issues in the cloud environment. To this end, utilization of a standard policy creation language XACML is highly recommended. The purpose of XACML, an OASIS standard, is to express the authorization policies in XML together with the request/response operations [93].

Another important specification for providing an effective ACS for cloud is that it should be a generic and comprehensive framework in the form of authorization application that will allow secure authorization of resources for cloud-hosted applications. This would allow enterprises to focus on the functional requirements of their business logic and not spend time and money figuring out the complexities of creating a robust access control system. In this regard, an effective authorization layer in the form of a plugin or an API should be implemented that could potentially be used by different types of cloud applications (on the SaaS layer) for authorized access to their resources (data).

Similarly, the extensibility of the ACS is also a rather challenging problem that needs to be further explored. Cloud hosts a plethora of applications that have certain business-specific parameters; therefore, any access control mechanism being layered on top of such an application should factor these parameters and make policies accordingly. This feature will provide autonomy to the users of the ACaaS to choose the desired model such as role-based or fine-grained access control according to their own authorization requirements.

Typically, the ACaaS layer is implemented over the SaaS layer and the more advanced solutions focus on this service model. Although the same rules apply for ACaaS, PaaS and IaaS, there is a lot of room for improvement, providing the service on top of those deployment models since they still provide the very basic authorization mechanisms. For instance, adequate partitioning of policy domains and secure delegated administration is required for PaaS. IaaS, on the other hand, is less likely to be web based and so the access management service will have to be customized accordingly. For this, access management will have to be on a per-customer basis, so that the passwords and privileges given to one customer do not enable them to access other customer environments [9].

Other issues include privacy of DOs and compliance of the access control system with country- and organization-specific privacy laws; extensibility to formulate policies and rules for each level of user, support for delegation rights in cross-cloud domain, dynamic specification of entities involved in data sharing, etc.

3.9   Conclusion

Cloud technology has garnered a great amount of research interest due to its various benefits and promising potential. Because of economical nature of its services, it has gained popularity in enterprises as well. However, in spite of the fact that cloud technology affords attractive service packages for the business world, its adoption is still rather slow, mainly due to the security and privacy concerns that exist in the domain.

Consumers need to be assured that the confidentiality and integrity of their data in cloud is maintained and that only those authorized can access them. Ongoing research in the area so far has resulted in many proposals that cater to a few select issues, but until the advent of SECaaS, there were no mature solutions that provided comprehensive data security in the cloud. Even so, focus on providing robust ACaaS for cloud is required.

The cloud community is quickly learning the importance of a holistic ACaaS, which is the reason why the last few years have seen an increased number of solutions. However, there are numerous challenges associated with providing such a service that mainly include coming up with a standard policy format and translating said policies for different deployment environments among administrative issues, and technical concerns like unauthorized access to administrator interfaces or data tampering. An adequate access control mechanism for cloud would be one that overcomes both technical and administrative challenges, and is extensible and reliable, allowing complete control over who gets to access what resources hosted on cloud.

In this chapter, we have performed an in-depth analysis of the various state-of-the-art access control models and highlighted their issues. In addition to this, we have emphasized the impact and various challenges in providing a comprehensive ACaaS solution to the CSCs, as reported in the literature. After conducting a thorough study on access control mechanisms in cloud and the related work that exists within the domain, we come to the conclusion that extant access control solutions for cloud are not generic and do not cover all the required features holistically. Therefore, there is a need for a meticulous research in order to develop and design an effective ACaaS for cloud environment that allows CSCs and CSPs to securely manage access to their resources.

References

1. Ahmad R, Janczewski L (2011, July) Governance life cycle framework for managing security in public cloud: from user perspective. In: IEEE International Conference on Cloud Computing (CLOUD), Washington, DC, 4–9 July 2011, pp 372–379
2. Al-Aqrabi H, Liu L, Xu J, Hill R, Antonopoulos N, Zhan Y (2012, April) Investigation of IT security and compliance challenges in Security-as-a-Service for cloud computing. In: 15th IEEE International symposium on object/component/service-oriented real-time distributed computing workshops (ISORCW), IEEE, Guandong, 11 April 2012, pp 124–129
3. Alhamad M, Dillon T, Chang E (2010, April) Conceptual SLA framework for cloud computing. In: 4th IEEE international conference on digital ecosystems and technologies (DEST), IEEE, Dubai, 13–16 April 2010, pp 606–610
4. Alliance C (2011) Security guidance for critical areas of focus in cloud computing V3.0. Cloud Security Alliance, 2011
5. Almutairi A, Sarfraz M, Basalamah S, Aref W, Ghafoor A (2012) A distributed access control architecture for Cloud computing software. IEEE Softw J 29(2):36–44
6. Amazon Web Services (2013) AWS identity and access management (IAM). http://aws.amazon.com/iam/. Accessed July 2013
7. American Medical Association Health Insurance Portability and Accountability Act. (2013, September) http://www.ama-assn.org/ama/pub/physician-resources/solutions-managing-your-practice/coding-billing-insurance/hipaahealth-insurance-portability-accountability-act.page. Accessed May 2013
8. Arasu A, Eguro K, Kaushik R, Ramamurthy R (2013, April) Querying encrypted data. In: IEEE 29th International conference on data engineering (ICDE), Brisbane, 8–12 April 2013, pp 1262–1263
9. Axiomatics Cloud scenarios. https://www.axiomatics.com/cloud-scenarios.html. Accessed May 2013.
10. Bates A, Mood B, Valafar M, Butler K (2013) Towards secure provenance-based access control in cloud environments. In: Proceedings of the third ACM conference on data and application security and privacy, ACM, New York, 2013, pp 277–284
11. Bazargan F, Yeun CY, Zemerly MJ (2012) State-of-the-art of virtualization, its security threats deployment models. Int J Inf Secur Res 2(3/4):335–343
12. Behl A (2011, December) Emerging security challenges in cloud computing: an insight to cloud security challenges and their mitigation. In: World congress on information and communication technologies (WICT), IEEE, Mumbai, 11–14 Dec 2011, pp 217–222
13. Bennett CJ (1992) Regulating privacy: data protection and public policy in Europe and the United States. Cornell University, Ithaca
14. Bhadauria R, Chaki R, Chaki N, Sanyal S (2011) A survey on security issues in cloud computing. arXiv preprint arXiv:1109.5388
15. Bhardwaj A, Kumar V (2011, December) Cloud security assessment and identity management. In: 14th International conference on computer and information technology (ICCIT), IEEE, Dhaka, 22–24 Dec 2011, pp 387–392

16. Biggs S, Vidalis S (2009, November) Cloud computing: the impact on digital forensic investigations. In: International conference for internet technology and secured transactions, ICITST 2009, London, 9–12 Nov 2009, pp 1–6
17. Bisong A, Rahman M (2011) An overview of the security concerns in enterprise cloud computing. Int J Netw Secur Appl 3(1):30–45. arXiv preprint arXiv:1103. 5613
18. Calero JMA, Edwards N, Kirschnick J, Wilcock L, Wray M (2010) Toward a multi-tenancy authorization system for cloud services. Secur Priv IEEE 8(6):48–55. (Threats and Countermeasures for Web Services, 2010)
19. Cloud A (2011) Access management system. http://www.cloudaccess.com/access-management. Accessed June 2013
20. Cloud Security Alliance (2011) Security as a service defined categories. https://cloudsecurity alliance.org/wp-content/uploads/2011/09/SecaaS_V1_0.pdf. Accessed July 2013
21. Cloud Security Alliance (2012, September) SECaaS Email security implementation guideline. https://cloudsecurityalliance.org/download/secaas-category-4-email-security-implementation-guidance/. Accessed June 2013
22. Cloud Security Alliance (2012, September) SECaaS Access control and identity implementation guideline. https://cloudsecurityalliance.org/download/secaas-category-1-identity-and-access-management-implementation-guidance/. Accessed June 2013
23. Cloud Security Alliance (2012, September) Web security as a service implementation guideline. https://cloudsecurityalliance.org/download/secaas-category-3-web-security-implementation-guidance/. Accessed May 2013
24. Cloudera I (2013) Introducing Sentry. www.cloudera.com/content/cloudera/en/campaign/introducing-sentry.html. Accessed July 2013
25. Cohen JE (2003) DRM and privacy. Commun ACM 46(4):46–49
26. Council IA (2012) Federal Risk and Authorization Management Program (FedRAMP), 2012
27. Danwei C, Xiuli H, Xunyi R (2009) Access control of cloud service based on UCON. In: Jaatun MJ, Zhao G, Rong C (eds) Cloud computing, vol 5931. Springer, Berlin, pp 559–564
28. Dell software (2013) Access manager. www.quest.com/access-manager/. Accessed June 2013.
29. Demchenko Y, Gommans L, de Laat C, Oudenaarde B (2005) Web services and grid security vulnerabilities and threats analysis and model. In: Proceedings of the 6th IEEE/ACM international workshop on grid computing, vol 33(1), IEEE Computer Society, 2005, pp 262–267
30. Dillon T, Wu C, Chang E (2010, April) Cloud computing: issues and challenges. In: 24th IEEE International conference on advanced information networking and applications (AINA), IEEE, Perth, 20–23 April 2010, pp 27–33
31. Dykstra J, Sherman AT (2012) Acquiring forensic evidence from infrastructure-as-a-service cloud computing: exploring and evaluating tools, trust, and techniques. Digit Invest 9: S90–S98
32. Evgeny M (2009) The RSA algorithm. http://www.math.washington.edu/ morrow/336_09/papers/Yevgeny.pdf. Accessed July 2013
33. Goldwasser S, Micali S, Rivest RL (1988) A digital signature scheme secure against adaptive chosen-message attacks. SIAM J Comput 17(2):281–308
34. Gonzalez N, Miers C, Redígolo F, Simplício M, Carvalho T, Näslund M, Pourzandi M (2012) A quantitative analysis of current security concerns and solutions for cloud computing. J Cloud Comput 1(1):1–18
35. Goswani B, Singh DS (2012) Enhancing security in cloud computing using public key cryptography with matrices. Int J Eng Res Appl 2(4):339–344
36. Gouglidis A, Mavridis I (2011, January) Towards new access control models for cloud computing systems. In: Kaspersky Lab—IT security for the next generation, conference for Young Professionals, University of Applied Sciences, Erfurt, 28–30 Jan 2011
37. Gowrigolla B, Sivaji S, Masillamani MR (2010, December) Design and auditing of cloud computing security. In: 5th International conference on information and automation for sustainability (ICIAFs), IEEE, Colombo, 17–19 Dec 2010, pp 292–297

38. Gupta S, Horrow S, Sardana A (2012, June) IDS based defense for cloud based mobile infrastructure as a service. In: IEEE eighth world congress on services (SERVICES), Honolulu, 24–29 June 2012, pp 199–202
39. Hamlen KW, Kagal L, Kantarcioglu M (2012) Policy enforcement framework for Cloud data management. IEEE Data Eng Bull 35(4):39–45
40. Harnik D, Kolodner EK, Ronen S, Satran J, Shulman-Peleg A, Tal S (2011) Secure access mechanism for cloud storage. Scalable Comput: Pract Exp 12(3):317–336
41. Howgrave-Graham NA, Smart NP (2001) Lattice attacks on digital signature schemes. Des Codes Cryptogr 23(3):283–290
42. Hu VC, Ferraiolo D, Kuhn DR (2006) Assessment of access control systems. US Department of Commerce, National Institute of Standards and Technology, 2006
43. Hussain M, Abdulsalam H (2011, April) Secaas: security as a service for cloud-based applications. In: Proceedings of the second Kuwait conference on e-Services and e-Systems, ACM, New York, 2011, p 8
44. ISO 270001 Directory An introduction to ISO 27001 (ISO27001). http://www.27000.org/iso-27003.htm. Accessed May 2013
45. IT world (2010) Access control to cloud servers. http://www.itworld.com/answers/topic/cloud-computing/question/what-kind-access-controls-cloud-servers-are-important. Accessed May 2013
46. Jain P, Rane D, Patidar S (2011, December) A survey and analysis of cloud model-based security for computing secure cloud bursting and aggregation in renal environment. In: World congress on information and communication technologies (WICT), IEEE, Mumbai, 11–14 Dec 2011, pp 456–461
47. Jansen WA (2011, January) Cloud hooks: security and privacy issues in cloud computing. In: Proceedings of the 44th Hawaii international conference on system sciences (HICSS), Jan 2011, pp 1–10
48. Jensen M, Schwenk J, Gruschka N, Iacono LL (2009) On technical security issues in cloud computing. In: CLOUD'09, IEEE International conference on cloud computing, IEEE, Bangalore, 21–25 Sept 2009, pp 109–116
49. Juniper N (2013) Junos pulse access control service 4.4R1 supported platforms document. http://www.juniper.net/techpubs/software/uac/4.4xrelnotes/j-ic-uac-4.4r1-supported-platforms.pdf. Accessed July 2013
50. Kandukuri BR, Paturi VR, Rakshit A (2009, September) Cloud security issues. In: IEEE international conference on services computing, SCC'09, 517–520, Bangalore, 21–25 Sept 2009
51. Kantarcıoǧ§lu M, Clifton C (2005) Security issues in querying encrypted data. In: Jajodia S, Wijesekera D (eds) Data and Applications Security XIX, vol 3654. Springer, Berlin, pp 325–337
52. Karger PA, Zurko ME, Bonin DW, Mason AH, Kahn CE (1990, May) A VMM security kernel for the VAX architecture. In: Proceedings of 1990 IEEE computer society symposium on research in security and privacy, IEEE, Oakland, 7–9 May 1990, pp 2–19
53. Khan AR (2012) Access control in cloud computing environment. ARPN J Eng Appl Sci 7(5):613–615
54. Khan KM, Malluhi Q (2010) Establishing trust in cloud computing. IT Prof 12(5):20–27
55. Kumaraswamy S, Lakshminarayanan S, Stein MRJ, Wilson Y (2010) Domain 12: guidance for identity & access management V2.3. Cloud security alliance https://cloudsecurity alliance.org/guidance/csaguide-dom12-v2.10.pdf, Accessed August 2012
56. Lang U (2010) Openpmf scaas: authorization as a service for cloud & SOA applications. In: 2nd International conference on cloud computing technology and science (CloudCom), IEEE, Indianapolis, 30 Nov–3 Dec 2010, pp 634–643
57. Lang B, Foster I, Siebenlist F, Ananthakrishnan R, Freeman T (2006) A multipolicy authorization framework for grid security. In: Fifth IEEE international symposium on network computing and applications NCA, IEEE, Cambridge, 24–26 July 2006, pp 269–272

58. Lazouski A, Mancini G, Martinelli F, Mori P (2012) Usage control in cloud systems. In: International conference for internet technology and secured transactions, IEEE, London, 10–12 Dec 2012, pp 202–207
59. Li D, Liu C, Wei Q, Liu Z, Liu B (2010) RBAC-based access control for SaaS systems. In: 2nd International conference on information engineering and computer science (ICIECS), IEEE, Wuhan, 25–26 Dec 2010, pp 1–4
60. Li J, Zhao G, Chen X, Xie D, Rong C, Li W, Tang Y (2010) Fine-grained data access control systems with user accountability in cloud computing. In: IEEE second international conference on cloud computing technology and science (CloudCom), IEEE, 2010, pp 89–96
61. Li XY, Shi Y, Guo Y, Ma W (2010) Multi-tenancy based access control in cloud. In: International conference on computational intelligence and software engineering (CiSE), IEEE, Wuhan, 10–12 Dec 2010, pp 1–4
62. Lombardi F, Di Pietro R (2011) Secure virtualization for cloud computing. J Netw Comput Appl 34(4):1113–1122
63. Lv H, Hu Y (2011, August) Analysis and research about cloud computing security protect policy. In: International conference on intelligence science and information engineering (ISIE), IEEE, Wuhan, 20–21 Aug 2013, pp 214–216
64. Mahmood Z (2011, September) Data Location and Security Issues in Cloud Computing. In: International conference on emerging intelligent data and web technologies (EIDWT), IEEE, Tirana, 7–9 Sept 2011, pp 49–54
65. Mather T, Kumaraswamy S, Latif S (2009) Cloud security and privacy: an enterprise perspective on risks and compliance. O'Reilly, Gravenstein, USA
66. Mell P, Grance T (2011) The NIST definition of cloud computing, version 15. National Institute of Standards and Technology (NIST), Information Technology Laboratory, www.csrc.nist.gov. Accessed 7 Oct 2011
67. Microsoft (2011) ACS overview. http://msdn.microsoft.com/en-us/library/gg429788.aspx. Accessed June 2013
68. Microsoft (2013) Introduction to the AppFabric access control service 2.0. http://msdn.microsoft.com/en-us/identitytrainingcourse_introtoacslabsv2.aspx. Accessed May 2013
69. Microsoft (2013) Server and cloud platform. http://www.microsoft.com/en-us/server-cloud/identity-access/default.aspx. Accessed June 2013
70. Microsoft (2013) Identity and access management. http://www.microsoft.com/government/ww/safety-defense/solutions/Pages/identity-access-management.aspx. Accessed May 2013
71. Microsoft (2013) Threats and countermeasures for web services. http://msdn.microsoft.com/en-us/library/ff650168.aspx#ThreatsAttacksVulnerabilities. Accessed May 2013
72. Mon EE, Naing TT (2011, October) The privacy-aware access control system using attribute- and role-based access control in private cloud. In: 4th IEEE international conference on broadband network and multimedia technology (IC-BNMT), IEEE, Shenzhen, 28–30 Oct 2011, pp 447–45
73. Narayanan HAJ, Gunes MH (2011) Ensuring access control in cloud provisioned healthcare systems. In: Consumer communications and networking conference (CCNC), IEEE, Las Vegas, 9–12 Jan 2011, pp. 247–253
74. Ohta K, Koyama K (1990, January) Meet-in-the-middle attack on digital signature schemes. In: Seberry J, Pieprzyk J (eds) Advances in cryptology—AUSCRYPT'90. Springer, Berlin, pp 140–154
75. PCI SSC Data Security Standards Overview. https://www.pcisecuritystandards.org/security_standards/. Accessed June 2013
76. Pearson S, Benameur A (2010, November) Privacy, security and trust issues arising from cloud computing. In: IEEE second international conference on cloud computing technology and science (CloudCom), IEEE, Indianapolis, 3 Nov–3 Dec 2010, pp 693–702
77. Pointcheval D, Stern J (2000) Security arguments for digital signatures and blind signatures. J Cryptol 13(3):361–396
78. Popa L, Yu M, Ko SY, Ratnasamy S, Stoica I (2010) CloudPolice: taking access control out of the network. In: Proceedings of the 9th ACM SIGCOMM workshop on hot topics in networks, ACM, New York, 2010, p 7

79. Popovic K, Hocenski Z (2010, May) Cloud computing security issues and challenges. Paper presented at MIPRO, 2010 proceedings of the 33rd international convention, IEEE, Opatija, 2010, pp 344–349

80. Priebe T, Dobmeier W, Kamprath N (2006) Supporting attribute-based access control with ontologies. In: The first international conference on availability, reliability and security ARES, IEEE, 20–26 April 2006, p 8

81. Reflex (2009) Access control. http://www.reflexsystems.co.uk/areas-of-expertise/access-control. Accessed May 2013

82. Reflex (2011) VTrust Features. www.reflexsystems.com/Products/vTrust. Accessed May 2013

83. Rimal BP, Choi E, Lumb I (2009, August) A taxonomy and survey of cloud computing systems. In: NCM'09, Fifth international joint conference on INC, IMS and IDC, Seoul, 25–27Aug 2009, pp 44–51

84. Rivest RL, Shamir A, Adleman L (1978) A method for obtaining digital signatures and public-key cryptosystems. Commun ACM 21(2):120–126

85. Rutkowska J (2006) Subverting VistaTM kernel for fun and profit. Black Hat Briefings, Las Vegas

86. Sandhu RS, Samarati P (1994) Access control: principle and practice. IEEE Commun Mag 32(9):40–48

87. Sanka S, Hota C, Rajarajan M (2010) Secure data access in cloud computing. In: 4th International conference on internet multimedia services architecture and application (IMSAA), IEEE, Bangalore, 15–17 Dec 2010, pp 1–6

88. Santos N, Gummadi KP, Rodrigues R (2009, June) Towards trusted cloud computing. In: Proceedings of the 2009 conference on hot topics in cloud computing, USENIX Association, Berkeley, 2009, pp 3–8

89. Sato H, Kanai A, Tanimoto S (2010, July) A cloud trust model in a security aware cloud. In: 10th IEEE/IPSJ International symposium on applications and the internet (SAINT), IEEE, Seoul, 19–23 July 2010, pp 121–124

90. SETECS (2010) OneCLOUD PIV Authentication and Authorization System. http://security. setecs.com/Documents/4_SETECS_Cloud_Portal_Security_System.pdf. Accessed May 2013

91. Sirisha A, Kumari GG (2010) API access control in cloud using the Role Based Access Control Model. In: Trendz in information sciences & computing (TISC), 2010, IEEE, 2010, pp 135–137

92. Somani G, Agarwal A, Ladha S (2012, December) Overhead analysis of security primitives in cloud. In: International symposium on cloud and services computing (ISCOS), Mangalore, 17–18 Dec 2012, pp 129–135

93. Standard OASIS (2013) eXtensible access control markup language (XACML) Version 3.0. 2008. http://docs.oasis-open.org/xacml/3.0/xacml-3.0-core-spec-os-en.pdf. Accessed July 2013

94. Standard OASIS (2013) eXtensible access control markup language (XACML). https://www. oasis-open.org/committees/tc_home.php?wg_abbrev=xacml. Accessed June 2011

95. Subashini S, Kavitha V (2011) A survey on security issues in service delivery models of cloud computing. J Netw Comput Appl 34(1):1–11

96. Suresh NR, Mathew SV (2011, December) Security concerns for cloud computing in aircraft data networks. In: International conference for internet technology and secured transactions (ICITST), IEEE, Abu Dhabi, 11–14 Dec 2011, pp 132–136

97. Takabi H, Joshi JB, Ahn GJ (2010) Security and privacy challenges in cloud computing environments. IEEE Secur Priv 8(6):24–31

98. Technologies INM IBM Software Value Plus Authorization. http://www-304.ibm.com/ partnerworld/wps/servlet/ContentHandler/swg_com_sfw_svp_cca . Accessed June 2013

99. The identity (2012) Ping identity adds authorization to strengthen enterprise access controls for applications in the cloud. https://www.pingidentity.com/about-us/press-release. cfm?customel_datapageid_1516=62363. Accessed May 2013

100. The Identity security company (2013) The 4 A's of cloud identity. https://www.pingidentity.com/resource-center/authentication-authorization-audit-logging-account-management.cfm. Accessed June 2013.
101. The identity security company Enterprise Identity Bridge. https://www.pingidentity.com/products/pingfederate/. Accessed July 2013
102. The Sarbanes-Oxley Act (2002) http://www.soxlaw.com/. Accessed June 2013
103. Tripathi A, Mishra A (2011, September) Cloud computing security considerations. In: International conference on signal processing, communications and computing (ICSPCC), IEEE, Xi'an, 14–16 Sept 2011, pp 1–5
104. Phan T (2013) Trusted I FedRAMP Security Authorization Solution. http://www.trusted-integration.com/FedRAMP-Compliance.htm, Accessed December 2013
105. Wang JJ, Mu S (2011, September) Security issues and countermeasures in cloud computing. In: IEEE International conference on grey systems and intelligent services (GSIS), IEEE, Nanjing, 15–18 Sept 2011, pp 843–846
106. Roberts II, J. C., Al-Hamdani, W (2011, September) Who can you trust in the cloud?: A review of security issues within cloud computing. In Proceedings of the 2011 Information Security Curriculum Development Conference, ACM, pp. 15–19
107. Yu S, Wang C, Ren K, Lou W (2010). Achieving secure, scalable, and fine-grained data access control in cloud computing. In: Proceedings IEEE INFOCOM, IEEE, San Diedo, 14–19 March 2010, pp 1–9
108. Zhang Y, Chen JL (2012) Access control as a service for public cloud storage. In: 32nd International conference on distributed computing systems workshops (ICDCSW), IEEE, Macau, 18–21 June 2012, pp 526–536
109. Zhu J, Wen Q (2012, November) SaaS Access Control Research Based on UCON. In: Fourth international conference on digital home (ICDH), IEEE, 2012, pp 331–334
110. Zissis D, Lekkas D (2012) Addressing cloud computing security issues. Future Gener Comput Syst 28(3):583–592

Part II
Standards, Brokerage Services and Certification

Chapter 4
Realization of Open Cloud Computing Standards, Forums and Platforms

G M Siddesh and K G Srinivasa

Abstract With the increased popularity of cloud computing, there is an increase in demand for resources among the heterogeneous workload types in the cloud environment. However, major concerns in this domain refer to the issues like scalability, security, trust, interoperability, loss of control and the problem of vendor lock-in. The hype of this emerging technology has resulted in a huge number of standards and frameworks in this domain. In this context, open standards present the solution to manage the cloud environment by integrating openness in the standards so that everyone benefits by reducing the time to switch among the service providers. In this regard, there is a great need for an *open cloud* in the present information technology (IT) domain that needs to manage thousands of resources with applications, which are distributed in nature to handle the issues in the cloud. Open cloud guarantees the users to select the best technologies now and in the future. There is a great need among users and developers for standardizing the cloud frameworks, which lead to the evolution of different open cloud forums. These forums have the responsibility to define and design standards for various services in the cloud so that openness and interoperability can be achieved. Open cloud forums do not aim towards achieving a single homogeneous cloud environment, but as the cloud matures several key principles of cloud must be followed to ensure openness. Open cloud forums are community driven and ensure universal acceptance of open standard formats and interfaces. This chapter presents the understanding of open clouds and their underlying principle, provides an introduction to open cloud standards and their benefits, and discusses the understanding of open cloud forums, their goals and contributions. The chapter also presents a discussion of some well-known open-source cloud platforms, in particular OpenStack, Nimbus, Open Nebula and Eucalyptus.

Keywords Cloud computing · Eucalyptus · Nimbus · Open cloud · Open cloud forum · Open cloud standard · Open Nebula · OpenStack

G M Siddesh (✉)
Department of Information Science & Engineering, M S Ramaiah Institute of Technology, MSR Nagar, Bangalore, Karnataka 560054, India
e-mail: siddeshgm@msrit.edu

K G Srinivasa
Department of Computer Science & Engineering, M S Ramaiah Institute of Technology, MSR Nagar, Bangalore, Karnataka 560054, India
e-mail: srinivasa.kg@msrit.edu

Z. Mahmood (ed.), *Continued Rise of the Cloud,* Computer Communications and Networks, DOI 10.1007/978-1-4471-6452-4_4,
© Springer-Verlag London 2014

4.1 What is Open Cloud?

With cloud computing gaining popularity, there is an increased demand for commoditization of typical computing resources which are available as a service. Cloud computing is leading to an exemplar shift in the way the research and business domains have started outsourcing their information technology (IT) and computational needs to data centres rather than maintaining their own infrastructure. The main idea is to offer elastic access to dynamically provision IT resources on a pay-on-use basis to service users. Cloud users are able to access the services of cloud from anywhere in the world on demand Hence, cloud computing can be classified as a new paradigm for the dynamic provisioning of computing services supported by state-of-the-art data centres containing ensembles of networked virtual machines (VMs). The loss of control and risk involved in this model is a major concern among the IT domain. The open clouds embrace cloud computing as an opportunity to open up siloed IT departments and engage the business units to help drive their success. There is a great need for an open cloud in the current market to have a secured and reliable cloud environment. Open clouds need to support the current IT domain to continue their work similar to GNU and Linux forums. Open clouds matter because there is a need for the cloud to be bigger than the proprietary companies so that the users and organizations have as much control over their computing destiny at scale as they have on their stand-alone servers by avoiding the problem of vendor lock-in [1, 2].

In the upcoming years, there will be a great deal of research in the public clouds to manage the issues of scalability, security, trust, service offerings, interoperability, loss of control and the problem of vendor lock-in. The open cloud architecture makes it possible to take advantage of these researches without interrupting the current business. Further, it simplifies to utilize these options at the proper time and for the suitable applications. The closed cloud architectures limit the choices to a small set of providers and provide the vendor control of the user infrastructure [3, 4]. The key principles of open cloud solution are as follows [1, 2]:

- **Openness**. Allows building and managing a heterogeneous hybrid cloud infrastructure. Openness spans to open access to rich information, open economical model and different service providers.
- **Choice of deployment**. Provides a choice to the end users to select the deployment platform and service providers, and this resolves the problem of vendor lock-in.
- **Portability**. Allows creating *cloud-ready* solutions that can be easily deployed among multiple cloud service providers. Further supports easy switching between providers without disrupting the service.
- **Standards based**. Defines a standardized interface for cloud environments while enabling service providers to differentiate their service offerings at the same time. Open cloud standards drive the new level of interoperability across clouds.
- **Application programming interface (API)**. Offers flexible open APIs with high degree of extensibility, so that services can be accessible at the inter-cloud level. Standardizing the APIs solves the problem of integration and interoperability.
- **Integration**. Allows building a *global cloud of clouds*—inter-clouds—*interconnected by open standard interfaces*. Services can be integrated among the multiple service providers achieving a true hybrid cloud environment.

Fig. 4.1 Potential risks in the adoption of clouds [6]

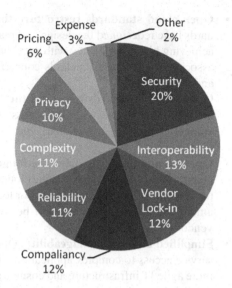

- **Extensible**. New application classes and service classes may require new features; it allows extending while retaining useful features.
- **Commodity based**. Must leverage extensive catalogue of open-source software offerings.

This chapter presents the understanding of open clouds and their underlying principles, provides an introduction to open cloud standards and their benefits, and discusses the understanding of open cloud forums, their goals and contributions. The chapter also presents a discussion of some well-known open-source cloud platforms, in particular OpenStack, Nimbus, Open Nebula and Eucalyptus.

4.2   Open Cloud Standards

Cloud computing is the latest trend which is grabbing the attention of IT domain, there is a paradigm shift in the usability of cloud because of its cost-effective model. As noted in Fig. 4.1, there are some major concerns among the consumers of potential risks involved in the adoption of clouds. These potential risks demand defining of standard management and service policies that are initiating towards the development of open standards in clouds [5].

4.2.1   Benefits

Adoption of open cloud standards leads to the following advantages [7–9]:

- **Open cloud standards restructure the cloud computing**. Open cloud standards have redesigned the design and management issues in cloud computing by achieving higher efficiency with maximum return on investment (ROI). Vendors associated with these standards concern customers interoperability, portability and other issues.
- **Open cloud standards improved the IT domain effectively**. The success behind the cloud is its cost-effectiveness. The adoption of open standards in cloud computing has led to a remarkable improvement in the IT deployment and management
- **Open cloud standards drive the longevity of the vendor**. Adoption of open cloud standards guarantees that the cloud vendors gain trust and reputation among the customers. Further, fear of vendor lock-in, integration, interoperability issues among the cloud consumers will be resolved, leading to the longevity of the vendor.
- **Simplified and self-manageability**. Open cloud standards provide simple, self-service access to complex applications. It provides the business with access to a more agile IT infrastructure and ensures applications and data are portable across the clouds.

4.3   Open Cloud Forums

Open forums help to build an open cloud by delivering the cloud standards: it not only brings openness in building hybrid clouds but also helps achieve coalition among the different communities and business models in cloud domain. Open cloud forums aim to provide the solution for vendor lock-in problems among the cloud users. Further, open cloud forums strongly focuses on portability, interoperability, integration, efficiency, agility, extensibility and cost benefits of cloud to IT infrastructures' applications [7].

Open cloud forums involve community consensus and advocate for universal acceptance of open standard formats and interfaces. These forums provide open framework which aims to support user autonomy and success of service providers' business. Interfaces and frameworks delivered by open cloud forums are suitable to support three service models of cloud computing: infrastructure as service (IaaS), platform as service (PaaS) and software as service (SaaS). Open cloud forums in turn help to build proficient cloud usage model and challenges.

4.3.1   Goals

Following are the key goals of open cloud forums [7]:

- Define and manage principles of open cloud with the consent of open community.

- Convince service providers and cloud community to follow the open cloud principles.
- Promote the cloud service providers to contribute in development of open cloud products and services.
- Educate the cloud community about open cloud products and services that comply with open standards.
- Support to integrate the advantages of different benefits of cloud services in the construction of a hybrid cloud.
- Offer simple solutions in the process of migration, by allowing enterprises to leverage existing infrastructure that is already in place.
- Prevent a vendor to take over the economical model of a costumer.
- Allow IT to offer all of the agility and benefits of cloud, preserving the control on the workloads.

4.3.2   Open Cloud Forums and their Contributions

The success of open cloud forums has driven the open standards to achieve efficiency in the usage and operations of clouds in the IT domain. Some of the key open cloud forums and their contribution towards standardization of cloud components are [10]:

- **Open cloud computing interface (OCCI).** OCCI consists of a set of open community-led specifications delivered through the open grid forum. OCCI is a protocol and API for different cloud management jobs. OCCI was originally initiated to create a remote management of API for IaaS model-based services, allowing the development of interoperable tools for common tasks including deployment, autonomic scaling and monitoring. It has since evolved into a flexible API with a strong focus on integration, portability, interoperability and innovation while still offering a high degree of extensibility. The current release of the OCCI is suitable to serve many other models in addition to IaaS, including, e.g. PaaS and SaaS. The OCCI has found wide acceptance among many of the cloud projects like OpenStack, OpenNebulla, FiWare project, Reservoir: an European Union FP7 project, Big Grid project: an Dutch e- science grid project, R2AD, PyOCNI, etc. [11, 12]
- **Cloud standards customers council (CSCC).** The CSCC is an end user support group committed to increase the cloud's successful adoption, by handling issues of standardization, security and interoperability in the clouds. The CSCC provides the cloud users with the opportunity to drive client requirements into standard development organizations and deliver materials such as best practices and use cases to assist other enterprises. The CSCC has been followed by IBM, Kaavo, CA Technologies, Rackspace and Software AG [13].
- **Open cloud initiative (OCI).** OCI is a non-profit organization established to advocate open standards in cloud computing. It is inspired by the open-source initiative (OSI) and aims to find a balance between protecting important user freedoms and enabling providers to build successful businesses. OCI focused on

interoperability, avoiding barriers to entry or exit, ensuring technological neutrality and forbidding discrimination. They define the specific requirements for open standards and mandate their use for formats and interface [14].

- **Distributed management task force (DMTF)**. The DMTF is an industry forum that develops, manages and promotes standards for system management in the IT domain. It enables system management interoperability among different services in the IT environment. The DMTF's Cloud Management Working Group (CMWG) aims at developing interoperable cloud infrastructure management standards and promoting adoption of those standards in the industry [15].
- **Open cloud consortium (OCC)**. The OCC aims at developing standards and frameworks for interoperating between clouds. The OCC focuses on large data clouds. It has developed the MalStone Benchmark for large data clouds and is working on a reference model for large data clouds [16].
- **Open cloud standards incubator**. The DMTF's open cloud standards incubator focused on standardizing interactions between cloud environments by developing cloud management use cases, architectures and interactions. Currently this group is managed by the CMWG [17].
- **CMWG**. The CMWG is responsible for the development of specifications that deliver architectural semantics and implementation details to attain interoperability among the cloud service providers and consumers. The CMWG has proposed a resource model that captures the key artefacts identified in the use cases and interactions for managing clouds document produced by the open cloud incubator [18].
- **Open data Centre alliance (ODC-A)**. The ODC-A helps in building expertise in cloud usage models and challenges. The ODC-A supports all the three service models of clouds: IaaS, PaaS and SaaS. The use cases of ODC-A include security, quality of service (QoS), storage in clouds [17].
- **Open management group (OMG)**. The OMG focuses on modelling, deployment of applications and services on clouds for portability, interoperability and reuse. The OMG supports all the three service models of clouds, that is, IaaS, PaaS and SaaS. The use cases of OMG include provisioning, metering, billing, development associations and platforms [18].
- **Open grid forum (OGF)**. The OGF is a standard development organization working in the areas of grid, cloud and related forms of advanced distributed computing. The OGF community pursues these topics through an open process for development, creation and promotion of relevant specifications and use cases. The use cases of OGF include provisioning, metering and billing in IaaS service model of the cloud [19].

4.4   Open-Source Cloud Platforms

Some of the major open-source cloud platforms like OpenStack, Nimbus, Open Nebula and Eucalyptus will be discussed in the next session.

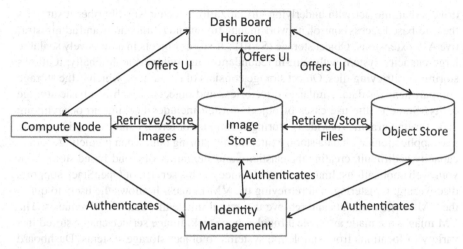

Fig. 4.2 Architecture of OpenStack [21]

4.4.1 OpenStack

OpenStack is an open-source technology to build private and public clouds. It was originated at NASA with Rackspace dedicated to massive infrastructure. OpenStack project is licensed under Apache 2.0; it aims at providing a dedicated environment to build a cloud hosting architecture, massive scalability, flexibility, openness by overcoming the problem of vendor lock-in. The success of OpenStack is because of its openness, and it consists of open-source components to deliver public and private cloud service. Being open it supports a validation process for the adoption and development of new standards. OpenStack supports scalability, where a massive scalability of up to 1 million physical machines, 60 million VMs and billions of stored objects can be achieved. OpenStack project is a compatible and flexible solution for implementing different drivers by supporting various hypervisors like XEN, KVM, Hyper-V, ESX, etc. [20].

Features Following are the features of openstack [21]:

- Leverage resource pools on demand
- Focus on high-performance computing (HPC) deployment
- Provide dashboard to allow cloud administrators to create and manage projects
- Simultaneously launch and manage multiple resource instances
- Launch and customize instances in the OpenStack dashboard within the limits the user's administrators have set

Architecture Figure 4.2 shows the architecture of OpenStack. The components of OpenStack include compute (Nova) : This component offers computing power through VMs on demand. This is similar to the Amazon's EC2 service, further it provides volume services similar to the elastic block services (EBS). Compute defines drivers that interact with underlying virtualization mechanisms. Further it supports the role-based access control, network management and IP allocation and administrative API extensions. Object storage (Swift) : It stores objects in a massively scalable large-capacity system with built-in redundancy and failover; additionally, it allows storing or retrieving files. Object storage consists of containers, which is the storage compartment for data, similar to directories, and objects, which is a basic storage entity. Some of the use cases of object storage includes backing up or archiving data, serving graphics or videos, storing secondary or tertiary static data, developing new applications with data storage integration, storing data when predicting storage capacity is difficult, creating the elasticity and flexibility of cloud-based storage for your web applications. Image service (Glance) : This service of OpenStack supports discovering, registering, and retrieving the VM images. It allows the users to query the VM image metadata and retrieve the actual image through HTTP requests. The VM images are made available through OpenStack. Image service can be stored in a variety of locations from simple file systems to object-storage systems. Dashboard horizon: It is a modular web-based user interface for all the OpenStack services. Identity keystone : It provides authentication and authorization for all the OpenStack services [22, 23].

4.4.2   Nimbus

Nimbus is an open-source toolkit which is a cloud IaaS via Amazon's Elastic Computing Cloud (EC2) and Web Service Description Language (WSDL) web service APIs. Nimbus was designed with the goal of turning clusters into clouds mainly to be used in scientific applications; it is a science cloud solution. Nimbus provides a special web interface known as the Nimbus Web. It is under the affiliation of the GLOBUS project, it uses the features of GLOBUS like GRID FTP and Cumulus for image repository, GLOBUS credentials for authentication. Nimbus is highly flexible and customizable in handling different sized virtual networks and creating VMs based on the user requirements. It poses restriction on the scalability by limiting the number and size of the VMs created [24, 25].

Features Following are the features of Nimbus [26]:

- It is an open-source IaaS
- Storage cloud service
- Remote deployment and life cycle management of VMs
- Compatibility with Amazon EC2 and S3
- Support for X.509 credentials
- Easy to use cloud client
- Fast data propagation
- Per user quota allocation
- Easy user management
- Contextualization
- VM network configuration
- Local resource management plug-in

Fig. 4.3 Architecture of
Nimbus [26]

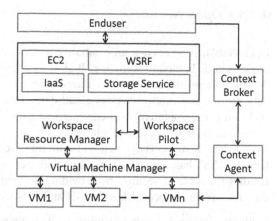

Architecture   Figure 4.3 shows the architecture of the Nimbus platform, that is, tools
that deliver the power and versatility of infrastructure clouds. The infrastructure of
Nimbus is an open-source EC2/S3-compatible IaaS targeting features that interest
the scientific communities, like support for proxy credentials, batch schedulers, best-
effort allocations and others. Nimbus is a set of open-source tools which includes
cloud client: It is a command line-based tool. Cloud client provides users up and running instances and clusters in minutes even from laptops. *Nimbus interfaces:* Nimbus
provides the interfaces of elastic computing cloud (EC2) and web service resource
framework (WSRF). *Nimbus IaaS Service:* It is a workspace manager, which is a
stand-alone site VM manager which distributes the VM images. *Cumulus:* It works
as an independent storage service, which is a repository of the VM image. Cumulus
is an open source for simple storage service (S3) REpresentational State Transfer
(REST) API. *Workspace resource manager:* It is an open-source resource manager
for multiple different VMMs. The workspace resource manager implements dynamic
leases. *Workspace pilot:* This component achieves virtualization, without disrupting
the current cluster it integrates with the local resource managers and it is a best effort
service. *Virtual machine manager (VMM)*: It is a stand-alone component responsible
for handling the VM control, image management and reconstruction and contextualization information management. The VMM communicates with the workspace
using Secure Shell (SSH). Further, the VMM handles the network-related settings
for VMs in assigning media access control (MAC) addresses and IP addresses, DHCP
delivery tool, building up a trusted networking layer. *Context broker:* Allows clients
to coordinate large virtual cluster for launching, controlling, and monitoring cloud
applications. It works with different cloud service providers. *Context agent:* It is a
lightweight agent on each VM which securely communicates with the context broker
using a secret key [26].

4.4.3   Open Nebula

Open Nebula is an open-source initiative towards designing, managing and promoting standards in cloud computing. It aims to achieve innovation in providing open, flexible, extensible, and complete management layer for the operation of virtualized data centres and enterprise-class cloud data centre management. It is designed to build on private/public/hybrid environment to provide open IaaS. Open Nebula is flexible enough in supporting heterogeneous configurations of storage, network and hypervisors. It supports open cloud forum interfaces such as OGF OCCI service interface, REST based interface, Amazon Web Service (AWS) EC2 API. Open Nebula handles the issue of security by providing authentication based on the lightweight directory acess protocol (LDAP), SSH and X.509 certificates [27].

Features Following are the features of Open Nebula [28]:

* Provides AWS-based EC2, EBS, OGF OCCI interfaces
* Supports automatic installation and configuration
* Fine-grained accounting and monitoring
* Easy integration with any billing system
* Powerful and flexible scheduler for the definition of workload and resource-aware allocation policies
* It is an high availability architecture and provides cost-effective failover solutions
* Fully platform independent
* Dynamic creation of virtual data centres
* Modular and extensible architecture
* Customizable plug-ins for integration with any third-party data centre service
* API for integration with higher-level tools such as billing, self-service portals
* Fully open-source software released under Apache license

Architecture Figure 4.4 demonstrates the architecture of Open Nebula. Open Nebula architecture is divided into three layers: Tools: This layer contains the management tools such as Command Line Interface (CLI), Scheduler, the Cloud RESTful interfaces, and third-party tools created using the XML-RPC interface or the new Open Nebula Cloud API. Core: The Open Nebula core controls and monitors the VMs, virtual networks, storage and hosts. Open Nebula core components are request manager, VMM, transfer manager, virtual network manager, host manager and database. Drivers: plug-in different virtualization, storage and monitoring technologies and cloud services into the core [28, 29].

4.4.4   Eucalyptus

Elastic Utility Computing Architecture Linking Your Programs To Useful System is an open-source software framework for cloud computing that implements IaaS in a private/hybrid environment. Eucalyptus efficiently enhances the private and

Fig. 4.4 Architecture of Open Nebula [28]

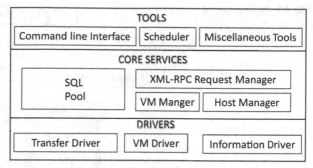

hybrid clouds within an enterprise's existing IT infrastructure. The eucalyptus IaaS platform is fully compatible with AWS API (Amazon EC2) [25]. It is a simple, flexible and hierarchal modular architecture. Eucalyptus supports Xen hypervisor. It is a Linux-based solution with the support of limited scalability when compared to massively scalable solutions. Eucalyptus implements a distributed storage system called walrus which is similar to Amazon s3 storage solution. Eucalyptus is not completely open, some modules are closed in nature. It may be called as an open solution for commercial EC2 cloud [30–32].

Features Following are the features of Eucalyptus [33]:

- It is compatible with AWS API
- It supports for Linux and Windows VMs
- It supports multiple cluster as a single cloud
- It has configurable scheduling policies and service-level agreements (SLAs)
- It provides web user interface (UI) and command-line tools for cloud administration and configuration
- It is a massively scalable architecture
- Its installation is available from binary packages for Centos, openSUSE, Debian, and Fedora. Also available on Ubuntu as Ubuntu Enterprise Cloud (UEC).

Architecture Figure 4.5 shows the architecture of Eucalyptus. A Eucalyptus cloud setup consists of five types of components. Cloud controller and Walrus : The cloud controller (CLC) and walrus are the top-level components, with one of each in a cloud installation. The cloud controller is a Java program that offers the EC2-compatible SOAP and Query interfaces as well as a web interface to the outside world. In addition to handling incoming requests, the cloud controller performs high-level resource scheduling and system accounting. Walrus, also written in Java, implements bucket-based storage, which is available outside and inside a cloud through the S3-compatible SOAP and REST interfaces. The top-level components can aggregate resources from multiple clusters. Each cluster needs a cluster controller (CC) for the cluster-level scheduling and network control and a storage controller (SC) for the EBS- style block-based storage. The two cluster-level components would typically be deployed on the head node of a cluster. Every node with a hypervisor will need a node

Fig. 4.5 Architecture of
Eucalyptus [33]

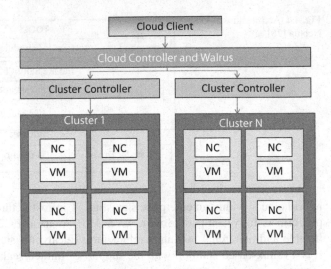

controller (NC) for controlling the hypervisor. Both CC and NC are written in C and
deployed as web services inside Apache: the SC is written in Java. Communication
among these components takes place over SOAP with the WS security [34, 35].

4.4.5   Comparison of Open-Source Cloud Platforms

Table 4.1 discusses a brief comparison of different open-source cloud platforms.

4.5   Conclusion

Cloud computing is a hot topic in the current trend among the IT domain, which makes
the IT firms to move from the traditional IT cost model to cloud computing model.
Cloud computing is attracting people because of its economical model, wherein
people rather than investing on static IT costs are investing only on cloud operational
costs which is cost effective. Cloud consumers will get on-demand computational
capacity and pay for whatever they have used. Cloud is a pay-as-you-go model.

In spite of these advantages, the cloud computing is facing a major step back because of its inherent characteristics like loss of control, security risks, vendor lock-in.
Openclouds in cloud computing provide cloud consumers the control of their future,
their technology roadmap. It helps users to integrate with other communities and
service providers to take up innovation in their areas. Open cloud tries to involve in
the success of cloud computing by solving the inherent characteristics of the cloud
mentioned earlier. The open forums help to build an open cloud by delivering open
cloud standards. These open standards, interfaces and principles are globally acceptable. Open standards provide a common framework in achieving easy portability,

Table 4.1 Comparison of open-source cloud platforms [36–40]

Features	OpenStack	Nimbus	Open Nebula	Eucalyptus
Philosophy	Unified authentication system, virtualization portability	Nimbus context broker, scientific clouds	VM migration support, highly customizable cloud	User management web interface, mimic Amazon EC2
Cloud service model	IaaS	IaaS	IaaS	IaaS
Cloud deployment model	Public and hybrid	Public	Private, public and hybrid	Private and hybrid
Hypervisors	KVM, Xen, Hyper-V, LXC	Xen and KVM	KVM, XEN and VMWare	Xen, KVM and VMware
Interfaces	EC2, S3, OCCI, REST interface	EC2, S3, REST, interface	Native XML/RPC, EC2, S3, OCCI, REST Interface	EC2, S3, OCCI, REST interface
Code base	Python	Python, Java	C, C++, Ruby, Java, Shell Scripts, yacc, Lex	Java, C
OS	Linux	Linux	Linux	Linux, Windows VMs
Networking	Flat, VLAN, Open vSwitch	IP is assigned using DHCP	Support Open vSwitch, Ebtable and 802.1Q	Managed, managed-novLAN, system and static
Storage (disk image)	Swift, nova, Unix file system	GridFTP, cumulus	Unix file system	Walrus
Security	Authentication using X.509 credentials, LDAP	Authentication using X.509 credentials	Authentication using X.509 credential, ssh rsa keypair, password, LDAP	Authentication using X.509 credentials
License	OpenSource—Apache2.0	OpenSource—Apache2.0	OpenSource—Apache2.0	OpenSource and commercial

providing full user control on their resources, avoiding vendor lock-in and handling the issues of security. To struggle with some proprietary standards, interfaces and principles of cloud, there is an open-source movement in cloud computing. This growing movement has led to many open-source cloud platforms like OpenStack, Open Nebula, Nimbus, Eucalyptus, etc.

Some of the goals, principles, contributions of open clouds, open forums, open standards are discussed in this chapter. Further, this chapter discusses the features and architectures of some major open-source cloud platforms. Over the past many years, it is proved that the IT solutions are strengthened when built over open architectural foundations. In this regard, the growth of cloud computing will have a positive impact with the introduction of open standards and open clouds.

References

1. Massachusetts Open Cloud (MOC) (2012) About the Massachusetts open cloud (MOC). http://www.bu.edu/cci/files/2012/11/MOC.pdf. Accessed Jan 2013
2. Haff G (2012) Red hat cloudforms: open clouds under your control. http://in.redhat.com/resourcelibrary/whitepapers/red-hat-cloudforms-open-clouds-under-your-control. Accessed Jan 2013
3. Edmonds A, Metsch T, Papaspyrou A, Richardson A (2012) Towards an open cloud standard. Internet Comput IEEE 16(4):15–24
4. Díaz-Sánchez D, Almenarez F, Marín A, Proserpio D, Cabarcos PA (2011) Media cloud: an open cloud computing middleware for content management. IEEE T Consum Electr 57(2):970–978
5. Henlin EH (2012) Open standards are dissolving cloud Silos. Report Technology Business Research (TBR) Inc, May 2012
6. Future clouds (2011) www.futurecloudcomputing.net. Accessed Aug 2011
7. Haff G (2012) Why the future of the cloud is open. http://www.redhat.com/f/pdf/cloud/Cloud_FutureCloud_WP_8847147_0212_dm_web.pdf. Accessed Jan 2013
8. Sher-DeCusatis CJ, Carranza A, DeCusatis CM (2012, Sept) Communication within clouds: open standards and proprietary protocols for data center networking. IEEE Commun Magazine 50(9):26–33
9. Zeller M, Grossman R (2009) Open standards and cloud computing KDD-2009 Panel Report. ACM, Jul 2009
10. Cloud standards (2013) Welcome to the cloud standards. http://cloud-standards.org. Accessed Mar 2013
11. Behrens M et al (2011) Open cloud computing interface-infrastructure. OGF Document Series, 2011
12. Open Cloud Computing Interface (2013) An open community leading cloud standards. http://occi-wg.org/. Accessed Mar 2013
13. Cloud Standards Customers Council (2013) Cloud standards. http://www.cloud-council.org/. Accessed Apr 2013
14. Open Cloud Initiative (2013) Open clouds. http://www.opencloudinitiative.org/. Accessed Mar 2013
15. Distributed Management Task Force (2013) Open standards. http://dmtf.org/standards/cloud. Accessed Apr 2013
16. OCC (2013) Open cloud consortium. http://opencloudconsortium.org/. Accessed Mar 2013
17. Open Data Center Alliance (2013) ODCA. http://www.opendatacenteralliance.org/. Accessed Apr 2013
18. Object Management Group (2013) OMG specifications. http://www.omg.org/. Accessed Apr 2013
19. Open Grid Forum (2013) Open standards. http://www.ogf.org/gf/docs/. Accessed Apr 2013
20. Takako P, Estcio G, Kelner J, Sadok D (2010) A survey on open-source cloud computing solutions. In: WCGA—8th workshop on clouds, grids and applications, Gramado, 3–16, May 2010
21. Open Stack (2013) Operations guide. http://docs.openstack.org. Accessed May 2013
22. Pepple K (2011) Deploying openstack. OReilly Media, Sebastopol
23. Sefraoui O, Aissaoui M, Eleuldj M (2012, Oct) OpenStack: toward an open-source solution for cloud computing. Int J Comput Appl 55(3):38–42
24. Hoffa C, Mehta G, Freeman T, Deelman E, Keahey K, Berriman B, Good J (2008) On the use of cloud computing for scientific workflows. In: IEEE fourth international conference, SWBES 2008, Indianapolis, Dec 2008
25. Keahey K, Figueiredo R, Fortes J, Freeman T, Tsugawa M (2008) Science clouds: early experiences in cloud computing for scientific applications, Aug 2008
26. Nimbus (2013) Nimbus infrastructure 2.10.1 documentation. http://www.nimbusproject.org/docs/. Accessed May 2013

27. Evoy GVM, Schulze B, Garcia EL (2009) Performance and deployment evaluation of a parallel application in an on-premises cloud environment. Proceedings of the 7th international workshop on middleware for grids, clouds and e-science, 2009
28. Open Nebula (2013) Open Nebula 3.8 guides. http://opennebula.org/. Accessed May 2013
29. Yang C-T, Huang K-L, Liu J-C, Chen W-S, Hsu W-H (2012) On construction of cloud IaaS using KVM and Open Nebula for Video Services. In: 41st International conference on parallel processing workshops (ICPPW) IEEE, Pittsburgh, pp 212–221, Sep 2012
30. von Laszewski G, Diaz J, Wang F, Fox GC (2012) Towards cloud deployments using FutureGrid. In: FutureGrid draft paper, Indiana University, Bloomington, Apr 2012
31. Montero RS, Moreno Vozmcdiano R, Llorente IM (2010) An elasticity model for high throughput computing clusters. J Parallel Distrib Comput 71:750–757
32. Eucalyptus (2013) Administration guide. http://www.eucalyptus.com/docs/3.1.0/ag.pdf. Accessed May 2013
33. Eucalyptus (2013) http://www.eucalyptus.com/learn/what-is-eucalyptus. Accessed May 2013
34. Nurmi D, Wolski R, Grzegorczyk C, Obertelli G, Soman S, Youseff L, Zagorodnov D (2009) The eucalyptus open-source cloud-computing system. In: IEEE/ACM international symposium on cluster computing and the grid (CCGRID '09), IEEE, Shanghai, pp 124–131, May 2009
35. Tan T, Kiddle C (2009) An assessment of eucalyptus version 1.4 (Technical report 2009-928-07). Grid Research Centre, University of Calgary, Canada, 2009
36. Lei Z, Zhang B, Zhang W, Li Q, Zhang X, Peng J (2009) Comparison of several cloud computing platforms. In: Second international symposium on information science and engineering, IEEE, Shanghai, pp 23–27, Dec 2009
37. Mahjoub M, Mdhaffar A, Halima RB, Jmaiel M (2011) Comparative study of the current cloud computing technologies and offers. In: First international symposium on network cloud computing and applications (NCCA), IEEE, Toulouse, pp 131–134, Nov 2011
38. Sotomayor B, Montero RS, Llorente IM, Foster I (2009) Virtual infrastructure management in private and hybrid clouds. IEEE Internet Comput (Special issue on cloud computing) 13(5): 14–22
39. Llorente M, Moreno-Vozmediano R, Montero RS (2009) Cloud computing for on-demand grid resource provisioning. Adv Parallel Comput 18:177–191
40. Pillai AS, Swasthimathi LS (2012) A study on open source cloud computing platforms. EXCEL Int J Multidiscip Manage Stud 2(7):31–40

Chapter 5
Role of Broker in InterCloud Environment

Saswati Mukherjee and Shyamala Loganathan

Abstract Cloud computing represents a great promise of quickly delivering the more efficient information technology (IT) systems to companies and enterprises, encouraging small- and medium-sized companies to make use of more intensive and widespread technology and, therefore, stimulating a strong recovery on a new basis of the information and communications technology (ICT) market. Two major challenges in cloud computing are scalability and consistent achievement of quality of service (QoS) standards set by the consumers. Various cloud resources can be acquired from the cloud service providers (CSPs) at different abstraction levels based on the services provided by the CSPs and requirements of the users. A uniform solution of delivering the promised services with proper performance metrics is to implement a federated environment with the help of an agent or a broker. This chapter presents the vision, the challenges, and the architectural elements of brokerage services of a federated cloud computing environment. It provides a basic overview and expectations and sets the background for the rest of the chapters in this book.

Keywords Cloud computing · Federation · Inter-cloud · Multi cloud · Broker · Brokerage services · CBS · Scheduling · QoS

5.1 Introduction

Cloud computing has evolved as a new paradigm that fulfils the dream of utility service in computing. It offers the promise of quickly delivering more efficient information technology (IT) solutions to companies and enterprises, encouraging small- and medium-sized companies to exploit the computational resources offered by a third party. Utilizing the pay-as-you-go model, the cloud stimulates a strong recovery on a new basis of the information and communications technology (ICT)

S. Loganathan (✉) · S. Mukherjee
Department of Information Science and Technology, CEG, Anna University,
Chennai 600025, India
e-mail: lshyamlabi@gmail.com

S. Mukherjee
e-mail: msaswati@yahoo.com

Z. Mahmood (ed.), *Continued Rise of the Cloud,* Computer Communications
and Networks, DOI 10.1007/978-1-4471-6452-4_5,
© Springer-Verlag London 2014

market. The main aim of the evolution of cloud computing is perhaps to deliver services providing dynamically scalable virtualized resources to the users. Cloud computing exploits the technologies of virtualization and web services to provide an environment where the customers can enjoy complete on-demand provisioning and elasticity [1].

A major challenge faced by a cloud service consumer is the increasing complexity offered by various cloud providers. Cloud resources can be acquired from the cloud service providers (CSPs) in different abstraction levels based on various factors. In this business model, the major concern of a service consumer is to select the CSPs who offer services that best fit the user's needs. This poses as a major problem since the functionality and usability of the exposed cloud services would differ based on the type of cloud providers and platforms. Further variation depending on the issues such as the methods for packaging and managing images, heterogeneity of resources and technologies used by the CSPs, use of providers' own metrics or properties, etc., would bring in added complexity. The types of instances offered, the level of customization allowed for these instances, the price and charging time periods for different types of instances, whether the pricing models are on demand, reserved or spot prices, etc., would impose more variations. In the absence of standardization, the choice becomes harder since different CSPs offer their proprietary services using the interfaces they find suitable. For example, consider the cases of Amazon and Rackspace, two giants in the cloud space. The central processing unit (CPU) capabilities are expressed by Amazon in terms of the number of cores and computation units. Rackspace, on the other hand, defines CPU capabilities in terms of physical host machine. Therefore, the task to choose the suitable service from a plethora of services available, each perhaps expressed in a different way, is far from trivial. After choosing a CSP based on any premise or even arbitrarily, a serious hurdle for a consumer is to decide an appropriate offering of the chosen CSP for its current requirement. Gartner has predicted that the complexity of combined cloud services is far too heavy a burden for an individual consumer [2].

On the other hand, the prime most concern of the CSPs in a cloud environment is to be able to satisfy the users' needs. Two major problems for the CSPs are the requirement of scalability and conformance to the negotiated service-Level agreement (SLA) based on the quality of service (QoS) targets. These are particularly challenging since a cloud scenario works under changing workload and dynamic resource requirements. To be able to face the challenges, a computing environment has to be created that would enable the expansion of capabilities such as virtual machines (VMs), files, databases, services, storage, etc. Only then a cloud provider will be equipped to handle sudden spikes in service demands.

The aspect of user satisfaction is tied partially to the ability of a CSP to provide a service locally for a user or at least from a geographically nearby location. Since a client request can come from any location, it is virtually impossible for any single cloud provider to deal with the requirement of having established data centres in multiple locations to meet the users' demands locally. This inability may lead to the service providers not being able to provide adequate responsiveness and usability to consumers distributed worldwide, thereby causing serious problems especially during a sudden high demand of workload. In a cloud environment such spikes are not only expected but also a way of life. The failure to meet these spikes of demands is fraught with problems of having inconvenienced consumers who are left without essential yet paid for resources. To meet these requirements, the CSPs need to adopt a mechanism that allows them to dynamically expand or shrink their provisioning capability on demand.

From the above-mentioned discussion, one can conclude that whether it is an individual consumer trying to make a right decision amongst many offerings or it is a cloud provider trying to expand its footprint, both need assistance beyond what is currently available.

An elegant and easy solution to all the problems mentioned can be achieved by making a pool of services in the form of a cloud federation. Leasing available services from the other cloud providers, when required would ensure that every CSP can, provide better support for specific consumers' local needs. On the other hand, finding similar services together in a federated environment would make the job of comparing various factors and making the right choice easier for a cloud consumer. However, this necessitates building mechanisms for seamless federation of data centres of various cloud providers supporting dynamic scaling of applications across multiple domains by interconnecting the CSPs for the purpose of providing a platform for quick comparisons, diverting traffic, managing loads and accommodating spikes on demand. This chapter strives to look into the various issues in building a cloud federation.

The organization of this chapter is as follows. We will first look at what is the motivation behind cloud federation and brokering, discussing the types of cloud federation and benefits thereof. Next, a quick look at the basic cloud architecture proposed by the National Institute of Standards and Technology (NIST), wherein an overview of cloud broker (CB) or agent and the types of brokers are discussed. The chapter further proceeds to see how a federation of cloud can be achieved using broker. Since cloud essentially has a layered architecture with abstractions in the higher layers, broker in different layers are discussed next. Brokers can be of various types and the next section discusses the taxonomy of brokerage in cloud, Two important aspects that a broker or an agent must be aware of are how to schedule different consumer requests and how to handle SLAs. The chapter discusses these aspects from the perspective of brokering finally drawing up the architecture of a generic cloud.

5.2 Motivation

A cloud federation offers direct benefits to every participating entity, be it a CSP, both as provider and as consumer who can be an individual consumer user or a consumer enterprise. For an individual consumer and enterprise, the federation provides the platform that consists of services and/or computing facilities from different CSPs. The federation may further extend its services to be integrated and composed based on the requirements of the consumer. For a consumer CSP, the federation creates an environment to extend the business footprints to all possible geographical locations, thereby expanding business and obtaining customer satisfaction. On the other hand, the providers in the federation are those that have available and idle resources at the time of offering the service in the federation. Thus, for a CSP provider, idle and underutilized resources earn at lean period. In fact, the usage pattern of a typical data centre shows that there is an equal divide between the peak time and lean time. While during the peak time, it needs a large amount of resources; but during the lean time, a major part of these resources are underutilized. Hence, federation is a profitable way of ensuring that every data centres have their resources utilized at all times.

Although there are multiple choices of how to achieve interoperable cloud federation, one of the most important options of implementing the federation of multiple clouds is perhaps through CBs or agents that serve, at the very basic level, as intermediaries between the CSP consumers and providers. In the federated scenario, a broker is an entity that has responsibilities such as provisioning and managing resources across various cloud platforms and automatically deploying various application components utilizing the resources assigned.

These cloud middlemen will also help individual consumers to make the right choice in selecting the right platform, deploy apps across multiple clouds, and even provide cloud arbitrage services that allow end users to shift between platforms to capture the best options from amongst all the available options for an individual. As Gartner predicts, cloud services are to be adopted by individual consumers such that the cloud service brokerages will develop the ability to govern the use, performance and delivery of the integrated cloud providers. According to Daryl Plummer, managing Vice President and Chief Gartner Fellow: "Unfortunately, using services created by others and ensuring that they'll work—not only separately, but also together—are complicated tasks, rife with data integration issues, integrity problems and the need for relationship management. Hence the role of brokers to add value to services and to deliver on top of old services" [2]. Figure 5.1 shows the basic structure of a CB.

Whether it is the requirements of the CSP or the consumers or whether it is the current and future requirements, cloud brokering is the need of the day and it is virtually impossible to overlook brokers in the cloud, given the complexity of the cloud ecosystem today.

5.2.1 How Many Clouds?

Since the current cloud ecosystem is complex, added to the future promise of an exponential increase of such complexity, it is not only expected but also required that the cloud providers of the next generation equip themselves with certain capabilities to be able to meet the requirements and demands of the complex usage of the cloud services [3]. These include:

- A mechanism of dynamically growing or shrinking resources on demand as sudden spikes in demands rise and disappear.
- The ability to participate in the market-driven resource provisioning system, maximizing resource utilization while still surviving in the business, satisfying negotiated SLAs with the customers. These SLAs are negotiated and finalized based on the factors such as availability, competitive market prices, etc.

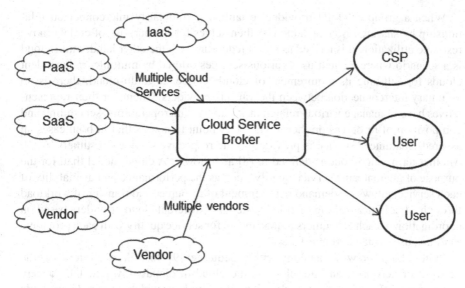

Fig. 5.1 Structure of a cloud broker

- The capability to provide authentication and security when such providers are dealing with multiple consumers and other client CSPs.
- A method to adhere to strict QoS standards while delivering on-demand, reliable and cost-effective services exploiting technologies such as virtualization and web services.
- The ability to provide effective post-deployment support to consumer enterprises and customers ensuring that they obtain maximum value for their investments.

Any CSP, be it the software as a service (SaaS), platform as a service (PaaS) or infrastructure as a service (IaaS) provider, has to necessarily ensure conformance to QoS parameters as part of their fundamental promise to the customer while facing infrastructure constraints, budget constraints as well as scalability constraints. Therefore, when a CSP, especially the small and medium providers whose resources are limited and hence either due to a sudden spike or due to a lack of a certain type of resource in some location, is unable to fulfil the demand of a consumer, it would willingly participate and exploit any relationship with other providers leasing additional resources from other clouds (mixing multiple public and private clouds) as well as renting out its own idle or underutilized resources. This automatically helps the provider to better support its specific user needs without trying to acquire new resource every time such needs arise.

As enterprises struggle to sort out the array of cloud computing requirements, options and services, analysts see a growing opportunity for some form of cloud federation. Various researchers have used different terms to specify different flavours of the basic concept of federated cloud [4]. This section looks at three such terms: cloud federation, multi-cloud and inter-cloud.

When a group of cloud providers establish a voluntarily interconnected relationship by sharing resources amongst themselves for the purpose of collaborative resource utilization, it is termed as cloud federation. On the other hand, multi-cloud is a scenario where a client uses various services offered by multiple, independent clouds for fulfilling its requirement of cloud service. In multi-cloud, there is no voluntary interconnection between the various providers. Clients or their representatives have to manage various related tasks such as interoperability, scheduling and composition of resources on their own [5]. A point to note is that in both cases an assured, guaranteed service is provided to the respective service consumers [6, 7]. Another term, inter-cloud is defined in [8] as follows: "A cloud model that, for the purpose of guaranteeing service quality, such as the performance and availability of each service, allows on-demand reassignment of resources and transfer of workload through a [sic] interworking of cloud systems of different cloud providers based on coordination of each consumers requirements for service quality with each providers SLA and use of standard interfaces."

"Inter-cloud" draws an analogy with the Internet [9]. Just like the Internet is the network of networks, an inter-cloud is the cloud of clouds. Overall, the concept of bringing different clouds together, where multiple providers are made available for each other or for their consumers, having the capabilities of a federation of clouds, offers substantial benefits to all the participants of the federation. Some of these include:

- Ability of a service provider to create the best possible service in the market within the budget requirement of the consumer.
- Reduced execution time of a task since multiple CSPs can be used for the fulfilment of one provider's commitment to the consumer, thereby fulfilling the SLAs.
- Ability of the cloud providers to expand and diversify to all geographic locations and to easily accommodate sudden spikes in demand without having to build a cloud footprint in multiple geographic regions.
- Ability for the cloud providers to maximize profit by successfully handling more customers than would be possible with the single owner infrastructure. This also ensures that the service providers are able to meet the SLA requirements, thereby locking in satisfied customers even during demand spikes.
- Ability of the providers to offer fault tolerance by completely avoiding cloud service outages.
- Increase in the providers' revenue by renting out computing resources that would otherwise be idle or underutilized during lean period.
- Ability of the clients or consumers to avoid the need of vendor lock-in.
- Ability of the providers to better adapt to market conditions quickly.
- Ability of the consumers to choose from amongst all the available services the best one as their budgets may permit.
- Ability to use the infrastructure and tools with automated provisioning and managing mechanism along with an effective self-supporting deployment capability.
- Since a cloud service may be atomic in the sense that a consumer would need to actually handle an array of services all from different providers to obtain a complete solution, the federation provides such ability to a customer.

Although providing federation capabilities amongst the CSPs brings forth substantial economic advantage for the participating CSPs and substantial performance gain as well as economic advantage for the participating consumers, it gives rise to a series of critical concerns. Since there are many cloud providers and platforms with various exposed cloud service interfaces that are different on different parameters, when a CSP looks for another CSP to serve a client request in a federated environment, some conflict may arise. The job of selecting the right service offered by a right provider with the right parameters that match the original service provider is nontrivial. To this end, the cloud instances in the federated environment must be able to do a set of work. Let us take an example. CSP1 is a service provider that agrees to provide some service to a consumer client, say CL1. CSP1 and CL1 frame a set of SLAs that define all the necessary terms suitable for both. However, if due to overload, CSP1 is now unable to provide all the resources needed by CL1, it cannot violate the agreed upon SLA. Hence it will turn to the federated environment to hire resources temporarily from another provider, say CSP2. CSP1 will combine its own resources with these leased resources for the service of CL1. However, this task is far from trivial, given the fact that both CSP1 and CSP2 may use completely different standards.

A uniform solution of dealing with this is perhaps to have all cloud vendors to agree on some standardized protocols for sharing resources such as information, files, computing resources, etc. and also sharing identity amongst themselves. However, currently there are no set interoperability standards in cloud environments that can seamlessly federate and interoperate amongst disparate clouds.

To this end, researchers propose two major methods to tackle the cloud federation scenario:

- One is a decentralized inter-cloud topology that is self-organizing [10]. The proposed inter-cloud or the cloud of cloud protocol supports one-to-one, one-to-many, and many-to-many use cases and provides a standard for exchange of resources such as content, storage and computing power in a network of clouds.
- The other, a more popularly accepted method, is the use of CB. In this method, the need is to provide and implement a CB or agent to federate different cloud providers' abilities. The next section discusses the NIST reference architecture, which has put forward the idea of a broker [11].

5.3   The National Institute of Standards and Technology Architecture

Figure 5.2 presents a high-level view of the NIST reference architecture called cloud computing reference architecture (CCRA) [11]. Various factors such as requirements, uses, characteristics and standards of cloud computing can be better understood using this generic high-level diagram.

It consists of five major actors, each playing a role and performing a set of specific functions. The major actors of the architecture are (i) cloud consumer, (ii) CSP, (iii)

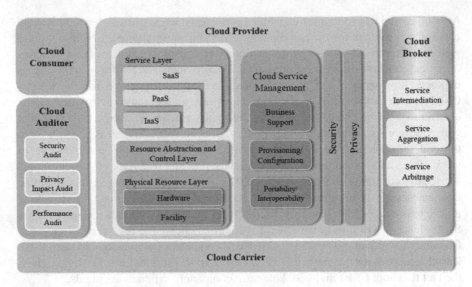

Fig. 5.2 NIST Cloud computing reference architecture (CCRA) 2.0 [11]

cloud auditor, (iv) CB, and (v) cloud carrier. Each actor has well-defined activities according to the role it plays in the architecture. As specified by the NIST, these actors, besides having a specific role to play, also interact with each other in a well-defined manner. A short description of each actor is provided subsequently.

Cloud Consumer The most important stakeholder is perhaps the cloud consumer. Any entity, a person or an organization with the intention of consuming one or more of the services offered by a provider comes in the category of cloud consumer. Typically SLAs are the means of an understanding between consumers and providers. A cloud consumer can look around to find a cloud provider most suitable for the consumer's requirements, pricing and any other terms.

Cloud Provider A cloud provider is an entity, a person or an organization, which is responsible to develop the infrastructure and offer services to be consumed by the consumer. Depending on the type of services offered, SaaS, PaaS or IaaS, a provider builds a suitable infrastructure. It is the sole responsibility of the service provider to ensure that the SLAs are adhered to. Further, security and privacy of the services has to be also ensured by the service provider.

Cloud Auditor A cloud auditor is an entity that evaluates various parameters and assesses whether a service provider is having conformance to the standards. Based on any objective evidences available and measuring these against standards, an auditor is able to assess a service provider on the basis of various parameters.

Cloud Carrier A cloud carrier is the conduit between cloud consumers and cloud providers. It provides connectivity and transport of the cloud services. Depending on the requirement of a cloud consumer and the SLAs between the provider and the consumer, a provider will engage in an SLA with the cloud carrier so that proper distribution of the services is provided to the consumer.

Cloud Broker The CB acts as an intermediary that helps the user integrate various cloud services offered by the cloud providers. Instead of requesting a service from a service provider directly, a cloud consumer may request cloud services from a CB. The NIST architecture adopts various categories of brokering services suggested by Gartner [12], and these are (1) intermediation, (2) aggregation and (3) arbitrage.

- Service intermediation. The term intermediation implies that the broker should be between a provider and a consumer. According to the NIST, intermediation brokers should be able to enhance a certain service by adding capabilities. Such a service may further be improved by providing the value-added services before a consumer uses the service. Such additional services may be identity management, performance reporting, enhanced security, etc.
- Service aggregation. An aggregation service of a broker would require a broker to be in contact with one consumer and multiple CSPs. The job is to successfully combine various services offered by the CSPs and form a service specifically required by the consumer. The NIST suggests that since there are different components involved from different providers, it is the responsibility of the broker to ensure that an appropriate data model suitable for all is adopted. It is further the responsibility of the aggregation service to ensure movement and security of data across such diverse CSPs.
- Service arbitrage. Service arbitrage, while being similar to service aggregation, differs in the fact that arbitrage service is free to choose from all CSPs offering a certain service based on some criteria. This automatically provides flexibility to such a service that is not available to the aggregation scenario. Therefore, if a certain service is available, an arbitraging broker has the opportunity to make a choice from multiple agencies.

Although many researchers and organizations have adopted the NIST architecture to deploy cloud, there are some limitations in the architecture. Especially the scope of the proposed broker architecture is very limited.

5.3.1 Limitations

In spite of being a good mechanism for describing service and business or operational relations, the NIST CCRA falls short on some critical criteria [11]. These include:

- CCRA is not suitable for large-scale enterprise applications
- It does not have any provision for multilayer and multi-domain cloud services or infrastructure
- It does not provide for virtualization as a cloud feature
- No mechanism is offered for provisioning and enforcing QoS
- The CCRA has no provision for distinguishing between customer organization and end user
- Although the CB is included, there can be several issues:

- It does not provide a uniform definition of what a CB is, and it serves no clear role in the CCRA
- The scope of the broker is not well defined in the context of either the cloud provider or the cloud consumer
- Broker acts more as an intermediary role between the consumers and providers, rather than providing a proper brokerage service
- There is a mismatch between the way the NIST has presented the idea of a broker and the general idea of what a typical broker is supposed to be.
- Various roles proposed by the NIST for a CB are not well accepted by the research community [13, 14].

With the above-mentioned background, this chapter bridges the gap between the accepted understandings of what a traditional brokering is supposed to do and how this can be adapted in the current cloud scenario. Finally a generic architecture is proposed for the purpose of cloud federation.

5.4   Cloud Broker

"The future of cloud computing will be permeated with the notion of brokers negotiating relationships between providers of cloud services and the service customers," commented L. Frank Kenney, Research Director, cited by Gartner [2].

The CB acts as an agent, just like a broker in any field. A broker might be the software, appliances, platforms, another cloud or suites of technologies that can add value to the base services available through the cloud. Addition of values may be managing identity of the users, providing access control to these services, providing and ensuring security, supervise and monitor the previously created agreements or even creating completely new services. Essentially, a CB can act in two different roles: as an intermediary and as an independent gateway.

As an intermediary, the broker acts between the consumer and provider, saving the consumer time by obtaining advance knowledge about the various services provided by different CSPs and providing the consumer with necessary business and technical information about how best to use the cloud computing resources and/or services available. In this model, a broker must acquire complete knowledge about the customer regarding the work processes, possible budget flexibilities, restrictions about data movement and any other requirements/restrictions to be able to successfully inform or provide the necessary information as is needed by the customer. Typically, a broker is expected to provide a list of recommended cloud providers for a requirement and the customer, armed with this knowledge, independently makes a choice and contacts the service provider to negotiate the SLA and eventually arrange the needed service. In this situation, the buyer is a client and the seller is the provider or both the buyer and the seller are the CSPs.

As an independent gateway, on the other hand, the CB has to directly negotiate contracts with cloud providers on behalf of the customer. This is the broker as defined by Gartner [2], "A cloud services brokerage is a business model in which a company or other entity adds value to one or more (generally public or hybrid, but possibly private) cloud services on behalf of one or more consumers of those services."

Here, a broker, besides having knowledge about the customer, is also allowed to get into contracts with the service providers on behalf of the customer. The broker is free to make decisions about whether services should be distributed across multiple vendors in an effort to get the best service at the lowest cost. Such brokers offer the customer a single consistent interface to different and multiple providers, both for business purpose and for technical purpose. In this case, the CB has the ability to offer "transparent visibility" regarding the provider or providers in the background [15]. Negotiation here is obviously more complex since multiple vendors might be involved. The broker hides any complexity and makes it appear to the customer as if all the services are being purchased from a single vendor.

Cloud brokerage strategies are still in its nascent state and are an evolving phenomenon. In the existing business practice, a CB charges a customer on an hourly basis for the customer's time, although a broker may charge different customers differently depending on the type, kind and the duration of the brokerage service it is providing.

5.4.1 Existing Work

Buyya et al. [16] presented an early vision of cloud interconnection, a market-oriented architecture for resource allocation within the clouds. The authors also discussed about the global cloud exchanges and markets. The inter-cloud system architecture proposed in a recent article on cloud computing by Rajkumar Buyya [3] includes a cloud exchange comprising directory, auctioneer and financial settlement functions. In the proposed architecture, the cloud coordinators handle scheduling and resource allocation, and the CBs negotiate with cloud coordinators for resource allocation that meets the users' QoS needs. In RESERVOIR [7], considering the reduction of costs and QoS as the main management objectives, services with multiple VMs are transparently provisioned and managed across clouds in an on-demand basis. Vecchiolaet al. [17] discussed the architecture of using multiple clouds to reduce the completion times for deadline-driven tasks. Celesti et al. [9] propose that architecture enables cloud federation based on a three-phase model, namely discovery, matchmaking and authentication. Brokering functionality in their architecture is provided by a matchmaking agent, which is responsible for choosing more appropriate cloud/clouds to establish a federation based on information collected at the different layer levels.

5.5 Broker in Layered Service Model

There is extensive literature classifying the services offered by cloud providers in various ways. Perhaps the most generic architecture is the layered service model where each cloud supports a vertical stack containing a minimum of three types of services, viz. SaaS, PaaS and IaaS. In this architecture, each layer interacts with the lower layer, thereby providing an increasing abstraction and isolation. Perhaps thus, it is most fitting to incorporate broker-mediated federation in the layered architecture [18]. In this model, each service layer is mediated by brokers specific to that layer, and these brokers handle the specific concerns of that layer for all the participating clouds.

Brokering at the Software-as-a-Service Layer In cloud, perhaps the most popular layer is the SaaS layer. In this layer, a provider provides an application service that is used by a consumer. Major emphasis of this layer is proper fulfilment of the user's requirements and conformance to the SLAs between the provider and the consumer. A cloud provider guarantees a given level of service that is specific to an application. Some typical services are security, time taken (either completion or response time), pricing of running the application, characteristics and input parameters specific to the application, etc., in addition to a set of generic QoS parameters such as availability/up time, etc. On the other hand, in a federated scenario, the requirement is that the CSP1 is able to find a CSP2 that conforms to the SLA and other parameters already agreed upon between CSP1 and CL1.

While it is possible for a broker in this scenario to look at all the possible parameters, but it is sufficient for a generic SaaS layer broker to include the requirements such as offering real-time usage monitoring and looking at the requirements of billing and ensuring very strict adherence to security requirements. The SaaS broker's services at this layer may include:

- **Tracking:** The SaaS brokers need to offer real-time usage tracking to keep a track of the exact usage for billing based on multiple pricing models offered by various providers. This job is particularly challenging in the face of changing requirements of the consumers as well as dynamically modifiable pricing models of the providers.
- **Billing and payment**: In a cloud environment, billing can be very complex and also expensive for an individual provider due to various factors such as different policies that may be applicable for different customers for the same service, various modes of payment used by various customers, flexible payment terms customized for each client, etc. However, a broker can afford to make a large investment in this respect and can provide billing service. The SaaS brokers would also be responsible for the generation of periodic reports about the business trends.
- **Security**: The SaaS level security may include protecting the servers, which is used to deploy the SaaS solution, ensuring that the users are properly identified and proper access control mechanism is in place.
- **Analytical ability**: Providing business intelligence by applying analytics to the large amount of data available to the broker can also benefit all parties.

Brokering at the Platform-as-a-Service Layer PaaS is explained by the NIST [19] as follows: "The capability provided to the consumer is to deploy onto the cloud infrastructure consumer-created or acquired applications created using programming languages, libraries, services, and tools supported by the provider. The consumer does not manage or control the underlying cloud infrastructure including network, servers, operating systems, or storage, but has control over the deployed applications and possibly configuration settings for the application-hosting environment."

So, essentially in PaaS, a provider offers computing platform to its consumers that allows the creation of web applications quickly and easily without the complexity of buying and maintaining all the software and infrastructure required. Since the PaaS layer uses frameworks, tools, libraries and runtime environments, these may require different licensing conditions, different pricing and performance criteria based on various parameters such as versions, manufacturers, make, etc. A PaaS layer broker needs to take into account all these. In addition to these, the generic requirements of the PaaS layer broker also needs to provide fault tolerance, security, etc. Brokering policies at the PaaS layer will try to optimize the requirements and the cost.

Brokering at the Infrastructure-as-a-Service Layer The IaaS is explained by the NIST [19] as "The capability provided to the consumer is to provision processing, storage, networks, and other fundamental computing resources where the consumer is able to deploy and run arbitrary software, which can include operating systems and applications. The consumer does not manage or control the underlying cloud infrastructure but has control over operating systems, storage, and deployed applications; and possibly limited control of select networking components (e.g., host firewalls)."

A provider has to offer the infrastructure to its consumers in this layer. A federation at this layer would require dynamic provisioning of various resources being pulled from different types of cloud, private as well as public. In the infrastructure layer, this has a serious impact since various infrastructures may have different capabilities and even characteristics depending on whether the resource belongs to a private or a public cloud. Thus, a broker at this layer must be able to thoroughly look into the various classes and pick and choose as per the requirements and constraints of the application.

Initially, an IaaS broker should enable resource provisions by matching the requirements of the resource classes with the requirements of the application coordinating on parameters such as throughput and constraints such as pricing, budget and performance of the resource. However, the broker's job is not complete once the provisioning is done. It also needs to continuously monitor the progress of the application since a sudden failure or unavailability of a resource should not cause any problem to the consumer. In case of a failure or any such problem due to which a resource is not accessible to the application, the broker should immediately re-provision a similar resource obtaining it from another CSP. This is resource adaptation that is typically done on runtime.

5.6 Brokerage Taxonomy

There are different ways of classifying various types of cloud brokering. The first one is based on the ways brokers are implemented. There are three possible schemas in this scenario:

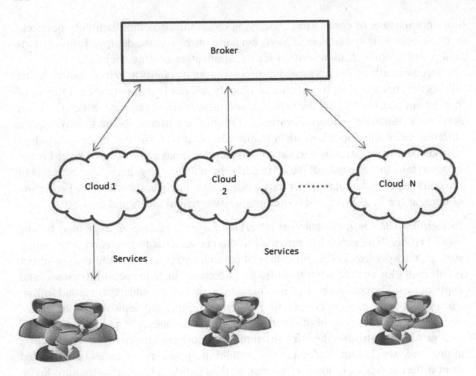

Fig. 5.3 Centralized federation scheme using a broker

Centralized Single Broker In this strategy, a third-party broker takes care of the federation. Figure 5.3 depicts a centralized broker, which does matchmaking of the providers on behalf of a cloud requester based on the requirement and offerings, after performing a proper discovery of such offered services.

In a multi-provisioned SLA-driven world of brokers, it is the responsibility of a broker to compare the SLAs of each provider to match the requirement of a user and to select the most appropriate one on behalf of the user. Thus, a single broker environment enables heterogeneous set of clouds to interact with each other through the broker interface. However, all these imply that the whole picture of the available providers' capabilities along with all constraints must be known to the broker. This works fine for a small cloud set-up; however, for a large cloud environment this solution is vulnerable to bottleneck and a single point of failure. An alternative is a hierarchical scheme.

Hierarchical Broker In this scheme, instead of one centralized broker, different clouds are connected to different brokers. These brokers, in turn, are connected to each other. Interactions happen at different levels, between brokers at the higher levels and between a broker and a provider at the lower level as given in Fig. 5.4.

In hierarchical brokering, matchmaking happens through interactions between brokers. Since there are a number of options at each level, the single point of failure

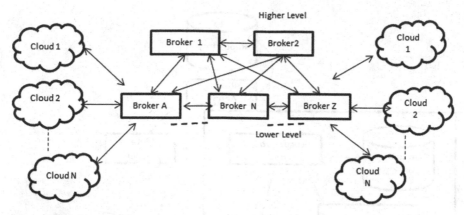

Fig. 5.4 Hierarchical federation scheme

is taken care of easily. However, this model is fraught with the problem of high communication cost and delay. Even when there is a straightforward requirement that can be fulfilled with simple or no brokering, a hierarchical brokering will still involve a fixed set of communications.

Meta-Broker A typical scenario is to abstract away some of the information to a special broker that acts as a meta-broker. In this scenario, there is a local broker for each cloud, in addition to a meta-broker. While a meta-broker provides the point of communication with the federated environment for the resource requester, local brokers are the point of contact for the service providers.

Meta-broker can be either centralized or distributed. In a centralized environment, there is one meta-broker across the federated environment. When a requester contacts the meta-broker with a specific requirement, it in turn checks the repository to decide the appropriate cloud and contacts the correct local broker. The local broker does the matchmaking after obtaining the requirement from the meta-broker and initiates SLA negotiation for the required resources available with the prospective consumer. Once the negotiation completes, the local broker does the actual provisioning, execution and managing the rest of the interactions. Figure 5.5 illustrates a centralized meta-broker.

This scenario is a little different in a decentralized meta-brokering. In the decentralized scenario, each cloud has a local broker and a meta-broker component. Like a centralized environment, the resource requester would contact the meta-broker component with a request. Meta-broker would first try to fulfil the request from its own cloud through its local broker component. In case a request cannot be fulfilled locally, either due to lack of resource or due to SLA constraints, the meta-broker would contact other meta-brokers and their local brokers to start negotiation. Eventually the requested resource would be provisioned from one of these clouds.

Whether it is centralized or decentralized, meta-broker facilitates request provisioning in a federated cloud environment. While centralized meta-broker has the problem of single point of failure, decentralized meta-brokers are devoid of this

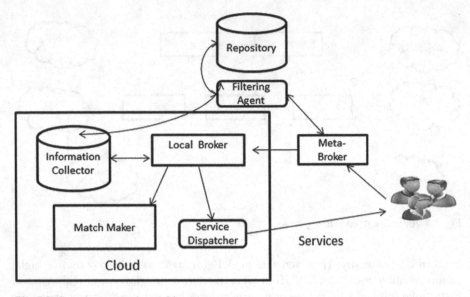

Fig. 5.5 Generic meta-broker architecture

problem. Further, since in case of meta-broker, communication is only between meta-brokers and between a local broker and the corresponding meta-broker, unnecessary communication cost is also avoided.

A second way of classifying CB is on the basis of the two parties which it serves. Since, a broker can bridge the gap between the various end points, we can use this to investigate the various types of brokers.

Single-Consumer-Multiple-Providers Broker Sometimes a cloud consumer requires an integration of various services provided by different cloud providers. This broker helps the consumer obtain and use various services provided by different providers. For example, a consumer, for some initiative, may need to use a software provided by an SaaS provider such as salesforce [20] and requires to exploit a large amount of internal data already captured and stored in cloud storages like S3 or databases like SimpleDB [21]. Further, the same consumer may also need to process the gathered data using an IaaS service, may be from Sun or Google App Engine. The necessary technical support to achieve such integration would be provided by this broker who would examine the requirements and help the consumer to integrate, compose and orchestrate the required services obtained from various vendors. This broker can act either as an intermediary broker or as an independent gateway providing transparent visibility to its customer.

SLA-Based Broker This broker's main aim is to provide the best possible SLA to the consumer while conforming to the imposed functional constraints. Thus, the consumer would provide a set of functional requirements along with the corresponding SLAs. The broker does the matchmaking and selects, on behalf of the consumer, providers that offer the required functions with the best pricing model and any other non-functional requirements provided through the SLAs. The main aim of this broker is to negotiate the best deal for the consumers. This broker provides transparency to its customers in terms of negotiation. However, once the negotiation is done, it does not have a necessary responsibility to keep the various vendors transparent from its customer.

Broker for Provider Clients In this scenario, a broker is used in a federated environment by a cloud provider to obtain resources for certain services that it is unable to provide to its consumer. Here, the cloud provider is the service requester. The requester CSP may have certain capability to partially fulfil the client's request. In that case, the requester would wish to obtain, from the federation, only those services that it is unable to offer. Thus, this CSP needs the broker not only to shop for the required services with the most fitting SLA parameters but also to be able to seamlessly integrate the services of the client CSP with the ones obtained from the federation.

Cloud Aggregation Broker This is an advanced concept where the broker is capable of building and offering a new service [22]. This broker can incrementally build new service by obtaining common capabilities from different vendors and mixing together other components from the third-party cloud platforms. In this scenario, the broker truly provides value-added service to its customers in the sense that beyond integrating services, it also adds new capabilities and provides a single access point to this upgraded composition. From the perspective of the application consumer, complete transparency about the service providers not only during integration but also through the lifetime of the service is an integral part of this brokering.

5.7   Scheduling in Cloud Broker

Scheduling forms a major part in cloud since it allows users to plug-in anytime from any place to utilize large-scale resources, be it storage or computing. The providers are responsible for accommodating requests on demand by dynamically expanding and contracting their resources in the form of virtual instances on the resource pool. These providers also need to have a mechanism of dispatching the execution of these virtual instances on their physical resources.

This need becomes multiplied in a scenario containing many clouds, as the federated approach expands the cloud capabilities in terms of services, with the aim of achieving a wider distribution of resources. However, since the global resource utilization equilibrium amongst the various resource pools in the federated environment would still need to be maintained, resource scheduling strategy becomes a very important design issue in a federated environment.

Resource scheduling in a federated environment is, however, not an independent strategy. It has to take into account the corresponding local data centre scheduling plans. The data centres have to focus on how to automatically and dynamically distribute and schedule the involved tasks according to the current workloads experienced in their infrastructures. Specifically, the approach implies that a local data centre should participate in the on-demand resource provisioning process at both local (intra-) and global (inter-) scale as well as manage the resource provisioning, demand allocation and queuing of user tasks at a local level by considering the characteristics of the actual system as well as the requirements of the user demands.

Cloud federation is fraught with inherently formidable challenges. Since the basic framework of cloud is virtualization, VMs form the base of cloud. These VMs are deployed on physical machines by the data centre scheduling mechanism. A typical cloud environment consists of multiple data centres. Since strict adherence to SLAs is a requirement in cloud, failure or even an overload of a physical machine necessitates that a deployed VM be migrated immediately. However, on the operational side, it is hard enough to determine even within a single service provider the best host for a VM for an optimal end-user performance, migrating such VMs flexibly and quickly is a very hard task. Cloud federation just multiplies the difficulty level since now the consideration of interoperability has to be included.

For scheduling in a federated scenario, the following factors need to be considered [23]:

• Heterogeneous pool of resources
• Need of interoperability amongst local schedulers
• Dynamicity of the environment
• Geographical distribution between different pools of resources
• Need for collaboration amongst the various data centres for job sharing amongst different infrastructures
• Load balancing across the federated ecosystem
• Proper resource allocation mechanisms
• Virtualized environment
• Self-management of resources

To handle all of the above-mentioned considerations in a dynamic federated environment, special attention needs to be given to the mechanism of scheduling. Meta-scheduler is a term found frequently in the grid computing, whose purpose is to establish a wide policy control amongst disperse resources. Policies used by such meta-schedulers include negotiation and management of a pool of resources bounded to different administrative domains. Hence, meta-schedulers possess functionalities required to offer interoperable resource management. Further, meta-schedulers are proficient in handling sudden spikes in demand and are equipped to dynamically bridge the gap amongst local and remote participants. Considering all the properties inherent to a meta-scheduler and the architectural issues in federated cloud scenario, the meta-schedulers seem to be the right choice for a federated cloud. The meta-scheduler scheduling strategies are classified into centralized, hierarchical, and decentralized scheduling [21]. We now investigate these strategies in detail.

Centralized Meta-Scheduling In the centralized model, meta-scheduling happens directly by a central instance that maintains information of all resources. Each time new jobs are submitted, the centralized meta-scheduler either sends the jobs for execution or arranges the jobs in a queue as there is no availability of resources. Specifically, the centralized meta-schedulers do not perform scheduling decisions [24] but only act as dispatchers. A central component is responsible for managing and communicating to various local schedulers of different providers. It gathers the information about job completion and availability of computational resources from the local sites. The dispatching decision is taken by the central component. The advantage of the centralized model is that a complete knowledge of the actual environment through central administration is achieved; therefore, common concerns in scheduling such as starvation could be easily predicted. In addition, the meta-scheduler assigns jobs constantly from the centralized pool list to the best possible resource for execution, which improves the performance. However, for each centralized meta-scheduler, a local system administrator maintains the complete control, thus making systems' dynamic changes unpredictable. In addition, possible situations such as bottleneck in responses and centralized failure are very important to be overcome.

Hierarchical Meta-Scheduling The hierarchical meta-scheduling scheme is similar to the centralized scheduling. In this setting, jobs are submitted to a central instance of the scheduler, which communicates with other schedulers belonging to its hierarchy. An advanced solution of hierarchical scheduling has been presented by Lucas-Simarro et al. [25] as a geographically distributed high-performance computing (HPC) setting. It is a layered architecture and offers a modular and autonomous solution on each layer. It is also reliable and scalable as it is hierarchically organized and performs scheduling in a space-sharing manner using deadlines. However, since there is only one central scheduling instance in the proposed system in which all jobs are to be submitted, this solution cannot be claimed as a truly hierarchical one.

Distributed Meta-Scheduling The distributed meta-scheduling theme originally defines that each resource has a local and a meta-scheduler. Thus, jobs are directly submitted to a meta-scheduler and the meta-schedulers decide whether it is possible to schedule the job in their own cloud or decide to which local schedulers to relocate it. A federated cloud encompasses resources from various infrastructures that may enter and leave dynamically. Allowing this denotes that real-time coordination is essential in decentralized interoperable collaborations so that the meta-schedulers are aware of the infrastructures available at any point in time in the ever-changing scenario. In the simplest of the cases, meta-schedulers query each other at regular intervals to collect the current load data [26], and hence use this information to find a suitable site with the lowest load for a certain job. Though distributed meta-scheduling is complex compared to the centralized and hierarchical themes, it is more scalable and flexible.

The scheduling mechanism in a broker should be adopted based on the type of broker and the kind of service it provides.

5.8 Role of Service-Level Agreement in a Cloud Broker

The SLA is a contract between a service provider and a customer that describes the service, responsibilities, terms, guarantees and service level to be provided and a mutually agreed upon set of consumer expectations and provider obligations. Typical QoS parameters that are included in the SLAs are resource availability, response time and deadlines. The authors in [27] came up with a list of factors to consider when defining the terms of an SLA:

- *Responsibilities of both parties*: It is important to define the balance of responsibilities between the provider and consumer. For example, the provider will be responsible for the SaaS aspects, but the consumer may be mostly responsible for the consumer's VM that contains licensed software and works with sensitive data.
- *Business continuity/disaster recovery*: The consumer should ensure the provider maintains adequate disaster protection.
- *Maintenance*: Consumers should know when providers will do maintenance tasks and what will happen to consumer's task at that time.
- *Data location and security*: There are regulations that certain types of data can only be stored in certain physical locations. Providers can respond to those requirements with a guarantee that a consumer's data will be stored in certain locations only and the ability to audit that situation.
- *Provider failure*: Make contingency plans that take into account the financial health of the provider.
- *Jurisdiction*: Understanding the local laws that apply to the provider as well as the consumer.
- *Brokers and resellers*: If the provider is not the one who is offering the service but is a middleman, the consumer should have a clear understanding of the policies of not only the middleman's but also the actual provider in the background.
- *Business-level objectives*: An organization must define why it should use the cloud services before it can define exactly what services it will use.

A CB requires that it should define, implement and apply cloud service management within and across mixed cloud services through strict negotiation and monitoring of formalized business SLAs [28]. The SLA management should include all three deployment models: IaaS, PaaS and SaaS. A broker not only negotiates, on the behalf of its customer but also continuously monitors the service against a set threshold of the SLAs. Violation can be tolerated only up to the threshold. Upon crossing the defined threshold, it is declared as an SLA violation and alarms in the form of an automatic notification, adjustment and some provisioning actions till the service does not come back in line with its SLA guides.

The key goal of a broker is to provide cloud service management and real-time control and agility to ensure that the cloud IT services are always applied in the right way, with the right amount at the right time to ensure the business services they support achieve their defined targets.

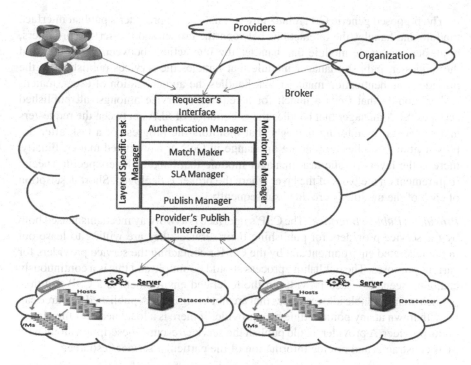

Fig. 5.6 Cloud ecosystem with generic CB architecture

5.9 Cloud Broker: Generic Architecture

In this section, the architecture of a broker is provided that possesses the functionalities of a single broker in a federated scenario having combined capabilities of both the SLA-based broker and the broker for cloud providers.

The proposed CB provides brokering service either between a client consumer and different provider CSPs or between a client CSP seeking resources and different provider CSPs. Thus, a service requester to this broker can be a client consumer, a user or an organization seeking a service from the federated cloud, or another CSP that is unable to provide service to its own consumer due to some temporary inability. The service providers, on the other hand, are cloud providers. These can be public cloud, private cloud, community cloud or hybrid cloud. The CB keeps a track of all the services available in the federated environment. Further the broker offers all other necessary services for interoperability between the requester and the providers such as intermediation, monitoring, portability, governance, provisioning, adapting, security, composition services and also negotiates relationships.

The CB has the capability of composing various services offered by different providers. Figure 5.6 shows a federated cloud ecosystem with the architecture of a generic CB. On one side, it has the service requesters who can be an independent client consumer, an organization seeking service/resource or a CSP who needs resource or service. On the other side, the CB has the CSPs that are ready to offer resources/services to the federation.

The proposed generic CB architecture consists of the provider's publish interface module that handles the interactions between the broker and the service providers, requester's interface module that handles the interactions between the broker and the requester, publish manager module that handles the services published by the providers, authentication manager that handles the authentication of users, matchmaker module that finds a match for a requested service amongst all published services, SLA manager that handles the negotiation of SLAs between the requesters and providers, monitoring manager that monitors the progress of a task after deployment and handles any failure or change in QoS or any related matter. Finally, there is the layer-specific task manager module that handles layer-specific special requirement on the basis of the layer where the broker is deployed. Short description of each of the module is provided subsequently.

Provider's Publish Interface The CSP's interface is a two-way mechanism used both by the service providers for publishing their services they are willing to lease out in the federated environment and by the CB for contacting the service providers for various purposes. The publishing process should be simple and this is a continuously changing scenario. Each provider in the federated environment is a CSP and they publish their available idle resources that are not being used. A published resource can be withdrawn at any point in time by a provider if there is a local need for the clients of the provider. A provider would publish the service/resource description along with SLA constraints and pricing information of the particular service/resource.

Publish Manager Publish manager maintains the information about different published services, both their pricing models and any constraint that they may impose. It helps the matchmaker module to select certain services for specific request. It also interacts with the interface on demand by sending cloud service subscription request in an attempt to fulfil a requester's requirement in case the aggregated published services cannot fulfil a certain requester's requirements. Some CSPs, under those circumstances, may respond their willingness to publish their resource if available.

It may be noted that the CB does not impose any restriction on the type of service/of resource being exposed through the published information. Thus, all types of services, for example, SaaS, IaaS, PaaS or data storage as a service (DSaaS) as well as all types of service providers, e.g. private cloud, community cloud, public cloud and hybrid cloud can use the CB's interface to notify their published information and obtain SLA negotiation, invocation of services based on matched and negotiated resources/services and the relevant data through this interface.

In this architecture, the composition of services can be dynamic in the sense that as a request arrives, the CB subscribes to the CSP using abstract logic and then eventually transfers this to the concrete service logic, finally invoking the service and passing on the obtained result to the requester.

It can receive requests from the cloud service consumers through requester's interface, analyse the requested cloud services, select appropriate service logic and function patterns based on CSB database information from subscription or internal integration, execute related operations, then invoke and adapt to the concrete cloud services and resources from the various CSPs.

Requester's Interface Requesters who need a resource/service would contact the CB through the requester's interface to first send the requirements and the corresponding constraints in terms of pricing and any other restrictions to the CB. These requests along with the constraints are stored in a request buffer (RB) till the requests are not provisioned. The CB goes through the RB and performs matchmaking, SLA negotiation and layer-specific tasks and ensures that the requester's job gets done successfully. On completion of the job, the appropriate result and/or messages are sent to the requester by the CB through this interface.

Authentication Manager The broker needs to authenticate the consumers in order to provide the result of some requests correctly as well as for billing purpose. The authentication manager maintains a database of requesters and stores all necessary information regarding the requests given by the requester such as the SLAs asked by the requester, the negotiated SLAs obtained by the broker on behalf of the requester, any special payment terms by some provider, etc. At the time of delivery of the result and payment, all these can be verified by the authentication manager.

Matchmaker The job of this module is to find a suitable service for a specific request. Matchmaker accepts the pending requests from the RB, request being an application request, platform-specific request or infrastructure request, and looks for a match amongst all available services published by the providers in the publish manager. All such matches are then forwarded to the SLA manager. In case no match is found, the CB sends a request to the CSPs for publishing resources that would match the pending request.

SLA Manager This module gets its inputs from the matchmaker. The job of this module is to understand and negotiate SLAs with each of the matching CSP on behalf of the requester and finalize the service for every request. To determine which provider best fits with the user's SLA needs, the SLA manager needs to evaluate the complete list of services of the CSPs chosen by the matchmaker, with special attention to factors such as service availability, the cost per unit of capacity for a provider, the mechanism and the metrics provided by the CSPs to monitor the leased out services. The SLA manager takes care of the problem of heterogeneous methods of service offerings and nonstandard SLA description by the CSPs. Thus, the responsibility of the SLA manager is to understand the requirements of the users, have a good idea of the descriptions of the offers by each of the chosen CSPs, to compare these in order to make a correct and efficient choice. To be able to achieve these, the SLA manager has to consider not only the technical requirements but *also* all the rules and conditions of the providers.

It not only has to understand the metrics provided by the CSP with whom the deal is finalized but also has to obtain proper information about how to monitor the service to determine whether the provider is delivering the service as promised, the responsibilities of the provider as well as what remedies are available if the terms of the SLA are not met by the providers. The SLA manager has to pass all these information to the monitoring manager whose responsibility is to monitor the services.

Monitoring Manager After a requester's job has been deployed, the monitoring manager takes over and monitors the CSP on behalf of the requester. It is the job of the monitoring manager to properly interpret the SLAs given by the CSPs and to ensure that these are strictly adhered to. It is also the responsibility of the monitoring manager to identify a violation of SLA when one surfaces. It can be non-conformance to any of the previously agreed upon SLAs. Inclusion of penalties in the SLA can also be previously agreed upon and in case there is a violation, it is the monitoring manager's responsibility to ensure that it is accurately compensated, as per the agreement.

Another job of the monitoring manager is to monitor the changing requirements on the consumers' side and reconfigure the cloud resources accordingly [26].

Layer-Specific Task Manager In many cases, a broker needs to give some service specific to a layer. The layer-specific task manager performs this task. For example, if a service composition is needed for a request in the IaaS layer with required specification from the requester, the layer-specific task manager takes care of this.

The above-mentioned architecture is generic and has no special functionality. However, rendering it for any special purpose the CB would only require the addition of specific modules to this architecture. It can be readily observed that the proposed CB can easily be converted to an SLA-based broker or a cloud aggregation broker by making simple modifications. Similarly, creating hierarchical broker or even decentralized meta-broker would be a simple task.

5.10 Conclusion

Cloud collaboration is currently the most attractive solution in the cloud world of high-demand and huge elasticity requirement. Even though there are various ways of bringing in such collaboration, federation definitely is the most attractive one from the perspective of both the service consumer and the provider. In a federation, cloud providers voluntarily form a collaborative environment and hence help consumers as well as providers, both small and medium, to a large extent. Such federation benefits the most when these are mediated by the brokers. A broker, on the other hand, can be classified based on the brokers' actions, centralized or decentralized. Although centralized brokers are more intuitively acceptable options, decentralized meta-brokers have a promising future since such brokers can avoid all the problems of a centralized architecture while providing the benefits of broker. However, the problem of cloud federation in general and the problem of implementing a CB for the purpose of federation in specific is a complex problem owing to the heterogeneity of actors and technologies involved. A fundamental aspect here is the definition of a common ground on which various federation techniques can refer to. The implementation of a federation, both with broker and without, is still a challenge.

This chapter introduces the concepts of cloud federation with the help of the CB and identifies the capability requirement of the entities in a broker. The cloud brokerage model is examined in great detail and a generic CB architecture is proposed.

The constituent entities of the architecture are discussed in detail. The proposed architecture can be easily adapted to accommodate all types of brokers. This is a novel area of intensive research whose body of knowledge is yet to be established properly. While most research projects focus on developing cloud federations, majority exploiting the usage of broker, most industry projects use brokers for the purpose of authentication, billing, etc., across clouds. Research in this area is in its nascent stage and a generic state-of-the-art solution is yet to arrive. These research and development activities of federation as well as brokerage would provide enhanced degree of scalability, flexibility and simplicity for management and delivery of services in a federated cloud environment. The cloud world would witness an enormous surge of brokerage in all fields, particularly in federation in near future.

References

1. Quarati A, Clematis A, Galizia A, D'Agostino D (2013) Hybrid clouds brokering: business opportunities, QoS and energy-saving issues. Simulat Model Pract Theory 39:121–134
2. Gartner (2009) Cloud consumers need brokerages to unlock the potential of cloud services. www.gartner.com/newsroom/id/1064712. Accessed 15 May 2013
3. Buyya R, Ranjan R, Calheiros RN (2010) InterCloud: utility-oriented federation of cloud computing environments for scaling of application services. In: Proceedings of the 10th international conference on algorithms and architectures for parallel processing ICA3PP' 10, Berlin, pp 13–31
4. Grozey N, Buyya R (2012) Inter-cloud architectures and application brokering: taxonomy and survey. Softw Pract Exp 44:369–390. doi:10.1002/spe.2168 (www.interscience.wiley.com)
5. Ferrer AJ, Hernndez F, Tordsson J, Elmroth E, Ali-Eldin A, Zsigri C, Sirvent R, Guitart J, Badia RM, Djemame K (2012) OPTIMIS: a holistic approach to cloud service provisioning. Future Gener Comput Syst 28(1):66–67
6. Agility A (2012) What is federation. http://www.arjuna.com/what-is-federation. Accessed 15 May 2013
7. Rochwerger B, Breitgand D, Levy E, Galis A, Nagin K, Llorente L, Montero R, Wolfsthal Y, Elmroth E, Caceres J (2009) The reservoir model and architecture for open federated cloud computing. IBM J Res Dev 53(4):1–11
8. Global Inter-Cloud Technology Forum (2010) Use cases and functional requirements for inter-cloud computing technical report. Global Inter-Cloud Technology Forum 2010
9. Celesti A, Tusa F, Villari M, Puliafito A (2010) How to enhance cloud architectures to enable cross-federation. In: Proceedings of the 3rd international conference on cloud computing (CLOUD 2010), pp 337–345
10. IEEE P2302—Standard for intercloud interoperability and federation (SIIF). http://standards. ieee.org/develop/project/2302.html. Accessed 15 May 2013
11. Liu F, Tong J, Mao J, Bohn B, Messina J, Badger L, Leaf D (2011) NIST cloud reference architecture. National Institute of Standards and Technology (NIST), Information Technology Laboratory. www.csrc.nist.gov. Accessed 5 May 2013
12. Gartner (2010) Cloud services brokerages: the dawn of the next intermediation age. www.gartner.com/. Accessed 15 May 2013
13. Cloud Broker Overload (2012) http://recursivedigressions.blogspot.in/2012/03/cloud-broker Overload.html. Accessed 15 May 2013
14. Redefine broker Service (2011) http://diversity.net.nz/nist-decides-to-redefine-the-english-language-broker-service-intermediary/2011/09/12/. Accessed 15 May 2013
15. NIST Special Publication 500–299 (2013) NIST cloud computing security reference architecture. http://www.nist.gov/itl/csd/cloud-061113.cfm. Accessed 25 May 2013

16. Buyya R, Yeo C, Venugopal S, Broberg J, Brandic I (2009) Cloud computing and emerging IT platforms: vision, hype, and reality for delivering computing as the 5th utility. Future Gener Comput Syst 25:599–616
17. Vecchiola C, Calheiros R, Karunamoorthy D, Buyya R (2011) Deadline-driven provisioning of resources for scientific applications in hybrid clouds with aneka. Future Gener Comput Syst 28:58–65
18. Villegas D, Bobroff N, Roderob I, Delgado J, Liu Y, Devarakonda A, Fong L, Sadjadi SM, Parashar M (2012) Cloud federation in a layered service model. J Comput Syst Sci 78: 1330–1344
19. Mell P, Grance T (2011) The NIST definition of cloud computing: recommendations of the National Institute of Standards and Technology (NIST). Information Technology Laboratory. www.csrc.nist.gov. Accessed 15 May 2013
20. salesforce.com (2011) http://www.salesforce.com. Accessed 5 June 2013
21. Amazon Simple Storage Service (2011) Amazon S3. http://s3.amazonaws.com. Accessed 5 June 2013
22. Nair SK, Porwal S, Dimitrakos T, Ferrer AJ et al (2010) Towards secure cloud bursting, brokerage and aggregation, web services (ECOWS). In: 8th IEEE European conference on web services, Ayia Napa, Cyprus, pp 189–196. doi:10.1109/ECOWS.2010.33
23. Sotiriadis S, Bessis N, Antonopoulos N (2011) Towards inter-cloud schedulers: a survey of meta-scheduling approaches. In: 2011 International conference on P2P, parallel, grid, cloud and internet computing (3PGCIC'11), pp 59–66
24. Sotiriadis S, Bessis N, Xhafa F, Antonopoulos N (2012) From meta-computing to interoperable infrastructures: a review of meta-schedulers for HPC, grid and cloud. In: IEEE international conference on advanced information networking and applications, pp 874–883
25. Lucas-Simarro JL, Moreno-Vozmediano R, Montero RS, Llorente IM (2012) Scheduling strategies for optimal service deployment across multiple clouds. Future Gener Comput Syst 29:1431–1441
26. Feitelson DG, Rudolph L (1995) Parallel job scheduling: issues and approaches. In: Proceedings of the workshop on job scheduling strategies for parallel processing (IPPS '95), pp 1–18
27. Cloud Computing Use Cases -A white paper (2010) Produced by the Cloud Computing Use Case Discussion Group. IBM, Version 4, 02 July 2010
28. Amato A, Di Martino B, Venticinque S (2012) Evaluation and brokering of service level agreements for negotiation of cloud infrastructures. In: 2012 international conference for internet technology and secured transactions ICITST-2012, pp 144–149

Chapter 6
Patterns of Trust: Role of Certification for SME Cloud Adoption

Alea M. Fairchild

Abstract Growth of cloud computing as a concept continues to pose challenges on how to deliver agile, yet secure, information technology (IT) services to enterprises. While the hype surrounding cloud computing may have peaked, the concept of "cloudwashing" (adding the term "cloud" to an existing service for marketing reasons) continues to cause confusion and inflated expectations with enterprise buyers. This fear, uncertainty, and doubt (FUD) just slows down the growth of a potentially larger market. This is especially true for small and medium sized enterprises (SMEs) who turn to IT providers to handle the underlying systems for their businesses. To assist cloud service buyers, a recent communication from the European Commission advocated voluntary certification for cloud service providers (CSPs). This has sparked a debate as to the relevance and authority of certification bodies in verifying the ability and capability of CSPs. In this research, we are developing an exploratory model looking at signaling quality, the independence of certifying authorities, and the impact of regulatory backing for trust of certification bodies, based on the existing academic literature on standards of adoption and trust. We are examining what role the third-party certifiers can play in adoption of cloud by SMEs, exploring the roles of certifiers in Europe already involved in market adoption to test our framework, together with four established cases of service providers seeking certification.

Keywords Adoption · Certification · Cloud governance · Information economics · SME · Trust

6.1 Introduction

Buyya et al. [1] defines cloud as: "... *a type of parallel and distributed system consisting of a collection of interconnected and virtualised computers that are dynamically provisioned and presented as one or more unified computing resources based on service-level agreements established through negotiation between the service provider and consumers.*"

A. M. Fairchild (✉)
Hogeschool Universiteit Brussel, Warmoesberg 26, 1000 Brussels, Belgium
e-mail: alea.fairchild@kuleuven.be

Z. Mahmood (ed.), *Continued Rise of the Cloud,* Computer Communications and Networks, DOI 10.1007/978-1-4471-6452-4_6, © Springer-Verlag London 2014

This definition shows a computing resource as a service being provided; there is an agreement for said service; and the fact that this service is negotiated between parties. The forms of service that cloud computing provides today may be broken down into managed services, software as a service (SaaS), utility computing, and platform as a service (PaaS). The ideas behind these forms of service are not new, but the fact that the users can tap into these services from web browsers via the Internet makes them "cloud" services [2].

Cloud-based software is often easier to use, quicker to install and implement, and provides far greater flexibility than on-premise solutions that need to be installed and maintained, especially for SMEs without resources for a dedicated IT staff. Cloud-based software can also help small businesses lower costs, often by a significant amount. A recent survey by market research firm IDC found that almost every SME that uses cloud services saves money, with many lowering costs between 10 and 20 %. Despite these benefits, the path to the cloud has been bumpy, particularly in Europe, and due to a convoluted web of privacy laws and other governmental regulations, as well as concerns about data security, analysts estimate that business cloud adoption in Europe lags behind the USA by about 2 years [3]. Cloud provides a big opportunity for Europe, and openness is the key attributed to provide opportunity for SMEs, with a concern that lock-in and barriers to entry could block that opportunity.

As part of their Europe 2020 strategy on cloud computing, the European Commission's recently released strategy to boost adoption of cloud computing services throughout Europe had a statement was that "cloud certification should be voluntary and industry driven, building on current and emerging international standards to foster global compatibility of cloud computing offerings" [4].

But is certification good for making and growing a marketplace? What is the role of certifiers in making a market, and how are they regulated? Auriol and Schilizzi [5] show us that there is a problem signaling the quality of goods and services when quality is never observable to consumers. Certification acts to transform unobservable credence attributes into observable search attributes. They then studied the cost of certification systems on market structure and performance in agricultural seed production. Given we are discussing an intangible deliverable, since this is a service, that is not available in bulk, we will take a slightly different approach.

The central research question is "What are the benefits of cloud service certification for building trust and establishing market growth for SME customers?" Our research objectives are the following:

- Define the role of the certifier in creating trust and establishing credibility
- Examine the impact of certification on market development
- Explore how best to regulate the certification process to protect user benefits, if needed

For our methodology, in this chapter, we will explore the role of the certifier by examining complementary markets where certification is active to see how trust has been created as well as the impact over time on market growth; and by examining the activities of one particular early market entrant in certification to see how stakeholder dynamics work between them, their customers, and the government bodies in the

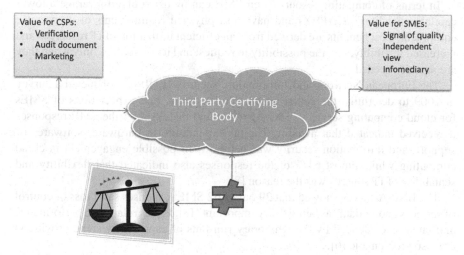

Model of Third Party Certifiers for CSPs and SMEs

Fig. 6.1 Role of the third-party certifying bodies—our model

countries where they are present. Using a case study in this research is motivated by seeing examples in the field to test and extend theory. Figure 6.1 visually demonstrates the role of the third-party certifier we are examining.

Our model examines the role of the third-party certifying body as an intermediary that is providing value to both the CSPs and the SMEs in their activities. As shown by the "not equal" sign, the definition of that intermediation role does not include oversight by one or more governmental bodies at this time, however, this is one element that would potentially change the balance between the parties if it became mandatory.

6.2   Adoption Issues for SMEs: Cultural, Economic, and Organizational

To start, we need to examine why a certifier would be needed for adoption, particularly for the SME. What sets this target group apart from larger enterprises? How would a certifier play a role in influencing this group of companies?

Cloud computing can be seen as an emerging computing service paradigm. And, like other services of this scale, complexity, and novelty, there are fears, uncertainties, and concerns about the technology's maturity. However, the most important can be listed as those relating to control, vendor lock-in, performance, latency, security, privacy, and reliability [6].

In Europe, SMEs are considered organizations of great importance, which is a fair assessment as they represent more than 95 % of the business sector of the developed economies [7] and which, due to reduced resources and difficult access to IT, are ideal candidates for adopting cloud computing.

In terms of computing resources, an SME can by using cloud leverage a lower capital expenditure (CAPEX) and have less physical requirements of on-premise equipment. Cost benefits are derived from an efficient utilization of IT resources and increased flexibility, i.e., the possibility to request and use resources only when they are actually needed.

The European Network and Information Security (ENISA) conducted a survey in 2009 to determine the actual needs, requirements, and expectations of SMEs for cloud computing services. This survey found that 68 % of the SME responses it received indicated that avoiding capital expenditure in hardware, software, IT support, and information security was behind their possible engagement in cloud computing while almost 64 % of the responses also indicated that flexibility and scalability of IT sources was the reason [8].

The ENISA survey showed that 29 out of 62 SME responses saw "loss of control of services and/or data" as being "very important" [8]. Issues relating to performance and latency (evidenced by the temporary run-outs of capacity by some providers) are also problematic [6].

Research conducted by Easynet Connect has shown that UK SMEs are increasingly eager to adopt cloud computing, with 47 % planning to do so within the next 5 years. Of those companies which indicated their preparedness to move to cloud computing, 35 % of them cited cost savings as the key driver [9].

6.2.1   Role of SME in Technology Adoption

The results shown below can be found in the ENISA report: *"Cloud computing Risk Assessment: Benefits, risks and recommendations for information security* (Table 6.1).

Most of the reasons shown above are business continuance and capital expenditure rationale. For an SME, given a limited budget and constrained resources, the economic rationale and benefits gained might even be of a higher priority, but the risk compared to a multinational enterprise (MNE) might also be perceived as higher with more to lose.

Cloud adoption for innovation of business processes was not highlighted in this ENISA study. Is there a culture in SME as early adopters or not? Thang and Yap [10] point out that the chief executive officer (CEO) often has a significant role in the adoption of IT by SMEs. An SME that is likely to adopt IT will most often have a CEO who has a positive attitude toward IT adoption, who is innovative and who is knowledgeable about IT.

Mehrtens et al. [11] show in their research three forms of SME organizational readiness as highly relevant to the adoption of the Internet: (a) the level of IT knowledge among IT professionals; (b) the level of IT knowledge among non-IT professionals; and (c) the level of IT use within the organization.

Table 6.1 Reasons for adoption of Cloud [8]

What are the reasons behind your possible engagement in the Cloud Computing area?		
Answer options	Response percent (%)	Response count
Remove economic/expertise barriers impeding to modernize business processes by the introduction of Information Technology	30.6	22
Avoiding capital expenditure in hardware, software, IT support, Information Security by outsourcing infrastructure/platforms/services	68.1	49
Flexibility and scalability of IT resources	63.9	46
Increasing computing capacity and business performance	36.1	26
Diversification of IT systems	11.1	8
Local and global optimisation of IT infrastructure through automated management of virtual machines	25.0	18
Business continuity and disaster recover/capabilities	52.8	38
Assessing the feasibility and profitability of new sen/ices (i.e. by developing business cases into the cloud)	29.2	21
Adding redundancy to increase availability and resilience	27.8	20
Controlling marginal profit and marginal costs	15.3	11
Other (please specify)	13.9	10
Answered questions		72

This research leads us back to the early comment of economic constraints for SME cloud adoption. Is the lack of IT personnel in a traditional SME one factor for cloud adoption?

The work of Sultan [6] examined the economic viability and efficiency of cloud computing for SMEs and its benefits. Sultan [6] tried to explain how cloud services differed from anything experienced so far by those businesses in terms of flexibility, availability, and cost structure. Furthermore, they examined the findings of some surveys which not only reveal the preparedness of many SMEs to use cloud computing and showed that many of those businesses are already using some of the cloud services on offer. This study concentrated mainly on the merit of "public" cloud services (where services are provided by "remote" suppliers who take responsibility for delivering those services to their clients), and not "private" and "hybrid" cloud offering. In working with public cloud providers such as Amazon and Rackspace, SMEs can take advantage of economies of scale that large cloud providers are able to offer, and leverage the potential of an outsourcing partner with industry expertise. However many SME enterprises with limited in-house IT support and limited knowledge about cloud technologies find it difficult to make the choice on private vs. public cloud. In examining organizational issues for adoption, one question to ask: Does size matter to a CSP? Several CSPs have developed specific packages geared toward SME needs.

Keung and Kwok [12] have recently developed a cloud deployment model assessment method called Cloud Deployment Selection Model (CDSM). The model has been validated in real case studies, and recommendations derived have been compared with real adoption cases. Based on the factors identified from many SME organizations, it could be an important tool for SMEs to decide between private or

Table 6.2 Processes that could be outsourced—$n = 72$ [8]

Which IT services/applications supporting business processes are most likely to be outsourced to a cloud computing service provider?

Answer options	Response percent (%)	Response count
Payroll	38.9	28
Human resources	19.4	14
Procurements	16.7	12
CRM/sales management	52.8	38
Accounting and finance	30.6	22
Project management	41.7	30
Application development on the cloud	44.4	32
Anonymised data analysis	29.2	21
Other (please specify)	12.5	9
Answered questions		72

public cloud solutions. Marston et al. [13] state that for SMEs, the prices and the terms and conditions (SLAs) are far better with a cloud provider than the SME could realize themselves with their moderate investment levels.

Another issue within the SME is expertise within horizontal applications outside of the core expertise of the business. Knowledge of the latest human resources (HR) and payroll applications may be outside of the employees of the business, therefore, the wish to outsource these applications to someone more knowledgeable may be a driver to external parties. Below, Table 6.2 highlights what processes companies want to be outsourced from the ENISA study on cloud adoption.

Given some of the economic and organizational drivers for SME cloud adoption, we then examine what role a third-party certifier might play in helping reduce the risk of CSP selection for the SME.

6.2.2 Role of Third-Party Certifiers

Fundamental concepts from information economics can provide a framework for examining the role of the third-party certifiers who are "external institutions that assess, evaluate, and certify quality claims" [14]. Five important concepts that we can use for this framework from an information economics perspective are:

- Uncertainty
- Information asymmetries
- Opportunistic behavior
- Divergences between private and social returns
- Signaling institutions

For the framework of our evaluation of the role of certifiers, we started with Spence's [15] article on Job Market Signaling, which provides an approach for thinking about countervailing institutions (institutions that emerge to address problems that arise from uncertainty and asymmetric information). Given uncertainty in the market some individuals or institutions may attempt to signal differences to prospective buyers or employers. Differentiation is critical to position a firm amongst its competitors.

We then looked at Tanner's [16] argument that third-party certifiers' key asset is their perceived independence. If third-party certifiers are truly independent, than the costs of obtaining third-party certification (for a quality attribute) will be inversely related to the quality of a firm and/or its product. If this were not the case, third-party certification would not allow for discrimination on the basis of quality. Masters and Sanoga [17] raise an additional point in that they argue that the emergence of third-party certifiers depends, in part, on the presence of a national standards authority. In a sense they provide a basis for certifying the certifiers.

We also have included other industry-specific certifications and quality seals in our evaluation of the role of certification and their role in trust with SMEs. The first example is ISO/IEC 27001, initially published in 2005, designed for information security management and assists firms in developing an independently assessed and certified information security management system. This standard allows SMEs to protect their reputation, as well as compete with bigger brands. We also explored SAS70 II certification, which is developed by the American Institute of Certified Public Accountants (AICPA) and used for audit control for activities and processes in services in ICT in the dedicated server and co-location hosting market. We also included in our analysis Eurocloud's Datacentre Star Audit (DCSA), which is a more niche seal of approval for data centers throughout Europe.

In examining existing related theory, we utilise Habib et al. [18] on trust and reputation in cloud environments. In online service environments, trust and reputation models have been proven useful in decision making [19]. We have also included research from Prezas [20] on trust and ISO/IEC 27001 certification.

Using a framework developed on these information economics concepts and information from other certification and quality seal market efforts, we will therefore be examining the dynamics of market adoption based on:

- Signaling quality in cloud service provisioning
- Independence of certification bodies in impacting market adoption
- Regulatory backing for trust of certification bodies

After structuring this framework, we will then examine the Cloud Industry Forum as an example of a certifying organization and how their offerings match with the framework as to impact of market growth and adoption.

6.3   Structuring the Framework on Trust and Adoption

As discussed above, we developed a framework to assess the role of the third-party certifier on trust and adoption for the SME. What did we synthesize from our literature research? Examples of relevant findings from Table 6.3 include:

Table 6.3 Synthesis of findings from literature

Topic	Findings
Signaling quality in cloud service provisioning	Fomin et al. [21] argue that the benefits of ISO 9001 certification have gradually shifted from earlier times when its certification was used as a signal to markets [22] to one where firms can actually gain direct benefits from the effective use of the quality management system itself. But opinion is mixed as to whether a formal accreditation process would actually provide large organizations in particular with the assurance required to participate seriously in the cloud world [23]
Independence of certification bodies in impacting market adoption	Tanner's [16] argument that third-party certifiers' key asset is their perceived independence. Masters and Sanoga [17] argue that the emergence of third-party certifiers depends, in part, on the presence of a national standards authority
Regulatory backing for trust of certification bodies	Empirical research has shown that communication about norms in cases of self-regulation is difficult, for both parties [24]. Backhouse et al. [25] suggest that in some cases for ISO/IEC27001, in the countries with the largest number of certificates for ISO/IEC 27001 the certification process is driven by either government regulation, as in Japan or supplier/buyer demands or the necessity of outsourcing and offshoring in markets such as Taiwan, Singapore and India

- A shift from earlier times when its certification was used as a signal to markets to one where firms can actually gain direct benefits from the effective use of the quality management system itself.
- In the countries with high participation in certification, the certification process is driven either by government regulation, supplier/buyer demands, or the necessity of outsourcing and offshoring the activity.

An additional point is **benefits creation**. Saint-Germain [26] argues that an important driver for ISMS certification is demonstrating to partners that the company has identified and measured their security risks and implemented a security policy and controls that will mitigate these risks In addition, international invitations to tender are beginning to require that organizations be compliant with certain security standards, and security audit demands from financial institutions and insurance companies are increasing. A further incentive is lower insurance premiums for ISO 27001 certified companies [27]. It has been seen that governments and other regulatory agencies are moving away from this labor intensive command and control approach of governmental certification and experimenting with various forms of self-regulation. Part of this self-regulation is adding benefits for the certification process to maintain compliance.

The next step to our research was to identify the rationale for CSPs to join a certification scheme. Do these kinds of schemes help make a market develop faster and/or more efficiently?

6.4 Cloud Service Providers Use Cases of Certification from the Cloud Industry Forum

The Cloud Industry Forum (CIF) is a non-profit organization based in the UK and was developed to assist in advocating cloud adoption. The CIF has been establishing research in cloud adoption, in order to create commonality in language and standards. They claim that they are trying to enable innovation in the marketplace, not restrict it [28].

The CIF has developed a code of practice that aims to provide transparency amongst CSPs, to assist the cloud service users (CSUs) in determining the core information necessary for decisions on adoption of cloud services, and to incorporate current standards and frameworks (e.g., ISO 9001, ISO 14001, and ITIL®) requiring provision of organizational, commercial and operational information which are independently reviewed. The CIF proposes an annual self-certification process for the CSPs, which would be an online submission based on off-line review [28].

The three pillars that provide the scope and framework for their certification are as follows:

- **Transparency:** Of the organization, its structure, location, key people, and services. This has to be reflected on your website.
- **Capability:** The processes and procedures in operation to support the delivery of services and customer experience.
- **Accountability:** Commitment of senior executive to the Code of Practice and behavior with customers.

If successful, this would lead to an approval to use certification mark and listed on the CIF site as a self-certified vendor.

For our research, we have randomly selected three CSP participants from the CIF certification program and looked at the framework criteria with the exception of regulatory backing. Using only three CSPs obviously is not reflective of the entire marketplace, but as all three have already joined a certification scheme, it gave us a good basis for CSP experience in this area. The rationale for the exclusion of regulatory backing was that as all three members had already joined CIF, who does not have regulatory backing, we held with Tanner's research [16] that the independence of the certification body was one of the features that drew these CSP firms to join, given their comments. We would have to survey other CSP firms that did not join to see if the independence was a factor in their not becoming certified by the CIF.

The three CSP firms selected for this study are the following:

- **ChannelCloud**: This CSP was established 10 years ago in the USA, launched in the UK and Ireland in January 2011. The goals of this CSP is to build a federation of ChannelCloud partners across the UK and Ireland toward its vision for a new, truly comprehensive method of delivering IT services to clients.
- **Unit4**: UNIT4 has been at the forefront of cloud computing for many years. The company's newest offering, Shared Journey, is a cloud-based deployment option designed for organizations looking to set up a shared services operation that is

quick to establish, easy to grow and responsive to change, which can be seen as ideal for SMEs.

- **Webroot**: Founded in 1997, the company provides best-of-breed security solutions that protect personal information and corporate assets from online and internal threats. Based in Broomfield, CO in the USA, the company is privately held and backed by some of the industry's leading venture capital firms, including Technology Crossover Ventures, Accel Partners, and Mayfield. The company was also one of the founding members of CIF.

Each of these three CSPs provided materials on their rationale for joining the CIF and some background on how much work the CIF audit was for them to do prior to their acceptance into the CIF. The management quotes in Table 6.4 came from the following sources, with the materials provided from the CIF:

- ChannelCloud: Paul Byrne, CEO, ChannelCloud UK/Ireland
- Unit4: Anwen Robinson, MD of UNIT4 Business Software Ltd.
- Webroot: George Anderson, EMEA Product Marketing at Webroot

6.5 Continuance of the Research

There are several options for continuing this research. One is to test if the enhanced quality of service that the certification audit requires benefits the SME in terms of trust and reliability. Other activities around this research could be to interview SME firms who work with these CSP firms to see if the certification was a factor in the selection of the cloud service. The challenge with this is two-fold: these schemes are reasonably new and the SME may not have seen enough service to verify how certification helped the process, and there may not yet be enough SMEs willing to participate in this kind of research to give us a good sample of the marketplace.

The concept of regulation of certification also needs to be addressed. As an initial part of this research, we interviewed lobbyists in Brussels on certification and governmental backing. The consensus from these interviews is that it could benefit certification, but that most European Union (EU) governments would not be willing to make the investment at this time as the governments feel this regulatory effort would slow down the pace of market development for cloud.

6.6 Conclusion

In this research, our goals were to explore the role of the third-party certification on adoption of cloud computing by SMEs. The literature base was established by examining other markets where certification has been used to see how trust has been created. We did not get enough empirical data on the impact of certification on other markets on growth over time and certification as a direct impact factor to market growth has not appeared in the literature we have examined in this regard.

Table 6.4 Quotes from CSP management on benefits of certification

	ChannelCloud	Unit4	Webroot
Signaling quality in cloud service provisioning	Crucial for us was the need to establish credibility in the market and that is why we aligned ourselves with the Cloud Industry Forum (CIF) code of practice. There is no doubt that gaining CIF certification has enhanced our position in the market. It has given us great credibility with our clients and prospects alike. Furthermore, it forced us to consider where we might have gaps in our documentation and business processes	CIF membership provides us with additional market credibility	The code of practice and the certification process enables professional cloud service providers such as ourselves, to demonstrate with clarity their ethics, practices and processes through an independently recognized and credible body in order to build trust by association with prospective customers
Independence of certification bodies in impacting market adoption	We share a view that we have in common with the CIF, one based on building trust and transparency throughout the market	By adopting a set of certifiable criteria, the cloud service provider enables the end user to have a transparent view of the vendor's business and the type of services and service levels they can expect from them	Vendors verified by the CIF are responsible for adhering to the CIF code of conduct covering following appropriate and secure data processing processes, ensuring robust and quality cloud service delivery and being accountable to customers for quality of service and support
Additional point: Benefits creation	The CIF has helped ChannelCloud UK/Ireland differentiate itself from those lacking the resources and capability to deliver a secure and robust cloud outcome for the business user	CIF requires its members to demonstrate ethical and transparent delivery of hosted and cloud services	The CIF has helped Webroot differentiate itself from those lacking the resources and capability to deliver a secure and robust cloud outcome for the business user. The CIF is aiding business' confidence in using cloud applications through educational endorsements and will ensure these organizations have the best chance to maximize benefit and reduce risk in their selection

Table 6.4 (continued)

	ChannelCloud	Unit4	Webroot
Ease of audit activity	We took this as an opportunity to tear up our existing legal and re-draft in line with the code of practice. This was the main reason behind the time investment we had to make. And in common with other organizations that have been through this process, we did have to create a number of new processes, systems and documents as it forced us to look at gaps in our existing business operations	It took our audit team only 3 weeks to deliver the necessary documentation for the accreditation process. Furthermore, we did not need a team of technical experts to do it. From a management perspective, this was critical to complete the CIF certification	When we started the certification process, the demands of external criteria really sharpened our view of our needs. We found a few "gaps" in the information we needed to supply, which not only provided a key incentive to create new materials but also brought home the reality of what we had and our perception

We utilized the case of one particular early market entrant in cloud certification to see how stakeholder dynamics work between them, their customers, and the government bodies in the countries where they are present. What we found was anecdotal evidence that the benefits to the CSP of certification lay more in the restructuring of their offer to achieve certification than to the SME than in the awareness of certification by the potential client.

In terms of the relations with the governmental bodies, in the jurisdictions where the certifier is located, there is no governmental backing of these schemes; therefore we were not able to see a dynamic in that relationship. The UK government has specifically stated that it is not interested in a regulator role in a debate with the CIF in November 2012 [30].

The success of cloud certification schemes toward SMEs can be seen as more longitudinal research. SMEs across geographies and industries are making major changes to their business models to be able to compete with larger firms by utilizing cloud services to improve operations and become more efficient. The adoption of cloud by SMEs initially have been driven by internal user demand [29] and horizontal application development (e.g., Dropbox and cloud e-mail), where a trusted partner does add a value component to the implementation.

Acknowledgments We would like to thank the Cloud Industry Forum and Andy Burton for their assistance in this research.

References

1. Buyya R, Yeo CS, Venugopal S (Sept 2008) Market-oriented cloud computing: vision, hype, and reality for delivering it services as computing utilities. In: HPCC '08 Proceedings of the 2008 10th IEEE International Conference on High Performance Computing and Communications. IEEE Computer Society, Washington, DC, pp 5–13
2. Kim W (2009) Cloud computing: today and tomorrow. J Object Technol 8(1):65–72
3. Guardian Professional (n. d.) Security, performance, fear or confusion: what's holding back cloud adoption? http://www.guardian.co.uk/media-network/media-network-blog/2012/apr/11/cloud-computing-adoption?INTCMP=SRCH. Accessed 8 Dec 2012
4. European Commission (2012) Steering board of the European cloud partnership. http://ec.europa.eu/digital-agenda/en/news/steering-board-public-statement. Accessed 8 Dec 2012
5. Auriol E, Schilizzi SG (2003) Quality signaling through certification. Theory and an application to agricultural seed market. IDEI Working Paper, p 165
6. Sultan NA (June 2011) Reaching for the "cloud": how SMEscan manage. Int J Info Manage 31(3):272–278
7. OECD (2010) Information technology outlook 2010 highlights. OECD publications. http://www.oecd.org/dataoecd/60/21/46444955.pdf. Accessed 10 Sept 2013
8. ENISA (2009) An SME perspective on cloud computing. http://www.enisa.europa.eu/act/rm/files/deliverables/cloud-computing-sme-survey/?searchterm=survey. Accessed 10 Sept 2013
9. Stening C (2009) Every cloud has a silver lining. Easynetconnect. http://www.easynetconnect.net/easynet-news/2009/01/every-cloud-has-a-silver-lining-chris-stening-easynet-connect/. Accessed 23 Aug 2013

10. Thong JYL, Yap CS (1995) CEO characteristics, organizational characteristics and information technology adoption in small businesses. Omega 23(4):429–442
11. Mehrtens J, Cragg PB, Mills AM (20 Dec 2001) A model of Internet adoption by SMEs. Info Manage 39(3):165–176
12. Keung J, Kwok F (2012) Cloud deployment model selection assessment for SMEs: renting or buying a cloud. Utility and Cloud Computing (UCC), 2012 IEEE Fifth International Conference on, p 21, 28, 5–8 Nov 2012
13. Marston S, Li Z, Bandyopadhyay S, Zhang J, Ghalsasi A (April 2011) Cloud computing—the business perspective. Decis Support Syst 51(1):176–189
14. Deaton BJ (Dec 2004) A theoretical framework for examining the role of third-party certifiers. Food Control 15(8):615–619
15. Spence AM (1973) Job market signaling. Quart J Econ 87(3):355–374
16. Tanner B (2000) Independent assessment by third-party certification bodies. Food Control 11:415–417
17. Masters WA, Sanogo D (2002) Welfare gains from quality certification. Amer J Agr Econ 84(4):974–989
18. Habib SM, Ries S, Muhlhauser M (October 2010). Cloud computing landscape and research challenges regarding trustand reputation. In: Proceedings of the 2010 Symposia and workshops on Ubiquitous, autonomic and trusted computing. IEEE Computer Society, pp 410–415
19. Jøsang A, Ismail R, Boyd C (2007) A survey of trustand reputation systems for online service provision. Decis Support Syst 43(2):618–644
20. Prezas N (2008) Advent of ISO/IEC 27001 certification and its role. In: Initial inter-organizational trust. iSChannel [Journal of the Information Systems and Innovation Group, Department of Management, The London School of Economics]. 3(1):37–50. http://www.lse.ac.uk/management/documents/iSChannel-Volume-3.pdf#page=37. Accessed 2 Feb 2014
21. Fomin VV et al (2008) ISO/IEC 27001 information systems security management standard: exploring the reasons for low adoption. EUROMOT 2008 Conference, Nice, France
22. Rodríguez-Escobar JA, Gonzalez-Benito J, Martínez-Lorente AR (2006) An analysis of the degree of small companies' dissatisfaction with ISO 9000 certification. Total Qual Manage Bus Excell 17(4):507–521
23. Everett C (June 2009) Cloud computing—a question of trust. Comput Fraud Secur 2009(6):5–7
24. Burgemeestre B, Hulstijn J, Tan YH (2010) Value-based argumentation for justifying compliance. In: Deontic Logic in Computer Science. Springer, Berlin, pp 214–228
25. Backhouse J, Hsu CW, Silva L (2006) Circuits of power in creating *de jure* standards: Shaping an international information systems security standard. MIS Quarterly 30(Special Issue):413–438. (Standard making: a critical research frontier for information systems research)
26. Saint-Germain R (2005) Information security management best practice based on ISO/IEC 17799. Info Manage J 39(4):60–66
27. von Solms B, von Solms R (2005) From information security to... business security. Comput Secur 24:271–273
28. Cloud Industry Forum (2012) 'Certification' within cloud computing. Hero or villain? Presentation of Andy Burton at of a round table 23rd November 2012. Brussels, Belgium
29. Kim W, Kim SD, Lee E, Lee S (Dec 2009) Adoption issues for cloud computing. In: Proceedings of the 11th International Conference on Information Integration and Web-based Applications & Services. ACM, pp 3–6
30. OpenForum Academy (2012) Certification within cloud computing: hero or villain? http://www.openforumacademy.org/library/round-table/OFAReport231112final.pdf/at_download/file. Accessed 10 Sept 2013

Part III
Frameworks for ERP, Big Data and Interoperability

Chapter 7
A Framework for Evaluating Cloud Enterprise Resource Planning (ERP) Systems

T. Chandrakumar and S. Parthasarathy

Abstract Cloud computing is a new paradigm, transforming the information technology (IT) industry, and the commercial sector, that is involved in reshaping the way enterprise services are designed, implemented, and deployed. Rather than using complex software systems, customers are beginning to spotlight on their core business processes while obtaining all required IT functions as cloud services. Enterprise resource planning (ERP) systems attempt to integrate data and processes in organizations. These systems are among the most adopted IT solutions in organizations. This chapter explores the literature available on cloud ERP systems, suggests the factors accounting for cloud ERP, and proposes a framework for evaluating cloud ERP systems. This framework is grounded on software engineering parameters involved in the development of cloud ERP. The validity of the framework is illustrated with the help of a case study.

Keywords Business process · Cloud · Customization · ERP · Evaluation · Software engineering

7.1 Introduction

Enterprise resource planning (ERP) systems are integrated software packages with a common database that support business processes in companies [29]. They involve distinctive functional modules that reflect the departmental structure of an organization (bookkeeping, acquisition, sales, production, warehousing, and so on.). They are created and offered by ERP outlets and sold as "standard software" that fits the necessities of numerous organizations, regularly improved for certain commercial ventures (industry or vertical solutions). Since ERP systems help the core processes and need to reflect the organizational structure of an organization, they come in numerous diverse sizes and specializations. They ordinarily experience a considerable

T. Chandrakumar (✉) · S. Parthasarathy
Department of Computer Applications,
Thiagarajar College of Engineering, Madurai, India
e-mail: t.chandrakumar@gmail.com

S. Parthasarathy
e-mail: parthatce@gmail.com

Z. Mahmood (ed.), *Continued Rise of the Cloud,* Computer Communications and Networks, DOI 10.1007/978-1-4471-6452-4_7,
© Springer-Verlag London 2014

customization procedure to make them fit to the necessities of a specific organization, and they frequently need to be electronically joined with other software systems (e.g., legacy systems or partner systems). The possibility of such adaptations needs to be tended to after the choice for distributed computing is taken. Executives included in managing enterprise operations and advancing corporate ERP systems progressively need to assess the suggestions and effect of distributed computing. For executives included in selecting, executing, man maturing, and streamlining ERP systems, the coming of cloud computing may well be one of the more critical and disruptive events that they will see in their professions [11]. As awareness and use of cloud and software as a service (SaaS) offerings press on to develop, ERP decision makers are progressively being asked to survey and impart the suggestions and impacts. Notwithstanding, the radical updates guaranteed by cloud computing joined together with the developing nature of numerous cloud services are making this a troublesome undertaking. Heading organizations of all sizes and in each part are now well-attentive to the formal that cloud-based services can convey to organizations especially as far as expense, speed, and adaptability. The energy is additionally building quickly on the supply side, with essentially all major software organizations now taking dollars from on-commence incomes and steering further investment at the improvement of SaaS products or variants. Cloud computing is a developing reality because of the pervasiveness of the Internet and Internet technologies, joined together with developments in hardware virtualization, and advanced more adaptable software architectures. The extra profit of multi-tenancy (or offering) carries enormous cost saving to software vendors through the upgrade and support of one form of code [17, 23]. Likewise, a key stimulator has been the different presentations of cloud services by organizations, for example, Google, Amazon, Netsuite, Salesforce, and Workday, and in addition accepted mega software companies like Microsoft, Oracle, and SAP.

Cloud computing, like similar forms of IT outsourcing, is heralding certain promises to user companies, such as:

- The decrease of capital cost because the customer does not acquire hardware or licenses up front any more [24]
- Cost transparency, e.g., through pay-per-use or subscription models [25]
- The decrease of operational costs [24]
- Increased flexibility for business processes due to lower switching cost [15]
- Guaranteed service level [22]
- Simplicity through commodity services [25]

"Cloud computing is a standout amongst the most examined and advertised innovations of later years. Engagement in cloud computing is basically impelled by its potential to reduce capital utilization and to pass on versatile IT services at simpler variable costs" [24]. The practicality of such modification need to be had a tendency to not long after the decision for cloud computing is taken. While there is small mistrust that cloud computing could be helpful in the zones of office computing and work group joint effort [6], it is intriguing to analyze distinctive types of working an unpredictable business software system (such as an ERP system) in a cloud environment.

7.2   Review of Literature

The new cloud ideal model is rolling out in the complete IS/IT domain. Numerous companies base their IT-procedures conforming to this movement. While minor complex frameworks, such as cloud customer relationship management (CRM) are as of now effectively offered and actualized in the cloud, the reception inside the enterprise frameworks space faces more many-sided quality and safety aspects [27]. Cloud computing is a chance to totally change how business and its individuals work. Safeguarding the organization from capital consumptions that keep going more extended on the accounting report than in the server room may be the regularly referred to profit; however, there are some you might not have acknowledged. The development of services for cloud computing (as a particular form of IT outsourcing) has been stimulated by three complementary and very influential technological achievements: Asynchronous JavaScript and XML (AJAX) technology, multitenancy, and virtualization [5, 19, 30]. Every revolutionary paradigm shift brings along new opportunities for doing business and cloud computing is not an exception. Incumbents, as well as new providers of IT services are positioning themselves horizontally and/or vertically along the cloud computing layers. However, one of the biggest questions being asked is how to effectively price IT services. Different pricing models have been studied [12] among them, e.g., fixed/variable [16], negotiating [32], service-level agreement (SLA)-related ones [10], or pay as you go [2, 8]. Developing nations are also seeing the opportunity of providing cheaper hosting services [4]. We believe there is a need to look at cloud computing from the interdisciplinary perspectives as well, in order to establish the viability of this model and provide guidance for practice. A study [3] looked at the problems faced by cloud service providers as how providers can price infrastructure in such a way that it may impact resource utilization.

Enterprises can hope to face numerous exchange offs when they move IT into the cloud. Cloud-based services exhibit options regarding cost, speed, and adaptability. Presently, the ERP is attempting to respond to the requirements of the industry. Accenture brought up the vitality of this change as ERP's relocation to cloud is not an inquiry of "if" but "when" [21]. Cloud ERP gets consideration by decreasing the usage, support and foundation expenses of result in correlation to on-premise ERP [9]. Enterprises can hope to face numerous exchange offs when they move IT into the cloud. Security is one of the central points to the cloud model, and it is frequently a passionate one besides. As cloud offerings burgeon, there will be continuous challenges with interoperability, portability, and migration. To make sure, interoperability is likewise an issue for on-start requisitions, yet this test is amplified in the cloud. An alternate component is the absence of generally demarcated SLAs by cloud providers. The cloud is frequently touted as an answer for organizations with extensive varieties in registering request. Cloud computing is not simply a matter of adding an infinite number of servers. Some problems and processes cannot be solved simply by adding more nodes. They require different architectures of processing, memory, and storage [14].

Cloud computing has advanced as a key processing stage for imparting assets that incorporate infrastructures, software, applications, and business processes. Virtualization is a center innovation for empowering cloud asset offering. On the other hand, generally existing cloud computing platforms have not formally received the service-oriented architecture (SOA) that might make them more adaptable, extensible, and reusable [33]. Enterprise cloud computing becomes more and more prevalent in the IT and business application industry. The scientific approach is to overcome most of the disadvantages of legacy on-premise solutions. Therefore, the existing different research streams, requirements, and semantic perspectives need to be converged into one central ubiquitous, standardized architectural approach [1]. A study reported in [28] presents the cost savings and reduction in the level of difficulty in adopting a cloud computing service-enabled ERP system.

ERP systems, relational databases, and other mature information technologies are undergoing commoditization and facing challenges from SaaS players moving into front-end enterprise applications [13]. Most of the Indian SMEs have adopted the traditional ERP Systems and have incurred a heavy cost while implementing these systems.

7.3   Cloud Computing—An Overview

Cloud computing is defined by the National Institute of Standards and Technology (NIST) *as a model for empowering ubiquitous, helpful, on-demand network access to an imparted pool of configurable computing resources (e.g., networks, servers, storage, applications , and services) that could be quickly provisioned and discharged with insignificant administration exertion or service provider collaboration.* The cloud is including us. We use the cloud normally if picking up passage to e-mail, Facebook, doing online banking, purchasing goods, and services online— even when using iTunes or Xbox Live! These are not; one or the other liable for it, as it is directed and cared for purpose, or do the majority of us grasp the force and flexibility distributed computing carries a small and medium business (SMB). At its core, cloud computing means providing computing services via the Internet. The "cloud" idea is tightly connected with the "as a service" idea. The public cloud, case in point, addresses a set of standard possessions of altering sorts that could be joined to collect procurements. Public clouds offer virtual machines to furnish outfit power, file systems, data storage systems, network devices, and other elements. They are regularly alluded as infrastructure as a service (IaaS). Various forms of public cloud providers and SaaS companies also offer a development platform as a service (PaaS).

In general, the public cloud has significant limitations when used to construct business applications. These constraints are testing enough that the movement to the cloud will fundamentally comprise a private cloud framework that looks little resemblance to the public cloud.

In the simplest of terms, cloud computing refers to end users connecting to software applications and information that runs in a shared environment rather than a dedicated environment. Rather than conventional figuring situations, from the most recent 30 years, where every provision was doled out to a particular bit of equipment dwelling in a data center, cloud computing enables end users to connect to applications of their choice at any day, any time, and on any Internet-connected device. The term "computer cloud" is overloaded as it covers infrastructures of different sizes, with different management, for a diverse user population. Several types of cloud environments are envisioned:

- Private Cloud—the infrastructure is operated solely for an organization. It may be managed by the organization or a third party and may exist on or off the premises of the organization.
- Community Cloud—the infrastructure is shared by several organizations and supports a specific community that has shared concerns (e.g., mission, security requirements, policy, and compliance considerations). It may be administered by the associations or an unbiased gathering and might exist on premises or off premises.
- Public Cloud—the infrastructure is made available to the general public or a large industry group and is owned by an organization selling cloud services.
- Hybrid Cloud— the infrastructure is a composition of two or more clouds (private, community, or public) that remain unique entities but are bound together by standardized or proprietary technology that enables data and application portability (e.g., cloud bursting for load-balancing between clouds).

There are three cloud delivery models, SaaS, PaaS, and IaaS deployed as public, private, community, and hybrid clouds. SaaS gives the users capability to use applications supplied by the service provider but allows no control of the platform or the infrastructure. Paas gives the capacity to convey buyer made or procured requisitions utilizing modifying dialects and instruments backed by the provider. Iaas permits the client to convey and run subjective programming, which can incorporate working frameworks and requisitions.

7.3.1 Software as a Service (SaaS)

SaaS applications are supplied by the service provider in a cloud infrastructure. The provisions are open from different customer units through a dainty customer interface, for example, a Web browser (e.g., Web-based e-mail). The provision of an application which is hosted (off premise) by a provider as a service to customers who access it via the Internet. In contrast to application service providing (ASP), SaaS is based on a multi-tenant model where many customers are using the same program code but have their own private data spaces. SaaS is only suited for the software "out of the box" that does not require much customization or integration with other applications [15]. The client does not supervise or control the underlying cloud base incorporating system, servers, working frameworks, storage, or even singular provision competencies, with the conceivable exemption of restricted client particular requisition setup settings. Services offered include:

- Enterprise services, for example, workflow administration, aggregate ware and community-oriented, supply chain, communications, digital signature, CRM, desktop software, financial management, geo-spatial, and look.
- Web 2.0 provisions, for example, metadata administration, social networking, blogs, wiki services, and portal services.

7.3.2   Platform as a Service (PaaS)

It gives the competence to convey buyer made or procured requisitions utilizing customizing dialects and tools supported by the supplier. The client does not administer or control the underlying cloud base incorporating network, servers, operating systems, or storage. The provision of resources required to build applications and services (software development environment) to a customer by an outsourcing provider. Typical use scenarios are application design, development, testing, and deployment [30]. The user has control over the deployed applications and, possibly, application hosting environment configurations. Such services include: session management, device integration, sandboxes, instrumentation and testing, contents management, knowledge management, and Universal Description, Discovery and Integration (UDDI), a platform- independent, Extensible Markup Language (XML)-based registry providing a mechanism to register, and locate Web service applications. PaaS is not particularly useful when the application must be portable, when proprietary programming languages are used, or when the under laying hardware and software must be customized to improve the performance of the application. Its major application areas are in software development when multiple developers and users collaborate and the deployment and testing services should be automated.

7.3.3   Infrastructure as a Service (IaaS)

With the capability to provision processing, storage, networks, and other fundamental computing resources; the consumer is able to deploy and run arbitrary software, which can include operating systems and applications belonging to diverse domains. The IaaS allows provisioning of computing resources (CPU cycles, memory, storage, network equipment) to a client. In this service model it is possible to share a server among multi tenants. The service is typically billed on a utility computing basis (resource consumption) [30]. The consumer does not supervise or control the underlying cloud infrastructure yet has control over operating systems, storage, deployed applications, and possibly limited control of some networking components, e.g., host firewalls. Services offered by this delivery model include server hosting, Web servers, storage, computing hardware, operating systems, virtual instances, load balancing, Internet access, and bandwidth provisioning. The IaaS cloud computing delivery model has a number of characteristics, such as the resources are distributed and support dynamic scaling, it is based on a utility pricing model and variable cost, and the hardware is shared among multiple users. This cloud computing model is particularly useful when the demand is volatile and a new business needs computing resources and it does not want to invest in a computing infrastructure or when an organization is expanding rapidly.

7.4 Cloud ERP—The Present Scenario

When evaluating technology within the business, total cost of ownership (TCO) is an important measurement of value. The technology vendor and buyer focus on one thing, the acquisition cost. This is fundamentally because of budgetary cycles that have a tendency to be concentrated on the short or close term. Indeed, it is usually acknowledged that the expense of support, updates, streamlining, administration, and preparing speak to roughly 3–5 times the expense of the obtaining—in excess of a 5-year proprietorship period. Because of this, it is critically important that a small business person look beyond the acquisition and implementation costs to the long-term view as to how much will the solutions actually cost the business. In the same way that one might survey the TCO of an "on-introduce" innovation result, the same assessment must be attempted for a cloud/SaaS solution. The assessment criteria and estimation may include factors, such as the following:

- Cost for every client, for every month
- Consulting/implementation fees
- Training costs
- Ongoing user support costs
- Upgrade costs
- Maintenance costs
- Extra application integration costs (third-party applications and information)
- Application/environment backup/restoration/recovery costs
- Ease and cost of adding new functionality or modules
- Ease and cost of adding new users to the solution/system
- Uptime commitments and cost of business downtime

Surely, cloud computing offers numerous attractive profits to ventures. The cloud model moves the IT base from a forthright capital expenditure to an operational one. Today's enterprise IT portfolio consists of a hybrid ecosystem of services that includes a mix of internal and external IT providers as well as private and cloud-based IT infrastructures. According to a recent international data corporation (IDC) survey (www.idc.com/prodserv/idc_cloud.jsp), private cloud frameworks in ventures mostly have IT administration requisitions, endeavor wide correspondence and joint effort instruments, and business provisions, for example, CRM and ERP. Furthermore, there is an improving example to outsourcing message, particular gainfulness applications, site creation, hosting, and administration; and on-demand compute and storage services. Provisions, for example, the IT help desk, data backup, and archival services fall some place between these procedures. Diverse enterprises decide to have these requisitions in-house or on public cloud bases. Legacy IT systems in the undertaking have a tendency to underpin custom enterprise requisitions and those with sensitive data.

Organizations can utilize public cloud for huge batch-oriented tasks, those involving substantial spikes in necessities for handling power that overall might be out of achieve or require tremendous speculation. Many enterprises procurement processing resources for top loads are regularly surpassing normal use by a component of 2 to 10. Thus, server usage in data centers is frequently as low as 5 to 20 %. One key profit of cloud computing is that it saves organizations from needing to pay for these underutilized resources. Organizations can utilize the cloud to quickly scale up or down; they can additionally purchase or discharge IT resources as required on a pay-as you-go model. As one aggregation of specialists from the University of California, Berkeley noted, "This versatility of resources, without paying a premium for vast scale, is remarkable in the history of IT" [21].

Cloud services are an example that parts up consolidated stacks of undertaking system and procurements into services either inner or outer service providers fulfill. In spite of the fact that SOA modeling rebuilt requisitions into composable services, it just tended to the requisition incorporation issue inside enterprises. Cloud services unfold that engineering plan and execution design into business relationships between service consumers and providers. In IaaS, PaaS, and SaaS, providers own the infrastructure, platforms, or software functions. As their part updates from straight furnishing IT systems to supervising services that vendors deliver, IT staff need to advance new skills. Instead of simply being technology masters, they will require the abilities to intercede and reconcile legacy innovation and new services while sticking to undertaking prerequisites, for example, compliance, accessibility, and cost control.

An alternate pattern is the consumerization of IT. The border between individual and business requisitions is rapidly vanishing, and representatives now routinely utilize versatile apparatuses and systems to trade a noteworthy divide of business-identified data. Notwithstanding routinely utilizing Internet provisions for business purposes, from desktop hunt to connectivity suites, more workers are carrying their own customer units to work to use in gaining entrance to administrations, for example, instant messaging networks and social networking sites.

A bigger number of as a business need than a pattern, the adequate cooperation between organizations and their clients and suppliers is likewise evolving IT. Cross-enterprise joint effort presupposes sharing, exchanging, and managing information across enterprise IT dividers. Such coordinated effort has extended past virtual gathering rooms and meeting calls to incorporate provisional regulated access to internal in-formation systems, knowledge bases, or information distribution systems.

Collaboration could reach out into incidentally taking advantage of the workforce and IT holdings of different enterprises and crowd sourcing services. This development will make new environments that depend on viably and specifically empowering access to the needed systems and services. On the grounds that such biological systems must be more open and receptive than universal IT, supervising them will require granular and subjective access control components.

7.5   Framework for the Evaluation of Cloud ERP

There are various components that executives might as well recognize in choosing whether and how to utilize cloud-based services for their ERP systems. Industry type, organization measure, result unpredictability, security needs, and a few other organizational issues should all be tended to. From the viewpoint, we analyze the pros and cons of moving ERP services to the cloud and present a framework that can be used to evaluate the viability of cloud-based ERP systems for their organizations. Cloud-based technology solutions require companies to loosen their control of critical data. Organizations should take a complete approach to the risks, from both the business and the IT security points of view. Industry security gauges are developing quickly, and cloud-based ERP suppliers have contributed a huge number of dollars in building state-of-the art security competencies and data administration forms. Accordingly, IT security directors need to reexamine how they group requisitions and information dependent upon level of danger, better recognize particular security necessities and the controls needed to administer hazard, and more completely comprehend the capability of cloud suppliers to meet their security prerequisites. An evaluation framework can also help in finding the most cost-effective solution for the business, which is a key consideration in the process. All the same, one of the most amazing offering purposes of cloud ERP frameworks is their beginning cost funds. Two key factors found from the literature stand out from all the others: implementation size and system complexity. These issues tackle distinctive intensities hinging upon if the organization is actualizing an ERP answer despite anything that might have happened before, moving from its current ERP solution, or enlarging its current framework's capacities to incorporate additional functionality. The decision framework for evaluating Cloud ERP System software component is depicted in Fig. 7.1. The highest level of hierarchy represents the goal, second level represents the main attributes (Level 1), and third level represents the sub-attributes (Level 2) represents the components.

Figure 7.2 indicates the different approaches in cloud ERP implementation. Providers are investing significantly in enhancing their offerings, expanding the functionality and availability of their services, and reducing the risks of adoption. More diminutive organizations that need to add the profits of scale to bring down their expenses and drive standardization might as well consider this choice now, as well bigger organizations looking to lower expenses and drive institutionalization inside divisions or practical units. ERP in the cloud is what is to come, and even organizations that have exceptional explanation for why not to take the plunge yet ought to be observing improvements and acknowledging their more drawn out extent plans.

7.5.1   Implementation Size

At present, small- to medium-sized organizations are the probable hopes for the cloud-based ERP systems, since execution and support costs are generally low. Numerous extensive, complex organizations will uncover that cloud-based systems do

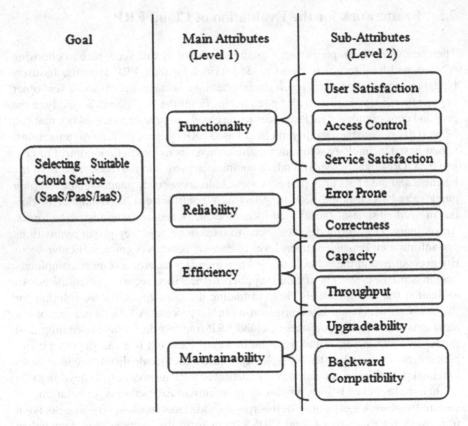

Fig. 7.1 Evaluation framework—Cloud ERP system

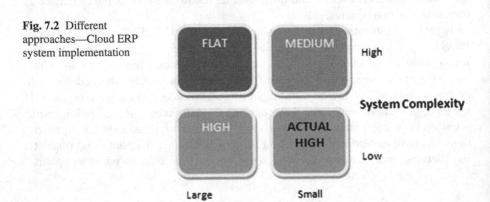

Fig. 7.2 Different approaches—Cloud ERP system implementation

not yet meet their enterprise-level needs, in spite of the fact that they may be suitable for littler divisions if the cloud-based result could be mixed into the existing enterprise-wide ERP platform. Companies with large-scale ERP systems may simply find the benefits of scale gained from in-house ownership to be greater than the potential cost savings offered by a cloud-based solution today. Rapid implementation is generally agreed to be among the top benefits of cloud-based ERP and also contribute to easier change of cloud service providers [7] and reduced time of providing new products in certain types of business [20].

7.5.2 System Complexity

The complexity of any ERP system is measured along three dimensions: the extent of integration, the amount of functionality, and the size of the footprint. Corporate environments that require essential usefulness, negligible customization, and restricted joining are especially suitable for cloud-based results. More complex organizations will probably uncover that cloud-based results are not the best choice at this time. A few organizations might profit from alleged half-breed models, where some ERP practicality is held in a conventional had environment while different requisitions are executed through the cloud. A large company with complex supply chain requirements, for example, might continue to maintain its customized ERP solution while using a cloud provider for selected business processes, such as talent management. A business with multiple subsidiaries might keep a centralized, hosted ERP solution to run the enterprise while providing its subsidiaries with a cost-efficient cloud-based solution to run their local operations. Cloud ERP has moved beyond the experimentation phase. The rising complexity when implementing and maintaining an ERP landscape along with a rising TCO is forcing enterprises to look for ways to standardize their landscape and optimize assets. Enterprises are quickening development by conveying cloud business systems over their worldwide vicinity.

7.6 Case Study

A case study was conducted in a manufacturing industry. The company had always stayed ahead with their streamlined operations and market-savvy products. The company was using different stand-alone software packages for different aspects of business. While this legacy system had served their purposes in the past, the company began to feel an increasing need for access to real time information. Instant access to information from a unified, online budgetary, and management information systems (MIS) report systems might give them an incorporated view crosswise over distinctive levels of the association. *The organization coveted experiences into their financials and business So, they really needed a system in place to standardize and streamline business processes across the organization and improve operational control through a comprehensive financial and management reporting system.* The interview was undertook with the employees in the mechanical as well as managerial position, who were employed throughout cloud-founded SAP implementation and the constituents of ERP vendor. These workers were employed with this cloud ERP scheme in their day-to-day job. It is discovered that for just a cloud ERP implementation in time, managerial issues considered already will do, but for reaping the full benefits of the cloud ERP software after implementation, technical factors highlighted in this study plays a crucial role.

The company was already using an in-house ERP system, using a combination of features from 5M and Tally. However, there was no coordination between the two systems and the information silos did not support business insights or growth. Moreover, the multi location structure made it difficult for the head office to get a clear perspective of the overall business scenario. *On-premise software was necessary for definite aspects that required specialized customization . However, there were other aspects where the major need was instantaneous access to real time information. For instance, having online information on inventory and accounts was extremely important.* The company then uses a SaaS- based cloud model that would not upset their existing framework and would work independently to provide business intelligence.

7.7 Findings and Discussion

The framework presented relies on parameters of software engineering in the development of cloud ERP, following a hierarchical structure of quality characteristics which are decomposed to sub-characteristics and attributes. The model adopts the strict approach of the ISO 9126 standard as regards its hierarchy, but also gives details on how to measure each attribute, an issue which is not addressed by the ISO model. The analysis of this new framework has helped us to reach the key construct of an as-is scenario, that is: history and development of Cloud ERP systems, the implementation lifecycle, critical success factors and project management, as well as benefits and costs. Having distinguished and arranged the profits, costs, risks, and limitations of cloud-based ERP rather than "traditional" ERP, we dissected them further keeping in mind the end goal to elucidate and analyze applicable aspects of cloud-based, hosted, and on-premise types of ERP systems through the literature survey. For instance, some drawbacks of cloud-based ERP referred to extensively in the literature as "security and confidentiality risks" were transformed into the feature of "high level of security and confidentiality".

Cloud-based ERP solutions have become one of the fastest growing segments of IT industry [26]. Moreover, the shift from traditional ERP to cloud-based ERP is clearly notable [18]. In particular many SME's shift to cloud-based ERP solutions [9]. First and foremost, with regard to cost profits of cloud-based ERP, generally investigated papers ordinarily concurred up-on more level upfront and working expenses. The explanation behind this is the way that undertakings do not have to make immense upfront venture in the IT base. Likewise, unlike the traditional ERP, cloud-based ERP might be designed on interest and looked after and duplicated quickly which prompts a greatly improved usage of the processing base. This thus will prompt more level upfront and operational cost. Second, basically all the inventors state that cloud-based ERP can rapidly be executed inside the endeavor unlike the accepted ERP which needs more exertion and time. Cloud-based ERP delivers a rapid deployment model that enables applications to grow quickly and match increasing usage requirements. The user can easily scale up or scale down depending on its needs [31]. Findings from interviews with ERP consultants provided partial support for the aforementioned proposed framework. In spite of the fact that there is ordinarily an understanding around them observing the stages of ERP life cycle and the determination procedure of selection process of ERP software, the larger part of interviewees has not been ever included with the arrangement of qualitative measures in the whatever time was spent selecting cloud ERP software. The explanations expressed are the accompanying high cost of making and measuring qualitative components, vagueness noticing the way of qualitative measures, absence of time to dedicate to qualitative estimation, and absence of directions by administration to build qualitative measures. Likewise, notwithstanding the way that the key component of ERP is usually affirmed by all, the assessment of cloud ERP software in practice does not explicitly take into account the various relevant strategic elements.

7.8 Conclusion

A cloud ERP solution is expected to offer a flexible ERP that supports the growth of the business within a fully managed private cloud environment—built on the proven platform. High-performance computing is one of the most important technology megatrends. By 2020, we will see 10 to 100 cores per server along with 100-TByte memory available for business applications. The big driver for high-performance computing is the cloud computing with virtual servers. This will change the IT landscape as the PC's acquaintance did with the computer landscape, which was ruled by water-cooled host machines. As such, software and hardware manufacturers have existed in close advantageous interaction. Every new software releases appetite for execution has been satisfied by faster computers with additional powerful processors.

For large organizations, the private cloud speaks to a choice to have a cake and consume it, as well. The point when contrasted with the standard components of the public cloud, the specially designed private cloud emerges as a drastically distinctive build. Unfortunately, numerous individuals press on to inexactly toss around the expression "cloud" without understanding that it might allude to altogether different demonstrates and without acknowledging its limitations. After a watchful examination of the cloud, numerous organizations may need to keep their CIOs for a long time to come. The cloud is bad or awful: it is only another ideal model with its own focal points and inconveniences. Over the long run, some of these concerns will be comprehended or the risks will be decreased to adequate levels. The cloud permits minor startups to overcome IT restraints and carry new on-demand offerings to medium sized organizations, yet it will be quite a while before it serves generally needs of larger enterprises. For generally associations, the inquiry of whether to move into the cloud will be a matter of weighing the pros and cons. There is a "sweet spot" for cloud business applications where the trade-off between rich business-specific functionality on the one side and ease of maintenance but little extensibility on the other is optimum. At this point, that spot is around ERP, CRM, and collaboration, especially between enterprises.

Enterprises are analyzing the use of cloud to carry out some of their processes. This put further new requirements to be addressed by this approach, contributing to its shaping. For example, many enterprise processes are time critical, with security and privacy requirements. Also the scale of enterprise applications is in the order of thousands of concurrent services. And this is in contrast with SMEs, which have a number of service orders of magnitude lower than enterprises. Cloud computing is converting how buyers, organizations, and governments store data, how they prepare that data, and how they use figuring power. It could be an engine of advancement, a stage for business endeavor, and driver of corporate effectiveness. While an undeniably normally term, confusion stays over what precisely constitutes cloud computing, how the businesses are unfolding, and what strengths will drive their development and dissemination. The evaluation of cloud ERP System requires the comprehension of the major effect cloud ERP has on the business technique, the organizational structure and the part of the individuals of the organization all through its existence cycle. The framework of ERP systems evaluation and selection proposed in this paper is significant in that it makes ERP managers bear in mind that ERP evaluation does not only refer to the analysis of the ERP product per se. In addition, and more crucially, it refers to the potential operational and strategic benefits and the total investment required for selecting, purchasing, implementing, operating, maintaining, and extending the proposed ERP system with additional applications throughout its life cycle. Failure to identify the full costs of ERP investment can have serious implications for the success of the ERP project.

References

1. Aalmink J, Balloul L (2009) Enterprise tomography driven governance of federated ERP in a Cloud. ICT innovations. Springer, Berlin, pp 257–264
2. Ahmed E, Paul L (2004) Negotiation in service-oriented environments. Commun ACM 47(8):103–108
3. Anandasivam A, Weinhardt C (2010) Towards an efficient decision policy for Cloud service providers. In: Proceedings of ICIS, 2010, Saint Louis, Missouri, USA, 12–15 Dec 2010
4. Armbrust M, Fox A et al (2010) A view of cloud computing. Commun ACM 53(4):50–58
5. Babcock C (2010) Management strategies for the cloud revolution: how cloud computing is transforming business and why you can't afford to be left behind. McGraw-Hill, New York
6. Barnatt C (2010) A brief guide to cloud computing: an essential introduction to the next revolution in computing. Robinson, London
7. Benlian A, Hess T (2011) Opportunities and risks of SaaS. Findings from a survey of IT executives. Decis Support Syst 52:232–246
8. Buyya R, Yeo CS et al (2009) Cloud computing and emerging IT platforms: vision, hype, and reality for delivering computing as the 5th utility. Future Gener Comput Syst 25:599–616

9. Castellina N (2011) SaaS and Cloud ERP trends, observations, and performances. Aberdeen Group
10. Choudhary V (2007) Comparison of software quality under perpetual licensing and software as a service. J Manage Inf Syst 24(2):141–165
11. Graupner S, Basu S, Singhal S (2011) Business operating environment for service Clouds. In: Proceedings of SRII Service Research and Innovation Institute conference-SRII 11, IEEE CS, pp 1–10
12. Hedwig M, Malkowski S, Neumann D (2010) Toward autonomic cost-aware allocation of Cloud resources. In: Proceedings of ICIS, pp 1–10
13. Hofmann P (2008) ERP is dead, long live ERP. IEEE Internet Comput 12(4):84–88
14. Hofmann P (2010) Cloud computing: the limits of public Clouds for business applications. IEEE Internet Comput 14:90–93
15. Iyer B, Henderson JC (2010) Preparing for the future: understanding the seven capabilities of Cloud computing. MIS Q Executive 9(2):117–131
16. Koehler P, Anandasivam A, Dan MA (2010) Cloud services from a consumer perspective. In: Proceedings of AMCIS, Paper 329
17. Kshetri N (2010) Cloud computing in developing economies. IEEE Comput Soc 43(10):47–55 (0018-9162/10)
18. Lin A, Chen NC (2012) Cloud computing as an innovation: perception, attitude, and adoption. Int J Inf Manage 4(1):533–540
19. Linthicum DS (2009) Cloud computing and SOA convergence in your enterprise: a step-by-step guide. Pearson Education, Boston
20. Marston S, Li Z et al (2010) Cloud computing—the business perspective. Decis Support Syst 51:176–189
21. Mattison BJB, Raj S (2012) Key questions every IT and business executive should ask about cloud computing and ERP. http://www.accenture.com/SiteCollectionDocuments/Microsites/cloudstrategy/Accenture-Cloud-ERP-PoV.pdf. Accessed 17 Aug 2012
22. Mell P, Grance T (2009) The NIST definition of Cloud computing. In: NIST website (National Institute of Standards and Technology). Available via DIALOG: http://csrc.nist.gov/groups/SNS/cloud-computing/clouddef-v15.doc (10/07/2009). Accessed 05 Dec 2010
23. Mell P, Grance T (2011) The NIST definition of Cloud computing., National Institute of Standards and Technology. Special publication 800-145
24. OECD (2010) OECD information technology outlook 2010. OECD publishing. Available via DIALOG: http://dx.doi.org/10.1787/it_outlook-2010-en. Accessed 29 Nov 2010
25. Ovum (2010) Planning for Cloud computing: understanding the organizational, governance, and cost implications. In: Ovum IT management and strategy report. Accessed 24 Nov 2010
26. Popovic K (2010) Cloud computing security issues and challenges, vol 2b. Institute of Automation and Process Computing, pp 344–349
27. Roos ST (2012) Shifting to successful ERP implementation projects in the Cloud
28. Sharma M, Mehra A (2010) Scope of cloud computing for SMEs in India. J Comput 2(5): 144–149
29. Staehr L (2010) Understanding the role of managerial agency in achieving business benefits from ERP systems. Inf Syst J 20:213–238
30. Velte AT, Velte TJ, Elsenpeter R (2010) Cloud computing: a practical approach. McGraw-Hill, New York
31. Verma B What is Cloud computing? What are its advantages and disadvantages? Available via DIALOG: http://www.techinmind.com/what-is-cloud-computing-what-are-its-advantages-and-disadvantages/. Accessed 18 Apr 2012
32. Wu S, Banker R (2010) Best pricing strategy for information services. J Assoc Inf Syst 11(6):339–366
33. Zhang L-J (2009) Cloud computing open architecture. In: Proceedings of IEEE international conference on web services-ICWS, pp 607–616

Chapter 8
DIPAR: A Framework for Implementing Big Data Science in Organizations

Luis Eduardo Bautista Villalpando, Alain April and Alain Abran

Abstract Cloud computing (CC) is a technology aimed at processing and storing very large amounts of data, which are also referred to as big data (BD). Although this is not the only aim of the cloud paradigm, one of the most important challenges in CC is how to process and deal with the BD. By the end of 2012, the amount of data generated was approximately 2.8 zettabytes (ZB), i.e., 2.8 trillion GB. One of the areas that contribute to the analysis of BD is referred to as *data science*. This new study area, also called big data science (BDS), has recently become an important topic in organizations because of the value it can generate, both for themselves and for their customers. One of the challenges in implementing BDS is the current lack of information to help in understanding this new study area. In this context, this chapter presents the define-ingest-preprocess-analyze-report (DIPAR) framework, which proposes a means to implement BDS in organizations and defines its requirements and elements. The framework consists of five stages define, ingest, preprocess, analyze, and report. It is based on the ISO 15939 Systems and Software Engineering—Measurement process standard, the purpose of which is to collect, analyze, and report data relating to the products to be developed.

Keywords Big data science · Data cleaning · DIPAR framework · ISO 15939 · Security · System requirements

L. E. B. Villalpando (✉)
Department of Electronic Systems, Autonomous University of Aguascalientes,
Av. Universidad 940, Ciudad Universitaria, Aguascalientes, AGS, Mexico
e-mail: lebautis@correo.uaa.mx

A. April · A. Abran · L. E. B. Villalpando
Department of Software Engineering and Information Technology,
ETS—University of Quebec, 1100 Notre-Dame St., Montreal, Canada
e-mail: alain.april@etsmtl.ca

A. Abran
e-mail: alain.abran@etsmtl.ca

Z. Mahmood (ed.), *Continued Rise of the Cloud,* Computer Communications
and Networks, DOI 10.1007/978-1-4471-6452-4_8,
© Springer-Verlag London 2014

8.1 Introduction

Cloud computing (CC) is a technology aimed at processing and storing very large amounts of data. According to the ISO subcommittee 38, the CC study group, CC is a paradigm for enabling ubiquitous, convenient, on-demand network access to a shared pool of configurable cloud resources accessed through services which can be rapidly provisioned and released with minimal management effort or service provider interaction [1].

One of the most important challenges in CC is how to process large amounts of data (also known as big data—BD) in an efficient and reliable way. In December 2012, the International Data Corporation (IDC) stated that, by the end of 2012, the total data generated was 2.8 zettabytes (ZB), i.e., 2.8 trillion GB [2]. Furthermore, the IDC predicts that the total data generated by 2020 will be 40 ZB. This is roughly equivalent to 5.2 terabytes (TB) of data generated by every human being alive in that year. In addition, according to the report, only 0.5 % of the data have been analyzed up to the present time, and one-quarter of all the currently available data may contain valuable information. This means that *BD processing* will be a highly relevant topic in the coming years.

One of the main areas contributing to the analysis of BD is *data science* (DS). Although this term has emerged only recently, it has a long history, as it is based on techniques and theories from fields, such as mathematics, statistics, data engineering, etc. [3]. The integration of these fields into the BD paradigm has resulted in a new study area called *big data science* (BDS).

BDS has recently become a very important topic in organizations because of the value it can generate, both for themselves and for their customers. One of the main challenges in BDS is the current lack of information to help in understanding, structuring, and defining how to integrate this study area into organizations and how to develop processes for its implementation. BDS involves implementation challenges not faced in DS, such as the integration of large amounts of data from different sources, data transformation, storage, security, the analysis of large data sets using high-performance processing technologies, and the representation of analysis results (visualization), to mention only a few.

This chapter presents the define-ingest-preprocess-analyze-report (DIPAR) framework, which proposes a means to implement BDS in organizations, and defines the requirements and elements involved. The framework consists of five stages: *Define, Ingest, Preprocess, Analyze, and Report (DIPAR)*, which we describe here. We also explain how to implement these stages, along with the components of the framework.

The rest of this chapter is organized as follows. Section 8.2 presents an overview of BDS, including its definition and history, as well as its relationships with other study areas, like data mining (DM) and data analysis (DA). Section 8.3 presents the ISO 15939 Systems and Software Engineering—Measurement process standard, the purpose of which is to collect, analyze, and report data relating to products to be developed. Section 8.4 constitutes the core of this chapter, in which we present our proposal of the DIPAR framework as a means to implement BDS in organizations.

Section 8.5 describes the relationships between this framework and the measurement processes defined in the ISO 15939 measurement process standard. Section 8.6 presents a case study in which the DIPAR framework is used to develop a BD product for the performance analysis of CC applications. Finally, Sect. 8.7 presents a summary and the conclusions of this chapter.

8.2   Big Data Science

The term big data science has been in common usage for only about 3 years, but it has evolved, in part, from the term *data analysis*. In 1962, Tukey [4] writes that, with the evolution of mathematical statistics, it will be possible to apply them to "very extensive data," which is the central interest in DA. Moreover, he points out that DA includes, among other things: procedures for analyzing data, techniques for interpreting the results of those procedures, ways of planning the data gathering process to make analysis of the data easier, and so on.

In recent years, DM has been the area of knowledge that has been responsible for DA in organizations. Authors like Han et al. [5] describe DM as an interdisciplinary subject which includes an iterative sequence of steps for what he calls *knowledge discovery*. These steps are data cleaning, data integration, data selection, data transformation, pattern evaluation, and the presentation of results. Han explains that these steps can be summarized in the extraction/transformation/loading (ETL) process. Extraction is the stage in which data are collected from outside sources, transformation is the stage in which methods and functions are applied to data in order to generate valuable information, and loading is the stage in which the data are inputted into the end target to generate output reports.

Although the ETL process has been applied in organizations for some years, this approach cannot be used in its entirety in BD, because the traditional data warehouse tools and processes are not designed to work on very large amounts of data. Some authors, like Lin [6], contend that "big data mining" is about much more than what most academics would consider simply DM. He goes on to say that a significant amount of tooling and infrastructure is required to operationalize vague strategic directives into concrete, solvable problems with clearly defined indicators of success. Other authors, like Thusoo et al. [7], note that the BD processing infrastructure has to be flexible enough to support optimal algorithms and techniques for the very different query workloads. Moreover, Thusoo emphasizes that what makes this task more challenging is that the data under consideration continue to grow rapidly. In one example, in 2012 alone, Facebook generated more than 500 TB of new data every day.

8.3   Big Data Science as a Measurement Process

One of the most important challenges for organizations is to turn available data into final products which generate value and create a competitive advantage for enterprises and institutions. Meeting this challenge is vital to the development of measurement

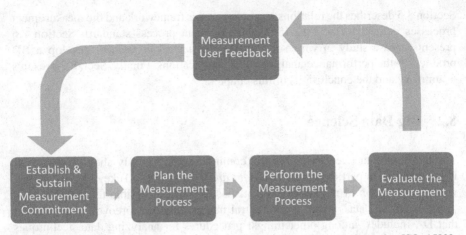

Fig. 8.1 Sequence of activities in a measurement process (Adapted from the ISO 15939 measurement process model [8])

processes that support the analysis of information related to the original data, with a view to defining the types of products that can be developed. According to ISO 15939 [8] *Systems and Software Engineering—Measurement process*, the purpose of a measurement process is to collect, analyze, and report data relating to the products developed and the processes implemented within the organizational unit to support effective management of the measurement process and to objectively demonstrate the quality of the products.

ISO 15939 defines a sequence of four activities to develop such measurements, which include establish and sustain measurement commitment, plan the measurement process, perform the measurement process, and evaluate the measurement. These activities are performed in an iterative cycle that allows for continuous feedback and improvement of the measurement process, as shown in Fig. 8.1.

The activities performed during the measurement process are described below:

Establish and sustain measurement commitment. This activity consists of two tasks: (1) define the requirements for measurement (2) assign resources. Defining the requirements for measurement involves defining the scope of measurement as a single project, a functional area, the whole enterprise, etc., as well as the commitment of management and staff to the measurement process. This means that the organizational unit should demonstrate its commitment through policies, allocation of responsibilities, budget, training, etc. Assigning resources involves the allocation of responsibilities to individuals, as well as the provision of resources to plan the measurement process.

- Plan the measurement process. This activity consists of a series of tasks, such as identifying information needs, selecting measures, defining data collection, and defining the criteria for evaluating product and process information. It also includes the activities related to reviewing, approving, and providing resources for measurement tasks.

Fig. 8.2 Stages to develop during implementation of the DIPAR framework

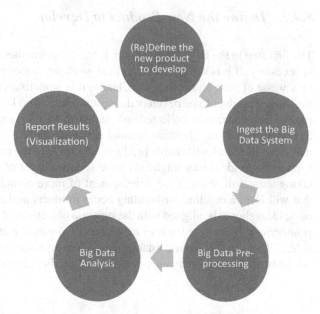

- Perform the measurement process. This activity consists of the tasks defined in the planning activity, along with the following sub activities: integrate procedures, collect data, analyze data, develop information products, and communicate results.
- Evaluate the measurement. This activity consists of evaluating information products against the specified evaluation criteria and of determining the strengths and weaknesses of the information products and the measurement process. This activity must also identify potential improvements to the information products. For instance, changing the format of an indicator, changing from a linear measure to an area measure, minutes to hours, or a line of code to a size measure, etc.

The next section presents the DIPAR framework, its stages, and its implementation process. It also describes the relationships that exist between the stages and how the framework is integrated into the measurement processes defined in ISO 15939.

8.4   The DIPAR Framework

The DIPAR framework integrates the four activities described in ISO 15939, and its main objective is to design BD products that have a high impact on organizational performance. Figure 8.2 depicts the five stages to be executed during the implementation of the DIPAR framework, as well as the order in which should be executed.

The following subsections describe each stage of the DIPAR framework and the elements they involve.

8.4.1   Define the New Product to Develop

The first step in the DIPAR framework is to define whether or not a new BD product is necessary. If it is not, all the analytical work developed to create the product will be a waste of time and resources. Clearly, it is sometimes not possible to establish the type of product to be developed, because there is no knowledge available on the type of data that can be collected and analyzed. Patil [9] suggests that this issue can be resolved by taking shortcuts in order to get products off the ground. He maintains that these shortcuts will enable products to survive to the finished state because they support good ideas that might not have seen the light of day otherwise, and that taking them will result in the development of more complex analytical techniques that will form a baseline for building better products in the future. Moreover, these basic ideas should be aligned with the strategic objectives of the organization, e.g., "*it is necessary to improve the user experience in the online store, in order to increase sales.*" This strategy would enable these ideas to form the basis for building new products, such as recommender systems and prediction systems.

8.4.2   Ingest the Big Data System

In order to clearly define the boundaries of the new product, large amounts of data need to be analyzed. One of the main challenges of ingesting a BD system is to define the ingestion sources, because most of the time data come from a number of sources, such as Web logs, databases, and different types of applications. This makes very difficult to know what type of data will be ingested by the BD system. For instance, an organization can gather behavioral data from users from very different sources, like Web page logs users visit, links users click, social media, the location systems included in mobile devices, etc. In addition, many of these data sources (services) are loosely coordinated systems which lead to the creation of a large number of isolated data stores. This distributed scheme makes it difficult to know the type of data that is being collected, as well as its state. In addition, the services provided by different systems change over time and as functionalities evolve; sometimes systems are merged into newer ones or replaced entirely. All these issues result in inaccuracies in the data to be analyzed, which must be kept in mind in the BD ingestion process.

One solution to this problem is to use BD software that is designed specifically to collect and aggregate data from different sources. Projects like Flume [10] and Scribe [11] allow large amounts of log data to be collected, aggregated, and moved from many different sources to a centralized data store. Moreover, since data sources are customizable, this type of software can be used to transport massive quantities of event data, including, but not limited to, network traffic data, data generated by social media, and email messages, in fact, pretty much any data source imaginable.

8.4.3   Big Data Preprocessing

One of the main problems that arises following the ingestion of a BD system is the *cleanliness of data*. This problem calls for the quality of the data to be verified prior to performing *BD Analysis (BDA)*. According to Lin [6], during the data collection process for Twitter, all the large, real-world data sets required data cleaning to render them usable. Among the most important data quality issues to consider during data cleaning in a BDS are corrupted records, inaccurate content, missing values, and formatting inconsistencies, to name a few. Another important issue in data quality assurance in BD preprocessing is formatting inconsistencies, caused by the very different forms that data can take. For example, the property *product ID* could be labeled *product_id* in one data service and *productID* in other service. Furthermore, the data type for this property could be assigned a numeric value in the first case and an alphanumeric value in the second case.

Consequently, one of the main challenges at the preprocessing stage is how to structure data in standard formats so that they can be analyzed more efficiently. This is often easier said than done: during the process of structuring and merging data into common formats, there is a risk of losing valuable information. This challenge is a current topic of investigation among researchers.

Another issue to address before embarking on BDA is to determine what data fields are the most relevant, in order to construct analysis models [12]. One way to resolve this issue is to sample the data to obtain an overview of the type of data collected, in order to understand the relationships among features spread across multiples sources. Of course, training models on only a small fraction of data does not always give an accurate indication of the model's effectiveness at scaling up [6].

8.4.4   Big Data Analysis

Once the data have been preprocessed, they are analyzed to obtain relevant results. For this, it is necessary to develop models which can be used in the creation of new products. One of the main problems arising during the design of such models is to recognize which of the available data are the most relevant to an analysis task. During a study of the BDA implementation process in organizations, Kandel et al. [12] found that almost 60 % of data scientists have difficulty understanding the relationships between features spread across multiple databases. He also found that the main challenge in this process is feature selection, which is an important step in the development of accurate models. Sampling is a good way to address these challenges.

In addition, according to Kandel, most data scientists have a problem with the size of their data sets. This is because the majority of the existing analysis packages, tools, and algorithms do not scale-up with BD sets. One way to solve this problem is to use one of the new BD technologies, which make it possible to process and analyze large data sets in a reasonable amount of time. For example, with Hive [13], this type of task can be performed very rapidly. Hive is a data warehousing framework created at Facebook for reporting ad hoc queries and analyzing their repositories. Other products, like Mahout [14], help to build scalable machine learning libraries which can be used on large data sets. Mahout supports four use cases in which machine learning techniques are used: recommendation mining, clustering, classification, and market basket analysis.

Once it becomes feasible to develop complex models and algorithms for DA, it is possible to create products with added value for the organization. However, to establish the direction to be taken during the product development process, we need to understand the results of the previous analyses. For example, once Amazon had analyzed its large data set, they found that they could use the historical record of Web pages visited by users to create a recommender system, for example: "*People who viewed product X also viewed product Y.*"

It is clear that a mechanism is required for presenting the analysis results so that they can be studied and understood, and, also communicated to the stakeholders involved in the design of the product. In the next section, we describe aspects that must be considered when reporting the analysis results.

8.4.5 *Reporting of Results (Visualization)*

Once BD are ingested, preprocessed, and analyzed, users need to be able to access and evaluate the results, which must be presented in such a way that they are readily understood. Often they are presented in statistical charts and graphs that contain too much information which is not descriptive enough for the end user. Although a number of BD analysts still deliver their results only in static reports, some end users complain that this system is inflexible and does not allow for interactive verification in real time [12]. According to the Networked European Software and Services Initiative (NESSI), in its technical paper entitled, "*Big Data, A New World of Opportunities*" [15], reports generated from DA can be thought of as documents. These documents frequently contain varying forms of media in addition to a textual representation. They add that the interface through which this complex information is communicated needs to be responsive to human needs ("humane"), user-friendly, and closely linked to the knowledge of the users. To achieve this, the NESSI proposes the use of Visual Analytics (VA), which combines the strengths of human and electronic data processing. The main objective of VA is to develop knowledge, methods, technologies, and practices that exploit human capabilities and the capacities of electronic data processing. They list the key features of VA, which are:

- Emphasizes DA, problem solving, and/or decision making
- Leverages computational processing by applying automated techniques for data processing, knowledge discovery algorithms, etc.
- Encourages the active involvement of a human in the analytical process through interactive visual interfaces
- Supports the provenance of analytical results
- Supports the communication of analytical results to the appropriate recipients

Furthermore, authors like Yau [16] maintain that data visualization is like a story in which the main character is a user who can take two paths. A story of charts and graphs might read much like a textbook; however, a story with context, relationships, interactions, patterns, and explanations reads more like a novel. Nevertheless, the former is not necessarily better than the latter. What this author suggests is that the content should be presented in a format somewhere between a textbook and a novel, so that BD can be visualized, that is, facts are provided, but context as well.

At the same time, authors like Agrin [17] focus on the real challenges that BD visualization developers face and what should be avoided when implement BD visualization. Agrin maintains that simplicity must be the goal in data visualization, suggesting, at the risk of sounding regressive, that there are good reasons to work with charts that have been in continuous use since the eighteenth century. In addition, he notes that the bar chart is one of the best tools available for facilitating visual comparison, as it takes advantage of our innate ability to compare side-by-side lengths. Agrin [17] also lists a number of tools and strategies which can be useful in the design of data visualization methods:

- Do not dismiss traditional visualization choices, if they represent the best option for your data.
- Start with bar and line charts, and look further only when the data requires it.
- Have a good rationale for choosing other options.
- Compared to bar charts, bubble charts support more data points with a wider range of values; pies and doughnuts clearly indicate part-to-whole relationships; tree maps support categories organized hierarchically.
- Bar charts have the added bonus of being one of the easiest visualizations to create: an effective bar chart can be hand coded in HTML using nothing but the cascading style sheet (CSS) and minimal JavaScript, or one can be created in Excel with a single function.

To summarize, it is important to consider the type of results to be presented in determining what scheme of visual representation will be used. On the one hand, if we need to show the degree of relationships between persons, graph representation may be the best option. On the other hand, if we need to show the degree of influence of certain factors on the performance of CC systems, perhaps the best option is the bar chart.

In the next section, we present the relationships among the elements of the DIPAR framework and the ISO 15939 Systems and Software Engineering—Measurement process standard.

8.5   DIPAR Framework and ISO 15939 Measurement Process

One of the main characteristics of the DIPAR framework is that it was designed taking into account the ISO 15939 measurement process activities. Each stage presented in the DIPAR framework is mapped to the activities described in the ISO 15939

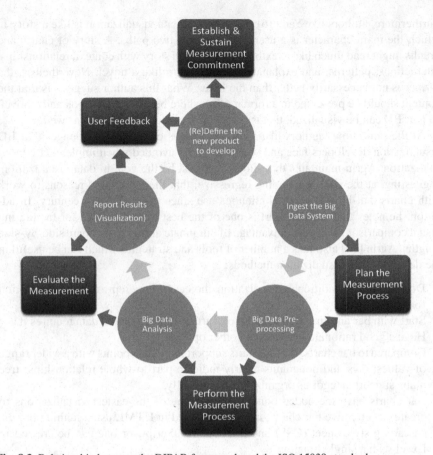

Fig. 8.3 Relationship between the DIPAR framework and the ISO 15939 standard

standard; both the stages and the activities follow the sequence defined in ISO 15939. Figure 8.3 shows the relationships that exist between the DIPAR framework stages and the activities defined in ISO 15939.

Once the DIPAR framework has been mapped to ISO 15939, it is necessary to present in a detailed form which of the stages described in the DIPAR framework are part of the ISO 15939 activities. Table 8.1 presents the relationships between the DIPAR framework and the ISO 15939 measurement process.

In the next section, we present a case study which uses the DIPAR framework to develop a BD product for analyzing the performance of CC applications.

Table 8.1 Relationship between the DIPAR framework and the ISO 15939 measurement process

ISO 15939 Activity	DIPAR Stage	Activities to Perform in the DIPAR Stages
1. Establish and sustain measurement commitment	1. Define the new BD product to develop	Define the new BD product requirements Align the product with the strategic objectives of the organization Define the scope of the product Devise a development plan Assign resources to the development of the product
2. Plan the measurement process	2. Ingest the big data system 3. Big data preprocessing	Define the data collection sources Sketch the type of data to collect Define the interfaces for data collection from the various data sources Verify data quality Perform data cleaning
3. Perform the measurement process	3. Big data preprocessing (cont.) 4. Big data analysis	Obtain an overview of the relationships among the collected data (e.g., sampling) Develop models and algorithms for the data analysis Implement the selected models using big data processing technologies
4. Evaluate the measurement	4. BDA (cont.) 5. Report the results (visualization)	Prepare the results in order to report them to the users Select the type of format to use to present results (graphs, charts, bar charts, etc.) Design flexible reports, in order to be able to update them in real time Design user-friendly interfaces to present results Support the results using a human-oriented analytical process
5. User feedback	6. Redefine the product to develop	Use the results to create or define more complex products, such as recommender systems, prediction systems, and market basket products, etc. Restructure new data to develop the new products

8.6   Case Study

8.6.1   Introduction

One of the most important challenges in delivering cloud services (CS) is to ensure that they are fault tolerant, as failures and anomalies can degrade these services and impact their quality, and even their availability. According to Coulouris et al. [18], a failure occurs in a distributed system (DS), like a CC system, when a process or communication channel departs from what is considered to be its normal or desired behavior. An anomaly is different, in that it slows down a part of a CC system without making it fail completely. It impacts the performance of tasks within nodes, and, consequently, of the system itself.

Developing products for CC systems, and more specifically for CC Applications (CCA), which propose a means to identify and quantify "normal application behavior," can serve as a baseline for detecting and predicting possible anomalies in the software (i.e., jobs in a cloud environment) that may impact cloud application performance.

The CS use different technologies for the data storage, processing, and development services they offer, through various frameworks for managing CCA. Hadoop is one of the technologies used most often in CS, because it offers open source tools and utilities for CC environments. Hadoop includes a set of libraries and subsystems which permit the storage of large amounts of information, enabling the creation of very large data tables or summarizing data with tools that are part of the data warehouse infrastructure. Although there are several kinds of application development framework for CC, such as GridGain, Hazelcast, and DAC, Hadoop has been widely adopted because of its open source implementation of the MapReduce programming model, which is based on Google's MapReduce framework [19].

According to Dean [19], programs written in MapReduce are automatically parallelized and executed on a large cluster of commodity machines. In addition, according to Lin's [20] approach to tackling large data problems today is to divide and conquer, which means that a large problem is broken down into smaller sub problems. Those sub problems can be tackled in parallel by different workers. For example, threads in a processor core, cores in a multi-core processor, multiple processors in a machine, or many machines in a cluster. Intermediate results from each individual worker are then combined to yield the final output.

CC systems in which MapReduce applications are executed are exposed to common-cause failures, which are a direct result of a common cause or a shared root cause, such as extreme environmental conditions, or operational or maintenance errors [21]. Some examples of common-cause failures in CC systems are memory failures, storage failures, and process failures. For this reason, it is necessary to develop a product capable of identifying and quantifying "normal application behavior" by collecting base measures specific to CCA performance, such as application processing times, the memory used by applications, the number of errors in a network transmission, etc.

In the next subsection, we present the implementation process of the DIPAR framework for the creation of a product that can identify and quantify the normal application behavior of CCA.

8.6.2 Define the Product to Develop

The first stage in the DIPAR framework implementation process is to define the product to be developed. Table 8.2 shows the BD product definition stage and the items involved in it .

Table 8.2 Product definition stage and the items involved

Product name: CCA performance analysis application	DIPAR stage: BD product definition
Item	Values
1. Product requirements	The product must improve CCA performance
	The product must include a performance measurement process (PMP)
	The PMP must be able to measure Hadoop performance characteristics
2. Product alignment with the strategic objectives of the organization	The product must improve the performance of the organization by increasing the quality of provision of services in BD processing
3. Scope of the product	The product must provide performance analysis for users, developers, and maintainers
	The product must be able to measure MapReduce and Hadoop system performance characteristics
	The product must not include analysis of elastic or virtualized cloud systems
4. Development plan definition	The product will be developed through the following steps:
	Install a Hadoop test cluster
	Collect system and application performance measures
	Develop a performance analysis model
	Report analysis model results
5. Resource allocation	Hadoop test cluster
	BD scientist
	MapReduce developer
	BD visualization developer

Table 8.3 BDS ingestion stage and the items involved

Product name: CCA performance analysis application	DIPAR stage: BD ingestion
Item	Values
Data types to be collected	Two data types must be collected: (a) Hadoop cluster measures (b) MapReduce application execution measures
Data source identification	Hadoop system logs
	MapReduce logs
	System monitoring tool measures (e.g., Ganglia, Nagios, etc.)
	MapReduce execution statistics
Interfaces for merging data	The data collected from the sources will be merged and stored in a BD repository like HBase [22]

8.6.3   Ingest the Big Data System

The second stage in the DIPAR framework implementation process is to ingest the BDS. In this stage, the type of data to collect is defined as well as their sources. Table 8.3 presents the elements involved in BDS ingestion.

Table 8.4 BDS preprocessing stage and the items involved

Product name: CCA performance analysis application	DIPAR stage: BD preprocessing
Item	Values
1. Data quality	The data collected from the various sources, such as logs, monitoring tools, and application statistics, are parsed and examined using the cleaning process provided by the Hadoop Chukwa [23] libraries
	Chukwa is a large-scale log collection and analysis system supported by the Apache Software Foundation
2. Data cleaning	The data cleaning process is performed using the Chukwa raw log collection and aggregation work flow
	In Chukwa, a pair of MapReduce jobs runs every few minutes, taking all the available logs files as input to perform the data cleaning process [24]
	The first job simply archives all the collected data, without processing it or interpreting it
	The second job parses out structured data from some of the logs and then cleans and loads those data into a data store (HBase)

8.6.4 Big Data Preprocessing

As already mentioned, one of the main problems that arises following the BDS ingestion stage is ensuring that the data are clean. To achieve this, preprocessing is necessary, in order to verify the quality of the data to be subjected to BDA. Table 8.4 presents the elements involved in preprocessing and the steps to be followed.

8.6.5 Big Data Analysis

Once the data have been preprocessed, they can be analyzed to obtain relevant results. In this case study, a performance measurement framework for CCA [25] is used, in order to determine the form in which the system performance characteristics should be measured. Table 8.5 presents the elements involved in the BDA stage and the steps required to execute BDA.

8.6.6 Reporting the Results (Visualization)

Once the BDS has been analyzed, the results are evaluated. They have to be presented in such a way that they are understood in statistical charts and graphs containing information that is descriptive for the end user. Table 8.6 presents the elements involved in the results reporting stage and the elements involved.

Table 8.5 BDA stage and the items involved

Product name: CCA performance analysis application	DIPAR stage: BD analysis
Item	Values
Overview of the relationships between collected data (sampling)	The Performance Measurement Framework for Cloud Computing [25] defines the elements necessary to measure the behavior of cloud systems using software quality concepts
	The framework determines that the performance efficiency and reliability concepts are closely related in performance measurement
	The framework determines five function categories for collecting performance measures, which are failure function, fault function, task application function, time function, and transmission function
Data analysis models and algorithms	In order to analyze and determine the types of relationships that exist in the measures collected from Hadoop, a methodology for the performance analysis of CCA is used [26]
	This methodology uses the Taguchi method for the design of experiments to identify the relationships between the various parameters (base measures) that affect the quality of CCA performance
	One of the goals of this framework is to determine what types of relationships exist between the various base measures. For example, what is the extent of the relationship between the CPU processing time and the amount of information to process?
Model implementation using BD processing technologies	Once the analysis method is determined, it is implemented by Apache's Pig and Hive technologies in order to apply it to the BD repository
	Apache Hive [13] is a data warehouse system for Hadoop that facilitates easy data summarization, ad hoc queries, and the analysis of large data sets stored in Hadoop-compatible file systems
	Apache Pig [27] is a platform for analyzing large data sets that consists of a high-level language for expressing data analysis programs, coupled with the infrastructure for evaluating these programs. The salient property of Pig programs is that their structure is amenable to substantial parallelization, which in turns enables them to handle very large data sets

Once the DIPAR framework implementation process was completed, the design team observed that the original product could be redefined to create a new product. This decision was based on the type of data and the results collected. Specifically, the results show a strong relationship between certain factors (base measures) and the performance of applications running on the cluster. Based on these results, we were able to develop a new performance analysis application. The new product has two main functions, the first as a recommender system, and the second as a fault

Table 8.6 Results reporting stage and the items involved

Product Name: *CCA Performance Analysis Application*	DIPAR Stage: *BD Report the Results*
Item	**Values**
1. Format to use to present the results	• Bar charts, line charts, and scatter charts were chosen to present the relationships between the various performance factors. • e.g. chart of factor contribution percentages

2. User interfaces to present the results	• A Web-based data visualization scheme was selected to present the results. The JavaScript and D3.js libraries were selected to design the data visualization Web site.
3. A human analytical process to support the results	• The charts were supported with textual explanations and classroom presentations by a data scientist.

prediction system. The performance analysis results can also be used to implement different machine learning algorithms in both systems to obtain new features.

The recommender system would propose different Hadoop configurations to improve the performance of CC applications, and the failure prediction system would propose different cases or scenarios in which a CC system could fail or simply have its performance degraded.

8.7 Summary

CC is a technology aimed at processing and storing very large amounts of data, and one of its biggest challenges is to process huge amounts of data, known as BD. In December 2012, the IDC released a report entitled, "The Digital Universe in 2020," in which the authors state that, at the end of 2012, the total amount of data generated was 2.8 ZB. As a result, BDS soon became a very important topic in organizations, because of the value it can generate, both for themselves and for their customers. However, a limiting factor in BDS is the current lack of information to help in understanding, structuring, and defining how to integrate BDS into organizations. The issues surrounding BDS integration are related to the large amounts of data from different sources that are involved, as well as to data transformation, storage, security, etc. In this chapter, we have presented the DIPAR framework, which consists of five stages: Define, Ingest, Preprocess, Analyze, and Report. This framework proposes a means to implement BDS in organizations, and defines its requirements and elements. The DIPAR framework is based on the ISO 15939 Systems and Software Engineering—Measurement process standard, the purpose of which is to collect, analyze, and report data relating to products to be developed. In addition, we have presented the relationship between the DIPAR framework and ISO 15939. Finally, we have presented a case study which shows how to implement the DIPAR framework to create a new BD product. This BD product identifies and quantifies the *normal application behavior* of CCA. Once we had completed the implementation of the DIPAR framework, we found that the original product could be redefined to create a new product. This new product has two main functions, one as a recommender system, and another as a fault prediction system. The DIPAR framework can be implemented in different areas of BD, and we are hopeful that it will contribute to the development of new BD quality technologies.

References

1. ISO/IEC (2011) ISO/IEC JTC 1 SC38: Study Group Report on Cloud Computing, International Organization for Standardization, Geneva, Switzerland
2. Gantz J, Reinsel D (2012) The digital universe in 2020: big data, bigger digital shadows, and biggest growth in the far East, IDC: Framingham, MA, USA, p 16
3. Press GA (2013) Very short history of data science. www.forbes.com/sites/gilpress/2013/05/28/a-very-short-history-of-data-science/. Accessed May 2013
4. Tukey JW (1962) The future of data analysis. Ann Math Stat 33(1):1–67
5. Han J, Kamber M, Pei J (2012) Data mining, concepts and techniques. Elsevier, Waltham, Morgan Kaufmann, USA, 633 p
6. Lin J, Ryaboy D (2012) Scaling big data mining infrastructure: the Twitter experience. In: Goethals B (ed) Conference on knowledge discovery and data mining 2012. Association for Computing Machinery, Beijing, pp 6–19
7. Thusoo A et al (2010) Data warehousing and analytics infrastructure at Facebook. In: ACM SIGMOD international conference on the management of data 2010. Association for Computing Machinery, Indianapolis, Indiana, USA
8. ISO/IEC (2008) ISO/IEC 15939:2007 Systems and software engineering—measurement process, International Organization for Standardization, Geneva, Switzerland
9. Patil D (2012) Data Jujitsu: the art of turning data into product. O'Reilly Media, Inc., Sebastopol
10. A.F.S. (2012) Apache Flume. flume.apache.org/. Accessed 13 June 2013
11. Facebook (2012) Scribe. https://github.com/facebook/scribe/wiki. Accessed 13 June 2013
12. Kandel S et al (2012) Enterprise data analysis and visualization: an interview study. In: IEEE visual analytics science & technology (VAST), 2012, Seattle, WA, USA, IEEE Xplore
13. Thusoo A et al (2010) Hive—a petabyte scale data warehouse using Hadoop. In: 26th international conference on data engineering, 2010, Long Beach, California, USA, IEEE Xplore
14. A.S.F (2012) What is Apache Mahout? https://cwiki.apache.org/confluence/display/MAHOUT/Overview. Accessed June 2013
15. N.E.S.S.I (2012) Big data, a new world of opportunities. Networked European Software and Services Initiative, Madrid, Spain
16. Yau N (2009) Seeing your life in data. In: Segaran T, Hammerbacher J (eds) Beautiful data, the stories behind elegant data solutions. O'Reilly Media, Inc., Sebastopol, pp 1–16

17. Agrin N, Rabinowitz N (2013) Seven dirty secrets of data visualisation. February 18, 2013, www.netmagazine.com/features/seven-dirty-secrets-data-visualisation#null. Accessed June 2013
18. Coulouris G et al (2011) Distributed systems concepts and design. 5th ed. Pearson Education, Edinburgh, Addison Wesley
19. Dean J, Ghemawat S (2008) MapReduce: simplified data processing on large clusters. Commun ACM 51(1):107–113
20. Lin J, Dyer C (2010) Data-intensive text processing with MapReduce2010. University of Maryland, College Park: Manuscript of a book in the Morgan & Claypool Synthesis Lectures on Human Language Technologies
21. Xing L, Shrestha A (2005) Distributed computer systems reliability considering imperfect coverage and common-cause failures. In: 11th international conference on parallel and distributed systems, Fuduoka, Japan, IEEE Computer Society
22. A.S.F (2013) Apache HBase, the Hadoop database, a distributed, scalable, big data store. http://hbase.apache.org/. Accessed 6 June 2013
23. Rabkin A, Katz R (2010) Chukwa: a system for reliable large-scale log collection. In: Proceedings of the 24th international conference on large installation system administration, USENIX Association, San Jose, CA, pp 1–15
24. Boulon J et al (2008) Chukwa, a large-scale monitoring system. In: Cloud Computing and its Applications (CCA '08), Chicago, IL
25. Bautista L, Abran A, April A (2012) Design of a performance measurement framework for cloud computing. J Softw Eng Appl 5(2):69–75
26. Bautista L, Abran A, Abran A (2013) A methodology for identifying the relationships between performance factors for cloud computing applications. In: Zaigham M, Saqib S (eds) Software engineering frameworks for the cloud computing paradigm. Springer, London, pp 111–117
27. A.S.F (2013) Apache pig. http://pig.apache.org/. Accessed 6 June 2013

Chapter 9
A Framework for Cloud Interoperability Based on Compliance and Conformance

José Carlos Martins Delgado

Abstract The current cloud computing panorama includes many cloud providers, each with their own model, set of services and Application Programming Interfaces (APIs), leaving users with an interoperability problem when trying to avoid a potential dependency on a specific provider. Current approaches tend to tackle this problem (user to cloud or cloud to cloud) by abstracting it, either by providing a common set of APIs, which have to map onto each cloud's APIs, or by introducing brokers that adapt the views of the user and of the cloud. This chapter proposes another approach that tries to solve the problem at its source, by defining a common service and resource model, a small set of common services (core API), an interoperability mechanism based on compliance and conformance and an extensibility mechanism that allows providers to build different clouds, based on this core and with support for interoperability. The chapter also presents an interoperability framework with three dimensions—lifecycle of services, levels of abstraction in interoperability and concerns, entailing aspects, such as security, quality of service, Service Level Agreement (SLA) and financial aspects. The main goal is not to provide an interoperability solution to existing systems but rather to establish a foundation layer for cloud computing that shows how clouds should be organized to cater for provider differentiation while supporting interoperability from scratch.

Keywords Cloud computing · Compliance · Conformance · Framework · Interoperability · Resource · Service

9.1 Introduction

In practical terms, *cloud computing* can simply be defined as the remote creation and use of computer-based resources and services, in a setting characterized by elastic, dynamic and automated resource provisioning, paid as used and managed in a self-service way [1].

J. C. M. Delgado (✉)
Department of Computer Science and Engineering, Instituto Superior Técnico,
Universidade de Lisboa, Taguspark, 2744-016 Porto Salvo, Portugal
e-mail: jose.delgado@ist.utl.pt

Z. Mahmood (ed.), *Continued Rise of the Cloud,* Computer Communications
and Networks, DOI 10.1007/978-1-4471-6452-4_9,
© Springer-Verlag London 2014

Resource virtualization is the key enabling factor. From a pool of physical resources (servers, storage, networks and so on), virtual resources can be dynamically allocated and provisioned, or decommissioned and released, to form an apparently elastic fabric of resources that are used on demand and paid as used. However, users want the services that resources support, not the resources themselves. Resources are becoming a commodity [2], allowing some Information and Communications Technology (ICT) enterprises, the providers, to specialize in providing resource infrastructures cheaper, more reliably, better managed, faster provisioned and in a more scalable way than any of the organizations that just require these resources for their lines of business, the users.

This growing dichotomy between users and providers, known as *utility computing* [3], is a marriage of convenience, as any outsourcing agreement. Providers alleviate users from many issues, including expertise, risks, costs and management, in what concerns resources and generic services. The user still has a share of the overall solution in application-specific services, but at least this means that the user is leaning more towards the core business than the ICT technologies that support it.

Moving on from an initial period of slow growth, in which concerns about security, privacy, performance and availability were inhibiting factors, cloud computing finally took the world by storm. Essentially, it becomes so easy, cheap and fast to get computing resources that conventional ICT simply cannot compete. The advantages have now more weight than the risks and disadvantages. It seems that there is no single large ICT provider who is not investing heavily in cloud computing.

This is clearly a market driven by providers, with users still cautious with the transition, but the scenario is evolving at a fast pace, including not only individuals but also enterprises as customers. Two of the most recent examples of this, at the time of writing (July 2013), are as follows:

- Amazon is driving a price war with other resource providers and has sliced prices of dedicated instances (virtual servers running on dedicated physical servers) by up to 80 % [4].
- Two giants, Salesforce and Oracle, signed a partnership to increase their combined weight over competition in the cloud computing service market [5].

Gartner [6] predicts that the worldwide market of public cloud services will grow 18.5 % in 2013, to a total of US$ 131 billion worldwide. The growth in 2012 has been 16.8 % and this rate should be sustainable for the next five years.

This is comparable only to the Web revolution, 20 years ago. It seems that both users and providers were just waiting for a technology that would interconnect them in a flexible and effective manner, so that the goals of everybody can be met. Two main factors also gave their precious contribution to the bootstrap of cloud computing:

- From the point of view of consumers, social networking and multiplatform mobility (laptops, tablets and smart phones) raised the pressing need of storing information in a server somewhere, always available to be accessed from anywhere and synchronized across platforms.

- From the point of view of enterprises and service providers, the market pressure from increasing global competition and ever-shortening turnaround times, combined with a sluggish global economy, emphasized the basic principle of concentrating on core business and (dynamically) outsourcing the rest.

However, we are still facing the same problem that drove the appearance of the Web: *interoperabil*ity. The goal is to endow distributed systems with the ability of meaningfully exchanging information in interaction patterns known as *choreograph*ies. Today, unfortunately, the problem is even worse than 20 years ago:

- The Web allowed uniform e-global access to media information and appeared before the market, creating it instead of reacting to it. This gave time to standards (HTTP, HTML and, later, XML) to be established before diversity could set in. This is why today we can use any browser to access any Web site. Even in the service realm, either with service oriented architecture (SOA) or representational state transfer (REST), the scenario is basically standardized (although standards are not enough to ensure interoperability [7]).
- The cloud enables global access to all kinds of computer-based resources, in a very dynamic environment, but these are more complex than mere hypermedia documents and the market exploded before standardization was achieved. This means that today there are many cloud providers with incompatible interfaces [8] and we cannot use the various clouds seamlessly.

Clouds are becoming the new data centres, now virtualized and much more dynamic. In principle, this means that it should be much easier to change the provider of resources and to discover and use the most convenient services. Unfortunately, this is usually not the case. Complexity, diversity and the lack of standardization in interoperability lead users to *lock-in*, since the costs of changing provider are typically higher than the benefits of the optimizations stemming from the free choice of a new provider. Market share and reputation become the main drivers for the initial choice of provider, instead of a continuous analysis of service quality.

Therefore, we have the problem of standardizing a market that is blossoming at a fast pace, with a war for market share between providers, battling with innovation, prices and alliances. Will current standardization efforts stand a change in such an environment, or will the stronger providers just impose de facto specifications? The main goals of this chapter are as follows:

- To discuss the interoperability problem and to get a better grasp of its dimensions.
- To assess the limitations and problems of current efforts towards solving this problem.
- To present a new approach and to discuss its relevance in dealing with concerns, such as adaptability, changeability and reliability.
- To contribute to the systematization of interoperability in the realm of cloud computing, by establishing a foundation layer that shows how clouds should be organized to cater for provider differentiation, while helping to deal with interoperability issues in a coherent way, right from scratch.

The chapter is organized pursuant to these goals. Section 9.2 provides some background information. Section 9.3 discusses the problem to understand it in a more profound way. Section 9.4 discusses the limitations of current approaches. Section 9.5 presents the new approach. Section 9.6 compares it to current approaches and discusses the benefits, the risks and limitations. Section 9.7 provides some hints into future directions of research. Section 9.8 draws conclusions on this matter.

9.2 Background

This section provides a brief review of the vast existing work on cloud computing, in particular in the interoperability slant, and by no means is intended as an exhaustive study. This is complimented by further information provided in Sects. 9.3 and 9.4.

9.2.1 Cloud Characterization

A cloud is a platform onto which computer-based resources and services can be deployed for later use, in a way that can be described as follows:

- Virtual (abstracting many deployment details);
- Elastic (deploy/decommission as much as needed);
- Dynamic (changes can be frequent and are quick to implement);
- Utility-like (payment proportional to use, which is measured);
- Self-service (automated, on-demand access);
- Omnipresent (accessed through a network, from anywhere).

One of the most cited definitions of cloud computing, encompassing these characteristics, is given by the US National Institute of Standards and Technology (NIST) [9]. Although many variants of the service models available are possible, the NIST considers the following three possibilities:

- *Infrastructure as a Sservice* (IaaS) —the user gets essentially raw resources and must deploy services to them.
- *Platform as a serv*ice (PaaS) —resources already have basic and common services, but the user must still deploy the application-specific services.
- *Software as a serv*ice (SaaS) —resources are provided ready to use, with services deployed. The user may have to configure them before use.

The NIST also considers cloud deployment models, namely private, community, public and hybrid clouds. The first three express the relationship between the owners and the users of the cloud, whereas the latter refers to composition of several clouds, in which the interoperability issue is of particular relevance.

Several survey papers [1, 10, 11] discuss the most relevant issues involving cloud computing.

9.2.2   Cloud APIs and Standards

There are many cloud providers at the IaaS level, the most developed of the cloud delivery models. Besides large providers with proprietary APIs, such as Amazon, Microsoft and Google, there is also a strong open-source movement in the cloud market [12], with cloud management platforms, such as OpenStack [13], CloudStack [14] and Eucalyptus [15]. Although not open source, VMWare's vCloud [16] is used as the underlying platform by several cloud providers. OpenStack and vCloud seem to be the most popular platforms among the non-proprietary IaaS providers.

Nevertheless, popular cloud management systems are not a solution to prevent lock-in. Each cloud ends up having its own features and characteristics, since cloud providers need differentiation to attract customers, and there are several proprietary cloud providers, usually the largest ones.

Several standards have been proposed to help solving the cloud interoperability problem. If clouds can interoperate, a user (individual or enterprise) can use several clouds and minimize lock-in.

At the IaaS level, cloud infrastructure management interface (CIMI) [17], a Distributed Management Task Force, Inc. (DTMF) standard since 2012, provides an API to provision and manage resources typically found in clouds (such as virtual machines, storage volumes and networks).

Open cloud computing interface (OCCI) [18] is another standard, produced by the Open Grid Forum (OGF) in 2011, which entails a more general and higher-level resource model. It is described by three documents, which specify a generic core (applicable to IaaS, PaaS, SaaS and even non-cloud environments), IaaS resources and a RESTful HTTP rendering of the API.

Cloud data management interface (CMDI) [19] is a Storage Networking Industry Association (SNIA) standard, adopted by the International Organization for Standardization/International Electrotechnical Commission (ISO/IEC) which provides a RESTful API to deal with storage resources in a cloud.

Open virtual format (OVF) [20], a DTMF standard adopted by ISO/IEC, allows applications to be packaged and deployed to virtualized systems. Given its low level and usefulness, it is the most used standard in cloud computing and constitutes a means to promote portability of applications between clouds.

Topology and orchestration specification for cloud applications (TOSCA) [21] is a specification being developed by advancing open standards for information systems (OASIS). At the time of writing (July 2013), a first version has been produced [22]. Like OVF, TOSCA is intended for application packaging and distribution, but at higher level, emphasizing the services in their entire lifecycle (design, deployment, monitoring and maintenance) rather than the infrastructure components that support those services.

DTMF is also working towards a standard for cloud audit and governance, Cloud Auditing Data Federation (CADF), to allow examining data and events in applications, even if they extend across several clouds. A working draft is available from the DTMF site.

Existing security standards and open specifications for distributed environments (such as OAuth, OpenID and security assertion markup language; SAML) are used in the cloud computing context, since there are no specific cloud security standards. Nevertheless, there are guidelines in the area of governance, risk and compliance (GRC), from the cloud security alliance (CSA), and in the area of security and privacy, by the NIST (cloud which has also produced a document on a security reference architecture).

The International Telecommunication Union (ITU) has a cloud computing focus group, which has produced a set of documents (available from the ITU site) regarding the cloud computing domain, with emphasis on the telecommunication services in a multiple cloud environment, in which interoperability is a major concern.

The Institute of Electrical and Electronics Engineers (IEEE) Cloud Computing Initiative (CCI) represents another standardization effort, with particular emphasis on cloud interoperability and two foreseen standards: IEEE P2301 (Guide for Cloud Portability and Interoperability Profiles) and IEEE P2302 (Standard for Intercloud Interoperability & Federation). The latter has produced a working draft, outlining the architecture of the intercloud, a network of interconnected clouds that establishes, at a higher level, a parallel with the Internet (seen as a network of interconnected servers).

In [23], a good summary of existing standardization efforts is provided, with particular emphasis on cloud interoperability and on the role that standards can play in the field of cloud computing.

9.2.3   Other Approaches to Interoperability

Without immediate standardization concerns, there is a vast literature on the cloud interoperability problem [24–26], encompassing many aspects and proposals. Cloud interoperability is a complex issue, but we can distinguish two main situations in a service's lifecycle that require it: at deployment time (*portability*) and at operation time (*integration*).

Portability [27] entails the ability to deploy the application that implements a service to several clouds, or to dynamically migrate it from one cloud to another, with minimal effort. Specifications for service packaging and distribution, such as OVF [20] and TOSCA [21], are fundamental to achieve this goal, by providing a common means to deploy and to migrate services. Nevertheless, portability is not enough. A user may need to use or to manage services in several clouds, or a service may be deployed across several clouds and its components need to interoperate and to be managed in an integrated fashion. This requires integration, for which several approaches exist.

One of the approaches is to recognize that working with a cloud implies invoking the features of its API and therefore interoperability can be achieved by using a common API, most likely organized into layers. This provides an abstraction that needs to be mapped onto the specific APIs of cloud providers. Examples of this approach are a cross-platform API [28], an object-oriented abstraction of cloud resources [29] and an abstraction layer for cloud storage resources [30]. However, syntactic integration is limited because the semantics of services cannot be expressed and have to be dealt with tacitly, by users and developers. Besides basic semantic information (e.g. semantic Web services), we need semantic registries [31], semantic frameworks [32, 33] and cloud ontologies [34–36].

The interoperability in the context of multiple clouds has been tackled by active research [8, 37–39]. The organization of multiple clouds as an intercloud, considered by the IEEE CCI, has been described in the literature [40–42].

We should also be aware that interoperability is not an exclusive problem of cloud computing or any virtualized ICT system. Distributed applications, whether supported by a cloud or by a conventional data centre, have the same basic interoperability problems. There is an ongoing effort to systematize an interoperability body of knowledge, as a foundation for an interoperability science [43], and several interoperability frameworks have been proposed [44, 45].

9.3   Understanding the Interoperability Problem

Deriving a good solution implies that the corresponding problem must first be well understood. The Cloud Computing Use Case Discussion Group defines cloud interoperability in terms of writing code that is able to work with more than one cloud provider simultaneously [46], whereas in [25] it is defined as the ability for multiple cloud providers to work together. A broader set of situations that require cloud interoperability is described in [47].

The goal of this section is to describe scenarios, actors, concerns and use cases that require interoperability, as a first step to identify foundational interoperability concepts and to derive a model that can express them in an orthogonal way.

9.3.1   Basic Scenarios

The current global computing scenario is not limited to clouds and neither is interoperability. The classical ICT setting is rather static, with typical N-tier enterprise information systems deployed to a single data centre, eventually including a cluster of servers. Users and developers are typical actors, both accessing applications in that data centre and in other Web servers. Figure 9.1 illustrates this scenario.

Today, the scenario can be drastically different, with a plethora and mix of disparate computing systems that need to interoperate, as illustrated by Fig. 9.1.

The following situations are now likely to occur:

- The data centre still exists, to hold critical or sensitive data, but it will probably include a private cloud instead of a mere cluster.
- The enterprise applications will be deployed to a hybrid cloud setting, integrating the enterprise's owned infrastructure with one or more public clouds.

Fig. 9.1 Classical ICT
scenario, with enterprise
applications in data centres
and global access to web
servers

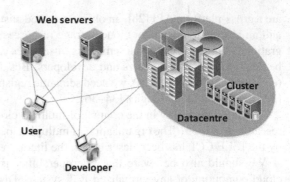

- Mobile cloud computing [48] is another possibility, given the ever increasing pervasiveness of smartphones and tablets that created a surge in the bring your own device (BYOD) tendency [49].
- The explosive development of the Internet of things (IoT) [50] and of radio frequency identification (RFID) tags [51] in supply chains raises the need to integrate the enterprise applications with the physical world, namely through sensor networks [52].
- Grids [53] and P2P systems [54] can be used for batch processing and specific applications.

For simplicity, not all possible connections are depicted in Fig. 9.1, but the inherent complexity of integrating all these systems is easy to grasp. Such heterogeneous scenarios have been compared to a jungle of computer-based systems, by using the designation *jungle computing* [55].

Tables 9.1 and 9.2 provide a characterization of the main types of these systems. Table 9.2 distinguishes resources (provider view) from the services (user view) that they implement. This distinction is important in systematizing the problem because it provides a mapping between an idealized vision (the world as a set of interconnected services) from a more practical one (a heterogeneous set of computing infrastructures that provide resources to implement services).

9.3.2 Actors, Roles, Goals and Expectations

In complex systems, there are usually many *actors* involved, each with a different set of motivations, assumptions, expectations, goals and contributions. This richness is fundamental to understand the full scope of the interoperability problem.

We must distinguish *role* from *actor*. Each individual or organizational actor can play, at a time or simultaneously, more than one role in the system. For example, a programmer is an individual actor that performs both the roles of *developer* (creating services) and *user* (invoking services during development or any other activity). We use the role, rather than the actor, to establish the motivations for interoperability, because it is the best way to organize needs and expectations in an orthogonal way.

Table 9.1 General characterization of the main types of computing infrastructures

Infrastructure model	Simple description	Main distinguishing features	Network	Dispersion
Server	Physical or virtual	Always on computing resource	None	None
Cluster	Set of servers	Load balancing, reliability	LAN	None
Data centre	Set of servers/clusters	Centralized management and physical infrastructures	LAN	None
Web	Global set of HTTP servers	Global access to information and services	Internet	Global
Peer to peer	Set of peers	Decentralized cooperation	Any	Large
Grid	Set of workers	Opportunistic performance	Internet	Large
Cloud-IaaS	Set of raw resources	Utility-style provisioning of raw resources	Internet	Small
Cloud-PaaS	Set of resources with basic services	Utility-style provisioning of preconfigured resources	Internet	Small
Cloud-SaaS	Remote resource with an application	Utility-style use of an existing application	Internet	Small
Multi-cloud	Set of clouds	Brokered or seamless usage of more than one cloud	Internet	Large
Intercloud	Global set of clouds	Brokered or seamless usage of all clouds	Internet	Global
Jungle	Global set of networked resources	Brokered or seamless usage of all networked resources	Any	Global

Table 9.3 contemplates some of the most relevant roles and, in a simplified way, describes the main motivations and expectations of each with respect to interoperability. The cloud is used as the archetype of a computer-based infrastructure, but the issues are basically the same in all the infrastructure types described in Tables 9.1 and 9.2.

In summary:

- Users, developers and auditors are not fond of heterogeneity or variability, but users and developers want to be able to choose among competing providers or development environments.
- Providers acknowledge that being compatible with others may bring more customers due to a lower entry barrier, but the same argument is also valid to lose them to competitors. Therefore, extensibility, innovation and differentiation are of prime importance.
- Brokers and consultants get their business from variability, by reducing its effects to other roles. Therefore, they require interoperability (so that solutions exist) but not normalization (so that variability is possible).
- SDOs try to counter market variability by producing widely adopted specifications. However, SDOs are not globally coordinated and standards partially overlap and/or compete. Also, the fast pace of technology evolution hinders most current standardization efforts. The realm of cloud computing is still ruled by the strongest providers.

These goals are somewhat conflicting and actors performing more than one role may adopt different postures, according to the project in which they happen to be involved.

Table 9.2 Detailed characterization of the main types of computing infrastructures, providing a distinction between resources and services

Infrastructure model	Resources					Services			
	Scale	Size (servers)	Heterogeneity	Owners	Node manager	Elasticity	Nature	SLA	Cost to users
Server	Small	1	None	One	Owner	Virtualization	Generic	Ownership	Full
Cluster	Medium	10–100s	None	One	Owner	On-supply	Generic	Ownership	Full
Data centre	Large	100–1,000s	Medium	One	Owner/users	On-supply	Generic	Ownership	Full
Web	Global	Millions	High	Many	Owners	On-supply	Generic	As allowed	Free/contract
Peer to peer	Large	100–1,000s	High	Many	Owners	On-supply	Specific	As allowed	Free/contract
Grid	Huge	1,000s	High	Many	Owners	On-supply	Specific	As allowed	By use
Cloud-IaaS	Large	100–1,000s	Low	One	Owner/users	On-demand	Generic	As needed	By use
Cloud-PaaS	Large	100–1,000s	Medium	One	Owner/users	On-demand	Generic	As needed	By use
Cloud-SaaS	Small	1	Low	One	Owner	On-demand	Specific	As needed	By use
Multi-cloud	Huge	1,000s	High	Several	Owners/users	On-demand	Generic	As needed	By use
Intercloud	Global	Millions	High	Many	Owners/users	On-demand	Generic	As needed	By use
Jungle	Global	Billions	Huge	Many	Mixed	Mixed	Mixed	Mixed	Mixed

Table 9.3 Motivations and expectations regarding interoperability of the main roles performed by actors involved in computer-based systems

Role	Simple description	Wish list
User	Configures, uses and pays services (no distinction made between individual and enterprise users)	Compatible cloud APIs (to use, configure and manage applications)
		Compatible security, SLA and business models
		Transparent choice of provider, for best SLA/cost ratio
		Single point of contact (provider or broker)
Developer	Creates, deploys and manages services	Compatible platforms and service libraries
		Choice of a single development environment
		Develop once, run anywhere
		Transparent support for dynamic migration and cloud bursting
Provider	Owns resources and rents them by dynamic provisioning	Compatible cloud APIs (to get more customers and third-party services, to use other clouds for resource bursting, to act as a broker with innovative services)
		Mechanism for cloud API extension, to enable differentiation from competition
		Standards with several layers of conformance
		Sectorial standards (covering specific topics), instead of large standards covering everything
Broker	Adapts and aggregates services	User + Developer + Provider, since a broker is a mix of all three roles
		Many different providers and third-party services, to increase the broker's value
Auditor	Audits and certifies services and infrastructures	Abundant standards, covering almost all aspects
		Conformance to standards by almost all providers
		Very limited extension mechanisms, to avoid variability that is difficult to audit
Consultant	Provides knowledge and solutions	Many standards
		Many different providers and third-party services
		Many extension mechanisms
Standards Developing Organization (SDO)		Universal adoption of its standards
		Breadth of applicability
		Completeness of specifications

Table 9.4 Typical categories of features of a cloud API

Service model	Category	Main aspects/features
IaaS	Workload (virtual machine images)	Hypervisors, image format, deployment, migration, load balancing, management
IaaS	Persistent data	Data models, storage and migration
IaaS	Network	Virtual networks, name resolution, policies, management
IaaS	Identity access management	Authentication, authorization, account management
PaaS	Queue and notification	Asynchronous messaging and eventing
PaaS	Database	Queries, management and administration
PaaS	Workflow management	Task coordination, scheduling
PaaS	Content delivery	Web caching, request routing, server load balancing
PaaS	Middleware and libraries	Support for application development
SaaS	User application	Web Services, RESTful interface

9.3.3 Use Cases and Concerns

To understand interoperability, we need to identify which situations require it. A good description of use cases is made in [23], including seven use cases (on the topic of deployment) from the cloud computing use cases white paper [46], 21 from NIST (on management, use and security) and 14 from DTMF (on management). A list of requirements for multi-cloud interaction is presented in [8], regarding development, deployment and execution of applications, spanning across the lifecycle of applications.

This plethora of use cases, scenarios and requirements is not detailed here, for simplicity. If we compare the APIs of large clouds, such as Amazon AWS, Microsoft Azure and Rackspace, we can easily understand why standardization is so difficult in cloud computing. Too many providers, specifications and users have appeared into play before the technology had the change to follow an organized and controlled route.

Many of these use cases are high level and depend on the architecture of the specific cloud, but others are recurrent and are present in all clouds (such as virtual machine provisioning and storage access), although differing in the details. The former refer to specific services, representing the differentiation of each provider, and are not particularly interesting to include in an interoperability effort. The latter constitute the basis for an interoperability systematization and an eventual standardization proposal.

Any interaction with a cloud (from another cloud, user, developer, etc.) requires interoperability, even if it pertains to some feature exclusive of that cloud. Here, we are interested in the most common features, those that a typical cloud implements. A cloud API can be structured in categories of features, according to each type of resources or services with most relevance, as illustrated by Table 9.4.

These categories of features exist, in one form or another, in most clouds currently offered on the market (if they support the indicated service models). However, the underlying resource and service architectures, as well as the APIs, can be quite different. The higher-level the service model is the more difficult interoperability becomes.

There are also transversal concerns, present in most, if not all, interactions with a cloud. These include the following:

- Security
- SLAs
- Reliability and disaster recovery
- Metering and monitoring
- Cost and charging models
- Regulatory compliance and legislation
- Auditing and risk management
- Strategy and governance
- Policies and rules
- Management and control frameworks and standards

Some of these concerns need to be addressed explicitly and programmatically (by using the API), whereas others can only be dealt with in a tacit manner or at the documentation level.

9.4 Analysis of Current Solutions to the Interoperability Problem

Standards are the canonical solution to interoperability problems but, depending on the perspective (Table 9.3), the obligation to adopt some specification can be seen as both a bonus and a curse. On one hand, it puts everyone on the same ground, provides a concrete target for development and testing and enables interoperability. Only lack of conformance to the standard can still originate problems. However, on the other hand, a standard can behave as a straightjacket and hamper innovation, differentiation from competition and customization.

In the general case, standards are more effective (with a broader acceptance) when:

- They stem from real cooperation between competing specifications. This was the case of the genesis of unified modelling language (UML) in which three leading gurus of the modelling domain, James Rumbaugh, Grady Booch and Ivar Jacobson truly cooperated to fuse their three approaches, respectively object-modelling technique (OMT), object-oriented design (OOD) and object-oriented software engineering (OOSE).
- They appear as the result of a perceived need and before the market expands (e.g. HTTP, HTML, XML, Web services).
- What a standard specifies is not the core business in itself (although supporting it) but is seen as useful. This is typically the case of standards pertaining to low-level aspects, such as Open Virtual Format (OVF) [20].

Unfortunately, in the case of cloud computing, the market expanded before standards, driven by innovation and perceived customer needs. When this happens, either we have a set of incompatible specifications or one dominates and takes the form of a de facto standard. Amazon and Salesforce have been early adopters and became leaders in their cloud market segments. Others, such as Microsoft, appeared later in the scenario with enough quality to establish their presence, but until now none had enough strength to impose de facto cloud standards.

Deficient standardization leads to incompatibilities and lock-in, which is an undesirable situation to all involved actors (with the probable exception of eventual dominant providers). As described in Sect. 9.2.2, the number of standardization efforts in cloud computing interoperability is significant. However, the main cloud providers seem to be able to add features and capabilities at a much faster pace than standards can settle and mature. In such a dynamic, market-oriented field, the standards that survive tend to be more de facto, spurred by real usefulness and market acceptance, than de jure, designed by working groups in standardized bodies.

Since an all-encompassing standard is not likely to appear in the near future, the current main alternative solutions are as follows:

- *Set of standards*—each covering a range of aspects of cloud computing interoperability. Some overlap and even compete and not all aspects are covered. The main problem for a standard is gaining sufficient market traction, in particular taking into account that cloud providers need to maintain their differentiation and added value regarding competition. Also, in some cases standardization seems to be more SDO-driven than required by cloud providers.
- *Abstraction layer over several cl*oud APIs [28, 30]—this corresponds to mapping a given specification (a portable API) onto the APIs of the various clouds, but it entails losing performance and dealing with compromises resulting from conflicting requirements.
- *Brokerage* [56–58]—in which a set of services provide an API implemented by invoking the APIs from several cloud providers. This can involve adapting services, choosing the best service from a set of alternatives or adding new services, probably by aggregating services from one or more providers. This is a flexible solution, capable of custom adaptations, but again it can involve loss of performance and compromises. The aggregated services can add value, but the fact is that brokerage leads to a new API that may simply be one more contender, increasing the problem instead of solving it.

Analysing this stack of solutions, we can identify several relevant issues:

- Standards tend to be an all or nothing solution, although in some cases the standard includes limited extension mechanisms, such as options and levels of conformance in OVF [20], the modular design of OCCI [18] and the provision for external extensions in TOSCA [21].
- Standards tend to be specification silos. Each tries to solve all the aspects of the area it tackles. Different standards usually deal with similar aspects with different underlying models, ontologies and APIs. For example, the concept of container is rather universal, but each standard deals with it differently.

- In the same track, the current approaches to cloud interoperability and its standardization start with the current layered conception of a cloud (IaaS, PaaS and SaaS) and impose rules and constraints to what we can do and cannot do, in each layer and between layers. This brings much complexity because, instead of considering a small set of foundational concepts and then deriving interoperability rules from them, the starting point is a working cloud, already a very complex system.
- Standards tend to be over-encompassing and over-specifying, instead of being modular (each dealing with a separate issue) and foundational (sticking to core specifications, not to every detail).
- There should be a backbone standard specifying which are the areas and topics that make sense standardizing and how these can be related. Each standard, tackling one area or topic, would then fit a slot in that backbone. Unfortunately, there is no such standard, as it would require global coordination of SDOs.
- The approaches using an abstraction layer and brokerage lead to APIs that suffer from the same problems than standardized APIs, with the added problem that they have neither SDOs nor large cloud providers to back them.
- Open source software, such as OpenStack [13] is sometimes heralded as a solution to interoperability, avoiding provider lock-in. This works up to some level, since a common specification is a good starting point. However, clouds based on open specifications quickly gain extensions and new services that hinder transparent interoperability. The main advantage of open source software is lowering the entry barrier for cloud providers, which avoid building the cloud management platform from scratch, not interoperability.

We contend that a different approach is needed, so that a better response to the cloud interoperability problem can be given. This is the purpose of the next section.

9.5 A New Approach to the Cloud Interoperability Problem

9.5.1 The Strategy

We need to make clear that the cloud interoperability problem is unsolvable in its entirety, given its nature, mainly due to the following reasons:

- Not all aspects are equally amenable to interoperability, because not all roles in Table 9.3 have the same goals.
- The market innovates faster than it organizes. This means that the pressure to provide more and better services than competitors is far greater than the need to interoperate with them. Laggards desire interoperability, but innovators and early adopters cannot (and usually do not want to) wait for specifications that support it.
- When the interoperability problem is solved at a given abstraction level (which happens when that level becomes a commodity and everybody just wants a standard), the need for differentiation by providers or the evolution in applications

makes the interoperability problem move to the next upper abstraction level. An example of this is the OSI model [59], which structured interoperability at the communication level but then higher levels of interoperability started to be tackled explicitly and today, 20 years later, we are still struggling with (certainly not less) interoperability issues.

Therefore, it is not strange that the most successful specifications are low-level standards, such as OVF and CMDI (because they are near the commodity level), and open source platforms, such as OpenStack and CloudStack (because the open source cloud market appeared after, and as a result of, the development of these platforms).

The obvious starting point to cloud interoperability is the IaaS service model, and it has been questioned [23] whether it makes sense to standardize other service models, such as PaaS and SaaS, which exhibit more variability and complexity. The fact is that complex systems can be (recursively) described by the composition of simpler systems, which means that even in complex systems we can identify repeatable patterns which are amenable to standardization. We just need to discover the basic concepts that constitute the fabric of clouds.

Chemistry and Physics have taught us that much that we observe and deal with daily are just macroscopic and complex manifestations of very small and very simple elementary components while interacting with each other. Chemistry devised the periodic table of elements, the basic properties of atoms and of other elementary particles. Physics has gone even further, by studying ever-smaller particles and other artefacts, in search of a Theory of Everything that is able to unify all the fundamental forces of nature (such as gravity and electromagnetism) and explain all observable phenomena.

Clouds are very complex systems at a much higher level than elementary particles, but the same composition principle should apply. There must be a set of concepts and of their interactions that, by multiple and arbitrarily complex composition, should be able to fully describe the behaviour and characteristics of clouds.

Instead of considering what to do with complex cloud subsystems and how to make them interoperable, we propose to tackle cloud interoperability by adopting an approach based on the composition principle, along the following guidelines:

- To try to discover which are the fundamental and primitive artefacts and aspects that underlie the entire cloud computing domain and, if possible, the entire spectrum of computing infrastructures described in Tables 9.1 and 9.2
- To devise an interoperability framework that shows how to make them interoperable and under which conditions
- To model system interoperability as determined by the composition of the primitive artefacts

Taking into account these guidelines and the problems of current approaches described in the previous section, our strategy to tackle the cloud interoperability problem can be outlined in the following way:

- To devise a generic framework, valid for any computing infrastructure in Tables 9.1 and 9.2. This can be the basis for a standard that can act as a backbone of other more specialized standards and includes.
  - A generic model of foundational artefacts, including a composition mechanism.
  - An extensible mechanism for self-description of artefacts.
  - A foundational interoperability mechanism (the basis of all interactions).
  - A framework to express the relevant aspects to interoperability between these artefacts.
- To define a core specification based on this framework, built with a set of primitive resources and their compositions.
- To define and to build clouds, and other infrastructures, by composition and extension of existing resources.

The following sections detail the interoperability framework. The core specification outgrows the context of this chapter, but a simple example of the approach is given in Sect. 9.5.5.

9.5.2   A Generic Model of Foundational Artefacts

Our foundational artefact model, depicted in Fig. 9.3, is very simple and includes only two main kinds of artefacts, resources and services, a composition mechanism for resources and an interaction mechanism for services. In spite of its simplicity, it can be used to build any arbitrarily complex computing infrastructure, including heterogeneous scenarios, such as the one depicted in Fig. 9.2.

This model can be described in the following way:

- A *service* is the set of *capabilit*ies (involving behaviour, state or both) that as a whole model some abstraction. Services can invoke one another, in the roles of consumer and provider. All interactions relevant to the interoperability context occur between services.
- A *resource* is the artefact providing the implementation of services and is either primitive or recursively composed of other resources. A resource implements at least one service (its management service), which exposes its inherent capabilities, but it can implement any number of other services.
- *Services* refer to each other by *references*, which are resources. Services interact by sending each other *messages*, which are also resources.
- One of the inherent capabilities of a *resource* is to incorporate and to expose some of the capabilities of a message sent to its management service. This can be accomplished by exposing a new service or changing that resource's own capabilities (behaviour or state).
- *All services* expose a capability that, upon a request message from a consumer, responds with a message describing all its capabilities, thus supporting self-description.

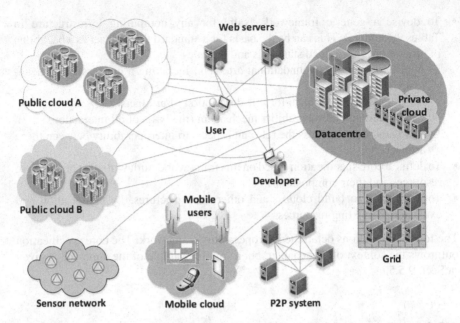

Fig. 9.2 Modern ICT scenario, with enterprise applications deployed to hybrid clouds and integrated with non-cloud systems

Exposed capabilities correspond essentially to exposed operations in an API. Behaviour capabilities are operations that execute specific actions, whereas state capabilities correspond to data getter and setter operations. A server and a storage container are examples of resources (most likely virtual, but not necessarily). The server will certainly have a management service that exposes a deployment operation, which receives a resource with the code that describes the service to be deployed and creates a new service with that code. The storage container will have a management service that includes getter and setter operations.

Figure 9.4 illustrates the relationship between resources and services in two different clouds. There are two resources, *A* and *B*, each with its own management service. Developers invoke operations in these services to deploy two new services, *X* and *Y* (by sending them resources with the service descriptions), which interact and need runtime interoperability. At this generic level, management services provide essentially the same functionality, which can translate to deployment-time interoperability by using compatible resource formats, such as OVF.

Resource composition corresponds to clustering a set of resources and then using them as a new, composed resource, in a higher-level system. For example, a full cloud in Fig. 9.2 is a composed resource that can be used to build a multi-cloud by composition. The concept of system composition is recursive and universal.

Virtualization now makes possible to change dynamically the structure of composed resources. Migration of a service can be accomplished by moving the resource that implements it from one place to another in the global resource tree. This is

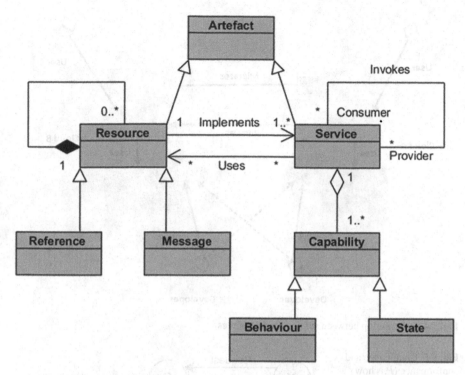

Fig. 9.3 A foundational artefact model

illustrated in Fig. 9.4, in which each cloud is the top container resource for all the resources it contains and a resource has migrated from one cloud to the other.

The migration of a service running on virtual machine corresponds to stopping the service, generating a resource with its code and state, and sending that resource as a message to the management service of another server, creating a new instance of the service there and resuming execution.

In a grid, the worker resources will have operations to receive jobs, execute them and sending back the results. Migration involves data, not code, but the resource model applies exactly in the same way. References will probably implement uniform resource identifiers (URIs), but not necessarily. Non-Internet networks, such as sensor networks, may use other addressing schemes and formats.

The concept of resource in this model is similar to the resource of the REST architectural style [60], but lower-level and more general. There is also a clear distinction between resources and services, with the operations offered by services not limited to a fixed set. This model combines the structural nature of REST with the service flexibility of SOA [61] It has been designated *structural services* and it is described in more detail in [62]. In any case, the most important aspect of this model is that it treats all kinds of resources and of services in the same way, under a common abstraction. Specific features will be introduced by specializing capabilities in resources and services, but at least now we have a common ground on which to base interoperability.

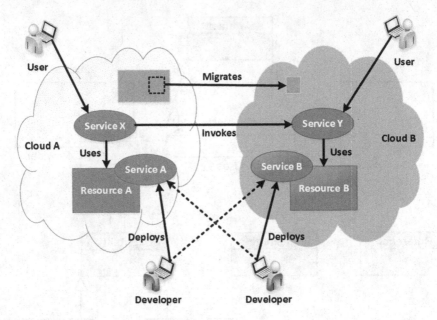

Fig. 9.4 Relationship between services and resources

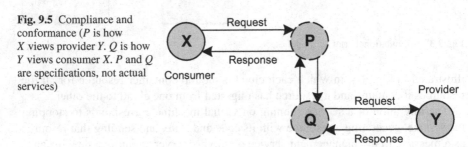

Fig. 9.5 Compliance and conformance (P is how X views provider Y. Q is how Y views consumer X. P and Q are specifications, not actual services)

9.5.3 A Foundational Interoperability Mechanism

This section considers the basic interaction between two services and discusses how interoperability can be established. This is valid not only for runtime interoperability, such as between services X and Y in Fig. 9.4, but also at deploy-time, because deploying a service to a resource corresponds to sending a message with the description of the service to that resource's management service. Therefore, deploy-time for a service corresponds to runtime for the management service of the target resource.

Figure 9.5 considers the two services X and Y of Fig. 9.4, in which X plays the role of consumer (sending a request) and Y plays the role of provider (honouring that request and sending a response).

If X and Y were designed to work together, in these roles, there would be no interoperability problem (assuming that the design was correct). Unfortunately, this is not always the case. Suppose that X was designed to interact with a provider P and Y was designed to expect a consumer Q. Having X interoperable with Y involves two conditions [63]:

- *Compliance* [64]—P must *comply* with Q in terms of requests, which means that P must satisfy all the requirements of Y to honour requests. Therefore, X can use Y as if it were P.
- *Conformance* [65]—Q must *conform* to P in terms of effects (including eventual responses), which means that Q must fulfil all the expectations of P regarding the effects of a request. Therefore, Y can replace (take the form of) P without X noticing it.

Note that given these definitions, interoperability is inherently asymmetric in nature. Apparently, symmetric interactions are the result of role reversal, in which interacting services alternate between consumer and provider roles. Partial interoperability has been achieved by *subsumption*, with the set of capabilities that X uses as a subset of the set of capabilities offered by Y and as long as Y (or another service that replaces it) supports the specification Q.

In many cases, services are conceived and implemented to work together, i.e. made interoperable by design. When systems are complex and evolve in an independent way, ensuring interoperability is not an easy task. A typical and pragmatic solution is to resort to Web services and XML data, sharing schemas and namespaces, or to RESTful APIs, which are simpler to use and require that schemas (media types) be standardized or pre-agreed. In these technologies, both customer and provider are forced to implement full interoperability (for example, sharing a XML schema), even if only a fraction of the possible interactions is used. This leads to a greater coupling than needed.

Other solutions involve discovering Web services similar to what is sought, by performing schema matching with similarity algorithms [66], and ontology matching and mapping [67]. However, manual adaptations are usually unavoidable.

The notion of partial interoperability, illustrated by Fig. 9.5, introduces a different perspective, stronger than similarity but weaker than commonality (resulting from using the same schemas and ontologies). The trick is to consider only the intersection between what the consumer needs and what the provider can offer. If the latter subsumes the former, the degree of interoperability that the consumer requires can be granted, regardless of whether the provider supports additional features or not.

9.5.4 A Multidimensional Interoperability Framework

Compliance and conformance describe the basic interoperability mechanism in abstract terms but do not give the full picture. This section outlines a framework that provides further insight into this mechanism. We consider the following three main dimensions, corresponding to fundamental perspectives of interoperability:

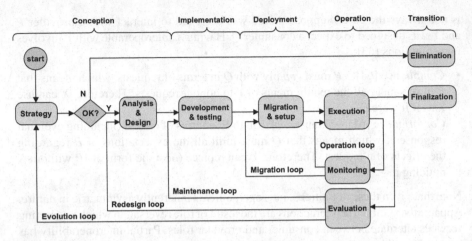

Fig. 9.6 A typical service lifecycle, including redeployments as migrations

- *Lifecycle* of the services—interoperability is not merely about the operation stage but starts much earlier in the system's lifecycle, in the conception stage. After all, what happens during operation is a consequence of what has been conceived and designed. In current agile and virtualized environments, development, deployment and migration are frequent operations. In the same line of thought, OCCI [18], TOSCA [21] and [8] consider explicitly several stages in the lifecycle.
- *Abstraction*— interoperability (compliance and conformance) can be considered at several levels of abstraction, such as semantics and syntax. Considering these levels separately leads to a better structuring of the interoperability aspects.
- *Concerns*— interoperability is not limited to functional objectives (the intended effect by invoking another service). There is a range of other concerns that need to be considered, mostly non-functional, such as configuration, SLA, reliability, security, policy management, legislation and regulatory compliance, financial aspects and so on. If, for example, the provider cannot meet (cannot conform to) the service level requirements of the consumer, interoperability will not be properly achieved.

For simplicity, we will not consider here a fourth dimension, *evolution*, which corresponds to successive versions of the interacting services obtained by successive iterations of their lifecycles.

Figure 9.6 illustrates a typical lifecycle. Different software engineering methods may use different lifecycles, but the general idea is that it flows along phases such as conception, implementation, deployment, production (also known as operation, or execution) and finally transition. During conception, a strategy assessment determines if the lifecycle proceeds to subsequent phases or the service is not worthwhile and is terminated. During operation, monitoring may determine reconfiguration or migration (for load balancing, for instance) and evaluation of management metrics (key performance indicators; KPIs) may determine changes to the service, with deployment of a new version of the service (and the current one is finalized).

The lifecycle is very important for interoperability, because not only interaction with other services must be considered by design (not as an afterthought) but also it constitutes a way of managing what happens to the service, including migration, in a controlled way. This is even more important in dynamic provisioning environments, such as clouds.

When a service sends a message to another, there is a full spectrum of aspects that both sender and receiver must understand, from low-level protocols up to the intentions that motivated the interaction. These aspects can be organized into levels of interoperability abstraction. We use a scale of five levels, which can be further refined as follows:

- *Symbiotic*, reflecting the *intent* (motivation and goals) of a service when engaging in an interaction with another. This can be tackled at levels of governance, alignment, collaboration or mere outsourcing.
- *Pragmatic*, dealing with the *effect* of the interaction on the other service. This can be specified at the choreography, process and service levels.
- *Semantic*, which expresses the *meaning* of the messages exchanged and of the resulting behaviour at the levels of rules, knowledge and ontology.
- *Syntactic*, which deals with the *format* of the messages, in terms of schema, primitive resources and their serialization.
- *Connective*, establishing the *protocol* at the message, routing, communication and physical levels.

Interoperability is possible only if all these levels contribute to it. For example, if the intended effect is expressed correctly at the upper levels but one service sends a message in XML and the other is expecting JavaScript Object Notation (JSON), they will not be able to interact. The same happens if services use exactly the same technologies and tools, but one expects an effect (such as receiving a payment) that the other does not provide.

In most practical cases, only a few levels are dealt with explicitly. The most common are syntactic and pragmatic, with semantic gaining ground. The others can be dealt with as follows:

- *Tacitly*, by assuming that what is missing has somehow been previously agreed, is obvious or described in the documentation that the developer will read. Inferring intent and semantics from documentation or undocumented behaviour constitute examples of this.
- *Empirically*, by resorting to some tool or technology that deals with what is necessary to make interoperability work. An example is using Web Services without caring about the details of how they work.

The correlation between the lifecycle and interoperability dimensions of the framework is illustrated by Fig. 9.7 (in which the lifecycle has been simplified) and can be described in the following way:

- All the levels of abstraction of interoperability must be considered in every stage of the lifecycle. Intentions behind interactions are still present during execution,

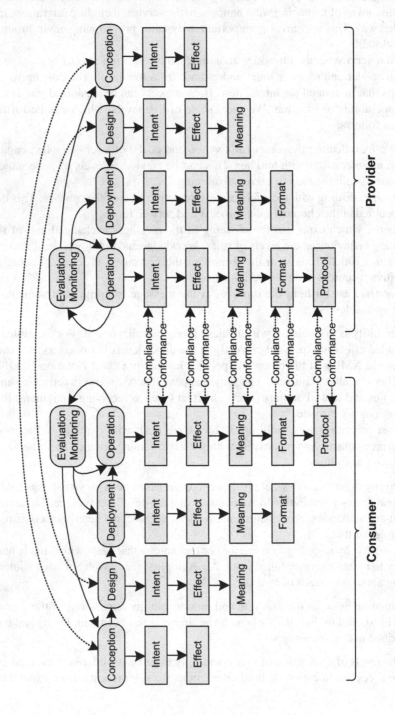

Fig. 9.7 Service lifecycle combined with interoperability abstraction levels

although in a tacit way, and connectivity is already needed in the conception stage, although in an empiric way. However, it is only natural that the method used to evolve the service along its lifecycle considers interoperability at an abstract level in the initial stages and at full detail in the operation stage. The progression illustrated by Fig. 9.7 is just an example, since it depends on the method used.

- There must be compliance (in the consumer to provider direction) and conformance (in the provider to consumer direction) in each corresponding cell (in a given stage and abstraction level) in both interacting services. Figure 9.7 illustrates this in detail in the operation stage only. However, the same should happen in other stages (the dashed arrows at the top of the figure indicate this). The rationale for this is twofold:
  - Services must be interoperable at each abstraction level of interoperability, be it at the intention level (one must understand and accept the intentions of the other), at the meaning level (interoperable ontologies and semantic relationships) or at the basic protocol level (there must be message connectivity).
  - Each stage in the lifecycle is a consequence of the previous stage, in a model-driven fashion. For systems to be interoperable at operation time, their conception and design must also be made interoperable.
- Evaluation and monitoring need not be made interoperable. Each service can evaluate its design or operation independently, although the specifications for interoperability must not be overlooked and need to be considered in the context of the partners' relationship. This is the case of SLA, for example, but these types of aspects are dealt with by the third dimension of the framework (concerns).

Figure 9.8 depicts the framework in its three dimensions. The plane (two dimensions) of Fig. 9.7 is repeated for each of the concerns relevant to interoperability. Besides the functional interoperability (resulting from the specification of the services), we need also to consider non-functional aspects such as security, SLA and financial aspects. Compliance and conformance still apply in the non-functional realm, e.g.:

- The consumer must comply with the provider's security policies when sending a request. The provider must conform to the consumer's security policies when sending a response.
- The consumer must comply with the SLA metrics and policies that the provider is able to provide and accept. In turn, the provider must conform to the requirements (such as performance and reliability) sought by the consumer. If this is not accomplished, interoperability can be achieved in functional terms, but not entirely because non-functional requirements have not been met.
- The same can be said about financial aspects, in which cost and payment terms need to be agreed under basically the same principles as an SLA.

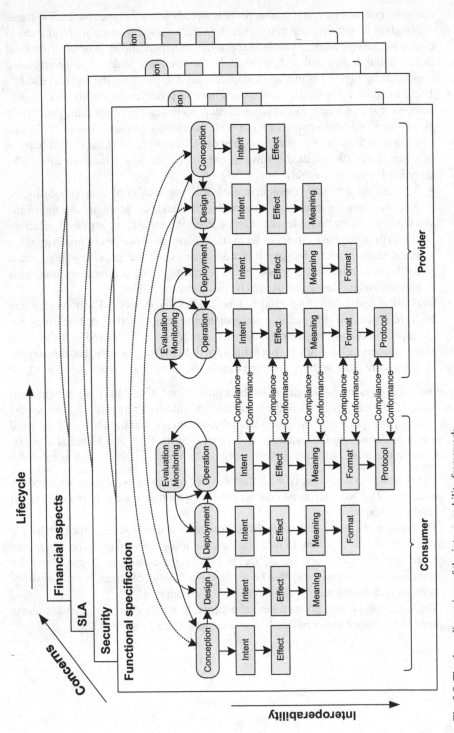

Fig. 9.8 The three dimensions of the interoperability framework

9.5.5 A Simple Example

This section provides a very simple example of how partial compliance and conformance can be used in a structural way and how it can promote API interoperability. We will illustrate data compliance and conformance only, for simplicity, but it should give an idea of what is involved. We use JSON to illustrate the details because it is easier to read than XML.

Suppose that we want to use a cloud to create a virtual server. First, we need to know which types of servers the cloud is able to create. To support self-description, the cloud's API should have an operation to return that information. In the light of the model described in Sect. 9.5.2, that operation could return a JSON structure such as the one in Listing 9.1.

```
{
    "cpu": {
        "architecture": ["x86", "x64", "powerPC"],
        "cores": [1, 2, 4, 8],
        "performance": ["extra", "high", "medium"],
        "ram": [4, 8, 16, 32, 64],
        "reliability": ["extra", "high"]
    },
    storage : {
        "size" : { "min" : 0.1, "max" : 1000 },
        "performance" : ["high", "medium"],
    },
    "zone" : ["Europe", "US", "Asia"]
}
```

Listing 9.1 JSON example describing the characteristics of a server

The JSON array elements express alternatives that the server can support. Object members correspond to characteristics of the resource (central processing unit (CPU) or storage). Note the structural organization of the server's characteristics. They are not just a linear list.

Listing 9.1 acts as a schema for the servers in this cloud, including all the characteristics and possible values and alternatives. Servers are composed of a CPU, a storage and are located in one of three alternative zones. The CPU and storage also have their characteristics (self-explanatory, at the level of this example). Random access memory (RAM) and storage sizes are expressed in gigabytes.

The cloud will have several server types available, each with a subset of the possible combinations of characteristics. The cloud should also have an operation to retrieve a list of available server types. For example, that list could include the two following server types described in Listing 9.2.

```
{
    server_type_1 : {
        "cpu" : {
            "architecture" : ["x86", "x64", "powerPC"],
            "cores" : [2, 4, 8],
            "performance" : ["extra", "high", "medium"],
            "ram" : [8, 16, 32],
            "reliability" : ["extra"]
        },
        storage : {
            "size" : { "min" : 1, "max" : 50 },
            "performance" : ["medium"],
        },
        "zone" : ["US", "Asia"]
    },
    server_type_2 : {
        "cpu" : {
            "architecture" : ["x86", "x64"],
            "cores" : [2, 4],
            "performance" : ["high"],
            "ram" : [4, 8, 16],
            "reliability" : ["high"]
        },
        storage : {
            "size" : { "min" : 0.1, "max" : 20 },
            "performance" : ["high", "medium"],
        },
        "zone" : ["Europe"]
    }
}
```

Listing 9.2 JSON example describing the characteristics of types of servers offered by a cloud

Now, imagine that we wanted to create a server with the following characteristics (Listing 9.3) (the array elements express the alternatives we are willing to accept):

```
{
        "cpu" : {
          "architecture" : ["x86", "x64"],
          "cores" : [4, 8],
          "performance" : ["medium"],
          "ram" : [16, 32],
        },
        storage : {
          "size" : { "min" : 1, "max" : 2 },
          "performance" : ["high"],
        },
        "zone" : ["Europe", "US"]
}
```

Listing 9.3 JSON example describing the server characteristics required by a customer

Although we have not discussed the algorithms to test compliance and conformance, an informal comparison between these JSON listings illustrates the following comments:

- server_type_1 cannot be used because it does not conform to the server required by the customer, in Listing 9.3. Checking the various characteristics, there is a matching solution for all except storage performance. The customer requires "high" but the server only offers "medium". If it were the other way around, conformance would be verified.
- server_type_2 conforms to Listing 9.3. For all characteristics, there is a matching solution. Note that the customer requires a "medium" performance CPU but the provider only offers "high". From the point of view of performance this is valid, but it may hinder conformance when cost is introduced (it may be higher than acceptable, since the CPU is better than required). All characteristics need to be taken into account when checking interoperability.
- The customer specified nothing regarding "reliability", in Listing 9.3. This means that anything is accepted in this characteristic and that it is not taken into account when checking conformance.
- Compliance is also needed when the customer requests the creation of a server. The operation to inquiry the cloud about the server types it supports exists to help in the design, but there must be another operation to make the actual request for the creation of the server instance. The type of the actual argument to pass to that operation is Listing 9.3 (what the customer requires) and the type of the formal argument is Listing 9.1 (what the cloud can provide). When operations are invoked, the actual arguments must comply with the formal arguments. In this case, Listing 9.3 must comply with Listing 9.1 (which we can verify by checking that there is a matching solution for all characteristics in Listing 9.3). After checking argument compliance, the server creation operation uses Listing 9.2 to search for a suitable server type, which it then creates.

- The names and structure of the elements in Listing 9.1 must be in accordance with the ontology used by the cloud. The customer needs not use exactly the same ontology in Listing 9.3. Another one that complies with it is enough. Compliance and conformance, as asserted in Sect. 9.5.4, must hold at all interoperability levels, namely semantics, ontology [68] included.

9.6 Discussion and Rationale

9.6.1 Usefulness of the Approach

How can this framework be useful in the current interoperability panorama? The main purpose of a framework is to aid in systematizing human thought, so that the problem can be better structured and a solution is easier to find. The structure of this chapter follows this approach, with a first structuring of the problem, analysis of current solutions, a framework and the outline of a solution.

Even at the standardization level, we believe that the interoperability problem (in any computing infrastructure and in clouds in particular), should use the same approach, which can be outlined in the following way:

- To define an interoperability framework, based on a generic artefact model and on orthogonal dimensions that cater for the lifecycle of artefacts, their interoperability at various abstraction levels and non-functional concerns (security, SLA, etc.).
- To define a set of primitive types of artefacts for each type of computing infrastructure, with a self-describing interface. This set may be organized into categories of artefacts.
- To define standard interfaces for the most used artefacts, in such a way that a basic computing infrastructure (such as a cloud or a grid) could be built in a standardized fashion, by composing the adequate types of artefacts.
- To define a backbone standard, corresponding to a minimalist computing infrastructure (with basic resources and services), which further standards could be laid upon.
- To define provider-specific artefacts (non-standardized, thus providing explicitly a mechanism for provider differentiation), either anew or by extension (based on compliance and conformance) of primitive or standardized artefacts.
- To build provider-specific computing infrastructures (namely, clouds), by using both standardized and provider-specific artefacts.
- To build an API centred on resources. This means that, instead of having a global API, each resource should have its own API. The advantage of this is that there are many operations common to different types of resources. Thanks to compliance and conformance, which behave as a distributed inheritance mechanism, common operations can be dealt with in the same way, as if we had distributed object-oriented polymorphism.

This is an incremental approach, which tries to standardize the minimum possible but with a structure that is designed to grow, instead of solving a reasonably sized chunk of the interoperability problem, which is the approach followed by most of the current standardization efforts.

The partial interoperability granted by compliance and conformance provides a better decoupling between services than a full standard specification that all services must use or implement. Better decoupling increases adaptability (fewer dependencies), changeability (it is easier to change a service if others depend on less of its features) and reliability (it becomes easier to find a replacement for a service that failed) [63].

9.6.2 Comparison with Other Approaches

Approaches, such as OCCI [18] and TOSCA [21] are more modular than other, but still try to solve most of the problems in the areas they tackle. In [29], the abstraction of cloud resources is presented in an object-oriented way, but without a framework that guides the interoperability aspects. In [8], guidelines and requirements for the functionality to include in a multi-cloud API are presented, along the service lifecycle, but the ideas to implement them start at existing technologies, platforms and tools. Although an evolutionary route, easier to implement, it does not solve the problem of the standardization of the underlying model.

The intercloud [40–42] is an attempt to integrate multiple clouds, in a parallel with the integration between servers provided by the Internet and the Web in particular. The problem is that in cloud computing the market expanded rapidly before the standards and the situation is quite different. The intercloud will only be as good as the interoperability between multiple clouds. Again, this is a top-level approach to interoperability, trying to integrate existing clouds without solving the lower level interoperability problems first.

The approach that consists in defining a common API, abstracting the actual APIs of cloud providers [28–30] is not without problems. It needs to abstract the different artefacts used by cloud providers (which means compromises that enable support only for the most used API patterns) and to deal with constant evolutions in the APIs, since the field is not mature yet.

One recent trend, seen in OCCI [18], TOSCA [21] and in the Meta Cloud [69] is the use of structural resource templates to describe the structure of a service, or the resources it requires, so that provisioning is simpler and more automated. This is in line with our artefact model (Fig. 9.3), which adds the benefit of compliance and conformance, as exemplified in Sect. 9.5.5.

It seems that everybody agrees that a single standard, encompassing all the aspects of cloud computing, namely interoperability, is not a viable solution. The main difference between the existing approaches is the subset of features to include, more vertically (a small number of aspects, but crossing the whole stack of cloud service models) or more horizontally (encompassing only one cloud service model) orientated.

Up to now, the most successful approach has been horizontal and low level, with the OVF and CMDI standards. The other efforts tend to go to upper levels and to build on what exists. Our proposal is different, starting by agreeing on a common artefact model, simple enough to be general but with extension mechanisms that enable each provider to build its own cloud model and platform. This approach starts at the simplest and lowest layer, providing a cleaner foundation for the computing infrastructure domain, not just for clouds.

9.6.3 Risks and Limitations

Freed from the compatibility burden, our approach lays down a clean model, based on active and interacting resources, with their services and solutions conceived specifically for them, instead of using established technologies designed for hypermedia document exchange and that simulate services on top of a document-based abstraction.

New approaches, such as ours, have the advantage of exploring new routes, which is an indispensable step for innovation, but are usually not exempt from their own limitations and incur the risk of never generating enough traction to be adopted by the market, thereby never progressing beyond the stage of an interesting solution. In our case, the following main risks and limitations are easily perceivable:

- Essentially, this is an untried approach. There is a prototype implementation, but it does not implement all the features and certainly has not been quantitatively assessed at a reasonably large scale, with a real comparison with current approaches, namely SOA and REST. Therefore, the claims made still need practical and meaningful validation.
- The approach is deeper than the mere domain of cloud computing. It goes back to the Web itself, since it is based on the service paradigm and not on the classical client-server hypermedia document exchange model. Although a potential better match to modern application requirements, this is a huge paradigm shift, with many possible problems in the way, yet to uncover.
- Any approach needs tools and middleware to support it, which requires market interest and takes time to develop, leading to a bootstrap problem. This has yet to be tackled, with a migration path that allows coexistence with current approaches.
- Compliance and conformance, in particular, constitute a rather different solution from the schema sharing approach currently used. It raises several problems, from formal treatment to performance, which have not been properly addressed yet in realistic scenarios.
- Although the polymorphism granted by compliance and conformance has the potential to support a common core of cloud service specifications, it has not been demonstrated yet how this can actually be done in a practical way, to really support useful standardization while allowing freedom for provider innovation.

9.7   Future Research Directions

From the point of view of the users, the ideal would be to treat providers in a cloud fashion, i.e. using services or installing their applications without really caring about which cloud provider they are using. This means virtualizing the cloud providers themselves, not just the infrastructure or the platform. We believe that the proposal presented in this chapter is a step in that direction, but much needs to be done before this vision can turn into reality, namely:

- There is currently no language that implements structural compliance and conformance as described in Sect. 9.5.3. We have presented a simple example in Sect. 9.5.5 using JSON as notation, but this is much more limited than what we can do with a language that supports better data structures and operations, not just data, and combines the best of SOA (flexible services) and REST (flexible resources). We are developing a compiler and platform for such a language (service implementation language; SIL) [70].
- The semantic level, namely compliance and conformance at the ontology and knowledge level, needs further study. At the moment, most of the research made on interoperability at the semantic level concerns similarity and matching [66, 67], not compliance and performance.
- The interoperability framework that we have presented has not been tested yet. We are still building the prototype of the SIL environment, but the interoperability problem in the domain of cloud computing is a very good match to the capabilities of the language. We will use it as one of the first practical examples. The goal is to build a very basic cloud platform, with a small number of universally used resource types and operations, and then derive two example clouds with different APIs, with additional resources and functionality. SIL itself serves to specify the structure of the resources (as shown in Sect. 9.5.5) and services of a compose application, allowing to test service and resource templates.
- One of the basic features of SIL is that it is compiled and serialized in binary. It has two representations, one with a look and feel similar to JSON for programmers and a binary format for computer processing. The compiler maintains the synchronism between the two. Native support for binary means that service images to deploy to resources no longer need to have a separate manifest or sent in a zip file. The same binary format used to serialize the resources (in a tag followed by length and value (TLV) approach) can be used to include these images. This allows us to study an alternative to OVF with the goal of providing a native implementation of the model depicted in Fig. 9.3.

9.8   Conclusions

The seamless interoperability that we enjoy today both at the Internet and Web levels cannot be achieved in the near future in the field of cloud computing. In the former cases, technology and standards had time to mature before the market expanded. In the latter, it happened the other way around. Under user pressure and by initiative of some early-adopter providers (in cloud storage), the market expanded and is evolving very rapidly, before standards had time to impose some order.

Today, large providers are not particularly interested in standardization. It seems that the value of compliance with standards (perspective of the users) is greater than the value of conformance to those standards (perspective of the providers). In other words, the absence of widely accepted standards endows large providers with the power of the lock-in law.

Only the lowest-level standards, such as OVF and CMDI, have enjoyed significant success. The reasons for this are simple. These are the oldest standards and, given their low level, do not contribute significantly to the differentiation that providers need to attract a larger customer base. Nevertheless, users continue with an interoperability problem, trying to defend themselves against provider lock-in. Current attempts to solve or reduce this problem use essentially high-level solutions, building common APIs over the existing providers and cloud computing concepts, or exposing brokers that hide the differences between providers.

In this chapter, we have presented a different approach, starting from a foundation artefact model, based on resources and services, adding a basic interoperability mechanism, based on structural compliance and conformance, and foreseeing extension mechanisms upon which providers can build their differentiating services. We proposed the idea of a core standard with the foundation concepts, which can serve as a backbone for higher-level standards.

In a sense, this approach tackles the interoperability problem in the incremental and generic way in which it should have evolved. However, it does not constitute an evolutionary route, and is therefore most likely longer and harder to implement than other approaches. Nevertheless, it has the merit of providing potential rewards in terms of accomplishing a cleaner structure and organization than what exists today in the cloud computing landscape.

References

1. Armbrust M et al (2010) A view of cloud computing. Commun ACM 53(4):50–58
2. Carr N (2004) Does IT matter? Information technology and the corrosion of competitive advantage. Business Press, Harvard
3. Brynjolfsson E, Hofmann P, Jordan J (2010) Cloud computing and electricity: beyond the utility model. Commun ACM 53(5):32–34
4. Morgan T (2013) Amazon slices prices on dedicated EC2 private cloud puffs. The Register, 10 July 2013. www.theregister.co.uk/2013/07/10/amazon_slashes_prices_on_dedicated_ec2_server_slices/. Accessed 16 July 2013
5. Clark J (2013) Salesforce and Oracle forge partnership to smash rivals. The Register, 25 Jun 2013. www.theregister.co.uk/2013/06/25/salesforce_oracle_partner_analysis/. Accessed 16 July 2013
6. Anderson E et al (2013) Forecast overview: public cloud services, worldwide, 1Q13 update. Gartner report. http://www.gartner.com/resId=2473016. Accessed 16 July 2013

7. Lewis G, Morris E, Simanta S, Wrage L (2008) Why standards are not enough to guarantee end-to-end interoperability. Proceedings of the seventh international conference on composition-based software systems, Feb 2008, pp 164–173
8. Petcu D (2013) Multi-cloud: expectations and current approaches. Proceedings of the international workshop on multi-cloud applications and federated clouds, New York, Apr 2013, pp 1–6
9. Mell P, Grance T (2011) The NIST definition of cloud computing. Special publication 800-145, National Institute of Standards and Technology, Sept. 2011. http://csrc.nist.gov/publications/nistpubs/800-145/SP800-145.pdf. Accessed 16 July 2013
10. Rimal B, Choi E, Lumb I (2009) A taxonomy and survey of cloud computing systems. Proceedings of the fifth international joint conference on INC, IMS and IDC, August 2009, pp 44–51
11. Zhang Q, Cheng L, Boutaba R (2010) Cloud computing: state-of-the-art and research challenges. J Internet Serv Appl 1(1):7–18
12. Bist M, Wariya M, Agarwal A (2013) Comparing delta, open stack and Xen cloud platforms: a survey on open source IaaS. Proceedings of the IEEE 3rd international advance computing conference, pp 96–100
13. Jackson K (2012) OpenStack cloud computing cookbook. Packt Publishing Ltd, Birmingham
14. Sabharwal N, Shankar R (2013) Apache cloudstack cloud computing. Packt Publishing Ltd, Birmingham
15. Nurmi D et al (2009) The eucalyptus open-source cloud-computing system. Proceedings of the 9th IEEE/ACM international symposium on cluster computing and the grid, May 2009, pp 124–131
16. Gallagher S, Dalgleish A (2013) VMware private cloud computing with vCloud Director. Wiley, Hoboken
17. DTMF (2012) Cloud infrastructure management interface (CIMI) model and REST interface over HTTP specification, document number: DSP0263, version 1.0.1., 12 Sept 2012. http://www.dmtf.org/sites/default/files/standards/documents/DSP0243_1.0.1.pdf. Accessed 16 July 2013
18. Edmonds A, Metsch T, Papaspyrou A (2011) Open cloud computing interface in data management-related setups. In: Grid and cloud database management, Springer, Berlin, pp 23–48
19. SNIA (2012) Cloud data management interface (CDMI) v1.0. 2, 18 Mar 2013. http://docs.oasis-open.org/tosca/TOSCA/v1.0/cs01/TOSCA-v1.0-cs01.pdf. Accessed 16 July 2013
20. DTMF (2012) Open virtualization format specification, document number: DSP0263, version 2.0. 0, 13 Dec 2012. www.dmtf.org/sites/default/files/standards/documents/DSP0243_2.0.0.pdf. Accessed 16 July 2013
21. Binz T, Breiter G, Leyman F, Spatzier T (2012) Portable cloud services using Tosca. IEEE Internet Comput 16(3):80–85
22. OASIS (2013) Topology and orchestration specification for cloud applications—version 1. 0, 4 June 2012. http://www.snia.org/cdmi. Accessed 16 July 2013
23. Lewis G (2012) The role of standards in cloud-computing interoperability, Software Engineering Institute, Paper 682, Oct 2012. http://repository.cmu.edu/sei/682. Accessed 16 July 2013
24. Loutas N, Kamateri E, Bosi F, Tarabanis K (2011) Cloud computing interoperability: the state of play. Proceedings of the IEEE third international conference on cloud computing technology and science, Nov 2011, pp 752–757
25. Zhang Z, Wu C, Cheung D (2013) A survey on cloud interoperability: taxonomies, standards, and practice. ACM SIGMETRICS Perform Eval Rev 40(4):13–22
26. Kostoska M, Gusev M, Ristov S, Kiroski K (2012) Cloud computing interoperability approaches-possibilities and challenges. Proceedings of the fifth Balkan conference in informatics, Serbia, Sept 16–20, pp 30–34
27. Petcu D, Macariu G, Panica S, Crăciun C (2013) Portable cloud applications—from theory to practice. Future Gener Comput Syst 29(6):1417–1430

28. Petcu D, Craciun C, Rak M (2011) Towards a cross platform cloud API—components for cloud federation. Proceedings of the 1st international conference on cloud computing and services science, The Netherlands, May 2011, pp 166–169
29. Nguyen B, Tran V, Hluchý L (2012) Abstraction layer for development and deployment of cloud services. Comput Sci 13(3):79–88
30. Hill Z, Humphrey M (2010) CSAL: a cloud storage abstraction layer to enable portable cloud applications. Proceedings of the IEEE second international conference on cloud computing technology and science, Nov 2010, pp 504–511
31. Mindrut C, Fortis T (2013) A semantic registry for cloud services. Proceedings of the 27th international conference on advanced information networking and applications workshops, Spain, March 2013, pp 1247–1252
32. Loutas N, Kamateri E, Tarabanis K (2011) A semantic interoperability framework for cloud platform as a service. Proceedings of the IEEE third international conference on cloud computing technology and science, Nov 2011, pp 280–287
33. Di Modica G, Petralia G, Tomarchio O (2012) A semantic framework to support cloud markets in interoperable scenarios. Proceedings of the IEEE/ACM fifth international conference on utility and cloud computing, Nov 2012, pp 211–214
34. Bernstein D, Vij D (2010) Using semantic web ontology for intercloud directories and exchanges. Proceedings of the international conference on Internet computing, Las Vegas, NV, July 2010, pp 18–24
35. Androcec D, Vrcek N, Seva J (2012) Cloud computing ontologies: a systematic review. Proceedings of the third international conference on models and ontology-based design of protocols, architectures and services, April 2012, pp 9–14
36. Jardim-Goncalves R, Cretan A, Coutinho C, Dutra M, Ghodous P (2013) Ontology enriched framework for cloud-based enterprise interoperability. In: Concurrent engineering approaches for sustainable product development in a multi-disciplinary environment, Springer, London, pp 1155–1166
37. Ardagna D et al (2012) MODAClouds: a model-driven approach for the design and execution of applications on multiple clouds. Proceedings of the workshop on modeling in software engineering, June 2012, pp 50–56
38. Paraiso F, Merle P, Seinturier L (2013) Managing elasticity across multiple cloud providers. Proceedings of the international workshop on multi-cloud applications and federated clouds, New York, NY, April 2013, pp 53–60
39. Grozev N, Buyya R (2012) Inter-cloud architectures and application brokering: taxonomy and survey. Software: practice and experience. doi:10.1002/spe.2168
40. Demchenko Y, Makkes M, Strijkers R, de Laat C (2012) Intercloud architecture for interoperability and integration. Proceedings of the 4th IEEE international conference on cloud computing technology and science, Taiwan, Dec 2012, pp 666–674
41. Bernstein D, Ludvigson E, Sankar K, Diamond S, Morrow M (2009) Blueprint for the intercloud-protocols and formats for cloud computing interoperability. Proceedings of the fourth international conference on internet and web applications and services, Venice, Italy, May 2009, pp 328–336
42. Bernstein D, Vij D (2010) Intercloud directory and exchange protocol detail using XMPP and RDF. Proceedings of the 6th World Congress on services, July 2010, pp 431–438
43. Jardim-Goncalves R, Grilo A, Agostinho C, Lampathaki F, Charalabidis Y (2013) Systematisation of interoperability body of knowledge: the foundation for enterprise interoperability as a science. Enterp Inf Syst 7(1):7–32
44. Ostadzadeh S, Fereidoon S (2011) An architectural framework for the improvement of the ultra-large-scale systems interoperability. Proceedings of the international conference on software engineering research and practice, Las Vegas, July 2011
45. Guédria W, Gaaloul K, Proper H, Naudet Y (2013) Research methodology for enterprise interoperability architecture approach. Proceedings of the advanced information systems engineering workshops, Springer, Berlin, pp 16–29

46. Ahronovitz M et al (2010) Cloud computing use cases, version 4.0, white paper from the Cloud Computing Use Case Discussion Group. http://opencloudmanifesto.org/Cloud_Computing_Use_Cases_Whitepaper-4_0.pdf. Accessed 16 July 2013
47. Petcu D (2011) Portability and interoperability between clouds: challenges and case study. Proceedings of the 4th European conference towards a service-based Internet, Poland, Oct 2011, pp 62–74
48. Fernando N, Loke S, Rahayu W (2013) Mobile cloud computing: a survey. Future Gener Comput Syst 29(1):84–106
49. Keyes J (2013) Bring your own devices (BYOD) survival guide. CRC Press, Boca Raton
50. Gubbi J, Buyya R, Marusic S, Palaniswami M (2013) Internet of things (IoT): a vision, architectural elements, and future directions. Future Gener Comput Syst 29(7):1645–1660
51. Aggarwal C, Han J (2013) A survey of RFID data processing. In: Managing and mining sensor data, Springer, US, pp 349–382
52. Potdar V, Sharif A, Chang E (2009) Wireless sensor networks: a survey. Proceedings of the international conference on advanced information networking and applications workshops, Bradford, UK, IEEE, May 2009, pp 636–641
53. Liu Y, Rong Z, Jun C, Ping C (2011) Survey of grid and grid computing. Proceedings of the international conference on Internet technology and applications, Wuhan, China, IEEE, Aug 2011, pp 1–4
54. Hughes D, Coulson G, Walkerdine J (2010) A survey of peer-to-peer architectures for service oriented computing. In: Handbook of research on P2P and grid systems for service-oriented computing: models, methodologies and applications, IGI Global, 2010, pp 1–19
55. Seinstra F et al (2011) Jungle computing: distributed supercomputing beyond clusters, grids, and clouds, In: Grids, clouds and virtualization, Springer, London, pp 167–197
56. Buyya R, Ranjan R, Calheiros R (2010) Intercloud: utility-oriented federation of cloud computing environments for scaling of application services. Proceedings of the 10th international conference on algorithms and architectures for parallel processing, Busan, Korea, May 2010, pp 13–31
57. Sundareswaran S, Squicciarini A, Lin D (2012) A brokerage-based approach for cloud service selection. Proceedings of the IEEE 5th international conference on cloud computing, Honolulu, HI, June 2012, pp 558–565
58. Nair S et al (2010) Towards secure cloud bursting, brokerage and aggregation. Proceedings of the IEEE 8th European conference on web services, Dec 2010, pp 189–196
59. ISO/IEC (1996) ISO/IEC 7498-1, information technology—open systems interconnection—basic reference model: the basic model, 2nd edn corrected, 15 June 1996, International Standards Office, Geneva. http://standards.iso.org/ittf/PubliclyAvailableStandards/index.html. Accessed 16 July 2013
60. Earl T (2012) SOA with REST: principles, patterns and constraints for building enterprise solutions with REST, Prentice Hall PTR
61. Earl T (2007) SOA: principles of service design, Prentice Hall PTR
62. Delgado J (2012) Bridging the SOA and REST architectural styles. In: Migrating legacy applications: challenges in service oriented architecture and cloud computing environments, IGI Global, 2012, pp 276–302
63. Delgado J (2012) Structural interoperability as a basis for service adaptability. In: Adaptive web services for modular and reusable software development: tactics and solutions, IGI Global, 2012, pp 33–59
64. Kokash N, Arbab F (2009) Formal behavioral modeling and compliance analysis for service-oriented systems. In: Formal methods for components and objects, Springer, Verlag, pp 21–41
65. Adriansyah A, van Dongen B, van der Aalst W (2010) Towards robust conformance checking. In: Business process management workshops, Springer, Berlin, pp 122–133
66. Jeong B, Lee D, Cho H, Lee J (2008) A novel method for measuring semantic similarity for XML schema matching. Expert Syst Appl 34:1651–1658
67. Euzenat J, Shvaiko P (2007) Ontology matching, Springer, Berlin

68. Mizoguchi R, Kozaki K (2009) Ontology engineering environments. In: Handbook on ontologies, Springer, Berlin, pp 315–336
69. Satzger B et al (2013) Winds of change: from vendor lock-in to the meta cloud. IEEE Internet Comput 17(1):69–73
70. Delgado J (2013) Service interoperability in the internet of things. In: Internet of things and inter-cooperative computational technologies for collective intelligence, Springer, Berlin, pp 51–87

Part IV
Management, Governance and Capability Assessment

Chapter 10
Survey of Elasticity Management Solutions in Cloud Computing

Amro Najjar, Xavier Serpaggi, Christophe Gravier and Olivier Boissier

Abstract Application Service Providers (ASPs) are increasingly adopting the cloud computing paradigm to provision remotely available resources for their applications. In this context, the ability of cloud computing to provision resources on-demand in an elastic manner is of the utmost practical interest for them. As a consequence, the field of cloud computing has witnessed the development of a large amount of elasticity management solutions deeply rooted in works from distributed systems and grid computing research communities. This chapter presents some solutions that differ in their goals, in the actions they are able to perform and in their architectures. In this chapter, we provide an overview of the concept of cloud elasticity and propose a classification of the mechanisms and techniques employed to manage elasticity. We also use this classification as a common ground to study and compare elasticity management solutions.

Keywords Classification · Cloud ecosystem · Cloud elasticity · Elasticity management · Survey

10.1 Introduction

Delivering computing resources as utility, similar to water and electricity is one of the key promises of cloud computing [6, 9]. Before the emergence of cloud computing technologies, ASPs were used to provision servers for their services in

A. Najjar (✉) · X. Serpaggi · O. Boissier
École Nationale Supérieure des Mines de Saint Etienne, FAYOL-EMSE,
LSTI, 42023 Saint-Etienne, France
e-mail: najjar@emse.fr

X. Serpaggi
e-mail: xavier.serpaggi@emse.fr

O. Boissier
e-mail: olivier.boissier@emse.fr

C. Gravier
Université Jean Monnet, 25 rue Docteur Rémy Annino, 42000 Saint-Etienne, France
e-mail: christophe.gravier@telecom-st-etienne.fr

Z. Mahmood (ed.), *Continued Rise of the Cloud,* Computer Communications
and Networks, DOI 10.1007/978-1-4471-6452-4_10,
© Springer-Verlag London 2014

in-house datacenters. Most of the time, they were forced to deploy enough resources to handle their peak-loads. Consequently, most servers in these datacenters remained idle [6].

With the emergence of the cloud computing technologies, the primary advantage for ASPs is to convert capital expenditure, previously dedicated to purchasing and deploying in-house servers, into operational expenditure. This results into better cost management. Moreover, the burdens of maintaining, upgrading and administrating the datacenters are offloaded to the CP.

Elasticity is the most important feature of the cloud computing paradigm [56]. Because of this feature, cloud users can acquire more resources from the cloud when the demand is high and relinquish unneeded resources when the demand decreases. However, in order to benefit from the elasticity, cloud users (or the ASPs) need to continuously monitor the end-to-end quality of service (QoS) of their cloud-hosted applications so that strategies built on this monitoring could drive the scaling up and down of resources allocated to each application. To relieve the cloud user from this burden, commercial and academic solutions have been proposed to automate the process and to minimize the cloud user intervention.

In the literature, some sources (e.g. [25, 48]) propose different classifications of these elasticity solutions. However, none of them captures the characteristics of most of the existing elasticity management solutions.

This chapter is organized as follows: Section 10.2 introduces the cloud ecosystem with its different actors that allow us to clearly set the context of elasticity management. Section 10.3 provides an overview of the problem of elasticity management and it introduces the taxonomy and the analysis grid used in this chapter to classify state-of-the-art elasticity management solutions. The following Sects. 10.4, 10.5 and 10.6 detail the features of current solutions along the three major axes of our analysis grid. Section 10.7 analyzes in detail three selected recent elasticity management solutions showing how the proposed taxonomy allows comparing them. This chapter concludes with Sect. 10.8 and points out to our future research perspectives.

10.2   Cloud Ecosystem

Attracted by the cost reduction, ASPs are increasingly migrating their business to the cloud. ASPs use resources rented from the *cloud provider* (CP) to build their service that, in turn, is going to be consumed by their *service users* (SUs) or end-users. CP, ASP and SU are the three main factors in this environment [6]. Their roles are as follows:

1. CP is usually a company owning large datacenters with advanced software systems that allow it to lease resources on-demand over the Internet in exchange for pay-per-use fees. From a service delivery model perspective [49], a CP can be classified as infrastructure as a service (IaaS) provider (e.g. Amazon EC2 [2]) or platform as a service (PaaS) provider, such as Google App Engine [27]. Note that in the literature the CP can be referred to as *cloud service provider* [57, 61] or as *cloud operator* [37].

2. ASP is the party that uses the cloud resources rented from the CP in order to build its services and applications, and to sell them to its clients in exchange for pay-per-use or monthly/annual subscription fees. In the literature, an ASP can be referred to as software as a service (*SaaS*) *provider* [6, 47, 81]. Dropbox [21] is an example of ASP proposing an online file storage service built over Amazon S3 [3]. In this chapter, in particular contexts, we may refer to the ASP as the *cloud user*.

3. SU is frequently named "end-user". It is the customer of the service provider. SUs use the service provided by the ASP in exchange for a fee. In this chapter, we may use the terms SU and end-user interchangeably.

Other actors, such as brokers, cloud aggregators and cloud tools providers [62] can also participate in the cloud ecosystem. However, we consider them to be beyond the scope of our study. In this chapter, we only consider the three main aforesaid actors.

Both kinds of provider in this ecosystem (i.e. CP and ASP) have to guarantee their service quality to their customers (i.e. ASP and SU, respectively). These guarantees and obligations are specified in *service level agreements* (SLAs). As mentioned in [61, 81], we distinguish between two types of SLAs:

1. SLA_{CP-ASP}: This SLA states QoS aspects provided to the ASP by the CP. The guaranteed level of each QoS aspect is specified as *service level objective* (SLO). It also stipulates penalties in case of violations of the SLOs that it contains.

2. SLA_{ASP-SU}: This SLA states the guarantees from the ASP to the SU ensuring the QoS to be delivered to the SU (e.g. maximum response time, availability and service-specific metrics).

Figure 10.1 illustrates an example of the cloud tripartite ecosystem in which the problem of elasticity management is situated. Note that Fig. 10.1 shows only three SUs and two CPs. Yet, in real cloud market settings, thousands of SUs may use the service provided by the ASP, which in turn rents cloud resources provided by several CPs.

From this global picture of the tripartite cloud ecosystem, the next section provides the definition and explanation of the elasticity management.

10.3 Global View of Elasticity Management

As the result of their survey on different definitions of cloud computing, Vaquero et al. [74] highlighted elasticity as one of the most important features of cloud computing. The CP is in charge of providing elasticity. To this aim it needs to implement adequate optimization and infrastructure management mechanisms to allow cloud resources access at will. On the other side, the ASPs that are sandwiched between the CPs and SUs, aim at performing rational *elasticity management*, so that they could achieve their business goals while serving their clients with adequate service quality.

In the following, we focus on elasticity management from the point of view of ASPs, i.e. as an ASP-centric problem. We consider that *infrastructure optimization* is

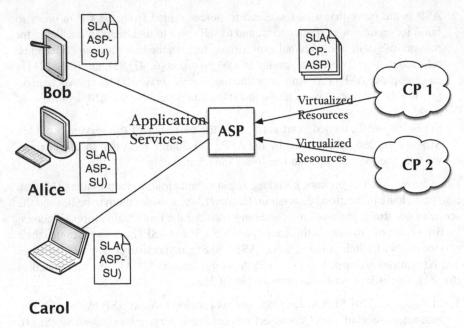

Fig. 10.1 Tripartite cloud ecosystem

beyond the scope of this chapter since it is a CP-centric problem tackling datacenter optimization (virtual machine; VM migration, energy-efficient physical machine scheduling, server consolidation, etc.) Also, we limit our study to ASPs renting resources from IaaS CPs. The next two subsections define *elasticity* and *elasticity management*, respectively.

10.3.1 Elasticity

Based on the US National Institute of Standards and Technology (NIST) definition of elasticity [54], Galante et al. [25] define elasticity as the ability of cloud user to *"quickly request, receive and later release as many resources as needed. The elasticity implies that the actual amount of resources used by the Cloud user may be changed over time, without any long-term indication of the future resource demands"* [25]. After presenting this widely accepted definition of elasticity, next subsection defines elasticity management.

10.3.2 Elasticity Management

In order to define and explain the process of elasticity management, we start by defining *scheduling* and *resource provisioning,* two sub-processes that are tightly related to elasticity management:

- Scheduling is a mechanism used by the ASP to assign each task or request submitted by its end-users to a virtual resource for execution [10]. A cloud-oriented scheduling mechanism takes into account different VM capacities, the VMs waiting queue length, the requirements of each submitted job, etc.
- Resource provisioning is a mechanism to acquire the necessary virtual resources from the CP. Given the workload and the end-user requests. It looks for the best CP and the optimal VM sizes to acquire.

Both scheduling and resource allocation can exhibit cost awareness, SLA- awareness or any other, ASP-defined, goal-awareness, such as end-user satisfaction. From these two definitions, we define elasticity management as follows: *"Elasticity Management is an ASP-centric problem. It concerns finding an optimal tradeoff between the satisfaction of the ASP customers and the ASP business goals. It may be achieved by using resource provisioning alone or in conjunction with scheduling . Elasticity management results in the acquisition or release of virtual Cloud resources".*

From this definition and the distinction between scheduling and provisioning, we can distinguish two kinds of elasticity management:

- In simple elasticity management the elasticity manager tackles only the question of Ccloud resource provisioning (when to provision resources, which resources, from which providers, etc.). Scheduling is delegated to a load-balancer that distributes the workload among the VMs provisioned by the elasticity manager. Examples of this type include [12, 29, 52, 64].
- In complex elasticity management, the resource provisioning decision arises as a result of the scheduling process. For instance, when the scheduler concludes that the current workload cannot be handled by the available VMs given the imposed QoS constraints and the current size of VM job queues, the elasticity manager provisions new VMs from the Ccloud in order to avoid service degradation or penalties and also maintain the end-user satisfaction. Examples of this type include [15, 26, 44, 81].

In the rest of this chapter, we use the term *elasticity management* to refer to both approaches. Since elasticity management is a complex process, elasticity management solutions usually consist of multiple components and services as mentioned as follows [14]:

- **Performance and workload monitors:** These are the sensors of the system that are in charge of collecting measures about the key performance and workload indicators.
- **Resource allocator:** This component actuates the resources provisioning actions determined by the elasticity manager.

- **Load balancer:** It distributes the requests among the instantiated resources. When the elasticity manager is a *complex* one, load-balancing is replaced by an ASP-customized cloud-oriented scheduling algorithm.
- **Elasticity manager:** It plays the central role of compiling the information received from the sensors, reasoning about this input using ASP-defined policies and deciding which actions to make (which resources to acquire, from which CP, etc.). This decision is then sent to the *resource allocator* that, using the application program interface (API) of the CP, executes the provisioning actions. When new VMs are provisioned, the *load-balancer* distributes the workload among them.

The *control level* enjoyed by the ASP defined by [14] depends on which of the aforelisted components are actually controlled by the ASP. Thus, Casalicchio et al. [14] distinguished four control levels ranging from *extreme ASP control*, where the ASP controls all the aforementioned components, to *limited ASP* control, where all of them are implemented and controlled by the CP.

Failing in managing the elasticity may lead to over-provisioning, hence, unnecessary costs paid to the CP, i.e. degrading the business return. It may also lead to under-provisioning which degrades the service quality delivered to the end-user and might force the ASP to compensate the committed violations by paying penalties.

In order to relieve the ASP from the complicated task of elasticity management, research works have been conducted to develop *autonomic elasticity management* solutions that enable the ASP to strike a balance between the tradeoffs it encounters. In the rest of this chapter, we use the terms *elasticity management* and *autonomic elasticity management* interchangeably.

This section presented cloud computing elasticity and defined the process of elasticity management. The different sub-processes and components of elasticity management were also introduced and discussed. In the coming sections, we provide taxonomy for classifying mechanisms and techniques employed to manage elasticity in the solutions described in the literature.

10.3.3 Analysis Grid

As more and more companies are migrating their business to the cloud, the question of *elasticity management* is gaining a considerable attention. Currently, there is an abundance of novel approaches addressing this issue. In the coming sections we propose a classification that:

- Draws the landscape of state-of-the-art elasticity management solutions, studies their characteristics and enumerates their different approaches
- Identifies the most important challenges and research directions currently shaping the research activity in this domain
- Provides an analysis grid that can be used as a base to better understand, compare, and eventually evaluate elasticity management solutions

This classification forms an analysis grid that has the following three major axes (c.f. Fig. 10.2):

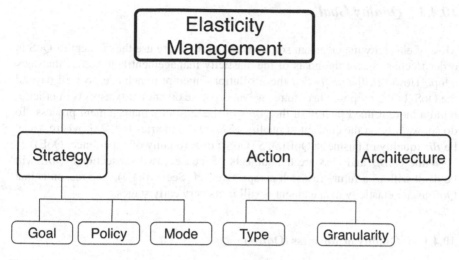

Fig. 10.2 Analysis grid of elasticity management solutions

- *Elasticity management strategy* identifying the strategy functions participating in the elasticity management decisions
- *Elasticity management actions* executed from the decisions issued by the strategy functions in order to provision resources from the cloud
- *Elasticity management architecture* that describes the overall organization of the elasticity management process

Each one of these major axes has a set of features. In the coming sections, we present an elaborate description of these axes and their features. For each of them, we also identify important research perspectives currently being investigated.

10.4   Elasticity Management Strategy

The problem of elasticity management can be seen as an optimization problem. Since the ASP is sandwiched between the CP and the SU, it seeks to deliver the optimal service quality to its SUs while satisfying its business goals (such as minimizing costs). Thus, the *strategy function* reflects:

- The strategic quality *goal*, or combination of goals, that the ASP is trying to achieve
- The *policies* that allow the *elasticity manager* to figure out *how* to achieve the strategic quality goals
- The *mode,* which indicates the manner in which the system interacts with the cloud ecosystem (either predictively or reactively)

In the next three subsections, we detail each one of these features.

10.4.1   Quality Goal

Most of elasticity management solutions in the literature use the concept of QoS in order to characterize the goals of the elasticity management approaches that they adopt. However, the *goals that* these solutions attempt to achieve go well beyond the QoS. In the proposed taxonomy, we incorporate other quality aspects in order to build a more refined picture of the *goals* of the elasticity management process. To do so, we rely on the concept of quality of X (QoX) metrics [68, 73], where X can be *Biz* (quality of business; QoBiz); S (QoS); or E (quality of experience; QoE).

While *QoBiz* and *QoS* are the subjects of the next two subsections, *QoE* will be dealt with as a future research perspective (c.f. Sect. 10.4.4). The reason is that QoE-aware elasticity management is still in its very early stages.

10.4.1.1   Quality of Business (QoBiz)

The QoBiz is a service provider-centric quality indicator that includes *quality attributes pertaining to business considerations, such as the service provider's revenue/profit, satisfaction* [20, 73]. QoBiz metrics are often expressed in monetary units. They include service price, revenue per user, revenue per transaction, provisioning cost and budget [69]. By combining these measures, QoBiz indicates the business profitability from the ASP perspective. Since cost reduction is the main reason pushing ASPs to migrate into the cloud, any efficient elasticity management solution must guarantee the optimal QoBiz.

Most of autonomic elasticity management solutions proposed in the literature take the ASP's QoBiz into consideration modelling it in different ways. From the study of 13 solutions dealing with QoBiz [12, 15, 26, 29, 42, 44, 47, 50, 52, 59, 64, 81, 83], we identified 7 key aspects that shape the QoBiz-awareness of elasticity management solutions:

- **ASP budget:** The ASP budget can be understood as the amount of money that the ASP is ready to pay to the CP in order to rent virtual resources. Many works taking ASP budget into account, consider it as a bound to be verified before renting new VMs.
- **Instance heterogeneity:** CPs may provide different VM sizes or flavors (Amazon EC2 offers small, medium, large and extra large instances). Each flavor may have a different computing capacity and cost. Being aware of the VM capacities and of their corresponding prices, the elasticity management solution can opt for the VMs configuration that minimizes the cost paid to the CP.
- **Multiple CPs:** As the cloud market is morphing into a highly competitive market, consulting resource prices from different CPs allows the elasticity manager to pick up resources with the minimal cost available in the market at any given moment. Nevertheless, currently this is still hindered by the *vendor lock-in* problem [6].
- **CP pricing policies:** CPs can adopt different pricing policies, such as *static-hourly pricing* or *auction-based pricing*. Choosing the offer with the most suitable

Table 10.1 QoBiz features in elasticity management solutions

QoBiz feature	Solution
ASP budget	[29, 50, 52, 59, 83]
Instance heterogeneity	[29, 47, 50, 64, 83, 81]
Multiple CPs	[52, 81]
CP pricing policies	
Static hourly pricing	[12, 26, 47, 50, 52], [64, 81]
Auction-based pricing	[15]
Fine-grained pricing	[29, 83]
BTU	[26, 42, 44, 47, 52]
Penalties	[12, 47, 44, 81]
Data transfer cost	[81]

pricing policy is important to optimize QoBiz of the ASP. Since the majority of CPs adopts static hourly pricing [14], the majority of elasticity management solutions assume a provider with this pricing policy.

- **Billing time units (BTU):** Most of CPs bill the ASP based on BTUs. Even if the VM is utilized only for a portion of the time unit and then released, the ASP pays the full time unit. Developing an elasticity management mechanism that takes BTUs into account and therefore does not release VMs if their BTU is not over might help the ASP in achieving optimal resource utilization.

- **Penalties:** Violating the SLA established with clients forces the ASP to compensate by paying penalties. The amount of this penalty is usually proportional to the amount of violation perpetrated and can also be a function of the client SLA type. Accounting for the penalties is important in order to maximize the QoBiz and manage the elasticity management accordingly.

- **Data transfer cost:** This is the cost charged by the CPs in exchange for transferring the data from the client machine to their datacenter. This cost, which is usually relatively high, is considered as an important problem obstructing the development of cloud computing [6].

As aforementioned, works in the literature approach the ASP's QoBiz from different perspectives and each one might account for one or more aspects as shown in Table 10.1.

Since cost saving is one of the most important factors encouraging ASP to move to the cloud, QoBiz is a very important quality goal. The study we conducted on state-of-the-art elasticity management solutions confirms this premise. QoBiz-awareness is a growing trend in elasticity management and is likely to play a central role as the cloud computing ecosystem morphs into a highly competitive and dynamic market. As for pricing policies, Table 10.1 shows that most of elasticity management solutions in the literature assume a CP with static-hourly pricing policy. This is mainly because the majority of CPs in today's market follows these pricing policies. In Sect. 10.4.4 we present some current research trends relevant to the CP pricing policy.

This subsection presented the first group of quality goals relating the ASP QoBiz. Next subsection introduces the second group of quality goals (i.e. QoS).

10.4.1.2 Quality of Service (QoS)

Unlike QoBiz, which is a subjective quality indicator, QoS is an objective one. As aforementioned in Sect. 10.2, QoS guarantees are stated in a contract called the SLA.

SLA is a legal document that establishes contractual relationship between a service provider and its users. The concept of SLA has been in use since the 1980s in a variety of areas [80]. Hence, there is no consensus on its definition. Verma *et al.* provide one of the widely accepted definitions [76]: *"An explicit statement of expectations and obligations that exist in a business relationship between two organizations: the service provider and the customer"*. Following the multiple definitions, numerous SLA languages have been proposed including WS-agreement by OGF [5] and WSLA [38] by IBM (for a comparison of different SLA languages see [80]).

In order to quantify the service level with regard to different QoS aspects (e.g. availability), the participating parties express that the service level should attain a specified Service Level Objective (SLO). According to Wilkes [79], SLOs *represent bounds on both the client and the service provider behavior.* Examples of SLOs include *maximal tolerated response time* or *the minimum guaranteed service availability*. What we call *SLO violation* occurs when an SLO condition is not met. In this case, most of the time, the party that caused the violation has to pay the penalty that is already specified in the SLOs.

Numerous QoS metrics can be used to measure each QoS aspect. For instance, *abandon rate* is a metric used to reflect the service *availability*. It consists in the ratio of the accepted service requests to the total number of user requests. The service *reliability* is another QoS aspect that is reflected by several QoS metrics, such as *mean time between failures* [63].

In the tripartite cloud system we introduced in Sect. 10.2, there are two types of providers (i.e. the CP and the ASP), as well as two types of clients (i.e. the ASP and the SU). For this reason, as introduced in Sect. 10.2, two types of SLAs are present (see Fig. 10.1). Since elasticity management is considered as an ASP-centric issue, we will limit our attention to SLA_{ASP-SU}.

Taking QoS goals into consideration when performing elasticity management means that the ASP allocates resources from the cloud in a manner that minimizes SLOs violation that in turn is likely to indicate the end-user satisfaction.

Next, we identify some of the key aspects that differentiate the approaches available in the literature. These aspects are important because the manner in which they are treated has significant implications on the elasticity management process. These are:

- **QoS metrics:** They are used to guide the elasticity management process. Some solutions use only low-level performance metrics derived from the monitoring services (e.g. central processing unit; CPU utilization), while other solutions rely on higher-level performance metrics stipulated as SLOs (e.g. response time).
- **Startup time:** This is the time needed to boot a VM instance and to make it ready to be used by the ASP.
- **Violations and penalties**: These are the penalties associated with SLA violations.

Table 10.2 QoS features in the literature

QoS related issues	Solution
Performance metrics	
CPU utilization or load balancer Data	[14, 26, 30, 46, 42, 51, 52, 59]
Response time	[12, 14, 26, 29, 30, 44, 46, 47, 50, 64, 81]
Startup time	[44, 50, 51, 81]
Violations and penalties	[12, 44, 47, 81]

As shown in Table 10.2, the majority of solutions included in this study utilize response time as a performance metric. CPU utilization level is only used by few solutions because it is a low-level performance indicator that is not used in SLAs as SLOs. In addition, the table reveals that most elasticity management solutions tend to ignore the VM startup time.

This subsection discussed *quality goal* the first feature of the *strategy* major axis. Next section presents *policy,* the second feature of the same axis.

10.4.2   Policy

After discussing the types of quality metrics (i.e. QoS, QoBiz) incorporated in the strategy function, this subsection discusses the method used to implement the strategy function. The classification proposed by Kephart et al. [40] to classify policies in autonomic systems is both valid and useful. Therefore, we use it to classify elasticity management policies. Their proposal distinguishes three main policy types used in autonomic systems:

1. Event—action rule policies;
2. Goal-based policies;
3. Utility and cost functions.

Event–Action Rules Event–action rules are used to specify *what* actions should be taken by an autonomic elasticity manager given the current situation or context (which is described as a set of events). A rule is triggered when an *event* happens. For instance, an event can be: the value of a performance metric (e.g. CPU utilization) crossing a predefined threshold. As discussed by [48], these rules might have one or more thresholds and can use one or more performance metrics. Also, some rules might utilize *inertia duration* to avoid oscillations.

The advantage of using rule-based control is that rules are easily expressed and understood by humans. However, event–action rules have also their drawbacks. First, specifying their parameters is a difficult task because setting the threshold needs precise ASP domain knowledge and might eventually require undertaking experiments. Still, the system can be subject to oscillations [23]. Second, since they are defined on the *state space*, the designer should ensure that this space is covered by the defined rules, which is not a straightforward task. Lastly, if the current state includes an event or more that activate more than one rule, the elasticity management system will have no clue on which rule to fire. Consequently, there is a possibility that the behavior of the system becomes non-deterministic. Assigning priorities to conflicting rules is a typical solution to this problem [40].

Multiple performance metrics can be integrated in one rule as done by [30] whose solution integrates CPU utilization, response time and network bandwidth utilization.

Because of their simplicity, numerous elasticity management solutions developed in the industry use rule-based systems, such as *Amazon Auto-Scaling* [4] and *Righ-Scale* [58]. However, beyond their apparent simplicity, choosing the right threshold is not an easy task. Furthermore, rules do not provide a powerful tool to achieve ASP QoBiz optimization. As consequence, most of rule-based elasticity management solutions are agnostic to ASP QoBiz.

Goal Policies In contrast to the rule policies that tell the system what to do in each state, goal policies define the desired states for the system. For instance, a goal policy can be expressed by the following expression: ResponseTime < t.

Hence, whereas event–action rules are defined on the *state space*, goal-based policies are defined on the *goal space*, which makes the latter easier to specify by human experts designing the ASP. However, goal policies can only tell the system what states are desirable and what states are not. All desired states are equally preferred and all undesired states are equally disliked by the system. Consequently, a system that uses goal policies cannot make appropriate tradeoffs [40].

Using goal policies in elasticity management solutions requires having a model of the system. Based on this model, the system knows how many resources are needed to achieve the specified goal. This model is constructed either analytically (e.g. queue theory) or empirically using benchmarking.

Whereas analytic models might work for a simple system, more complex systems require empirical performance models where the performance of each type of VMs is measured with different workloads, given different goals.

Utility and Cost Functions Utility functions are a concept borrowed from economics where *agents* are assumed to have *preferences*. A utility function maps these preferences into numerical values; a higher utility value means greater preferences [79]. In other words, the utility value is a measure of *the level of satisfaction an agent receives from any basket of goods and services* [8, 82]. Cost functions have the opposite meaning to utility functions. They define the cost a system needs to pay in a given situation. Intuitively, a rational system seeks to maximize its utility functions and to minimize its cost functions.

In contrast to rules and goal policies, utility/cost functions result in conflict-free decision strategies, because the system decides the actions that maximize/minimize its utility/cost. However, setting the utility function is not a straightforward task because they might require specifying multi-dimensional set of preferences [40].

When each party has a set of preferences, utility/cost function provide a powerful tool for making tradeoffs and thereby achieving the best possible outcomes. Similar to goal policies, using utility/cost functions requires having a performance model that is then used to seek optimal actions.

Table 10.3 Policy types in elasticity management solutions

Policy type	Solution
Rules	[14, 30, 42, 51, 59]
Goal policies	[14, 29, 46, 52]
Utility and cost functions	[12, 15, 26, 44, 47, 50, 52, 64, 72, 81, 83]

Table 10.4 Modes for elasticity management

Mode	Solution
Reactive	[12, 14, 15, 26, 29, 33, 46, 47, 52, 59, 72, 81]
Predictive	[12, 14, 33, 50, 64]

In the cloud computing ecosystem, utility and cost functions have been used to express the preferences of the CP and the ASP [72] and to capture the end-user (SU) preferences [15]. As noted by [15], using utility functions can be very efficient in the cloud ecosystem since it is composed of self-interested parties: the CP looks for optimizing the utilization of its cloud infrastructure and maximizing its revenue, the ASP seeks to minimize the price paid to the CP in exchange for the rented service and to maximize the revenue it obtains from its SU, and the SU desires an optimal service quality with the minimal cost.

Table 10.3 summarizes the policies followed by 18 elasticity management solutions.

As shown in Table 10.3, the majority of solutions studied in this chapter use utility/cost functions because, unlike goal-based policies they are capable of expressing tradeoffs; an inherent aspect of the elasticity management process.

This subsection presented *policy* the second feature of *strategy* the first major axis of our analysis grid. Next subsection introduces the third feature of the same axis.

10.4.3   Mode

Actions taken by the autonomic elasticity manager can be either *reactive* (i.e. actions triggered by measurements or events taking place in the cloud ecosystem) or *predictive* actions. In the latter case, the system is able, thanks to a prediction model, to forecast the workload coming to the system and to adapt accordingly. Predicting the environment behavior and acting in advance enable the autonomic elasticity management system to compensate for the delays caused by the VM startup time. Nevertheless, building a workload forecaster is an error-prone and complex task. Due to space limitations, we are not going to detail predictive elasticity management solutions in this chapter. Deep analysis of these techniques can be found in other works and surveys, such as [13, 34, 48].

As shown in Table 10.4, all rule policies are reactive because they can only be triggered when an event takes place (i.e. when a specified threshold is crossed).

The previous subsection presented the features of the first major axis of our analysis grid (i.e. *strategy*). Next subsection now presents some of the important challenges and research perspectives relating to this axis.

10.4.4 Research Perspectives

This subsection identifies some of the important challenges and research directions related to the *strategy function*. First, QoE, an SU-centric quality measure, is introduced and its potential utilization in the cloud ecosystem is discussed. Next, emerging alternative billing and pricing policies are presented. Finally, novel SLA models and languages will be introduced.

Quality of Experience (QoE)   Whereas QoBiz is an ASP-centric metric, QoE is a SU-centric metric. QoE is a subjective measure that captures the SU perception of the service quality and is defined by the ITU-T[1] to be: *"the overall acceptability of an application or service as perceived subjectively by the end-user"*.

In today's cloud computing market, where more personal and business applications are migrating to the cloud [32] and where competition drove prices to very low levels [22], the service quality will play the role of the differentiator [32]. Being user-centric makes QoE a suitable indicator of the SU satisfaction.

Using QoE as a tool to drive resource allocation is dubbed by the research community as *QoE management*. In order to perform QoE management, the QoE of the SU should be estimated. Then, remedies are applied, if needed, by the autonomic manager to restore the QoE to acceptable levels.

Mean opinion score (MOS) is probably the most popular subjective QoE measure. However, carrying out polls to estimate MOS can be a very tedious and costly task. Moreover, as noted by many scholars, MOS is not enough [31].

As more personal and interactive applications (e.g. cloud gaming [60]) are migrating into the cloud, recent research in the field of Cloud Computing pointed out that *"the concept of QoE has the potential to become the guiding paradigm for managing the quality in the Cloud"* [32]. However, most works that address the QoE in the context of cloud computing service still tackles this issue solely from network perspective (e.g. [35]). In addition to that, QoE is almost always used with video/audio services.

Integrating QoE in the cloud ecosystem is a promising research domain that is still in its early stages. In order to incorporate QoE metric in the elasticity management process, application-specific QoE models, relating the amount of the allocated resources from the cloud with the QoE of the SU, should be developed. In case of low (or unnecessarily too high) QoE levels, remedies should be applied in order to restore the QoE to acceptable levels.

In the field of computer networks, QoE has already been used by autonomic network managers as a metric to drive network resource allocation [1, 43, 55]. By capitalizing on these recent advances of QoE management in the field of computer networks, cloud QoE management can be developed to become an important factor in quality management in the cloud ecosystem.

---

[1] Telecommunication Standardization Sector (ITU-T) is a sector of the International Telecommunication Union (ITU).

Alternative Billing and Pricing Policies This subsection discusses two important aspects influencing the ASP QoBiz. First we introduce recent developments addressing the billing schemes and second we introduce novel alternative pricing policies.

Fine-grained Billing Schemes In today's cloud market, most of CPs adopt hourly-based static pricing schemes where virtualized resources are billed per hour according to the static price declared by the CPs [14]. A survey conducted by Casalicchio et al. [14] in 2011 showed that only 2 out of 20 CPs offer fine-grained BTUs of 5 min (CloudSigma [18]) and 1 min (VPSNET [78]), respectively. Almost all other CPs use one hour as the minimal BTU. Following this billing scheme, even when used for 5 min a VM will be billed for one hour. Fine-grained BTUs enhance the on-demand aspect of the acquired resources and enable the ASPs to benefit from real-time elasticity. Nevertheless, as a result of the current market constraints, only few works in the elasticity management considered using cloud resources rented with fine-grained BTUs.

Alternative Pricing Policies Although most of solutions in the literature address *on-demand* pricing policy, in which the CP declares a static per-BTU price, alternative pricing policies are already available in the Cloud market. In order to exploit idle resources in its datacenters Amazon EC2 leases these resources as *spot* instances. These *spot* instances follow an alternative pricing scheme: their prices are decided as a result of auctions, and therefore reflect the current offer and demand in the market. Since the introduction of spot instances, many research works have attempted to *deconstruct* and analyze their pricing polices [7, 36] and to develop optimal bidding strategies [53, 67, 77].

For instance in [15], Chen et al. presented an autonomic elasticity management solution that bids for spot instances from Amazon EC2. These instances are then used to build a video trans-coding application used by the client of this ASP. The algorithm proposed by the authors addresses the critical tradeoff between the SU satisfaction and the ASP profit.

The relatively low price of Amazon EC2 *spot* instances is the main driving force behind the significant increase in their adoption last year [45]. According to Matt Garman, the vice-president of Amazon EC2, the slope of adoption of Amazon EC2 *spot* instances is witnessing a significant increase because researchers in genomics and drug design as well as online advertising are increasingly using these instances to analyze terabytes of data.

The main disadvantage of using *spot* instances is their unreliability. When the market price exceeds the user bid price, *spot* instances will be de-allocated even without notifying the user. However, most of the aforementioned works address this problem by creating novel algorithms to maximize the reliability of *spot* instances.

Novel SLA Models and Languages SLA and QoS-management play essential roles in regulating the relationship between parties in the cloud ecosystem. Nevertheless, as noted by Serrano et al. in [63], QoS management in today's cloud computing market is done in an ad-hoc manner. The study we conducted on several elasticity management solutions confirms this conclusion. Solutions dealing with SLA/QoS awareness, each adopts an ad-hoc SLA and user-request model. Ad-hoc QoS management poses significant challenges to the performance and dependability of cloud service. To overcome this limitation, research efforts are being dedicated to propose unified SLA models and languages.

In [63], Serrano et al. introduce SLA-aware-Service (SLAaaS): a new cloud model that defines a non-functional interface, which exposes the SLA, associated with a cloud functional service. SLAaaS is orthogonal to the service delivery model (IaaS, PaaS, SaaS). Thus, it models SLAs binding different factors in the cloud ecosystem. For instance, in the tripartite ecosystem discussed in Sect. 10.2, SLAaaS can be employed to model both SLA_{CP-ASP} and SLA_{ASP-CP} (c.f. Fig. 10.1). In SLAaaS interface, the user selects QoS aspects he/she is interested in, and then specifies metrics he/she wants to use as indicators measuring this aspect (e.g. *response time*). Then, the user chooses the SLO (e.g. a threshold) she wants to apply for this metric.

In order to account for cloud-specific features and facilitate cloud SLA management, new SLA languages are being developed to reflect cloud-specific features, such as elasticity, agility and fluctuations [41].

CSLA [41] is a cloud SLA language based on WSLA [38] and the SLA@SOI project [65]. CSLA models QoS fluctuations and cloud uncertainty by introducing factors, such as *confidence* and *fuzziness*. The *confidence* variable indicates the compliance of SLO clauses, and *fuzziness* defines an acceptable margin around the target value of the SLO. In case of violation, the party that committed the violation must pay penalty proportional to the amount of the violation.

This section introduced and explained the *strategy function*, the first major axis of our taxonomy. Next section presents the second major axis, which describes actions that can be taken by the elasticity management process.

10.5 Elasticity Management Actions

In the last section, we described the facets of the strategy function focusing on metrics, policies and modes adopted by an elasticity management system. This section is about *actions*, the second major axis of such a system. This axis has two features:

- **Type** refers to the nature of actions usually defined by the API of the CP that can be executed by the elasticity manager to rent virtual resources from the CP.
- **Granularity** refers to the scope elasticity management actions: fine-grained level (i.e. per tier), or coarse-grained level (at the application level where an n-tier application is managed in a holistic manner).

Action *types* and *granularity* will be discussed in the coming two subsections.

10.5.1 Type

In our taxonomy, we distinguish between two types of elasticity management actions: *Replication* and *Resizing*.

Table 10.5 Actions type in elasticity management solutions

Action type	Solution
Replication	[12, 14, 15, 26, 29, 33, 44, 46, 47, 52, 59, 64, 72, 81]
Re-sizing	[29, 83]

Replication It is also called horizontal scaling. When the API of the CP allows replication, which is the case of most cps, the ASP (or its autonomic elasticity manager) adds or removes VMs on demand. VM instances come in different flavors. For instance, in Amazon EC2 the user can choose among the small, medium, large, extra-large sizes. In order to distribute the workload among the replicas, the ASP should either use a load-balancer as discussed in Sect. 10.3.2, or implement a customized Cloud-oriented scheduling algorithm that demonstrates useful properties, such as cost awareness or QoS-awareness.

Resizing It is also called vertical scaling. Replication offers only coarse-grained resources. This can be a limitation for elasticity management solutions. To overcome this problem, some research works are shifting toward resizing.

When resizing is enabled by the CP, CPU and memory resources can be added/removed to/from running VMs hereby giving the ASP a fine-grained control over the amount of resources to acquire and release from the cloud. Coupling fine-grained resource allocation with fine-grained pricing policies provides the ASP with more flexibility to cope with the varying demand of its clients. Nevertheless, as illustrated by [14] which provided a useful taxonomy of CPs in the market, the majority of CPs accepts only replication. Table 10.5 shows elasticity management action types used in the literature.

10.5.2   Granularity

Regardless of the *type* of the elasticity management actions executed, these actions can be undertaken on different abstraction or *granularity* levels. As discussed by [75] elasticity actions are implemented to perform either:

- **Per-tier management:** Most of works in the literature perform elasticity management for one tier only (the business tier) and ignore other tiers, such as storage tier, load-balancing tier, etc.
- **Multi-tier management:** This coarser granularity control spares the ASP from the burden of developing managers for each tier. Thus, a multi-tier application can be managed by a single high-level elasticity manager that can provision resources to different tiers in order to avoid bottlenecks, optimize resources and maximize the end-user satisfaction.

Most of the works discussed in this chapter fall into the first category, i.e. per-tier or tier-wise elasticity managers. Nevertheless, works presenting holistic (multi-tier) elasticity managers are gaining attention recently. Next, we discuss this feature.

The most common services hosted in the cloud have multi-tier topology. Typically, Web applications are composed of three tiers: (i) a front-end web service tier (ii) a middle application tier implementing the business logic (iii) a back-end hosting the storage tier (i.e. database). Thanks to the cloud's elasticity, each tier of the cloud-hosted application can be scaled to respond to the workload [29]. Works addressing multi-tier applications departs from the premise that these applications are subject to different types of workloads. Each type of workload stress one or more tiers. Thus, by detecting the bottlenecked tier and granting it enough resources, optimal resource utilization can be achieved.

In [33], Iqbal et al. present an elasticity management solution for a two-tier application composed of a Web server tier and a database tier. Two types of workloads are distinguished: static content requests which can be treated solely by the Web-server tier and dynamic content requests which stress both the Web service tier and the storage tier.

Based on the monitored response time and the request type, a proposed heuristic can detect bottlenecks and respond by adding new VMs to the corresponding tier. For instance, if the static request response time indicates saturation, the system responds by scaling the web server tier. As for releasing acquired VMs when the workload decreases, the authors utilize a predictive (c.f. Sect. 10.4.3) mode capable of estimating when to scale out resources.

Unlike the previous solution (i.e. [33]), which is agnostic to the cost paid to acquire cloud resources, Han et al. [29] present a cost-aware elasticity management solution. Their approach utilizes cost-aware criteria to detect and analyze bottlenecks within a 5-tier cloud-hosted application. The authors devise an algorithm that handles changing workloads of multi-tier applications by adaptively scaling up and down bottlenecked tiers. In order to estimate the current application performance model, i.e. the amount of virtual resources needed to restore the response time to the desired level, the Cost-Aware Scaling (CAS) algorithm relies on an analytic model that capture the application behavior.

Before closing this section, which introduced the second major axis used by our taxonomy, the next subsection introduces the most important challenges and research perspectives relating to *elasticity management actions*.

10.5.3 Research Perspectives

The research perspectives presented in this article are twofold: (i) First, novel approaches, adopting fine-grained cloud resource provisioning are discussed. (ii) Second, *autonomic cloud computing* is introduced. This concept is an emerging topic that applies *autonomic computing* as a method to administrate complex cloud systems.

Fine-grained Cloud Resource Provisioning As discussed in the previous section, most of elasticity management works presented in this chapter use replication in order to scale the applications hosted in the cloud, i.e. adding VMs when the demand increases and releasing them when the demand decreases. The main reason behind this tendency is that most of the CPs do not allow VM resizing. Nevertheless, the coarse-grained resource allocation mechanisms allowed by replication, even when multiple VM sizes are available, imposes important limitations on the effectiveness of the elasticity management process; it implies additional resource provisioning overhead and leads to over-provisioning.

As demonstrated by [19], developing elastic VMs that can be resized on-the-fly allows overcoming the aforementioned limitations of replication- based cloud resource provisioning. Using such elastic VMs implies less resource consumption and less SLO violations. However, in order to utilize these efficient elastic VMs, on-the-fly VM resizing should be offered by CP, which is rarely the case in today's market [14]. To overcome this obstacle, some elasticity management solutions are adopting *VM substitution* to simulate resizing [59]. A VM is replaced by a bigger or smaller VM according to the amount of needed resource.

Autonomic Cloud Computing *Autonomic cloud computing* is an emerging research subject that is motivated by the complexity of cloud systems and the need to develop automated cloud management mechanisms. Applying the recent developments of *autonomic computing* technology [39] can go beyond autonomic elasticity management. Furthermore, the potential benefits of such cooperation between these two domains are reciprocal. On the one hand, the main characteristics of autonomic computing [39] (i.e. self-monitoring, self-repairing, self-optimizing, etc.) can prove to be very useful to overcome several actual challenges in the cloud computing ecosystems including platform optimization and energy-efficient scheduling [10]. On the other hand, cloud computing constitutes an interesting domain to study the use of autonomic features because of their dynamic nature and complexity [10].

This section discussed the second major axis in our analysis grid. This axis classifies *actions* taken by elasticity managers, their types and granularities. Next section, discusses the third major axis of the proposed taxonomy.

10.6 Elasticity Management Architecture

Almost all elasticity management solutions both in the academic literature and in industry have centralized architectures. Even when the solution is decomposed in different modules following, for instance, the monitor-analyze-plan-execute (MAPE) architecture [39], still the planning and decision-making processes are centralized in one component. This section gives an overview of the few *decentralized* elasticity management solutions available in the literature.

In [72], the authors present a decentralized architecture inspired from *unity* [71]. Their architecture is composed of multiple *application managers* each being responsible for provisioning resources for a different cloud-hosted application. Each one of these managers looks for maximizing its utility function by acquiring sufficient resource to fulfil its application needs. A *resource arbiter* plays the main role in this architecture. It is responsible for allocating resources to the application managers in a manner that minimizes the provider cost.

Chieu et al. [16] develop an architecture capable of dynamic resource allocation via distributed decision in the cloud environment. In this architecture, each
resource is managed by a capacity and utility agent (CUA) that seeks to maximize
its own utility by making its own utilization decision based on the current system
and workload characteristics. This multi-agent system is coordinated and managed
by the distributed capacity agent manager (DCAMgr) which is responsible for managing and communicating with the participating agents and directing the resource
adjustment actions to the target systems.

In [15], the authors develop an elasticity management solution in which the ASP
agent integrates the end-user preferences in scheduling resource provisioning processes. The preferences of end-users are modelled by utility functions. Based on
this model, the ASP proposes tradeoffs or concessions to guarantee the end-user
satisfaction minimize the cost paid to the CP.

QoE4Cloud [37], uses distributed agents to collect information about the current
level of QoE of the end-user (c.f. Sect. 10.4.4). Whereas the monitoring service
is distributed in this architecture, the elasticity management decision making is
centralized.

Although most of elasticity management solutions in academia and the industry
are centralized, using multi-agent systems in the cloud ecosystem is an emerging
trend that will be discussed in the next subsection.

10.6.1 Research Perspectives

Because of the similarities between the multi-agent and cloud computing technologies, the near future is likely to carry important opportunities of synergy between
them [70]. On the one hand, since cloud computing offers on-demand and seemingly
unlimited resources, cloud computing technologies can provide a testbed for large
scale and computationally intensive multi-agent systems. On the other hand, multi-
agent systems can be used to endow the cloud ecosystem with intelligence needed
to manage this complex environment.

Recently, multi-agent systems are being used to realize intelligent assistant agents
capable of service composition and brokering in cloud ecosystems [17, 24, 28]. SLA
negotiation is a fertile domain in which the self-interestedness of multi-agent systems
can be exploited efficiently. However, most of works in the literature dealing with
SLA negotiation address the relationship between the CP and their clients (i.e. the
ASP) and ignore the relationship between the ASP and the SU.

Son et al. [66] present a multi-issue negotiation mechanism for cloud service
reservation. This mechanism supports both price and timeslot negotiations and enables the CP and the ASP to make tradeoffs between the price and timeslot and
therefore achieve win-win agreements.

In the same context, Zheng et al. [82], study the merits of different negotiation
strategies (i.e. concessions and tradeoffs) and their effectiveness in making mutually
accepted settlements between the CPs and their users.

In summary, multi-agent systems have the potential to scaffold cloud computing technology with the intelligence needed in the complex cloud ecosystems. As for elasticity management, we did not find any work proposing a decentralized multi-agent elasticity management system. In such a system, agents can be used to represent the conflicting interests and quality metrics (QoBiz, QoE, QoS) of different actors (CP, ASP, SU) in the cloud ecosystem. As noted by many authors, market-based mechanisms are likely to shape the future of cloud computing technologies. Decentralized and multi-agent systems have the potential to implement market dynamics in this agile and distributed computing ecosystem. Nevertheless, considerable efforts need to be dedicated in order to capture and represent the preferences and the business logic of each of the participating parties. Furthermore, advances in the fields of automated conflict resolutions and agreement technologies need to be adapted and utilized in the cloud ecosystem.

The previous three sections introduced and explained the three major axes used in the classification we propose. In the next section, we present and analyze three recent and representative elasticity management solutions to illustrate our purpose.

10.7   Analysis of Existing Solutions

In this section, we analyze in detail three [47, 81] recent elasticity management solutions. These solutions were selected based on their novelty and on their scientific contributions.

10.7.1   *Cost-aware Cloud Service Request Scheduling for SaaS Providers*

In the paper [47], Liu et al. develop a cost-aware elasticity management solution that takes into account a personalized user request and the current workload. The authors devise efficient resource provisioning and scheduling policies that (i) satisfy the end-user by meeting the SLA constraints and (ii) minimize the cost incurred to the CP. The authors formulate the problem as an optimization one. In order to solve it, the authors develop a genetic algorithm called cost-aware service request scheduling based on genetic algorithm (CSRSGA) that is able to achieve the specified objectives in reasonable time.

To verify the effectiveness of their algorithm, the authors conduct simulation-based experiments using EC2 on-demand instances. The obtained results demonstrate that the CSRSGA algorithm outperforms other cost-aware algorithms in terms of virtual resource utilization, rate of return on investment and operation profit.

Next we study this solution based on the analysis grid we presented earlier. First we discuss the *strategy used* by this work. Second, we describe the used *actions* and finally we study its *architecture*.

Elasticity Management Strategy As quality goals (c.f. Sect. 10.4.1), this solution incorporates both QoBiz and QoS goals as follows:

The CSRSGA algorithm seeks to optimize the QoBiz of the ASP. This algorithm takes into account penalties' costs and attempts to avoid them. The algorithm assumes that the cloud resources are rented from a CP following the *on-demand* pricing policy with different VM flavors (sizes). Prices depend on the capacities of the flavors and they are billed every hour. The algorithm accounts for coarse-grained BTUs (hours) and therefore it does not release an instance until its billing unit is completely over. As for QoS goals, this solution proposes its own SLA model that stipulates the following issues:

- t_s: is the standard request completion time by the standard VM instance (the capacity of the standard VM instance is defined by the user and is used to provide relative definitions of other instances capacity).
- *Mbdt*: is the maximum processing delay without any penalty. In order to achieve the maximum revenue, the ASP should try to complete the request within this time.
- *deadline*: is the request upper limit. If the processing time of the user's request crosses this limit, the ASP must pay a penalty.
- *pr* is the penalty rate which is a function of the violation that took place.

Unlike the majority of elasticity management solutions, which ignores the VM startup time, this solution takes it into account in order to achieve a better QoS.

As a policy, the authors use cost functions. They formulate the problem as an optimization problem subject to the aforementioned constraints. To find the optimal solution, the authors resort to a genetic algorithm, which identifies the most profitable VM configurations to provision in reasonable time. As shown in Table 10.4, the algorithm does not function in a predictive *mode*, instead it relies on a reactive elasticity management mode.

Elasticity Management Actions Similar to most of other elasticity management solutions, the action type adopted by this solution is *replication*. *Resizing* is not allowed. Concerning the actions' *granularity*, this solution implements one-tier elasticity management.

Elasticity Management Architecture The *architecture* of this solution is monolithic. Elasticity management is carried out by a single entity.

10.7.2 SLA-based Admission Control for an SaaS Provider

This paper [81] presents an innovative elasticity management solution that enables SaaS providers (ASP in our terminology) to effectively use public cloud resources to maximize their profit by minimizing the cost and improving the customer satisfaction level. The authors propose an admission control mechanism capable of maximizing the number of accepted requests while guaranteeing the needed service quality. The authors evaluate their proposed solution using CloudSim [11]. The results demonstrate that their algorithm achieve up to 40 % of improvement to the traditional techniques found in the literature.

As done with the previous paper, next we study this solution based on the analysis grid we presented earlier:

Elasticity Management Strategy As quality goals (c.f. Sect. 10.4.1), this solution incorporates both QoBiz and QoS goals as follows:

This paper elaborates an advanced model of the QoBiz of the ASP. Since the emergence of the cloud computing paradigm, data-transfer cost has been identified as an important cost concern hampering the adoption of the cloud computing paradigm [6]. To the best of our knowledge, only few elasticity management solutions model this important factor and this paper is one of them. In addition to that, the algorithms presented in this paper take into account multiple possible CPs, i.e. the ASP can choose to provision resources from the CP that minimize its costs. Moreover, this work takes into account different VM flavors (sizes), their different capacities and their corresponding costs. Also, in order to maximize the ASP profit, this solution presents strategies capable of minimizing the SLA violation, which also leads to customer satisfaction.

As for QoS goals, this solution proposes its own SLA model that stipulates the following issues:

- **Deadline:** The maximum time the user is ready to wait for the result.
- **Penalty rate ratio**: A ratio for consumer compensation if the SaaS provider misses the deadline.

Unlike the previous solutions (i.e. [47]), this one does not take into account VM startup time.

As an elasticity management policy, the authors devise costs functions that capture the ASP's QoBiz and the end-user satisfaction. Then, they develop four heuristic admission control strategies that can be coupled with three resource provisioning and scheduling algorithms. Based on its business objectives, the ASP chooses a suitable algorithm. This solution utilizes reactive resource provisioning mode and do not develop a predictive model.

Elasticity Management Actions Similar to [47], this solution uses only replication. Resizing is not allowed. In addition to that, the solution performs one-tier elasticity management.

Elasticity Management Architecture The *architecture* of this solution is monolithic. Elasticity management is carried out by a single entity.

10.7.3   Integrated and Autonomic Cloud Resource Scaling

In this work [30], the authors develop a rule-based elasticity management system called Autonomic Cloud Resource Scaler (IACRS) that addresses some of the limitations of traditional rule-based elasticity management mechanisms (c.f. Sect. 10.4.2). In contrast to the other two aforediscussed works [47, 81], the elasticity management solution proposed by [30] is completely agnostic of the cost-associated with VMs. Also, the article does not provide tests to evaluate the proposed algorithms.

Next we study this solution based on the analysis grid we presented earlier:

Elasticity Management Strategy Almost all rule based elasticity management solutions are agnostic of the QoBiz of the ASP and this article is not an exception.

As for aforesaid QoS goals, this article elaborates a rich rule engine capable of incorporating multiple performance metrics:

- CPU utilization.
- Response time.
- Network load.
- Delay and jitter.

In order to retrieve these different performance metrics, the authors employ various monitoring techniques.

Concerning the policy type used, IACRS utilizes rules. The authors develop a sophisticated rule-based system. IACRS uses elasticity management rules that take into account multiple events correlated with one another. For instance, the authors propose the following rule: *Add a new VM when both the CPU load of VM1 and the response time to it from a customer edge router are high.*

The author's assumption behind this rule is that the high CPU load may have caused high response time. Hence, the inferred solution is to acquire a new VM and split the load. In addition to its relatively rich performance metrics incorporation, the algorithm employs also an advanced thresholding mechanism. In particular, the algorithm uses four thresholds: an upper threshold *ThrU*, *ThrbU*—a threshold slightly lower than *ThrU*, *ThrL*—the lower threshold, and *ThoL* which is slightly above *ThrL*. In order to avoid oscillations, IACRS uses a *duration* parameter specified in seconds that is used for checking the persistence of the metric value above/below ThrU/ThrL and *ThrbU/ThroL*. Based on the four thresholds and the two duration parameters, the authors provide a set of heuristic rules that infer when it is necessary to provision resources from the cloud or release already acquired resources.

Elasticity Management Actions This solution adopts one-tier elasticity management granularity in which only replication is allowed.

Elasticity Management Architecture Like the other two discussed solutions, this chapter adopts a monolithic architecture.

The previous three subsections presented three selected elasticity management solutions in details. Table 10.6 provides a synthesis of these solutions using our analysis grid and shows how our analysis grid is used as a common ground to study and compare different elasticity management solutions.

Table 10.6 Comparison of selected solutions

Axis	Solution	Liu et al. [47]	Wu et al. [81]	Hasan et al. [30]
Strategy	QoBiz	Instance heterogeneity, BTU and penalties, static hourly-pricing	Instance heterogeneity, different CPs, penalties, data transfer cost, static hourly-pricing	Unaware
	QoS	RT, startup time	RT	CPU utilization, RT, network load, delay, jitter
	Policy	Cost functions	Cost functions	Rules
	Mode	Reactive	Reactive	Reactive
Action	Type	Replication	Replication	Replication
	Granularity	One-tier	One-tier	One-tier
Architecture		Monolithic	Monolithic	Monolithic

10.8   Conclusion and Future Work

This chapter introduced elasticity management in the domain of cloud computing. It is an ASP-centric process by which the ASP addresses the important tradeoff between its customers' satisfaction and its business goals. In addition to the ASP, we highlighted the SU and the CP that plays a role of utmost importance in this process. Being sandwiched between the CP and the SU, the ASP rents virtual resources from the CP to build its own services and sell them to its SUs in exchange for fees.

In order to help the ASPs manage the cloud elasticity, research efforts reported in the literature have proposed several autonomic elasticity management solutions. This chapter provides an analysis grid for studying and classifying the abundance of solutions in the literature. This analysis grid:

- Draws the landscape of state-of-the-art elasticity management solutions, studies their characteristics and enumerates their different approaches;
- Provides a common ground for comparing and understanding elasticity management solutions relatively to each other;
- Identifies the most important challenges and research directions currently shaping the research activity in this domain.

This analysis grid is organized around three major axes. The first axis describes the *elasticity management strategy* which characterizes the quality *goals* of the elasticity management process, defines the *policies* used to guide it, and describes its *modes* of interactions between this process and the cloud ecosystem. The second axis is focused on *actions* undertaken as a result of the elasticity management process. Actions have two features: the *type*, which describes the nature of the elasticity management actions, and the *granularity*, which characterizes the level on which these actions are applied. Finally, the third axis studies the *architecture* adopted by elasticity management solutions. In addition, for each one of these three major axes, we identified the most important research perspectives and challenges that are being addressed by the research community.

Based on this analysis grid, we have provided a detailed analysis of three selected elasticity management solutions.

As noted by [48], the domain of cloud elasticity management still lacks formal methodologies for comparing the merits of different solutions. The analysis grid that we presented in this chapter could be a step in this direction. For instance, based on the *quality goals* identified in this chapter, different scoring metrics could be developed to compare the performance of two given solutions.

A next step in this direction would be to develop elasticity management testbeds. These testbeds can be then used to define scenarios to compare different elasticity management solutions.

References

1. Agboma F, Liotta A (2006) QoE-aware QoS management. In: Proceedings of the 6th international conference on advances in mobile computing and multimedia, MoMM '08, ACM, New York, USA, 2008, pp 111–116
2. Amazon elastic compute cloud (amazon ec2). http://cloudcomputing.sys-con.com/node/612375. Accessed 20 July 2013
3. Amazon simple storage service (amazon s3). http://aws.amazon.com/s3/. Accessed 20 July 2013
4. Amazon Web Services Auto scaling http://aws.amazon.com/autoscaling/. Accessed 20 July 2013
5. Andrieux A, Czaikowski K, Dan A et al (2007) Web services agreement specification (ws-agreement). Open grid forum, 2007
6. Armbrust M, Fox A, Griffith R et al (2010) Above the clouds: a view of cloud computing. Technical report, 2010
7. Ben-Yehuda OA, Ben-Yehuda M, Schuster A, Tsafrir D (2011) Deconstructing Amazon ec2 spot instance pricing. In: IEEE third international conference on cloud computing technology and science (CloudCom). IEEE, 2011, pp 304–311
8. Besanko D, Braeutigam R (2010) Microeconomics. Wiley, Canada
9. Buyya R, Yeo CS, Venugopal S, Broberg J, Brandic I (2009) Cloud computing and emerging IT platforms: vision, hype, and reality for delivering computing as the 5th utility. Future Gener Comput Syst 25(6):599–616
10. Buyya R, Calheiros RN, Li X (2012) Autonomic cloud computing: open challenges and architectural elements. In: Third international conference on emerging applications of information technology (EAIT). IEEE, 2012, pp 3–10
11. Calheiros RN, Ranjan R, Beloglazov A, De Rose CA, Buyya R (2011) Cloudsim: a toolkit for modeling and simulation of cloud computing environments and evaluation of resource provisioning algorithms. Softw: Pract Exp 41(1):23–50
12. Cardellini V, Casalicchio E, Lo Presti F, Silvestri L (2011) Sla-aware resource management for application service providers in the cloud. In: First international symposium on network cloud computing and applications (NCCA), IEEE, 2011, pp 20–27
13. Caron E, Desprez F, Muresan A et al (2010) Forecasting for cloud computing on-demand resources based on pattern matching. Technical report, 2010
14. Casalicchio E, Silvestri L (2012) Mechanisms for sla provisioning in cloud-based service providers. Comput Netw 75(3):795–810

15. Chen J, Wang C, Zhou B, Sun L, Lee YC, Zomaya AY (2011) Tradeoffs between profit and customer satisfaction for service provisioning in the cloud. In: Proceedings of the 20th international symposium on high performance distributed computing, ACM, 2011, pp 229–238

16. Chieu TC, Chan H (2011) Dynamic resource allocation via distributed decisions in cloud environment. In: 8th international conference on e-business engineering (ICEBE). IEEE, 2011, pp 125–130

17. Clark K, Warnier M, Brazier FM (2012) An intelligent cloud resource allocation service. In: Proceedings of the 2nd international conference on cloud computing and services science (Closer 2012), 2012

18. Cloud sigma. http://www.cloudsigma.com/. Accessed 20 July 2013

19. Dawoud W, Takouna I, Meinel C, (2012) Elastic virtual machine for fine-grained cloud resource provisioning. In: Venkata Krishna P, Rajashekhara Babu P, Ariwa E (eds) Global trends in computing and communication systems. Springer, Berlin, pp 11–25

20. Di Nitto E, Karastoyanova D et al (2009) S-cube: addressing multidisciplinary research challenges for the internet of services. In: Future Internet Assembly, pp 263–272

21. Dropbox. https://www.dropbox.com/. Accessed 20 July 2013

22. Durkee D (2010) Why cloud computing will never be free. Queue 8(4):20

23. Dutreilh X, Rivierre N, Moreau A et al (2010) From data center resource allocation to control theory and back. In: IEEE 3rd international conference on cloud computing (CLOUD), 2010, IEEE, 2010, pp 410–417

24. Fan CT, Wang WJ, Chang YS (2010) Agent-based service migration framework in hybrid cloud. In: IEEE 13th international conference on high performance computing and communications (HPCC), 2011, IEEE, 2011, pp 887–892

25. Galante G, Bona L (2012) A survey on cloud computing elasticity. In: IEEE fifth international conference on utility and cloud computing (UCC), 2012, IEEE, 2012, pp 263–270

26. Genaud S, Gossa J (2011) Cost-wait trade-offs in client-side resource provisioning with elastic clouds. In: IEEE international conference on cloud computing (CLOUD), 2011, IEEE, 2011, pp 1–8

27. Google app engine. http://appengine.google.com. Accessed 20 July 2013

28. Gutierrez-Garcia JO, Sim KM (2010) Self-organizing agents for service composition in cloud computing. In: IEEE second international conference on cloud computing technology and science (CloudCom), 2010, IEEE, 2010, pp 59–66

29. Han R, Ghanem MM, Guo L et al (2012) Enabling cost-aware and adaptive elasticity of multi-tier cloud applications. Future Gener Comput Syst 32:82–98

30. Hasan MZ, Magana E, Clemm A et al (2012) Integrated and autonomic cloud resource scaling. In: Network operations and management symposium (NOMS), 2012 IEEE, 2012, pp 1327–1334

31. Hobfeld T, Schatz R, Egger S (2011) Sos: the mos is not enough! In: Third international workshop on quality of multimedia experience (QoMEX), 2011, IEEE, 2011, pp 131–136

32. Hobfeld T, Schatz R, Varela M, Timmerer C (2012) Challenges of QoE management for cloud applications. IEEE Commun Mag 50(4):28–36

33. Iqbal W, Dailey MN, Carrera D, Janecek P (2011) Adaptive resource provisioning for read intensive multi-tier applications in the cloud. Future Gener Comput Syst 27(6):871–879

34. Islam S, Keung J, Lee K, Liu A (2012) Empirical prediction models for adaptive resource provisioning in the cloud. Future Gener Comput Syst 28(1):155–162

35. Jarschel M, Schlosser D, Scheuring S, Hossfeld T (2011) An evaluation of QoE in cloud gaming based on subjective tests. In: 2011 Fifth international conference on innovative mobile and internet services in ubiquitous computing (IMIS), IEEE, July 2011, pp 330–335

36. Javadi B, Thulasiramy RK, Buyya R (2011) Statistical modeling of spot instance prices in public cloud environments. In: 2011 Fourth IEEE international conference on utility and cloud computing (UCC), IEEE, 2011, pp 219–228

37. Kafetzakis E, Koumaras H, Kourtis MA, Koumaras V (2012) QoE4CLOUD: a QoE-driven multidimensional framework for cloud environments. In: 2012 international conference on telecommunications and multimedia (TEMU), Aug 2012, pp 77–82

38. Keller LH (2003) The wsla framework: specifying and monitoring service level agreements for web services. J Netw Syst Manage 11(1):57–81
39. Kephart JO, Chess DM (2003) The vision of autonomic computing. Computer 36(1):41–50
40. Kephart JO, Walsh WE (2004) An artificial intelligence perspective on autonomic computing policies. In: Fifth IEEE international workshop on policies for distributed systems and networks, POLICY 2004, Proceedings, IEEE, 2004, pp 3–12
41. Kouki Y, Ledoux T (2012) CSLA: a language for improving cloud SLA management. In: Proceedings of the international conference on cloud computing and services science, Porto, Portugal, Apr 2012, pp 0–0
42. Kupferman J, Silverman J, Jara P, Browne J (2009) Scaling into the cloud. CS270-advanced operating systems, 2009
43. Latré S, De Turck F (2012) Autonomic quality of experience management of multimedia networks. In: Network operations and management symposium (NOMS), 2012 IEEE, 2012, pp 872–879
44. Leitner P, Hummer W, Satzger B et al (2012) Cost-efficient and application sla-aware client side request scheduling in an infrastructure-as-a-service cloud. In: 2012 IEEE 5th international conference on cloud computing (CLOUD), IEEE, 2012, pp 213–220
45. Levy (2013) Amazon's cheaper cloud services—up to a point. *BloombergBusinessWeek*. Online; accessed 20-July-2013.
46. Lim H, Babu S, Chase J, Parekh S (2009) Automated control in cloud computing: challenges and opportunities. In: Proceedings of the 1st workshop on automated control for datacenters and clouds, 2009
47. Liu Z, Wang S, Sun Q et al (2013) Cost-aware cloud service request scheduling for saas providers. Comput J 2013 57(2): 291–301
48. Lorido-Botrán T, Miguel-Alonso J, Lozano JA (2012) Auto-scaling techniques for elastic applications in cloud environments. Department of Computer Architecture and Technology, University of Basque Country, Technical Report. EHU-KAT-IK-09–12, 2012
49. Mahmood Z (2011) Cloud computing: characteristics and deployment approaches. In: 2011 IEEE 11th international conference on computer and information technology (CIT), IEEE, 2011, pp 121–126
50. Mao M, Li J, Humphrey M (2010) Cloud auto-scaling with deadline and budget constraints. In: 2010 11th IEEE/ACM international conference on grid computing (GRID), IEEE, 2010, pp 41–48
51. Marshall P, Keahey K, Freeman T (2010) Elastic site: using clouds to elastically extend site resources. In: 2010 10th IEEE/ACM international conference on cluster, cloud and grid computing (CCGrid), IEEE, May 2010, pp 43–52
52. Marshall P, Tufo H, Keahey K (2012) Provisioning policies for elastic computing environments. In: Parallel and distributed processing symposium workshops & PhD forum (IPDPSW), 2012 IEEE 26th international, IEEE, 2012, pp 1085–1094
53. Mazzucco M, Dumas M (2011) Achieving performance and availability guarantees with spot instances. In: 2011 IEEE 13th international conference on high performance computing and communications (HPCC), IEEE, 2011, pp 296–303
54. Mell P, Grance T (2011) The nist definition of cloud computing (draft). NIST Special Publication 800:145, 2011
55. Menkovski V, Exarchakos G, Liotta A (2010) Machine learning approach for quality of experience aware networks. In: 2010 2nd international conference on intelligent networking and collaborative systems (INCOS), IEEE, Nov 2010, pp 461–466
56. Owens D (2010) Securing elasticity in the cloud. Commun ACM 53(6):10
57. Qian H, Medhi D, Trivedi K (2011) A hierarchical model to evaluate quality of experience of online services hosted by cloud computing. In: 2011 IFIP/IEEE international symposium on integrated network management (IM), 2011, pp 105–112
58. Right scale cloud management. http://www.rightscale.com/. Accessed 20 July 2013
59. Rodero-Merino L, Vaquero L, Gil V et al (2010) From infrastructure delivery to service management in clouds. Future Gener Comput Syst 26(8):1226–1240
60. Ross PE (2009) Cloud computing's killer app: gaming. Spectrum IEEE 46(3):14–14

61. Sakr S, Liu A (2012) Sla-based and consumer-centric dynamic provisioning for cloud databases. In: IEEE 5th international conference on cloud computing (CLOUD), 2012, IEEE, 2012, pp 360–367

62. Schubert L, Jeffery KG, Neidecker-Lutz B (2010) The future of cloud computing: opportunities for European cloud computing beyond 2010: expert Group Report. European Commission, Information Society and Media, 2010

63. Serrano D, Bouchenak S, Kouki Y (2013) Towards QoS-oriented SLA guarantees for online cloud services. In: IEEE/ACM international symposium on cluster, cloud and grid computing (CCGrid 2013), 2013, pp 0–0

64. Sharma U, Shenoy P, Sahu S, Shaikh A (2011) A cost-aware elasticity provisioning system for the cloud. In: 2011 31st international conference on distributed computing systems (ICDCS), IEEE, 2011, pp 559–570

65. Sla@soi. http://sla-at-soi.eu/. Accessed 20 July 2013

66. Son S, Sim KM (2012) A price-and-time-slot-negotiation mechanism for cloud service reservations. IEEE Trans Syst Man Cybern Part B: Cybern 42(3):713–728

67. Song Y, Zafer M, Lee KW (2012) Optimal bidding in spot instance market. In: INFOCOM, 2012 Proceedings IEEE, Orlando, March 2012, pp 190–198

68. Stankiewicz R, Cholda P, Jajszczyk A (2011) Qox: what is it really? Commun Mag IEEE 49(4):148–158

69. Stojanovic M (2012) Factors affecting service provider's quality of business in ngn environment. Center for Quality, 2012.

70. Talia D (2012) Clouds meet agents: toward intelligent cloud services. Internet Comput IEEE 16(2):78–81

71. Tesauro G, Chess DM, Walsh WE et al (2004) A multi-agent systems approach to autonomic computing. In: Proceedings of the third international joint conference on autonomous agents and multiagent systems-Vol 1, IEEE Computer Society, Washington, DC, 2004, pp 464–471

72. Van HN, Tran FD, Menaud JM (2009) Sla-aware virtual resource management for cloud infrastructures. In: Ninth IEEE international conference on computer and information technology, 2009. CIT'09, volume 1, IEEE, 2009, pp 357–362

73. Van Moorsel A (2001) Metrics for the internet age: quality of experience and quality of business. In: Fifth international workshop on performability modeling of computer and communication systems, vol 34, pp 26–31. Citeseer, 2001

74. Vaquero LM, Rodero-Merino L, Caceres J, Lindner M (2008) A break in the clouds: towards a cloud definition. SIGCOMM Comput Commun Rev 39(1):2008

75. Vaquero LM, Rodero-Merino L, Buyya R (2011) Dynamically scaling applications in the cloud. ACM SIGCOMM Comput Commun Rev 41(1):45–52, 2011

76. Verma DC (2004) Service level agreements on ip networks. Proc IEEE 92(9):1382–1388

77. Voorsluys W, Garg SK, Buyya R (2001) Provisioning spot market cloud resources to create cost-effective virtual clusters. In: Xiang Y, Cuzzocrea A, Hobbs M (eds) Algorithms and architectures for parallel processing. Springer, Berlin, pp 395–408

78. Vps.net. http://vps.net/. Accessed 20 July 2013

79. Wilkes J (2008) Utility functions, prices, and negotiation. Market oriented grid and utility computing. Wiley series on parallel and distributed computing, pp 67–88

80. Wu L, Buyya R (2010) Service level agreement (sla) in utility computing systems. arXiv preprint arXiv:1010.2881

81. Wu L, Kumar Garg S, Buyya R (2012) Sla-based admission control for a software-as-a-service provider in cloud computing environments. J Comput Syst Sci 78(5):1280–1299

82. Zheng X, Martin P, Brohman K (2012) Cloud service negotiation: concession vs. tradeoff approaches. In: Proceedings of the 2012 12th IEEE/ACM international symposium on cluster, cloud and grid computing (ccgrid 2012), IEEE Computer Society, Ottawa, 13–16 May 2012, pp 515–522

83. Zhu Q, Agrawal G (2010) Resource provisioning with budget constraints for adaptive applications in cloud environments. IEEE Trans on Serv Comput 5(4):497–511

Chapter 11
From Cloud Management to Cloud Governance

Teodor-Florin Fortis and Victor Ion Munteanu

Abstract For some time now, with the full support of cloud computing technologies, it has become possible for enterprises of all sizes to access new business opportunities, thus repositioning themselves in the global IT market. Advancements in cloud interoperability, with important developments of platform as a service (PaaS) and cloud management solutions, have enabled an increasing number of cloud services which, in turn, have led to additional requirements for integration at a superior level: the cloud governance. Moreover, current cloud migration patterns suggest that additional mechanisms in cloud services automation and management are required, in close relation with a fully automated support for the lifecycle of cloud services. This chapter discusses existing trends in cloud migration focusing on solutions which facilitate it, with an emphasis on cloud management and cloud governance, and the relationship between them.

Keywords Cloud computing · Cloud governance · Cloud management · Cloud resource broker · Cloud service broker · Platform as a Service

11.1 Introduction

As the future of grid computing, cloud computing has become a popular environment of equal opportunity for enterprises of all sizes as *"developers with innovative ideas for new Internet services no longer require the large capital outlays in hardware to deploy their service or the human expense to operate it."* [1]

As a new paradigm, cloud computing builds upon existing technology in order to bring forth clear advantages exposed as core cloud characteristics [2] and technical

T.-F. Fortis (✉) · V. I. Munteanu
Faculty of Mathematics and Informatics, West University of Timisoara,
bvd. V. Pârvan, 4, 300223 Timisoara, Romania
e-mail: fortis@info.uvt.ro;

Research Institute e-Austria Timisoara, bvd. V. Pârvan, 4, room 045B,
300223 Timisoara, Romania

V. I. Munteanu
e-mail: vmunteanu@info.uvt.ro

Z. Mahmood (ed.), *Continued Rise of the Cloud,* Computer Communications
and Networks, DOI 10.1007/978-1-4471-6452-4_11,
© Springer-Verlag London 2014

ones [3] for delivering infrastructure at reduced costs to companies, a direct conse-quence being that "*an increasing number of SMEs [. . .] are thinking of migrating some aspects of their operations to the cloud.*" [4]

Unfortunately, a simple migration to the cloud is not possible, as it does not necessarily provide efficient exploitation means for this new environment. Addi-tional enablers, like infrastructure and platform abstractions, and cloud management support are required for an efficient cloud adoption in the case of small and medium-sized enterprises (SMEs), in order to achieve the desired efficiency and ease of use for cloud resources utilization and management.

Furthermore, despite the great progress achieved in the adoption of cloud com-puting, and the growing number of applications that are exposing their services in a cloud environment, there is still an increasing demand for integration as these newly deployed services are rather perceived as "*a mish-mash of SaaS silos and cloud is-lands, with very little attention paid to data consistency and integration, and even less to policy management and oversight.*" [5]

Cloud management is a collection of technologies and software which enable control and operation of cloud applications through a series of services ranging from monitoring to security and privacy management, resource provisioning, application scaling, etc. Focusing on improving the efficacy of the "*in the cloud*" activities and facilitating easy access to the cloud environment by hiding any unnecessary layers, cloud management complements existing PaaS solutions and simplifies cloud adoption through infrastructure management. A series of services could be identified in the context of cloud management, including resource provisioning, monitoring and reconfiguration, or service level agreement (SLA) and quality of service (QoS) management.

While existing PaaS and cloud management solutions focus on providing enter-prises of all sizes easy access to cloud environments and push on cloud adoption, cloud governance takes a more directional role by steering the underlying cloud man-agement solutions according to a set of predefined policies, processes and procedures.

The cloud broker, "*an entity that creates and maintains relationships with multiple cloud service providers*" [6], exists in close relation with both cloud management and cloud governance, exposing functionalities that are relevant for both layers. Current cloud broker solutions focus mainly on cloud management aspects by providing more infrastructure brokering and less service brokering.

Unlike cloud management which is in charge of low level processes like resource provisioning or resource monitoring, cloud governance enables formation of vir-tual enterprises, and controls all high level processes, including service lifecycle management, security, privacy, billing and others, spanning across execution and operations support. It is envisioned as a central entity whose purpose is to enable both service and data integration and create a unitary ecosystem where applications can be created, managed, discovered and can easily interact with each other.

Acting at the software as a service (SaaS) level, cloud governance revolves around providing service management and service lifecycle automation, complemented by a marketplace of services, and integrated with specific operations support in order to provide service across this dynamic and heterogeneous environment.

The cloud service lifecycle is central for cloud governance as it spans on all service layers and it also interfaces with cloud management. Its different aspects that could be considered and extended include, but are not limited to, service templates, offerings, contracts, service provisioning, runtime maintenance and service termination.

In the context of cloud governance, the cloud service brokering is the core service offered by the governance environment as it facilitates the consumer–producer model in that it enables service identification, selection and contracting, successfully exposing the three principles introduced in a later section of this chapter; and thus creating virtual environments for improved exposure of cloud services. In order to achieve cloud service brokering, a series of additional components are required, components that are linked with a cloud service ontology which is complementary in that it enables extensible semantic service descriptions.

11.2   Cloud Brokerage

The importance of cloud brokerage was identified at the early stages of cloud computing development, in a Gartner press release [7]. *"The future of cloud computing will be permeated with the notion of brokers negotiating relationships between providers of cloud services and the service customers,"* as L. Frank Kenney specified in the aforementioned document. In close relation with existing developments for cloud management and service lifecycle support solutions, different definitions for the cloud broker were identified and further refined.

The Gartner document first identified that the cloud broker *"might be software, appliances, platforms or suites of technologies that enhance the base services available through the cloud. Enhancement will include managing access to these services, providing greater security or even creating completely new services."* [7]

In a subsequent definition from Gartner's IT Glossary, the cloud broker was identified as an innovative service:*"cloud services brokerage (CSB) is an IT role and business model in which a company or other entity adds value to one or more (public or private) cloud services on behalf of one or more consumers of that service via three primary roles including aggregation, integration and customization brokerage. A CSB enabler provides technology to implement CSB, and a CSB provider offers combined technology, people and methodologies to implement and manage CSB-related projects"* [8].

The National Institute of Standards and Technology (NIST) cloud computing reference architecture document [9] puts the cloud broker in relation with the increasing complexity required for integration of cloud services, and the cloud broker is defined as *"an entity that manages the use, performance and delivery of cloud services and negotiates relationships between cloud provider s and cloud consumers"*.

A resource-oriented point of view for the cloud broker was identified in the white paper [10], where the cloud broker was mentioned as an agent that *"has no cloud resources of its own, but matches consumers and providers based on the SLA required by the consumer. The consumer has no knowledge that the broker does not control the resources"*. In the vision of the cloud computing use cases group (CCUCG), the

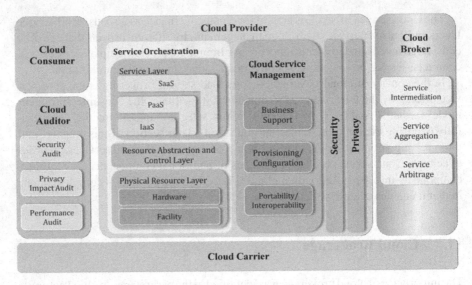

Fig. 11.1 The NIST conceptual reference model. (Source: [9])

cloud broker has some specific responsibilities in delivering hybrid clouds, where the cloud broker coordinates multiple clouds by federating "*data, applications, user identity, security and other details*" [10].

A distinctive definition was offered in a document from the DISA Department of Defense, where the responsibilities of an enterprise cloud service broker (ECSB) were identified to "*manage the use, performance and delivery of cloud services, and negotiate relationships between cloud providers and cloud consumers*".[1]

In another cloud computing strategic paper [6], the cloud broker was identified as "*an entity that creates and maintains relationships with multiple cloud service providers. It acts as a liaison between cloud services customers and cloud service providers, selecting the best provider for each customer and monitoring the services*".

Three main CSB-related businesses were identified by Gartner [7] and adopted in the NIST reference architecture document [9] (see also Fig. 11.1) as:

- **Cloud service intermediation** Service intermediation is related with various means for enhancing services, including SLAs and QoS- related activities, security and identity management support, managed access to cloud services, and others.
- **Service aggregation** As a core capability, the CSB is identified as being able to retrieve, combine and integrate multiple services in one or several services. During the aggregation process, new services could be offered, together with the necessary means for data integration and security between the cloud consumers and multiple cloud providers.

---

[1] http://www.disa.mil/Services/DoD-Cloud-Broker.

- **Cloud service arbitrage** In the case of service arbitrage, the cloud broker has the ability to dynamically choose services during the aggregation process. Different agencies and/or service repositories could be used for this process, in relation with some specific selection mechanisms.

11.2.1   Cloud Resource Broker

The cloud resource broker is necessary, according to the definition from [7], to establish relationships between consumers and providers. As the initial interest in cloud developments was primarily oriented towards resource consumption, early developments were highly oriented towards resource brokering, including negotiation and provisioning.

Current research being conducted focuses either on brokering architectures (all cloud service models) or on SLAs, in close relation with the QoS, in order to support consequent activities (monitoring, scaling, etc.).

Acting on top of the Infrastructure as a Service (IaaS) layer, the Gridbus project[2] developed a resource broker that was able to perform negotiations with resource providers [11], where a *"resource on a grid could be any entity that provides access to a resource/service"*.

Different approaches into SLAs were performed in [12], where the SLAs were broken into SLA objectives (SLOs) which enable individual resource monitoring based on performance metrics, and in [13], where SLAs are used for on-demand service provisioning, or in [14], where they are combined with policies for automatic negotiation. QoS-based approaches focused on mechanisms for resource allocation were covered in [15] and research into QoS metrics was performed in [16].

Additional standards are being developed to support service descriptions, of them the most noteworthy being open cloud computing interface (OCCI) [3] which was originally intended to work at IaaS level. However, it can be easily extended to work at different deployment levels, too. Built to use OCCI, SLA@SOI [4] was designed to tackle IaaS SLAs.

11.2.2   Cloud Service Broker

The CSB offers a full implementation of the brokering component, usually at the superior level of cloud governance, thus providing functionality related with *service intermediation* and *service aggregation*, eventually via *service arbitrage* [7, 9]. The CSB facilitates service consumers easy access in order to search, retrieve and

---

[2] http://www.cloudbus.org/broker.
[3] http://occi-wg.org/.
[4] http://sla-at-soi.eu/.

contract services (*service intermediation*). By doing so, it enables creation of virtual marketplaces where trading can be done (enabling *service arbitrage*), allowing applications that were previously running in isolation to be integrated (via *service aggregation*) within the larger cloud ecosystem, either as a virtual enterprise or a cluster of partners.

In a document detailing the European Union's vision for the future of cloud computing [17] the CSB was identified as an important element that is needed in order to foster competitiveness in the European space as, currently, it has fallen behind the USA on the cloud computing market. Moreover, a significant semantic support is necessary to facilitate better search of heterogeneous information, and thus there is a need for the development of a semantically enabled cloud services registry and repository.

Built on top of existing cloud taxonomies [2, 18], and cloud resource ontology [19], such a registry will enable the core requirements for the CSB, and provide further integration with cloud specifications, including OCCI [20, 21] Topology and Orchestration Specification for Cloud Applications (TOSCA),[5] Open Services for Lifecycle Collaboration(OSLC[5]), CloudML [22], or even ThingML [23, 24], technologies which aims to enhance the portability of cloud applications and services.

Two distinctive approaches are required for developing a fully specified registry for cloud services—resource representations and service representations.

11.2.2.1 Resource Representation

The FP7 mOSAIC project [6] developed an ontology for cloud resources, closely following the Oracle cloud resource model and OCCI specifications [19]. Specifying that "*the Resource class is the most complex in the mOSAIC, since, following the OCCI documentation, in Cloud Systems everything is a cloud Resource*", the ontology offers a good coverage for cloud resources, establishing at the same time some basic mechanisms for interrelations between services and resources.

The resource representation from the mOSAIC project was fully exploited by a semantic engine and integrated in the development of a semantically enabled, agents-based cloud management solution [25]. However, the mOSAIC Cloud Agency was rather concerned with the development of a brokering mechanism, in order to allow advanced mechanisms for resource provisioning and SLA monitoring [26, 27].

Other approaches include the ontology-based resource selection service (OReSS) mechanism described in [28], together with a resource selection engine; a selection mechanism for resources, based on user requirements and specified SLAs [29]; an extended representation of cloud resources, in the context of the *Cloud@Home* initiative [30]; or the definition of a meta-language, CloudML, to support resource provisioning in the cloud [22].

---

[5] http://open-services.net/.
[6] http://www.mosaic-cloud.eu.

Table 11.1 Relevant service brokering operations. (Source: [36])

Operation	Level	CSB operation (intermediation; aggregation, arbitrage)
Authenticate and authorize	Management	Intermediation
Analyze service information	Management	Intermediation
Build semantic query	Governance	Aggregation & arbitrage
Filter services	Governance	Aggregation & arbitrage
Solve dependencies	Governance	Aggregation & arbitrage
Retrieve offers	Governance	Intermediation
Validate offer	Management	Intermediation
Select offer	Governance	Intermediation, aggregation & arbitrage
Contract service	Governance	Intermediation
Lookup instance	Governance	Aggregation & arbitrage
Create instance	Management	Intermediation

11.2.2.2 Service Representation

While the mOSAIC approach is close enough to the IaaS and PaaS levels, additional information is required in order to have complete specifications of services at the SaaS level, and to fully enable the semantic registry that will allow the activation of the *intermediation-aggregation-arbitrage* mechanism.

Key concepts, including those of services, business, computing, quality and service types, were identified in the analysis of Sorathia et al. [31] in order to capture service representations. This analysis, complemented by previous results related with cloud taxonomies [18, 32], or the service-oriented mechanisms, as those from [33, 34], offered the necessary support for the identification of the core concepts in the development of a cloud services ontology, including service models, deployment models, service capabilities and functional properties, service availability, non-functional properties, SLAs, security and QoS, service characterization, service classifications, and service resources [35]. Closely related with these findings, a series of relevant brokering operations could be specified, as shown in Table 11.1, and detailed in [36].

11.3 Cloud Management

Cloud management revolves around the use of existing technologies and software in order to expose services which facilitate easy cloud migration by providing the means to create and manage portable cloud applications. In close relation with the existing PaaS solutions, cloud management focuses on alleviating users of the need to know all cloud layers' details by bypassing the unnecessary ones, and thus reducing the complexity of the development and the required time.

The necessity for cloud management was first described in a set of distributed management task force (DMTF) and CCUCG documents [10, 37, 38], which underline its role in cloud adoption and existing relationships with other cloud enablers while identifying its main focus in providing automation of services (e.g. resource provisioning), SLA management, resource monitoring and others.

Different cloud architectures and use-cases were considered, described and discussed during the last years for achieving a complete specification of various operational aspects of cloud computing, both at IaaS and SaaS levels. Thus, cloud management activities were identified as spanning over the two aforementioned layers. However, we are going to make a clear distinction between management activities at IaaS level, and corresponding activities at SaaS level, and limit cloud management to the IaaS level, while cloud governance includes specific management activities for cloud services.

Developed by IBM, the monitor-analyze-plan-execute (MAPE) cycle [39], along with the MAPE-knowledge base (MAPE-K), fits perfectly with cloud management in terms of desired automation and functionality, thus setting the guidelines for future developments.

The importance of SLAs is further highlighted in the work of Emeakaroha et al. [40] where he stresses that "*prevention of SLA violations avoids unnecessary penalties providers have to pay in case of violations [...] interactions with users can be minimized*".

Through the specification of QoS requirements, SLAs ensure correct and complete resource specification as well as offer the basis upon which monitoring can be performed as well as enable application reconfiguration based on a set of policies which use monitoring information in order to trigger [41] (Table 11.2).

11.3.1 Requirements for Cloud Management

Current requirements revolve around the management of cloud resources and the facilitation of easy integration within other cloud management solutions. In the case of cloud resource management, the focus is on:

- **Resource provisioning:** is the process of selecting the best cloud resources that fulfil the cloud application requirements. It is a process that runs on all deployment levels (IaaS, PaaS and SaaS) and is achieved by using existing parameters which help to define cloud resources in order to filter through the offers coming from cloud vendors, thus offering brokering capabilities to the client entity; the *Execute* phase from the MAPE-K model
- **Resource configuration:** involves the configuration of the provisioned resources as per application requirements, making sure that the environment is fit for application deployment; the *Execute* phase from the MAPE-K model
- **Application deployment:** is the final step which facilitates a running cloud application and involves the deployment of all application components and resolving of all their dependencies as well as additional application configuration which must be done, additionally, when migration is perform, it must handle data migration as well; the *Execute* phase from the MAPE-K model

Table 11.2 Functionalities and requirements for cloud management and cloud governance

Cloud management	Cloud governance
IaaS & PaaS	SaaS
1. Functionalities	
Management	
Resource management	Service management
Provisioning	
Resource provisioning	Service provisioning
Service deployment	Service catalogues & business standards
Security and privacy	
Resource monitoring	Lifecycle support & operations support
2. Requirements	
Service infrastructure (enabled by *provisioning*)	–
Security (enabled by *deployment*)	Security (enabled by *lifecycle operations*)
–	Service composition (enabled by *service catalogues & business standards*)
–	Service coordination (enabled by *lifecycle operations*)
–	Business & operations support (enabled by *lifecycle operations*)

- **Resource monitoring:** any cloud management solution must offer the monitoring of the provisioned cloud resources either by using vendor specific APIs to retrieve monitoring information or by installing custom software to achieve it. Monitoring is in close relation with SLA management and application reconfiguration; the *Monitoring* phase from the MAPE-K model
- **SLA management:** involves the storage, modification and retrieval of brokered SLAs which happens upon provisioning, monitoring or reconfiguration of the cloud application; the *Plan* phase from the MAPE-K model
- **Application reconfiguration:** is focused on analyzing monitoring information (metrics) and correlating it with information found in SLAs (policies) in order to trigger application reconfiguration: scaling up or down, replacing resources which breached SLAs; the *Analyze* phase from the MAPE-K model

Table 11.3 Cloud management solutions

Cloud management solution	PaaS	Description
4CaaSt (http://4caast.morfeo-project.org/)	Yes	PaaS designed for multi-tier applications featuring cloud management functionality
Cloudkick (https://www.cloudkick.com/)	No	Supports Amazon and Rackspace and libcloud (http://libcloud.apache.org/) python library was developed as a result of the project
CloudSwitch (http://www.cloudswitch.com/)	No	Supports Amazon EC2 and Terremark
Deltacloud (http://deltacloud.apache.org/)	No	Open source Apache project featuring a REST interface supporting all major cloud vendors
Open Cirrus (https://opencirrus.org/)	No	Cloud computing test bed designed to support research of service provisioning and management
OpenNebula (http://opennebula.org/)	No	Open source solution for the management of virtual machines
OpenShift (https://www.openshift.com/)	Yes	Both open source (community) and commercial PaaS with cloud management functionality designed based on JBoss AS

In the case of integration within other cloud management solutions, a good cloud management solution must provide interfaces (e.g. REST) and APIs through which its functionality can be accessed and executed.

11.3.2 Reference Architectures

The Open Cloud Standards Incubator from DMTF produced a couple of white papers that are most relevant for the cloud management area: a reference architecture, covering both aspects related with cloud resource management and cloud services management [37], and a companion use-case document [38]. While discussing relevant cloud management issues, the DMTF couple of documents set clear relations with aspects that are most appropriate for cloud governance.

More pertinent to cloud management at IaaS level, the DMTF Cloud Management Working Group developed a set of documents that deal with central aspects for resource management at infrastructure level. In the cloud infrastructure management interface (CIMI) model the typical IaaS resources *are modeled with the goal of providing Consumer management access to an implementation of IaaS and facilitating portability between cloud implementations that support the specification* [42].

A similar approach was used by the open grid forum (OGF) OCCI-WG with the OCCI specification, initially developed to address IaaS-related management tasks, and extended *to serve many other models in addition to IaaS, including PaaS and SaaS* [20].

A number of cloud management solutions exist, most of them being strictly limited to offering basic cloud management functionality like resource provisioning and monitoring, few also being hybrids between cloud management and PaaS as described in Table 11.3.

11.4 Cloud Governance

Cloud governance, thought as a natural extension of SOA governance, is an essential component for further development of an environment able to offer superior facilities for SMEs, on top of the core cloud characteristics. These facilities, built around cloud services lifecycle support, and strongly backed by the exploitation of a semantically enabled cloud services knowledge base, will allow the development of different virtual environments where SMEs could cooperate and develop tailored solutions, acting as a unique entity while they are still preserving the identity of their services.

These virtual environments, either virtual enterprises or virtual clusters, allow the implementation of different scenarios of grouping and collaboration between partners, requiring relevant technological support, and business and operational support, both aspects being integrated with the cloud service lifecycle support.

As mentioned in [43], a series of research challenges are extremely relevant in the context of the virtual environments activated by a cloud governance solution, including *novel cloud architectures, automated service provisioning, data security* and *software frameworks*, [44], together with *open standards interface, delivery of services supported by* SLA, or *security in various service delivery models* [45].

11.4.1 Requirements for Cloud Governance

An IBM *RedBook* identifies cloud computing as an enabler of a series of business models, most relevant for cloud service providers, where "*an ecosystem of businesses and individuals [...] extends the reach of cloud service providers by expanding the breadth of services that are offered and addressing niche or specialty markets and geographies*" [46]. In the same IBM document a series of adoption patterns for their cloud computing reference architecture (Fig. 11.2) were identified, with two distinct perspectives: the IaaS-based (IaaS as an entry point), and the SaaS-based one. Hosting, aggregation and '*whitelabel*' (rebranding of services) are seen as the most relevant choices a service provider will adopt.

Automatic aggregation and clear identification of policies, parameters and processes were also identified as being most relevant in the context of cloud governance [48]. Together with the patterns described in the IBM White Paper [47] and the set of steps that were identified for a governance framework for cloud security in [49], a set of four core requirements for cloud computing were identified, including security and privacy, lifecycle automation, service management and business standards [43, 50].

Security is a core requirement that also has implications in privacy and standards. Security considerations must cover both application developers and cloud providers. An important issue related to security is the lack of disclosure of security-related information of cloud providers.

Privacy is an important concern as many SMEs deal with sensitive information which poses migration concerns related to the storage and handling of this information as well as legal implications in terms of contracts and governmental laws.

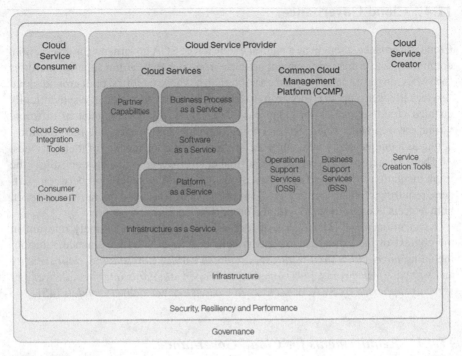

Fig. 11.2 The IBM cloud computing reference architecture with service creation details. (IBM CCRA, source: [48])

Another core requirement is standards, as most cloud providers implement their own proprietary technologies and do not always adhere to existing open standards thus making interoperability hard to achieve.

The last one, lifecycle management, is a core requirement which most cloud providers do not cover. It refers to the ability to manage various cloud applications in terms of, e.g. versioning, updating, monitoring, etc.

11.4.2 Relationship with Cloud Management

Standards like ISO/IEC 38500 for IT governance offer a foundation on which cloud governance can be built and can further allow interaction with frameworks and industry standards. This, in turn, enables interaction between cloud governance and cloud management through bridges that these standards facilitate.

Through the Monitor-Evaluate-Direct cycle brought by ISO/IEC 38500, one can establish links with the MAPE-K cycle, as defined by IBM [39], in order to better express the symbiosis between cloud governance and cloud management and how their services and functionality is complementary, as shown in Fig. 11.3.

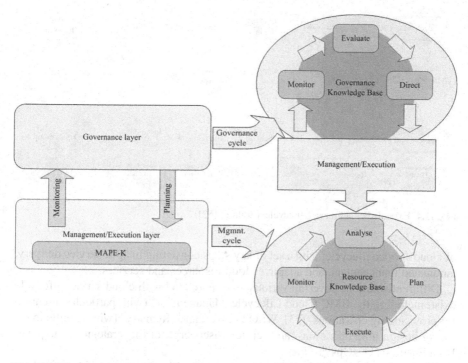

Fig. 11.3 The interrelationships between the MAPE-K and ISO 38500 models

11.4.3   Lifecycle Support

According to Bennett et al. [51], eleven stages could be identified in close relation with cloud governance requirements, including from a functional point of view service development, testing, deployment and maintenance, service usage and monitoring, service discovery, and service versioning and retirement. Each of these stages could be specified in close relation with cloud service lifecycle steps, as identified in [37, 52].

In [37] the cloud service lifecycle is presented rather from the perspective of cloud management. The description from [52], as presented in Fig. 11.4, is more comprehensive, offering a clear identification of the stages that are related with service template and specification (design time operations), service discovery and composition (provisioning operations), service deployment and execution (deployment and execution operations), and service versioning, archiving and retirement. With this level of details, links with the business and operations support could be easily specified.

Few solutions currently exist for supporting cloud service management. In the approach from adaptive computing[7], automation is central for the implementation

---

[7] http://www.adaptivecomputing.com/products/cloud-products/moab-cloud-suite/.

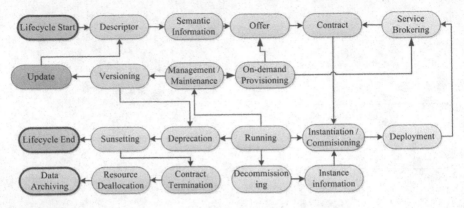

Fig. 11.4 Extended cloud service lifecycle. (Source: [52])

of cloud service lifecycle, with a set of key steps consisting in agile service delivery, automated management, and adaptive cloud resources and services.

Different solutions covering various aspects related with cloud service lifecycle exist, including the BMC Cloud Lifecycle Management[8] (with particular attention for provisioning operations) [53], WSO2 Governance Registry[9] (with specific interest for design time operations, and service discovery), or the strategic white paper from Enstratus DevOps[10].

Clotho, the service lifecycle manager from the Morfeo project [54], offers facilities for service orchestration, while offering support for automated "*service deployment and the dynamic provisioning of services*"[11]. The PaaSage project[12] aims to "*develop an open and integrated platform to support the lifecycle management of cloud applications*"[13], while the MODAClouds project intends to provide "*quality assurance during the application life-cycle and support migration from Cloud to Cloud when needed*"[14].

11.4.4 Service Registry

In order to meet the various requirements set for cloud governance, specifically for the service lifecycle, some support for the storage and retrieval of service-related information is necessary, thus underlining the need for a specialized service registry.

---

[8] http://www.bmc.com/products/cloud-management.
[9] http://wso2.com/products/governance-registry/.
[10] http://www.enstratius.com/devops-wp.
[11] http://claudia.morfeo-project.org/wiki/index.php/Service Lifecycle Manager.
[12] http://www.paasage.eu/.
[13] http://www.ercim.eu/news/345-paasage.
[14] http://www.modaclouds.eu/.

This service registry provides the means for the creation of virtual enterprises by providing support for collaboration between enterprises and, consequently, support for the composition of their services, as well as provide the means for cloud application automation for tasks related to application scaling, migrating, etc. Therefore, a semantic approach would be most suited in order to enable this functionality, as well as to provide semantic interoperability, which can be integrated both at cloud management and at cloud governance levels extending the level of automation that is achievable and enhancing the cloud service lifecycle.

While, at IaaS level, semantic interoperability is focused around resources [19] as was investigated in the FP7-ICT Project mOSAIC [15], PaaS semantic interoperability was considered in FP7 Project Cloud4SOA [16]. At SaaS level, semantic interoperability supports creation of cloud service marketplaces which enable service discovery, selection and composition.

The functionalities of a cloud governance service registry can be broken in:

- **Service management**—the registration, updating and removing of services and service related information both syntactic and semantic
- **Semantic discovery**—the ability to use semantic information of a service (functional and non-functional information) in order identify services
- **Semantic filtering**—the ability to manipulate semantic information of a service in order to achieve service selection
- **Execution support**—support execution activities though service information

Essentially, the service registry provides a catalogue of existing services on top of which governance clients, or even the governance itself, can run service discovery in order to support various stages of the service lifecycle from the planning stage to the execution and termination stage of cloud services.

11.5 Multi-Agent Approaches for Cloud Governance and Management

Multi-agent systems are complex asynchronous systems composed of a minimal of two homogeneous or heterogeneous agents which work in order to achieve some set of goals. Each agent composing the system can have various degrees of autonomy when deciding what to do and how to do it (individually or cooperatively, self-interested or benevolent). On the other side, having a completely asynchronous system can lead to it being highly distributed and, possibly, highly fault tolerant. Because of these abilities, multi-agent systems are ideal for the development of highly distributed, collaborative, autonomic applications, especially when dealing with cloud environments where there is a mix of heterogeneous technologies and where adaptability is critical.

---

[15] http://www.mosaic-cloud.eu.
[16] http://www.cloud4soa.eu.

According to D. Talia [55], *"the convergence of interests between multi-agent systems that need reliable distributed infrastructures and Cloud computing systems that need intelligent software with dynamic, flexible, and autonomous behavior will result in new systems and applications"*. Thus, an increasing interest in using multi-agent approaches for cloud applications exists. Furthermore, Sim states that *"agent-based cloud computing is concerned with the design and development of software agents for bolstering cloud service discovery, service negotiation, and service composition"* [56].

Multi-agent systems that handle various real life problems can benefit from cloud computing. For example, the cloud based multi-agent system described in [57] was used for the management of dynamic traffic environments by taking advantage of the available on-demand computing, storage and networking put forth by the cloud environment.

Another interesting approach was Unity, a multi-agent decentralized architecture for autonomic cloud computing, designed for the study and testing of ideas related to autonomic system, which features self-healing, real-time self-optimization and goal-driven self-assembly [58].

11.5.1   Multi-Agent Approaches for Cloud Management

Cloud management represents an important business segment of cloud computing, many enterprises offering cloud management solutions. From a multi-agent point of view, most agent solutions address parts of the problems, but few address it as a whole.

One of the most representative solutions for agent-based cloud management is mOSAIC's Cloud Agency [59]. Part of the mOSAIC project, the Cloud Agency offers resource provisioning and monitoring across public and private major infrastructure cloud providers and is *"in charge to broker the collection of Cloud resources from different providers that fulfills at the best the requirements of user's applications"* [41]. Another study focuses on platform level services as well as other native software applications providing the 'as' part of the +Cloud (masCloud) platform which is in charge of resource management, performing on-demand resource scaling [60].

One important aspect of cloud management is resource provisioning and in this regard there are many directions. Some multi-agent solutions deal with negotiation, though actual cloud resource negotiation is not currently possible with most cloud providers. Others focus on the discovery, selection and composition of cloud resources.

For example, the work performed in [56] highlights the use of agents in order to provide cloud resource management with focus on service discovery, negotiation and composition achieved through cooperating agents performing complex negotiations in order to provide a cloud search engine.

An approach for Web service discovery in the cloud environment is presented in [61] where agents, coupled with specific algorithms for matchmaking and ranking of Web services, are used for finding the best candidate that corresponds to the description provided by the client while considering QoS parameters of the Web services.

Cloud resource provisioning is also addressed in [62] through a distributed negotiation mechanism where agents act on behalf of the consumers and negotiate contracts which allow single-sided termination (consumer's side) upon paying a certain price. Semantic cloud resource negotiation is conducted in [63] where a multi-agent system is used in order to facilitate the adaptation and coordination of application execution across various cloud providers through a set of scheduling policies in order to achieve both consumer and producer satisfaction.

In their work [16], Cao et al. describe a multi-agent cloud management architecture focused on supporting QoS-assured cloud service provisioning and management. Another QoS-oriented cloud management solution is presented in [64] where *"an automatic resource allocation strategy based on market Mechanism (ARAS-M)"* is used, and *"a QoS-refectitive utility function is designed according to different resource requirements of Cloud Client"* and is combined with a genetic algorithm for automatic price adjustment.

Security considerations using agent-based approaches where a security audit system makes use of intelligent autonomous agents in order to tackle cloud-specific problems like infrastructure changes were presented in [65].

11.5.2 *Multi-Agent Approaches for Cloud Governance*

As it is a new research topic, there are few approaches in which multi-agents address issues related to cloud governance. Starting from mOSAIC's Cloud Agency, the work carried in [50] extends its functionality and complements it with specific governance functions.

Since cloud governance focuses on providing business aspects and one important one is virtual enterprises the work performed by Carrascosa et al. [66], though not being directly linked to cloud computing, is about THOMAS which is an open architecture which builds on the foundation of intelligent physical agents (FIPA) agent architecture in order to facilitate the design of virtual organizations using a service-oriented approach where agents are in charge of service management.

In order to enable virtual enterprises, cloud governance must facilitate easy composition of cloud services so that their developers and owners can benefit from adhering to new business models. In this regard, automated cloud service composition has been efficiently achieved in [67] using a three-layered self-organizing multi-agent system in which agents are in charge of cloud participants and resources and which addresses dynamic contracting under incomplete information.

Another approach that tackles service collaboration in cloud computing is presented in [68], where a multi-agent system is used in conjunction with *"a negotiation mechanism (mean algorithm and protocol) that allows nodes in a 'cloud' to achieve an effective collaboration among service providers".*

From the data perspective, cloud governance must facilitate privacy and security while providing data integrity for the information it holds. It must store complete information related to the cloud applications it services from service descriptions to run-time monitoring information used for audit.

Multi-agent approaches in the field cloud data storage typical focus on providing data integrity services, such as the solution presented in [69] called *'CloudZone'* where a multi-agent architecture is in charge of providing integrity through the use of two types of agents, one which provides a user interface for the client and one in charge of data integrity and reconstruction by performing regular data backup.

A specific approach shows how data warehouses can be deployed in the cloud environment using a multi-agent system designed around Web services in order to benefit from the core cloud characteristics while maintaining traditional data warehouse benefits [70].

In regard to the security concerns of cloud storage solutions, Talib et al. [71] propose a multi-agent based security framework built on top of Java Agent Development (JADE) for managing the security of cloud data storage in order to guarantee data correctness, integrity, confidentially and availability [71].

Tackling privacy and security, Angin et al. propose an identity management solution for cloud computing, a prototype being developed using mobile JADE agents, which has *"entity-centric mechanism for protecting privacy of sensitive data throughout their entire lifecycle [...] known as the active bundle scheme [...] is able to provide users with control over their data, allowing them to decide what and when data will be shared"* [72].

11.6 Conclusions

Current advancements have made cloud computing into a thriving market where enterprises of all sizes are fighting for their share, to take advantage of the business models it brings and of its core characteristics.

Unfortunately, since its inception, many problems have plagued this new paradigm and so it has become an active research topic for many communities worldwide. This has also constituted a strong deterrent for many enterprises which are reluctant to adopt it in fear of losing control over their data, over the services and applications they provide for their clients.

While some of its core problems like cross cloud development and interoperability are or have already been addressed through PaaS or cloud management solutions, problems that are related to the business layer or the support for cloud service lifecycle are yet or insufficiently addressed.

This chapter has provided a comprehensive overview of cloud management and cloud governance detailing interactions between them, showing how one complements the other, and emphasizing the role they play in general cloud adoption. In addition, many solutions that address the whole picture or just a partial one are analyzed, especially solutions which involve multi-agent systems.

Acknowledgements This work was partially supported by the grants of the European Commission FP7-ICT-2009-5-256910 (mOSAIC) and FP7-ICT 2011-8-318484 (MODAClouds). The work of the second author was also partially supported by Romanian Government national grant PN-II-ID-PCE-2011-3-0260 (AMICAS). The views expressed in this chapter do not necessarily reflect those of the corresponding projects' consortium members.

References

1. Armbrust M, Fox A, Griffith R, Joseph AD, Katz R, Konwinski A, Lee G, Patterson D, Rabkin A, Stoica I, Zaharia M (2009) Above the Clouds: a Berkeley view of Cloud computing, Berkeley report. http://www.eecs.berkeley.edu/Pubs/TechRpts/2009/EECS-2009-28.pdf. Accessed 30 Sept 2013
2. Mell P, Grance T (2011) The NIST definition of Cloud computing. White paper. http://csrc.nist.gov/publications/nistpubs/800-145/SP800-145.pdf. Accessed 30 Sep 2013
3. Gong C, Liu J, Zhang Q, Chen H, Gong Z (2010) The characteristics of Cloud computing. Parallel Processing Workshops, International Conference on 0:275–279. doi:10.1109/ICPPW.2010.45
4. Sultan NA (2011) Reaching for the Cloud: how SMEs can manage. Int J Inf Manage 31(3): 272–278. doi:10.1016/j.ijinfomgt.2010.08.001. http://www.sciencedirect.com/science/article/pii/S0268401210001143. Accessed 30 Sept 2013
5. Wainewright P (2011) Time to think about cloud governance. Blog entry. http://www.zdnet.com/blog/saas/time-to-think-about-cloud-governance/1376. Accessed 30 Sept 2013
6. Australian Government Department of Finance and Deregulations (2011) Cloud computing strategic direction paper. Strategic paper. http://agict.gov.au/files/2011/04/Draft-ICT-Strategic-Vision.pdf. Accessed 30 Sept 2013
7. Gartner, Inc (2009) Cloud consumers need brokerages to unlock the potential of cloud services. Press release. http://www.gartner.com/it/page.jsp?id=1064712. Accessed 30 Sept 2013
8. Gartner, Inc (2013) IT glossary. Cloud services brokerage (CSB). http://www.gartner.com/it-glossary/cloud-services-brokerage-csb. Accessed 30 Sept 2013
9. Liu F, Tong J, Mao J, Bohn R, Messina J, Badger L, Leaf D (2011) NIST Cloud computing reference architecture. http://collaborate.nist.gov/twiki-cloud-computing/pub/CloudComputing/ReferenceArchitectureTaxonomy/NIST_SP_500-292_-_090611.pdf. Accessed 30 Sept 2013
10. Cloud Computing Use Cases Group (2010) Cloud computing use cases white paper. http://opencloudmanifesto.org/Cloud_Computing_Use_Cases_Whitepaper-4_0.pdf. Accessed 30 Sept 2013
11. Buyya R, Yeo CS, Venugopal S (2008) Market-oriented Cloud computing: vision, hype, and reality for delivering it services as computing utilities. In: High performance computing and communications, 2008. HPCC'08. 10th IEEE international conference on, pp 5–13. doi:10.1109/HPCC.2008.172
12. Sim K (2010) Towards complex negotiation for cloud economy. In: Bellavista P, Chang RS, Chao HC, Lin SF, Sloot P (eds) Advances in grid and pervasive computing, lecture notes in computer science, vol 6104. Springer, Berlin, pp 395–406
13. Kertesz A, Kecskemeti G, Brandic I (2009) An SLA-based resource virtualization approach for ondemand service provision. In: Proceedings of the 3rd international workshop on virtualization technologies in distributed computing, ACM, New York, NY, USA, VTDC'09, pp 27–34
14. Zulkernine F, Martin P (2011) An adaptive and intelligent SLA negotiation system for web services. IEEE Trans Serv Comput 4(1):31–43

15. Buyya R, Yeo CS, Venugopal S, Broberg J, Brandic I (2009) Cloud computing and emerging IT platforms: vision, hype, and reality for delivering computing as the 5th utility. Future Gener Comput Syst 25:599–616
16. Cao BQ, Li B, Xia QM (2009) A service-oriented QoS-assured and multi-agent Cloud computing architecture. In: Proceedings of the 1st international conference on Cloud computing, Springer, Berlin, Heidelberg, CloudCom'09, pp 644–649
17. Lutz SKJ, Neidecker-Lutz B (eds) (2010) The future of cloud computing, opportunities for European Cloud computing beyond 2010. http://cordis.europa.eu/fp7/ict/ssai/docs/cloud-report-final.pdf. Accessed 30 Sept 2013
18. Youseff L, Butrico M, Silva DD (2008) Towards a unified ontology of Cloud computing. In: Grid computing environments workshop, 2008. GCE'08, pp 1–10. doi:10.1109/GCE.2008.4738443
19. Moscato F, Aversa R, Di Martino B, Fortis TF, Munteanu V (2011) An analysis of mOSAIC ontology for Cloud resources annotation. In: Ganzha M, Maciaszek LA, Paprzycki M (eds) Computer Science and Information Systems (FedCSIS), 2011 Federated Conference on, IEEE Computer Society, 18–21 Sept, Sczeczin, pp 973–980. http://fedcsis.eucip.pl/proceedings/pliks/154.pdf. Accessed 30 Sept 2013
20. Nyren R, Edmonds A, Papaspyrou A, Metsch T (2011) Open Cloud computing interface—core. OGF specification. http://ogf.org/documents/GFD.183.pdf. Accessed 30 Sept 2013
21. OASIS (2013) Topology and orchestration specification for Cloud applications. OASIS Committee Specification 01. http://docs.oasis-open.org/tosca/TOSCA/v1.0/cs01/TOSCA-v1.0-cs01.html. Accessed 30 Sept 2013
22. Brandtzæg E, Mosser S, Mohagheghi P (2012) Towards CloudML, a model-based approach to provision resources in the clouds. In: Model-Driven Engineering for and on the Cloud workshop (co-located with ECMFA'12) (CloudMDE'12), workshop, DTU, Copenhaghen, Danemark, pp 18–27
23. Hao R, Morin B, Berre AJ (2012) A semi-automatic behavioral mediation approach based on models@runtime. In: Proceedings of the 7th workshop on Models@run.time, ACM, New York, NY, USA, MRT'12, pp 67–71. doi:10.1145/2422518.2422529
24. Berre AJ (2012) An agile model-based framework for service innovation for the future internet. In: Grossniklaus M, Wimmer M (eds) Current trends in web engineering, lecture notes in computer science, vol 7703. Springer, Heidelberg, pp 1–4. doi:10.1007/978-3-642-35623-0
25. Petcu D, Macariu G, Panica S, Crăciun C (2013) Portable cloud applications-from theory to practice. Future Gener Comput Syst 29(6):1417–1430. doi:10.1016/j.future.2012.01.009
26. Aversa R, Di Martino B, Rak M, Venticinque S (2010) Cloud agency: a mobile agent based cloud system. In: Proceedings of the 2010 international conference on complex, intelligent and software intensive systems, IEEE Computer Society, Washington, DC, USA, CISIS'10, pp 132–137. doi:10.1109/CISIS.2010.143
27. Cretella G, Di Martino B (2012) Towards automatic analysis of cloud vendors APIs for supporting cloud application portability. In: Complex, intelligent and software intensive systems (CISIS), 2012 sixth international conference on, pp 61–67. doi:10.1109/CISIS.2012.162
28. Yoo H, Hur C, Kim S, Kim Y (2009) An ontology-based resource selection service on science cloud. Int J Grid Distrib Comput 2(4):17–26
29. Ma Y, Jang S, Lee J (2011) Ontology-based resource management for cloud computing. In: Nguyen N, Kim CG, Janiak A (eds) Intelligent information and database systems, lecture notes in computer science, vol 6592, Springer, Berlin, pp 343–352. doi:10.1007/978-3-642-20042-7_35
30. DiStefano S, Cunsolo V, Puliafito A (2010) A taxonomic specification of Cloud@Home. In: Huang DS, Zhang X, Reyes GC, Zhang L (eds) Advanced intelligent computing theories and applications. With aspects of artificial intelligence, lecture notes in computer science, vol 6216, Springer, Berlin, pp 527–534. doi:10.1007/978-3-642-14932-0n 66
31. Sorathia V, Ferreira Pires L, van Sinderen M (2010) An analysis of service ontologies. Pac Asia J Assoc Inf Syst 2(1):17–46. http://doc.utwente.nl/72509/. Accessed 30 Sept 2013
32. Katzan H (2010) On an ontological view of Cloud computing. Science 3(1):1–6. http://journals.cluteonline.com/index.php/JSS/article/view/795/0. Accessed 30 Sept 2013

33. Han T, Sim KM (2010) Cloudle: an ontology-enhanced cloud service search engine. In: WISE Workshops, pp 416–427
34. Kang J, Sim KM (2011) Towards agents and ontology for Cloud service discovery. Cyber-enabled distributed computing and knowledge discovery (CyberC), 2011 international conference, pp 483–490
35. Fortis TF, Munteanu VI, Negru V (2012) Towards an ontology for Cloud services. In: Barolli L, Xhafa F, Vitabile S, Uehara M (eds) CISIS 2012, IEEE, pp 787–792
36. Munteanu VI, Mîndrută C, Fortis TF (2012) Service brokering in Cloud governance. In: SYNASC 2012, IEEE Computer Society, pp 497–504. doi:10.1109/SYNASC.2012.50
37. DMTF (2010a) Architecture for managing Clouds. http://dmtf.org/sites/default/files/standards/documents/DSP-IS0102_1.0.0.pdf. Accessed 30 Sept 2013
38. DMTF (2010b) Use cases and interactions for managing Clouds. http://www.dmtf.org/sites/default/files/standards/documents/DSP-IS0103_1.0.0.pdf. Accessed 30 Sept 2013
39. Naick I (2004) Make autonomic computing a reality with IBM Tivoli. http://www.ibm.com/developerworks/library/ac-itito/index.html. Accessed 30 Sept 2013
40. Emeakaroha VC, Netto MAS, Calheiros RN, Brandic I, Buyya R, De Rose CAF (2012) Towards autonomic detection of SLA violations in cloud infrastructures. Future Gener Comput Syst 28(7):1017–1029. doi:10.1016/j.future.2011.08.018
41. Venticinque S, Aversa R, Di Martino B, Rak M, Petcu D (2011) A cloud agency for SLA negotiation and management. In: Proceedings of the 2010 conference on Parallel processing, Springer, Berlin, Heidelberg, Euro-Par 2010, pp 587–594
42. DMTF (2012) Cloud infrastructure management interface (CIMI) model and RESTful HTTP-based protocol an interface for managing Cloud infrastructure. DMTF Standard. http://dmtf.org/sites/default/files/standards/documents/DSP0263_1.0.0.pdf. Accessed 30 Sept 2013
43. Fortis TF, Munteanu VI, Negru V (2012) Steps towards Cloud governance. A survey. In: Information technology interfaces (ITI), proceedings of the ITI 2012 34th international conference on, pp 29–34. doi:10.2498/iti.2012.0374
44. Zhang Q, Cheng L, Boutaba R (2010) Cloud computing: state-of-the-art and research challenges. J Internet Serv Appl 1:7–18. doi:10.1007/s13174-010-0007-6
45. Subashini S, Kavitha V (2011) A survey on security issues in service delivery models of cloud computing. J Netw Comput Appl 34(1):1–11. doi:10.1016/j.jnca.2010.07.006
46. MacIntyre J (2012) IBM SmartCloud: becoming a Cloud service provider. IBM RedBooks. http://www.redbooks.ibm.com/redpapers/pdfs/redp4912.pdf. Accessed 30 Sept 2013
47. O'Neill M (2009) Connecting to the Cloud, Part 3: Cloud governance and security. http://www.ibm.com/developerworks/xml/library/x-cloudpt3/. Accessed 30 Sept 2013
48. IBMGlobal Technology Services (2011) Getting Cloud computing right. IBM White Paper. http://public.dhe.ibm.com/common/ssi/ecm/en/ciw03078usen/CIW03078USEN.PDF. Accessed 30 Sept 2013
49. Cecere T (2011) Five steps to creating a governance framework for Cloud security. Cloud Computing J. http://cloudcomputing.sys-con.com/node/2073041. Accessed 30 September 2013
50. Fortis TF, Munteanu VI, Negru V (2012b) Towards a service friendly Cloud ecosystem. In: Bader M, Bungartz HJ, Grigoras D, Mehl M, Mundani RP, Potolea R (eds) ISPDC 2012, IEEE Computer Society, pp 172–179
51. Bennett S, Erl T, Gee C, Laird R, Manes AT, Schneider R, Shuster L, Tost A, Venable C (2011) SOA governance: governing shared services on-premise & in the Cloud. Prentice Hall/PearsonPTR. http://www.soabooks.com/governance/. Accessed 30 Sept 2013
52. Munteanu VI, Fortis TF, Negru V (2012) Service lifecycle in the Cloud environment. In: SYNASC 2012, IEEE Computer Society, Los Alamitos, CA, USA, pp 457–464. doi:10.1109/SYNASC.2012.67
53. BMCSoftware (2010) Cloud lifecycle management. Managing cloud services from request to retirement. Solution White Paper. https://s3.amazonaws.com/Vendor_Uploads_Education/Ingram_Micro_-_Sponsor_Account_179317.pdf. Accessed 30 Sept 2013

54. Baryannis G, Garefalakis P, Kritikos K, Magoutis K, Papaioannou A, Plexousakis D, Zeginis C (2013) Lifecycle management of service-based applications on multi-clouds: a research roadmap. In: Proceedings of the 2013 international workshop on multi-cloud applications and federated clouds, MultiCloud'13, New York, NY, USA, ACM, pp 13–20. doi:10.1145/2462326.2462331

55. Talia D (2011) Cloud computing and software agents: towards Cloud intelligent services In: Fortino G, Garro A, Palopoli L, Russo W, Spezzano G (eds) WOA 741:2–6 (CEUR-WS.org, CEUR Workshop Proceedings)

56. Sim KM (2012) Agent-based cloud computing. IEEE Trans Serv Comput 5(4):564–577. doi:10.1109/TSC.2011.52

57. Li Z, Chen C, Wang K (2011) Cloud computing for agent-based urban transportation systems. IEEE Intell Syst 26(1):73–79. doi:10.1109/MIS.2011.10

58. Tesauro G, Chess DM, Walsh WE, Das R, Segal A, Whalley I, Kephart JO, White SR (2004) A multi-agent systems approach to autonomic computing. In: Proceedings of the 3rd international joint conference on autonomous agents and multiagent systems: vol 1, AAMAS '04, IEEE Computer Society, Washington, DC, USA, pp 464–471. doi:10.1109/AAMAS.2004.23

59. Venticinque S, Aversa R, Di Martino B, Petcu D (2011b) Agent based cloud provisioning and management-design and prototypal implementation. In: 1st international conference on Cloud computing and services science, CLOSER 2010, pp 184–191

60. Prieta F, Rodrguez S, Bajo J, Corchado J (2013) A multiagent system for resource distribution into a cloud computing environment. In: Demazeau Y, Ishida T, Corchado J, Bajo J (eds) Advances on practical applications of agents and multi-agent systems. Lecture notes in computer science, vol 7879. Springer, Berlin, pp 37–48. doi:10.1007/978-3-642-38073-0 4

61. Hamza S, Okba K, Acha-Nabila B, Youssef A (2012) Web services discovery, selection and ranking based multi-agent system in cloud computing environment. Int J Inf Stud 4(3):123–144

62. An B, Lesser V, Irwin D, Zink M (2010) Automated negotiation with decommit for dynamic resource allocation in cloud computing. In: Proceedings of the 9th international conference on autonomous agents and multiagent systems: vol 1, AAMAS '10, International Foundation for Autonomous Agents and Multiagent Systems, Richland, SC, pp 981–988

63. Ejarque J, Sirvent R, Badia R (2010) A multi-agent approach for semantic resource allocation. In: 2010 IEEE 2nd international conference on Cloud computing technology and science (CloudCom), pp 335–342. doi:10.1109/CloudCom.2010.30

64. You X, Wan J, Xu X, Jiang C, Zhang W, Zhang J (2011) ARAS-M: automatic resource allocation strategy based on market mechanism in Cloud computing. J Comput 6(7):1287–1295. http://ojs.academypublisher.com/index.php/jcp/article/view/jcp060712871296. Accessed 30 Sept 2013

65. Doelitzscher F, Reich C, Knahl M, Passfall A, Clarke N (2012) An agent based business aware incident detection system for cloud environments. J Cloud Comput 1(1):1–19. doi:10.1186/2192-113X-1-9

66. Carrascosa C, Giret A, Julian V, Rebollo M, Argente E, Botti V (2009) Service oriented mas: an open architecture. In: Proceedings of the 8th international conference on autonomous agents and multiagent systems: vol 2, AAMAS '09, International Foundation for Autonomous Agents and Multiagent Systems, Richland, SC, pp 1291–1292

67. Gutierrez-Garcia J, Sim KM (2010) Self-organizing agents for service composition in Cloud computing. In: 2010 IEEE 2nd international conference on Cloud computing technology and science (CloudCom), pp 59–66. doi:10.1109/CloudCom.2010.10

68. Paletta M, Herrero P (2009) A mas-based negotiation mechanism to deal with service collaboration in Cloud computing. In: International conference on intelligent networking and collaborative systems, INCOS '09, pp 147–153. doi:10.1109/INCOS.2009.21

69. Talib A, Atan R, Abdullah R, Azrifah M (2011) Cloudzone: towards an integrity layer of Cloud data storage based on multi agent system architecture. In: 2011 IEEE conference on open systems (ICOS), pp 127–132. doi:10.1109/ICOS.2011.6079311

70. Yang SY, Lee DL, Chen KY, Hsu CL (2011) Energy-saving information multi-agent system with web services for Cloud computing. In: Chang RS, Kim Th, Peng SL (eds) Security-enriched

urban computing and smart grid, communications in computer and information science, vol 223, Springer, Berlin, pp 222–233. doi:10.1007/978-3-642-23948-9 25

71. Talib AM, Atan R, Abdullah R, Murad MAA (2010) Security framework of Cloud data storage based on multi agent system architecture: Semantic literature review. Compu Inf Sci 3(4): 175–186

72. Angin P, Bhargava B, Ranchal R, Singh N, Linderman M, Othmane L, Lilien L (2010) An entity-centric approach for privacy and identity management in Cloud computing. In: 2010 29th IEEE symposium on reliable distributed systems, pp 177–183. doi:10.1109/SRDS.2010.28

Chapter 12
Towards the Development of a Cloud Service Capability Assessment Framework

Noel Carroll, Markus Helfert and Theo Lynn

Abstract Considering the complexity of today's service environment, Small-to-Medium sized Enterprises (SMEs) cannot afford to accept the status quo of service operations, and therefore, they must have some clear business analytics objectives to reach. Without clear metric objectives, organisations are almost destined for disaster since the allocation of resources may not have responded to the demand exerted from outside of the organisation. This is particularly true within a complex and rapidly changing cloud computing environment. The cloud dynamic ecosystem is moving toward a collection of services which interoperate across the Internet. This chapter offers a discussion on an approach to assessing cloud capabilities through cloud service capability assessment framework (CSCAF). Service metrics play a critical role in CSCAF that presents managers with a practical framework to carry out cloud capability assessments. The process may be simply described as publishing, retrieving, and managing cloud service descriptions, service publications which are matched with descriptions of consumer's requirements and service matching.

Keywords Capability assessment · Cloud assessment · Cloud computing · Cloud service capability assessment framework · Service capability

12.1 Introduction

Considering the complexity of today's service environment, SMEs cannot afford to accept the status quo of service operations and therefore must have some clear business analytics objective to reach. Without clear metric objectives, organisations are

N. Carroll (✉)
Department of Marketing and Management, University of Limerick, Limerick, Ireland
e-mail: noel.carroll@ul.ie

M. Helfert
School of Computing, Dublin City University, Glasnevin, Dublin 9, Ireland
e-mail: markus.helfert@computing.dcu.ie

T. Lynn
Irish Centre of Cloud Computing and Commerce (IC4), School of Business,
Dublin City University, Glasnevin, Dublin 9, Ireland
e-mail: theo.lynn@dcu.ie

Z. Mahmood (ed.), *Continued Rise of the Cloud,* Computer Communications
and Networks, DOI 10.1007/978-1-4471-6452-4_12,
© Springer-Verlag London 2014

almost destined for disaster since the allocation of resources may not have responded to the demand exerted from outside of the organisation. This is particularly true within a complex and rapidly changing cloud computing environment. The cloud dynamic ecosystem is moving toward a collection of services which interoperate across the Internet. This chapter is motivated by the findings of a literature review to assess the experiences of SMEs as they provide and/or try to avail of cloud solutions. More specifically, the initial research phase of a literature review identified the lack of capability assessment practices for cloud computing readiness and capabilities within SMEs. This chapter offers a step toward a solution to assess cloud capabilities.

This chapter presents the CSCAF. The chapter discusses the development of the CSCAF and how it can support organisations gain a thorough insight on their ability to migrate toward providing and/or availing of cloud solutions. Thus, service metrics play a critical role in CSCAF that presents managers with a practical framework to carry out cloud capability assessments. The author also adopts Universal Description, Discovery, and Integration (UDDI) as a platform to develop a cloud capabilities registry (CCR). The process may be simply described as publishing, retrieving, and managing cloud service descriptions, service publications which are matched with descriptions of consumer's requirements and service matching.

12.2   Literature Review

The interesting thing about cloud computing is that we've redefined cloud computing to include everything that we already do. . . . I don't understand what we would do differently in the light of cloud computing other than change the wording of some of our ads. . . . . [Larry Ellison (Oracle's CEO), Wall Street Journal, September 26, 2008].

This section draws on the current literature and discusses some the main themes which have emerged from the evolution of cloud developments. The objective of the literature review is to provide a platform for both academics and industry practitioners to gain an understanding of the current trends and issues surrounding the adoption of the cloud.

The influence of information technology (IT) continues to alter our understanding of the business environment. It continues to shift computing paradigms to afford greater accessibility to business capabilities. This is yet again evident through the emergence of cloud computing. Cloud computing allows various key organisational resources to become more efficiently available, for example, software, information, storage, and business processes. Cloud computing allows organisations to gain access to sophisticated services through Internet channels. The fundamental benefit of cloud computing is its ability to share resources "on demand" at considerably reduced costs. This has led to the explosive uptake of cloud computing. According to the latest Cisco report, *"Cloud is now on the IT agenda for over 90 % of companies, up from just over half of companies (52 %) last year* [1]." However, availing of services through a systematic manner can become a very complex entanglement of business processes. Understanding the complexity and value of "the cloud" offers immense opportunities through service analytics (i.e., measuring performance).

Thus, understanding and organising how cloud resource are exchanged while assessing organisational ability to provide services on-demand requires a capability maturity framework to assist in strategic business and IT alignment. If organisations are to enjoy the benefits of cloud developments, it is important to strategise how they can assess the business and technical factors to transform their cloud capabilities. This is particularly true for the survival of SMEs. While the author anticipates that cloud computing will revolutionise the way SMEs operate and compete on a global scale, there is little literature on SMEs assessment capabilities. This literature review offers a state-of-the-art in cloud computing across SMEs and examines methods of how cloud initiatives could be assessed. The author identifies a number of key factors for assessment and highlight significant gaps particularly in the realisation of cloud readiness and assessing "cloud value". The emphasis here is a change in organisational architecture and support how managers reengineer cloud provisions by orchestrating their capabilities to optimise return-on-investment (ROI). The chapter offers a discussion on addressing the literature gaps by introducing the CSCAF to support cloud computing assessment.

12.2.1   The Service Environment

The service industry continues to play a critical and dominant role within the global economy [2, 3, 4, 5]. A service may be defined as *"a means of delivering value to customers by facilitating outcomes customers want to achieve, without the ownership of specific costs and risks"* [6]. Nowadays, services are wrapped up in a complex business and IT environments. For example, the Internet offers a distributed platform to port services across the world and has become one of the most significant industrial drivers in recent years, referring to the networking and connectivity of objects. IT is described as the third wave of the world's information industry. It captures the importance of Internet tools and technologies to support computing utility. This has also led to the realisation of cloud computing. Cloud computing is considered to be the next "technological revolution" [7] which will transform the IT industry [8]. The National Institute of Standards and Technology (NIST) [9] define cloud computing as *"a model for enabling convenient, on-demand network access to a shared pool of configurable computing resources (e.g., networks, servers, storage, applications, and services) that can be rapidly provisioned and released with minimal management effort or service provider interaction."* Thus, understanding an organisation's capability to adopt this paradigm has become increasingly important as part of their strategic planning. Cloud readiness is one of the emerging concepts which support organisation's ability to take stock of their resources and their capability to adopt cloud solutions. Cloud readiness is a critical assessment strategy which examines the organisational ability to adopt a cloud service infrastructure to support service provision. However, while much of the literature is primarily concerned with large organisations and multinational organisations (MNOs), the author has identified the gap and need to examine cloud readiness of SMEs.

12.2.2 Defining Cloud Computing

Cloud computing has resulted in a number of technological and business shifts which provide an opportune period to promote the adoption of cloud initiatives. However, due to the explosive uptake of the cloud [10], there has been some blurred concepts as to what constitutes as cloud computing. In fact, according to Cohen [11], it is the "lack of understanding" which has held many organisations back from adopting the cloud. In effect, there is a resistance amongst managers with the expectation for organisation to swiftly move from a traditional business model which has served organisations well up until now to one which has yet to be proven. This section attempts to clear up the meaning of cloud computing as we examine what the literature defines as cloud computing (see Table 12.1).

Although Table 12.1 demonstrates the various understanding of what constitutes as cloud computing, they do share common characteristics. For example, this chapter defines cloud computing as an enabling effort and overarching philosophy which exploits Internet technologies as organisations provide or avail of resources and competences through flexible and economic IT-enabled infrastructures. Buyya et al. [12] highlights the economic promise of cloud computing and explains that it is "*a type of parallel and distributed system consisting of a collection of interconnected and virtualized computers that are dynamically provisioned and presented as one or more unified computing resources based on service-level agreements.*" This may be achieved through a number of service models. There are generally three main categories of the cloud computing models:

- *Public cloud:* It is a cloud is made available through a metered agreement for the general public [8].
- *Private cloud:* These are internal data centres of an organisation or other organisation, which is not made available to the general public [8].
- *Hybrid cloud:* It is a combination of public and private cloud environments.

These three categories may also be described as micro characteristics of cloud models. For example, see Table 12.2.

The adoption of these models is largely reflected in the service environment (i.e., the industry) and manager's confidence in their ability to become cloud providers/users. It is expected that as organisations become more accustomed to cloud capabilities they will become more tentative with experimenting with a combination of these models [1].

12.2.3 The Emergence of the Cloud

The exponential growth of technological developments has provided modern society with the expectation of rapid accessibility to services [17]. We have grown accustom to "on-demand" services to meet our daily routines making accessibility an essential requirement [2]. This had a significant impact within the business environment and how we now view services. IT has experienced the same phenomenon but at a much faster pace, i.e., utility computing. This was predicted back in 1969 when

Table 12.1 Cloud computing definitions

Author	Definition	Macro characteristics
Buyya et al. [12]	"…parallel and distributed system consisting of a collection of interconnected and virtualised computers that are dynamically provisioned and presented as one or more unified computing resources based on service-level agreements established through negotiation between the service provider and consumers"	Distributed system Interconnected Virtualised Dynamic Negotiations Provider Consumer
Armbrust et al. [8]	"…both the applications delivered as services over the Internet and the hardware and systems software in the data centres that provide those services"	Applications Delivery Internet Hardware Software Data centres
Gillett [13]	"A form of standardized IT-based capability, such as Internet-based services, software, or IT infrastructure offered by a service provider that is accessible via Internet protocols from any computer, is always available and scales automatically to adjust to demand, is either pay-per-use or advertising-based, has Web- or programmatic-based control interfaces, and enables full customer self-service"	IT capability Internet-based services Software Availability Self-service
Cearley [14]	"help enterprises improve the creation and delivery of IT solutions by allowing them to access services more flexibly and cost-effectively"	Improvement Create IT solutions Deliver IT solutions Accessibility Flexibility Cost-effective
Wang et al. [15]	"set of network enabled services, providing scalable, QoS guaranteed, normally personalized, inexpensive computing platforms on demand, which could be accessed in a simple and pervasive way"	Network services Scalability Quality of Service Guarantee Personalised Inexpensive Platform On-demand Pervasive
EC Expert Report [16]	"…an elastic execution environment of resources involving multiple stakeholders and providing a metered service at multiple granularities for a specified level of quality (of service)"	Elasticity Resources Multiple stakeholders Metered services Quality

Kleinrock envisaged that we would witness the evolution of computer utilities similar to that of electricity [18, 19]. This, coupled with increasing demands for greater mobility and customised software at reduced costs, has allowed service providers to become more competitive regardless of organisational size [20, 21]. In this sense, there is an apparent paradox with enabling greater competitiveness and shrinking market size. However, while more organisations choose to deliver and/or avail of the

Table 12.2 Cloud model characteristics

Model	Micro characteristics
Public	Flexible
	Distributed users
	Elastic
	Freedom of self-service
	Pay-as-you-use
	Secure
	Metered
Private	Internalised business processes
	Restricted access
	Scalable
	Accessible
	Elastic
	Shared
Hybrid	Elastic
	On-demand
	Abstracted locations and equipment from the user
	Combination of restricted and open access to services

cloud opportunities, this adds greater complexity to the business environment, often making it difficult to assess the "true value" of cloud developments [22]. Thus, cloud computing promises increased capabilities with little guidance as to how one can assess their capabilities within the cloud. In fact, it is suggested that cloud computing promises to transform the strategic value of an organisation through "incremental and evolving objectives, competencies, and value measures [23]." The question remains, *how can SMEs assess the value of cloud capabilities*? Therefore, at this stage, the attraction of cloud computing is exploratory in nature but some of the key benefits include the financial reward, ability to leverage existing investment, establish and defend a service franchise, leverage customer relationships, and to become a cloud platform [8]. Table 12.3 summarises the main advantages and disadvantages [24] of cloud computing. The disadvantages of cloud computing are often considered by Cloud service providers (CSPs) as opportunities and we will invert these and argue they can provide a service that improves upon each of these through what the author describes as "plug-in capabilities".

The disadvantages of cloud computing have been identified as "opportunities" by several large cloud providers an area which we will revisit later in this chapter. The advantages listed in Table 12.3 have resulted from a number of important shifts in the service ecosystem. The growth of the cloud computing is due to a number of key technological delivery factors (hardware and software) which came together over the last decade (Fig. 12.1).

Cloud computing comprises four main layers and an overarching management layer which, in a real world scenario, would operate in most of the layers. Due to improved technological hardware capabilities, organisations can enjoy the benefits listed in Table 12.3. However, understanding how we can measure these cloud computing capabilities remains unclear. In addition, Armbrust et al. [8] list what they describe as the three main hardware aspects which are considered "new" to cloud computing:

Table 12.3 Advantages and disadvantages of cloud computing

Advantage	Disadvantage
Enhanced service accessibility (greater access to resources)	Often an unknown fit for the needs of the organisation (reliability, availability, accessibility, robustness, resilience, recoverability)
Backup and recovery (increased storage capacity)	
Increased competitiveness (faster access to markets) through improved access to resources	Integrity (software functionality)
Scalability	Maintainability (remoteness, priorities, SLAs) suggesting a limited scope of solution
Greater flexibility	
Collaboration (sharing resources)	Contingent risks (high impact on service operations)
Lower investment/up-front cost	
Lower operational costs	Major service interruption (service survival, data survival)
Lower IT staff costs	
	The need to support a flexible business operation
	Security risks (service, data, authentication and authorisation, denial of service attacks)
	Risk management strategies (compliance and usage)

Fig. 12.1 Cloud stack

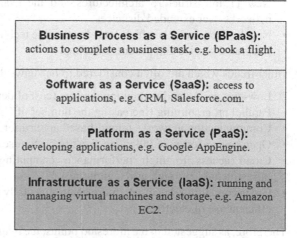

- *Agility*—creating the illusion of endless computing resources available on demand
- *Reduced cost and increased competition*—eliminates end-users up-front commitment and thereby costs
- *Resource efficiency*—supports short-term concept of "pay as you go" usage of computing resources

This offers an immediate insight on the primary drivers behind cloud computing, i.e., greater access to computing economies of scale to generate greater business value, for example *cloudonomics* [25]. Considering the promise of cloud computing, it is critical that organisation can evaluate the opportunities presented to organisations. This is particularly important in the context of core business solutions, drivers and business initiatives to sustain "value-added" activities.

12.2.4 Cloud Computing: Drivers and Trends

Over the last two decades, we witnessed two important key cloud computing developments: (1) increase in technology capability and accessibility, and (2) the emergence of new business models. Similar to the growth in IT throughout the 1990s [26], combined these developments opened up new opportunities to apply technology to address business needs. The cloud computing paradigm promises greater accessibility to computing capacity from domain expertise providers allowing consumers access (anytime-anywhere) to resources via Internet connectivity. The availability and low cost of large-scale commodity computing infrastructure and storage enabled the emergence of cloud computing. This was also timely with the emergence of cost of electricity, growth in broadband, and economies of scale in hardware and software development [8]. These factors also influence the location of data centres. According to Gillett [13] of Forrester Research, the main drivers which support the adoption of cloud developments include:

- Internet-based services (including social media)
- New IT infrastructure architectures and the availability of very high speed networks over extended distances
- New business models which cater for flexible technology usage
- Integrated service and product offerings

Other trends which are often considered to be "unwritten" [27] include:

- Low-cost access and computing devices (cost of devices continue to decrease)
- Parallel programming (increasing the number of CPU cores)
- Communication networks (cloud-based applications)
- Open source software (allowing users to customise SaaS)
- Cloud access to high performance computing (utilisation of global e-infrastructures through grid computing)
- Green computing (becoming more environmentally friendly computing and make efficient use of electricity)

Therefore, as suggested in the aforesaid points, the main rationale for adopting cloud computing may be summarised as opportunistic, cost, production, and catalytic. From a research perspective, we are reminded of Mooney et al. [28] where they suggest that there is a difference in the value drivers in the pre- and post-adoption of IT-enabled management and operational processes. Their framework examines the typology of business processes and impact of IT on processes. In addition, they suggest that by examining the impact of IT on processes, we can derive a "business value'" of IT. This research proposes the need to examine this in a cloud computing context. While there is much hype about the promise of cloud computing, industry analysts (for example, Gartner, Forrester, and Morgan Stanley) predict how it will transform our understanding of the "organisation" where boundaries continue to erode. However, there is no "'one size fits all'" approach [29]. The consumption of service varies drastically and influences the derived benefits from their requirements and application. The cloud does not represent a shift in how IT services are produced or even managed but rather it shifts our understanding on how IT is valued and accessed to deliver services. For example, pricing is a hot topic across cloud computing literature. Armbrust et al. [8] explain that one of the key drivers of the cloud is the elasticity of resources adding to the competitive armour of an organisation. While one of the benefits of the cloud is the "anytime-anywhere" factor, this also causes concern, particularly regarding the "anywhere". The physical location of the data centres are often influenced by the laws which govern that area and the techniques used to protect data. Buyya et al. [12] highlight how Amazon EC2 has introduced the concept of "availability zones" (i.e., a set of resources that have a specific geographic location) which appears to have set a trend regarding cloud storage and security. Service provision is also protected through service level agreements (SLAs). SLAs establish the terms and conditions upon which a service is provided, for example, pricing mechanism and quality of service (QoS). Thus, many of these factors influence the decisions in the transition toward cloud computing.

12.2.5   Transition Toward the Cloud

The transition toward the cloud is often considered a daunting process. It can be a time consuming process and is often hindered by the fear of "unknown" financial investments coupled with security risks (for example, see the Open Group, 2009; "Risk Taxonomy" [30]). However, prior to cost assessment, it is also important to gain an understanding on whether the service ecology is "ready" to make the move. This places emphasis on the need to incorporate a capability assessment tool. There are two key questions which managers must ask clearly answer regarding their motivation to adapt cloud computing [22]:

- Are you trying to reduce cost or add value?
- Who will benefit from the use of cloud computing? The IT group or business units in the enterprise (including clients or customers)?

The transition toward the cloud is also influenced by the presence of existing technological capabilities, for example, service orientated architecture (SOA) environment. The benefits of the cloud are similar to SOA. For example, some of the main characteristics of SOA are its flexibility in processes, its reusability of services, and its ability to reduce the complexity in service execution [31], making the transition more informed. Cloud computing and SOA may be viewed as complementary activities since both play critical roles in IT planning and management. Cloud computing presents a value- added offering to SOA but does not replace SOA initiatives. SOA components can leverage software over networks using standards-based interfaces which can benefit from the platform and storage services as a less expensive scalable commodity. Cloud computing and SOA share similar drivers, such as cost reduction. As illustrated in Fig. 12.2, there are significant overlaps in cloud computing and SOA [32]. However, we must be mindful that they have different focus to address problems within the organisation.

For example, SOA is primarily concerned with enterprise integration technologies to efficiently exchange information between systems. SOA implemented technologies include Web services standards which support greater integration across different

Cloud Computing	Overlap|	SOA via Web Services
• Software as a Service (SaaS) • Utility Computing • Terabytes on Demand • Data Distributed in a Cloud • Platform as a Service • Standards Evolving for Different Layers of the Stack	• Application Layer Components/Services • Network Dependence • Cloud/IP Wide Area Network (WAN)-supported Service Invocations • Leveraging Distributed Software Assets • Producer/Consumer Model	• System of Systems Integration Focus • Driving Consistency of Integration • Enterprise Application Integration (EAI) • Reasonably Mature Implementing Standards (REST, SOAP, WSDL, UDDI, etc.)

Fig. 12.2 Overlapping concepts from cloud computing and SOA [32]

development languages by providing a language neutral software layer. This allows organisations to maintain a certain level of consistency across enterprise architecture for additional integration. Cloud computing, on the other hand, focuses on using the network to outsource IT functions as commodities where it may be considered a more viable option than supporting the IT function internally. Therefore, cloud computing provides on-demand access to virtualised IT resources across the Internet. Thus, while SOA and cloud computing share many characteristics, they should not be considered synonymous [32].

In most cases however, managers require some form of guidance to support their ability to decide on their readiness for cloud strategy and enrolment. We examine some of the prominent assessment models which are used to assess IT-enabled business strategy. Assessment models have always been greeted with enthusiasm and criticism. For example, Mettler [33] explains that capability maturity model integration (CMMI) assessments are too forward-looking from a maturity assessment perspective. In addition, Gefen et al. [34] warns that one of the most common criticisms of CMMI is its excessive documentation which may "*lead to a loss in motivation and creativity.*" Thus, we must design assessment strategies which allow SMEs to easily explore and examine their cloud capabilities. This is critical as according to the EC Expert Report [16] one of the open research issues is that "*cloud technologies and models have not yet reached their full potential and many of the capabilities associated with clouds are not yet developed and researched to a degree that allows their exploitation to the full degree, respectively meeting all requirements under all potential circumstances of usage.*" Thus, this forms part of the author's motivation toward the assessment of cloud computing environments.

12.3 Assessing the Cloud

Cloud readiness is associated with service improvement. In order to assess process improvement Humphrey [35] suggests that one requires four key components:

- A framework to measure the improvement
- Advice on the approach to take
- Guidance on the methods to use
- The way to benefit and build on the experience of others

Assessing the cloud steers this research effort toward understanding cloud service metrics. Brooks [36] cautions that we must be careful when selecting service metrics. Just because a measure may be easily available does not ensure that we are making the correct choice of measures. He suggests some key principles when choosing metrics. IT Service Management (ITSM) practice recommends adopting the philosophy of the following principles [36]:

- Specific, measurable, achievable, realistic, and timely (*SMART*): Metrics should be realistic and concise within a specific timeframe.
- Keep it simple stupid (*KISS*): Metrics should be explained well in a simple format.
- Goal-questions-metrics Method (*GQM*): These are high-level goals which are used to decide what metrics to employ.
- Mean absolute percentage error (*MAPE*): It is a statistical technique used to establish reliability.
- *Customer relationship diagram*: It is a mapping method of the most immediate customer relationship which identifies the processes between the organisation and the customer in a simplistic manner, e.g., customer satisfaction.

While adopting these metric principles, Brooks [36] also suggests that a process should be designed to monitor appropriate status from the beginning. In addition, if changes occur, communication and training should be provided to develop a thorough understanding as to the impact of this change. Brooks [36] advises that we should not implement a "*catch-all statuses or categories*" as metrics in service management making it important to monitor and manage these statuses and categories, particularly in assessing cloud readiness.

According to Orand [37], the main issue associated with IT is the inability to improve service provision due to a lack of "proper" measurements. There is often a mismatch in IT personnel's ability to address the business needs as business demands more for IT support and functionality. The alignment of IT and business is often only experienced as an organisation matures [38] to support evolving strategies (if organisations survive to that point). While there is often a lot of discussion surrounding business and IT capabilities, consider for a moment that business do not "want" IT but rather, they want the "service" which is provided by IT (Fig. 12.3). This research describes this as cloud value co-creation [39], i.e., the alignment of business objectives and IT capabilities to supports organisation's ability to generate value. IT is a cost, and yet it enables business value. Thus, we ought to be interested in the output of a service and the capabilities employed to reach the desired output. What is of immense interest here is the ability to assess cloud capabilities in delivering the desired output.

Organisations rely on the alignment of business objectives and IT capabilities to create value. However, what if organisations identify a niche market which they can

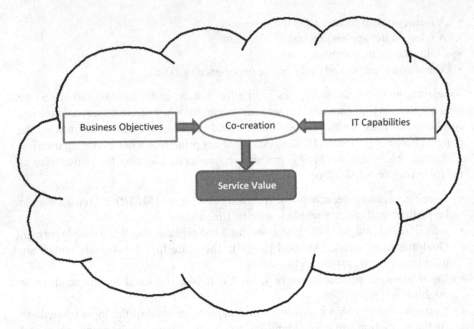

Fig. 12.3 Cloud co-creation

provide a solution but may lack one or two essential IT capabilities to be successful in this space. SMEs can view this as a hindrance or an opportunity. Consider the opportunity of SMEs offering "plug-in capabilities" to support external organisations ability to avail of greater cloud solutions. The author examines this in light of existing service management standards. Several efforts have surfaced as world leading standards in ITSM and IT quality initiatives for governance, quality, and operational guidance. These include (but not limited to):

- CMMI
- Control objectives for IT and related technology (COBiT)
- Open group architecture framework (TOGAF)
- ITSM
- IT infrastructure library (ITIL, ISO 20000)
- IT-capability maturity framework (IT-CMF)
- Service management index (SMI)

There have been a number of efforts to access cloud computing environments. It has become increasingly difficult for customers to decide on a CSP based on their individual requirements [40, 12]. Garg et al. [40] propose a framework which suggests that service quality may be matched with service requirements. However, this is once again from a technical (software) perspective rather than a business-oriented view (focusing on the business value of cloud "as-a-Service" components). The research focuses on how one could dissect service capabilities to improve capability assessment methods.

12.3.1   Capability Assessments

Capability assessments have been well documented throughout literature, particularly in the IT field. However, due to the explosive growth in cloud computing, efforts to assess the organisational capabilities of SMEs to adapt "the cloud" are almost non-existent. This presents a significant burden on SMEs to understand the benefit of cloud computing or to optimise their existing cloud operations. Therefore, to address this problem the author began to structure the capability assessment process following traditional approaches, such as the capability maturity model (CMM). There are five factors which must be considered in the assessment including:

- *Maturity levels*—presents a scale of one to five, where five is the ideal maturity state
- *Key process areas*—clusters specific business process or activities which are considered important to achieve a business goal
- *Goals*—goals of individual processes and to what extent they are realised indicates the capability and maturity of an organisation
- *Common features*—describe the practices which implement a process centred on performance mechanisms
- *Key practices*—the infrastructure and practice which contribute to the process

While this chapter adopts this structure and has based on it the development of CSCAF, one must be mindful of the need to examine cloud capabilities from a management level (i.e., business-oriented metrics rather than IT-oriented metrics). Processes are measurable and are therefore performance-driven. The main objective of developing a capability assessment is to provide some level of measurement which can generate data to support decision-making. These measurements can support managers determine process status and effectiveness being executed by their cloud strategy. It can also allow organisations identify where opportunity exists at various levels identified by CMM (discussed later in this chapter). Therefore, the initial step to assessing capabilities is to have a clear and concise understanding of how one can:

- Determine organisational goals of cloud computing initiatives
- Identify organisational objectives of how they set out to achieve the goals
- Define specific measures which influence decision-making
  - Determine individual process goals
  - Determine individual process objectives
  - Determine individual process measures
- Establish a cloud readiness and capabilities assessment framework

The assessment process is a significant contribution to both practitioners and academia. This work is also influenced by previous works, such as Sycara et al. [41] and Paolucci et al. [42] who examine the semantics of matching engines. The author attempts to simplify this approach in a business context.

Fig. 12.4 ITIL service
lifecycle V3 ([52])

12.3.2 IT Infrastructure Library

In order to achieve some level of consistency, good practice must be established and become a commodity of achieving desired results. The ITIL is an example of this approach which defines best practice and became "good practice" (see Fig. 12.3). One of the prominent ITSM practices which guide the alignment of IT service with business needs is the ITIL. The ITIL describes specific procedures, tasks and checklists which may not be organisation-centric but is employed to examine service compliance and to measure improvement. The ITIL was initially designed as a library of defined best practice (i.e., tried and tested in industry) which dates back to 1986. Nowadays, ITIL v3 presents a holistic view of the service lifecycle with particular attention on IT which support service delivery. Orand [37], describes ITIL as "*documented common sense*". While ITIL does not prescribe how to do things, it does highlights what ought to be carried out in order to reach a desired outcome. Thus, ITIL has become the de facto for over 20 years of ITSM. The author identified the potential of examining cloud readiness through this cyclical approach (see Fig. 12.4) while recognising the need to adopt ITIL to suit a cloud computing context. For the purpose of this chapter, the author examines the promise of ITIL in cloud computing.

As illustrated in Fig. 12.4, the service lifecycle comprises five stages:

- *Service strategy*—guidance to developing an overall strategy (for example, markets, customers, capabilities, resources, financial) to align business needs with IT capability. The main components covered within service strategy include:
  - Strategy management
  - Service portfolio management
  - Financial management of IT services
  - Demand management

- Business relationship management
- *Service design*—guidance to balance design and service constraints (for example, requirements vs. financial resources) to streamline automated processes. The main components covered within service design include:
  - Design coordination
  - Service catalogue
  - Service level management
  - Availability management
  - Capacity management
  - IT service continuity management (ITSCM)
  - Information security management system
  - Supplier management
- *Service transition*— guidance in transitioning a service into operation (i.e., technical and non-technical) through enterprise architecture. The main components covered within service transition include:
  - Service level management
  - Availability management
  - Capacity management
  - ITSCM
  - Information security management system
  - Service asset and configuration management
  - Release and deployment management
- *Service operation*—guidance on effective and efficient operation of the service, i.e., aligning strategy and objectives with service execution and technology
- *Continual service improvement*—ensuring continual improvements throughout the organisations lifecycle, not just a service (e.g., people and governance)

These stages play a fundamental part in our assessment of cloud readiness and capabilities and the development of the CSCAF. The author considers these stages to play a role in the assessment of organisational macro capabilities within which more detailed assessment may be carried out to pinpoint areas of weakness.

12.3.3   Control Objectives for Information and Related Technologies

The control objectives for information and related technologies (COBIT) is a framework [43] that supports the management and governance of IT. It supports managers' ability to identify business requirements, risks, and technological issues within their organisation. The COBIT was launched in 1996 to establish an international set of standards in the day-to-day operations of an organisation directed toward managers and IT staff. This section examines how this offers an agile support tool to provide cloud services. The COBIT framework consists of 34 core processes to manage IT, and validated from "*41 international source documents*" [44]. The processes identify the objective, input, output, and performance through a maturity model. These processes are also aligned with the business objectives, thus creating a better linkage between business and IT. In doing so, there are shared metrics and responsibilities of process owners within four main categories: (1) Plan and organise (2) Acquire and implement (3) Deliver and support (4) Monitor and evaluate.

COBIT is also known to act as an umbrella framework for a number of good practices including, ITIL, ISO 27000, CMMI, and TOGAF. Within the COBIT 5 framework (see Fig. 12.5), users can benefit from its process descriptions, control objectives, management guidelines, and maturity models. However, from a SME perspective, adopting COBIT can become a very time-consuming and cumbersome task guideline to support SME cloud operations. This motivates the author to establish an easily adoptable framework which integrates the benefits of COBIT.

As illustrated in Fig. 12.5, the latest version of COBIT (COBIT 5) provides and end-to-end view of enterprise IT governance. This highlights the important role that information and technology plays in the creation of value within an organisation. The principles and practice of COBIT 5 can also provide a valuable lens in cloud computing particularly in business and IT governance. COBIT 5 provides five key IT management and governance principles:

- Meeting stakeholders' needs
- Covering the enterprise end-to-end
- Applying a single integrated framework
- Enabling a holistic approach
- Separating governance from management

These are important principles for cloud computing initiatives. For example, COBIT 5 may be adopted in cloud computing to enjoy the benefits of supporting business decisions and strategic goals through the innovative use of cloud initiatives. In addition, COBIT 5 provides the tools to maintain an acceptable level of IT-related risk and cost control through various process compliance guidance.

12.3.4 Service Measurement Index

The service measurement index (SMI) is a performance-orientated service standard which is being developed to support organisation's ability to compare service provision based on business and IT requirements [45]. It examines and compares business objectives and business value to support decision-making tasks. The SMI provides a good platform upon which we can examine the quality of public, private, or hybrid cloud services. Considering the complexity of cloud service networks, measuring the performance and value of service offerings is of critical importance to managers regardless of their organisational size (for example [46]). At Carnegie Mellon University, the Cloud Service Measurement Initiative Consortium (CSMIC) [47] are currently exploring how they might adapt a SMI hierarchical framework. The SMI model examines six main measurement categories. It provides a relative index to compare and monitor services (scoring 1–99). Therefore, SMI is dependent upon consumers' ratings which evaluate six main factors or metrics of a service: (1) Quality (2) Agility (3) Risk (4) Cost (5) Capability (6) Security.

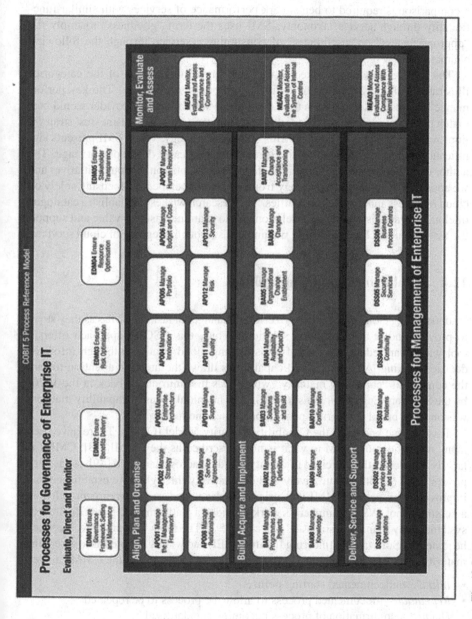

Fig. 12.5 COBIT 5 framework [43]

As the status of SMI grows their database may populate with rich data while indicating which metrics are of greater importance to various services (for example, security is of greater importance in email exchanges rather than cost). Therefore, a comparison is required to benchmark performance of services with similar functionality through service taxonomy. SMI uses the term "goodness" to imply the "appropriateness" or "usefulness" of consuming a service through the following characteristics (Fig. 12.6):

The service provider is asked to rate the service under each of the categories illustrated in Fig. 12.6 based on their desired business objective. The key performance indicators (KPIs) data is used to examine which service provider would best match their performance. In effect, this adds greater agility to a businesses' strategy, improves service quality, and "informs" business strategy. While SMI presents significant promise to the cloud world, it remains in an early development stage. The author identifies the need to support SMEs in their adaptation of cloud initiatives and we approach the assessment strategy from a different perspective focusing solely on cloud readiness and service capabilities. This research wishes to establish a catalogue of cloud characteristics and their relationship to examine business value and support the assessment of cloud capability within SMEs through a registry of cloud services.

12.4   Exploring Cloud Capabilities

Understanding cloud capabilities is a critical managerial task for SMEs as they strive to provide and/or avail of cloud solutions. Thus, this CSCAF approach offers a tool which can reduce the risk of transforming cloud strategies though informed decision-making. Assessing cloud capabilities draws the author's attention toward the concept of "capability maturity" which was first introduced back in the 1970s by the Software Engineering Institute (SEI). The initial focus of capability maturity was on three broad categories: people, processes and technology.

This became known as the Capability Maturity Model (CMM). There have been many reiterations of CMM to what is now described as the CMMI [48]. CMMI is largely adopted as the preferred IT quality standard across the world [49]. It has been proven to work both quantitatively and qualitatively through more established and improved work paths. CMMI was originally developed as a government software assessment tool. Watts Humphery's work provided a platform for the development of systematically managing software processes [50]. The model began to evolve when he joined the Software Engineering Institute (SEI) and widely adopted as to assess the maturity of processes. There are five main maturity levels within the CMMI model:

- *Initial*—undocumented starting point
- *Repeatable*—documented process to allow the process to be repeated
- *Defined*—confirmation of process becoming standardised
- *Managed*—agreed metrics to evaluate the process performance
- *Optimising*—managing the improvement of the process

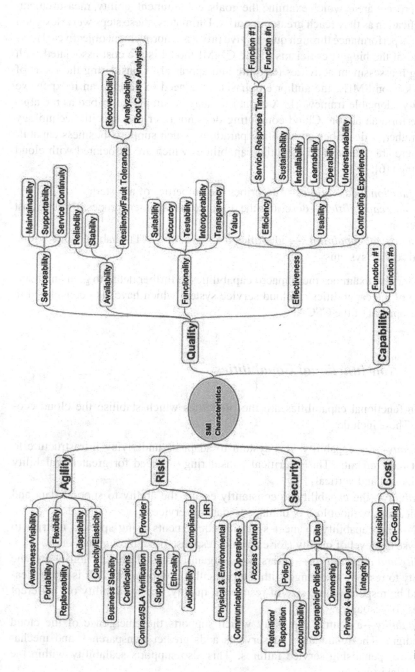

Fig. 12.6 SMI overview [45]

These levels provide a holistic view of process maturity. Within each phase, there are the key process areas which examine the goals, commitment, ability, measurement, and verification as they reach greater maturity. Ultimately, these steps were designed to improve performance through quantitative process-improvement objectives. However, one of the biggest criticisms of the CMMI model is the cost associated with adopting it assessment activities (training and appraisal). Considering the focus of this work is on SMEs, the author emphasises the need to develop an inexpensive and easily adoptable framework. A capability may be simply described as the ability to perform an action. Cloud computing does not refer to a specific technology per se; rather, it describes an enabling paradigm which supports business capabilities. There are a number of essential capabilities which are associated with cloud computing [16]:

- *Non-functional capabilities*— describes the properties of a system
- *Economic capabilities*— describes the resource management process through cost reduction
- *Technological capabilities*— identifies the realisation of IT-enabled value within cloud service systems

The author also examines these macro capabilities in further detail to gain an understanding of the capabilities of cloud service system which have also considered in the development of the CSCAF.

12.4.1   Non-functional Capabilities

The non-functional capabilities are the properties which stabilise the cloud ecosystem. These include:

- *Elasticity*—the capability of a system to adapt its underlying infrastructure to meet requirements. This is critical considering the need for greater scalability (horizontal and vertical)
- *Reliability*—the capability to constantly ensure the ability to support data and applications without loss or damage to data or services
- *QoS*— the capability to meet specific requirements using specific metrics to analyse the level of quality (for example, response time, throughput, etc.)
- *Agility and adaptability*— refers to an organisation's elastic capability and the ability to respond to change within a particular environment. This is often measured by response time, size of resources, quality, and availability of "different types" of resources
- *Availability*—a central capability which supports the emergence of the cloud paradigm. The redundancy of services adds greater transparency and mechanisms of penalising service failures. This also supports scalability within the cloud environment

12.4.2 Economic Capabilities

Economic capabilities play a central factor to the uptake of cloud computing. Cloud service systems support the following capabilities:

- *Cost reductions*: Organisations avail of reduced methods of infrastructure maintenance and acquisition costs which also influence human behaviour in a number of ways, for example:
  - *Pay-as-you-use*: This is a consumption-based cost model which allows organisations to bill customers for the resources they utilise. Customer requirements and quality are met by the cloud offering and allowing them to avail of resources without the initial upfront cost. This also allows SMEs to accelerate their service solutions development.
- *Time to market*: This supports SMEs' ability to sell more quickly without experiencing barriers with setting up the infrastructure to compete with MNOs. This allows them to remain competitive.
- *Return on investment (ROI)*: This determines whether the cost and effort is smaller compared to the commercial value and benefits of return. Therefore, it is crucial that an organisation understands where the cut-off point is in which cloud computing is no longer a viable option.
- *Turning capital expense into operating expense*: The benefits of cloud computing may be difficult to determine. Capital expenditure is associated with infrastructural costs but outsourcing capabilities allows organisations to convert capital expense to operational expense.
- *Green IT*: This applies to an organisations capability to reduce energy costs and the carbon emissions.

12.4.3 Technological Capabilities

There are many technological capabilities associated with cloud computing some of which are considered the main ROI in cloud computing. These include:

- *Virtualisation*—hiding the complexity of cloud computing is considered to be an essential characteristic. Virtualisation also enables greater flexibility though the following attributes:
- *Ease of use*—the management and configuration of the system is often integrated in an application to easily operate and control the system.
- *Infrastructure independency*—supports increased interoperability through an independent coding platform
- *Flexibility and adaptability*—a virtual execution environment allows organisations to meet requirements is a shorter timeframe
- *Location independence*—cloud environments facilitate access to resources through Internet connectivity channels.

- *Multi-tenancy*—data may be sourced by multiple actors across a network although location of data may be unknown. This impacts how data is hosted and how applications are developed to port the data.
- *Security, privacy, compliance*—organisations must consider the sensitivity of data which is created, stored, and shared across a virtual network.
- *Data management*— managing data is a critical component of cloud storage which orchestrates the distribution of data in a flexible and consistent manner. This is connected with the QoS and both the horizontal and vertical factors associated with scalability.
- *APIs*— provides a common programming interface to create and extend service provision
- *Metering*—organisations may offer an elastic pricing mechanics on the consumption of resources through a billing application
- *Tools*—supporting the development and adaptation of cloud service provision and usage capabilities

Commercial cloud tools are typically developed independently from one another which attempt to solve customers' problems. However, there is often little technical convergence between these solutions, except for the potential of what the author calls "plug-in capabilities". The cloud development lifecycle tends to begin in-house, provide internal solutions, and offer cloud capabilities through public cloud service offerings. Interoperability is considered one of the main issues associated with proposing a cloud interface which raises issues of an open cloud approach. This highlights the importance of this work in the need for cloud capabilities assessment and matching. The author presents an assessment approach to examine cloud capabilities using CSCAF as we consider the importance of the ITIL. This chapter examines these and summarise their main attributes which support the establishment of the CSCAF. This chapter examines cloud capabilities from a number of perspectives including, strategies, tactical, and operational (see Fig. 12.7).

Figure 12.7 illustrates how the author approached the task of assessing cloud capabilities emphasising the need to "drill down" to operational capabilities and establish cloud service metrics for SMEs. Each management level typically requires different levels of analysis to support their decision-making tasks.

12.4.3.1 Strategic Cloud Service Capabilities

Strategic capability is concerned with the survival and sustainability of an organisations ability to meet business goals and identify methods to generate additional opportunity and value. The four main activities of service strategy are as follows: (1) Defining the service market (2) Developing service offerings (3) Developing strategic assets (4) Executing the service plan.

Managers must be able to identify the factors which they deem controllable and also act upon the uncontrollable to adjust internal operations accordingly. Their decisions have a direct impact on both the short-term and long-term future of an

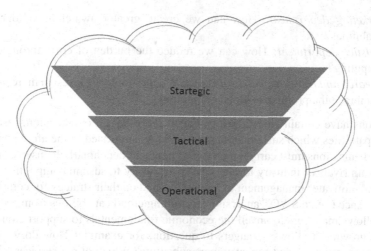

Fig. 12.7 Overview of cloud capabilities assessment

organisation. Many of their decisions are high level and driven by management vision. These may be categorised as tangible (for example increase market share) and intangible (enhance social and environmental image). Examining strategic capabilities requires a resource-based (i.e., skills, assets, and competence) lens to examine the service value chain though internal audits, benchmarking, or strengths, weaknesses, opportunities and threats (SWOT) analysis. Capabilities consist of what may be described as "soft assets" for example, management, organisation, processes, knowledge, and people [6]. This allows managers to scan the business landscape and identify how they can align and build on internal capabilities with external opportunities. For example, one should consider the following resources from a strategic capability perspective before planning to migrate to the cloud:

- *Human resources*: How does our human capital provide value to exploit cloud opportunities?
- *Physical resources*: How do our assets provide value and competitive advantage?
- *Technological resources*: How do our IT capabilities provide business value and competitive advantage?
- *Financial resources*: Is cloud computing a viable option for us and how will it optimise business value?
- *Intellectual capital*: Should we invest in R&D to become leaders in innovative cloud solutions?

In addition, managers must develop an understanding of how cloud computing can support organisational functional areas (i.e., performance for specific outcomes), for example:

- *Finance department*: Where can we improve on cost savings through cloud solutions?
- *HR department*: How can we attract new talent with expertise in cloud computing?

- *Marketing department*: How can we create greater awareness of our cloud capabilities?
- *Logistics department*: How can we reduce the burden of costs through cloud computing?
- *Research and Development department*: Where should we invest in more research to embrace the promise of cloud computing?

Functions have certain characteristics which represent an organisation, resources, and capabilities which sustain an organisation. As suggested in the aforementioned lists, organisations must carry out an assessment and benchmark themselves against their main rivals or industry levels. This is necessary to sustain competitive advantage and motivates management to remain focused on their strategy for comparative performance (i.e., a SWOT analysis). Examining cloud capabilities from a strategic level allows managers to unveil the economic fundamentals to support cloud computing growth. It allows managers to question, for example: How do we offer a distinctive service? What can customers substitute? Which of our services offerings and channels is most profitable? What is generating profit in cloud computing and where are we positioned to benefit from this? Which service process is the most effective? What are the significant game changing trends which are emerging in the business landscape, and where are the constraints which would allow us to gain improved competitive advantage? These are the fundamental questions which managers explore to examine the configuration of underlying drivers in cloud computing at a strategic level. Therefore, the following capabilities which we would associate with cloud computing at a strategic level (guided by ITSM) include:

- Business perspective metrics
- Continuous service improvement programme
- Risk management: (documentation management and competence, awareness & training)

The major output of service strategy is the service level package (SLP) which documents the business requirements and influences the service design [6]. Therefore, from a strategic perspective, it is important that managers understand the business desired outcomes and value of a service in business terms rather than IT terms. This requires managers to ask "why" they do things rather than "how" they do things [6].

Figure 12.8 illustrates a simplified view of service strategy of how managers must realise customers' expectations and value before they establish the strategy. This dual view highlights the need to identify the critical success factors (CSFs) which determine the underlying requirements of a service to ensure success. It also allows managers identify areas for opportunity or continual improvement. The service strategy is typically defined through a service portfolio which determines an organisations commitment to generate customer value. The author incorporates these views into the CSCAF where they can make a valid assessment contribution for SMEs in cloud computing.

Fig. 12.8 Dual view of
service strategy co-creation

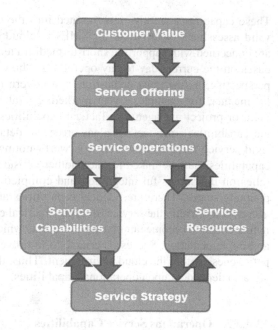

12.4.3.2   Tactical Service Capabilities

Tactical capabilities are largely concerned with managing how a strategy is to be realised through various implementation processes and a set of procedures. This draws
our attention toward the management of the service lifecycle since cloud computing enables service delivery. For example, some tactical capabilities would include
the implementation of CMMI and ITIL assessment practices to govern and monitor
service delivery. Adopting a tactical view of cloud capabilities allows managers to
examine the value chain and how operations align with cloud strategy. This also
encourages managers examine the strategic relevance of adopting or "the cloud".
Therefore the strategic value is reliant upon the successful execution of the tactical
strategy. In general, one can view tactical capabilities in how the cloud can fulfil the
organisational strategy as opposed to being just an organisational fad. From a tactical
perspective, the transformation of an organisation's ability to provide or adopt cloud
solutions would include the following capabilities which we can associate with cloud
computing (guided by ITSM):

- Service level management
- Problem management
- Financial management for IT services
- Capability management
- IT continuity management
- Availability management
- Security management

These capabilities are also incorporated into the CSCAF where they can make a valid assessment contribution for SMEs in cloud computing. Tactical capabilities are concerned with supporting short-to-medium term planning objectives which focuses on the current day-to-day operations ("how things are"). From a manager's perspective, he/she must orchestrate and govern business processes in a successful manner, for example, 1 year marketing strategy, a 1 year budget and finance plan, or project management. Tactical capabilities are more informed than strategic capabilities since tactical plans are more detailed and therefore require more rigid service metrics. However, it is worth noting that both strategic and tactical capabilities must be linked to one another considering that organisational success relies on the successful integration and completion of both strategic and tactical planning stages. Therefore, tactical capabilities are concerned with how business is conducted within the service lifecycle. Tactical capabilities must inform strategic management to become familiar with concepts which govern the success of planning and implementation. Success is critical to improve managers' confidence and competitiveness within the cloud environment. Thus, the success if tactical capabilities are also dependent upon operational capabilities.

12.4.3.3 Operations Service Capabilities

Operational management requires a more detailed approach toward designing, controlling, and managing business processes which directly impact on service operations. Operational management is entrusted with greater responsibility to ensure efficiency of service without jeopardising service quality to meet customer requirements. The author views it as a more "hands on" approach to generate service value within the cloud. Therefore, there is a direct link on how operational capabilities support the realisation of business strategy (strategic capabilities), often controlled by tactical planning. Thus, operational capabilities require the governance of detailed service metrics. We are guided by ITSM to implement cloud service operational metrics, for example, the author considers:

- Incident management
- Service desk
- Configuration management
- Change management
- Release management—application support; application development; and ICT infrastructure management

Service metrics are a critical part of supporting scientific management to quantify service operations and output. Cloud metrics are critical to aid decision-making and instil greater focus, vision, and cost savings within a business environment. In addition, cloud metrics assist managers to implement a "vocabulary" which acts as a "common language" to discuss cloud operations and cloud capabilities. The data which is derived from service metrics provide sufficient insight to report the "truth" (or tell the story) on cloud capabilities and performance indicators. Within a cloud environment the author considers operational capabilities and metrics to be extremely important. Defining cloud operational capabilities and metrics can be viewed as a daunting task but not a challenging one.

12.5 Establishing Cloud Capabilities and Metrics—The Process

One of the first tasks the author was faced with was to establish "what" was to be measured regarding cloud capabilities and determine "why" one ought to measure them. Therefore, establishing a common set of measures is paramount in order to begin a process of examining cloud capabilities. One must also consider whether we would like to establish cloud metrics across similar service organisations or in more holistic terms, across an industry. The author opted for the latter to support the exploratory nature of this research in establishing the CSCAF. However, as this research evolves, the author will aim to derive more organisational-specific measurement approaches. For now, the author would entrust organisations to customise the CSCAF accordingly to meet their individual needs. IT resources can be pooled together to centralise core service capabilities through a ubiquitous range of hardware and software network channels. The dynamics of cloud computing impacts on the demand to meet the adjustability of service level agreements (SLAs). This places greater importance of cloud capabilities, i.e., to optimise the value of core capabilities, for example:

- Business and strategy alignment
- Financial/value impact
- Architecture and infrastructure
- Information/data management
- Security and capacity planning
- Operations and project management
- Project portfolio and asset management
- Organisation and procurement
- Governance and roles

12.5.1 Exploring Operational Cloud Processes

In the previous section the author discussed the capabilities at various management levels: strategic, tactical, and operational. This section adopts this view in terms of understanding cloud capabilities as it allows us to establish a measurement program which provides a balanced and comprehensive view of a service environment. One may categorise service indicators as follows:

- Leading indicators (what we want in the future, i.e., desired results)
- Lagging indicators (how it was in the past or currently, i.e., customers' views)

Fig. 12.9 Assessment overview

It is common to incorporate and integrate both of these to determine how an organisation has progressed toward achieving their goals. Therefore, the measures which an organisation opts for must be repeatable to support the consistency of operational definitions. The operational definitions will define the specific purpose of a measure and it should address one of four broad categories: (1) Cost and effort (2) Status and progress (3) Non-conformance (4) Performance and satisfaction.

Identifying which cloud capability measures belong to the aforesaid listed categories will provide organisations with the first step to establishing a cloud measurement programme (see Fig. 12.9).

The steps described in Fig. 12.9 provide a holistic view of how managers should approach a measurement programme and the questions which managers might pose throughout the design phase. To support organisations achieve this one can expand on these steps and suggest that managers should:

- *Define the organisational goals*—("where do you plan to be in 10 years?")
- *Define the metrics associated with each goal*—("how will you know whether you have reached your goal?")
- *State the objective of the individual measures*—("what are you trying to answer through this specific metric ?")
- *List the characteristics of interest*—("what factors are associated with this particular measure?")
- *Choose a measurement tool*—("how will we measure our progress?")
- *Determine the current status of progress, i.e., benchmark*—("how do you compare yourself to the competition?")
- *Apply a method/formula to test metrics*—("how will we know whether we are on the right track?")
- *Monitor progress*—(who/what is enabling/inhibiting your ability to reach your goals?")
- *Communicate decision criteria*—(how have you got your team to support your vision to move in a particular direction?")
- *Review and repeat* ("what can I improve on when I repeat the process?")

As suggested from the aforediscussed list, it is critical that each measure is linked with a business objective to achieve business goals. Once the goals have been firmly established, we can also establish the entities and attributes associated with them. This is where we begin to dissect the goals into more quantifiable metrics (both quantitative and qualitative measures). This allows us to identify what factors contribute toward the goal (i.e., entities) and how their characteristics influence measures (i.e., attributes). This is an important exercise when establishing cloud capability metrics since it identifies which indicators support decision-making tasks. It is advised that if you identify measures which do not influence decision-making, they should not be included in the measurement programme since they will not serve any real tangible purpose [36].

12.5.2   Defining Operational Cloud Processes

Defining cloud capability measures steered the author toward examining what data should be collected to construct our indicators. Firstly, one should develop clear and concise definitions of the measures we identified. The author identified the service management index (SMI) assessment fields as an appropriate approach to generate cloud metrics (see Sect. 12.3.4). However, merely defining them is not enough. It is important that we test the measure to examine whether they derived any contributory value to the CSCAF. The measurements which reflect an organisations cloud environment must focus on the value generated by processes. Therefore, the selected measures should only be included if they can be acted upon. The simple test for this is to ask, *"what can I do if this process fails?"* [36]. If you cannot answer this, you should not consider this to be an important metric since it will not impact on the decision-making tasks. Therefore, it is important that measures reflect the cloud environment, its objectives, and the organisational priorities. It is also important that organisations do not over emphasise one measurement over another, for example, cloud service availability over customer satisfaction. In this case, although the service is available, customers may be dissatisfied with the QoS which can have drastic consequences for organisations. Managers must remain alert and faithful to all measures which are designed in their assessment program.

12.5.3   Establishing a Cloud Assessment Programme

Establishing a cloud assessment programme requires the commitment of the entire organisation, i.e., it must become institutionalised within the organisation's culture. To begin this process, Table 12.4 summarises four main phases which should be considered—explore, establish, guide, and share.

The first phase is similar to what is described in Sect. 12.4 which provides managers with the opportunity to analyse and reflect on the operations of their organisation. This exploratory phase may be categorised into two components:

- Exploring the cloud processes—identify the process which support and stabilise a service environment
- Exploring the cloud procedures—examine the practices which govern the processes

Once the process and procedures have been identified, the second phase requires managers to establish the process through two useful tools:

Table 12.4 Establishing the assessment programme

Phase	Description	Component	Description
1	Explore	Processes	Overall processes used to govern and manage the project
		Procedures	Supporting sub-processes to carry out the process
2	Establish	Templates	Outlines and guides how to create consistency
		Forms and checklist	Helps you plan and follow task completion and document progress
3	Guide	Guidelines	Instructions that people can execute within the program
4	Share	Repositories	Locations where you store your program elements for team members
		Training material	Develop and ensure that people can adopt the program elements in a directed manner

- Templates—supports consistency in defining the processes
- Forms and checklists—allows managers to follow the progress of the assessment programme

When the assessment metrics and practice has been established, it is important to document these in order to make it repeatable through the use of performance guides. This instructs people how to act within a specific guideline. The fourth phase is concerned with sharing the assessment programme and performance information through repositories and training material to ensure assessments are carried out in a structured format.

12.5.4 Reporting Cloud Service Metrics

Determining cloud service metrics is a data management and collection process. As highlighted throughout this chapter, data must support managers in their decision-making tasks upon which metrics are also tied to process ownership. The numeric objectives set out by managers must present some realistic rationale where improvements are made regularly. There are many components to the assessment processes. These components provide a solid foundation to develop service capabilities through rigorous assessment while identifying the following components (see Table 12.5):

Table 12.5 summarises some of the main components which one ought to consider when assessing a cloud environment. This begins to structure the assessment process in measuring specific processes which best capture the data on cloud capabilities. The measures must be communicated to a team and repeatable by others. The approach we chose was to adopt was the influenced by combining ITSM and SMI since the author considered both to be the most appropriate for assessing cloud capabilities (for example, see Table 12.6):

Table 12.5 Assessing cloud components

Component	Description
Description	Description of the purpose and use of the process
Entry criteria	Describe the previous activities and preconditions to successfully carryout the process
Inputs	Items that are required to conduct the activities (e.g., documents, plans)
Actors	Roles of people to undertake the activities
Roles	A set of responsibilities, activities, and authorities granted to a person or a team
Activities	Describe the steps to see the process through
Outputs	Identify what outputs should appear after the activities are executed
Exit criteria	The results that should be in place in order to conclude the process and responsibilities have been accounted for
Measures	Define the measures you will collect for the process which will give insight on performance

Table 12.6 CSCAF assessment criteria

Field	Description
Description	Explain need for the measure
Specification	What objective is met
Metric attribute	Which attributes it relates to
Justification	Why measure is included
Service(s) where it applies	The specific services to which the measure is applicable
Definition(s) where it applies	Define context of application
Formula(s) and calculations	How the measure is computed
Typical value range	What are the expected values
Examples	Links to a published use of the measure or description of its actual use

Table 12.6 presents the assessment criteria which are incorporated in our CSCAF assessment programme. These criteria appear to be the most suitable to quickly capture important data. It also establishes cloud metrics and supports the development of the CSCAF.

12.6 Developing the CSCAF

The CSCAF is designed to offer a simplified analytical approach toward the assessment of cloud capabilities for SMEs at various levels in the cloud provision models (i.e., BPaaS, SaaS, PaaS, and IaaS). There are a number of evolutionary phases in the development of the CSCAF (Fig. 12.10).

While examining the promise of cloud computing, it is important to establish a framework to assess the value of cloud-enabled technologies from a business perspective. The roadmap outlined in Fig. 12.10 is concerned with the exploration, design, and implementation of metrics for cloud readiness and adaptation while merging some of the key qualities of the frameworks that exists in ITSM and SMI. The aim

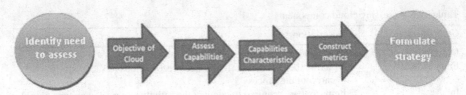

Fig. 12.10 CSCAF development roadmap

Table 12.7 Main IT assessment concerns

Major IT concern	Function
Money/value	Financial
	Impact/value
	Portfolio management
IT strategy	Business alignment
	Strategic planning
	Governance
IT products	Architecture
	Engineering, development, delivery
	Project management
IT services	Service, support, operations
	Security, compliance
IT assets	Asset management
	Capacity planning
Sourcing	Procurement
People	Organising, roles

of the CSCAF is to allow SMEs adopt the framework and customise it for their specific needs to realise the opportunities of value-based cloud analysis and improve capabilities. Many international standards, for example, the IT-capability maturity framework (IT-CMF) examine IT functions in terms of a number of functions as shown in Table 12.7.

While the factors listed in Table 12.7 are undoubtedly important in the assessment of an organisational IT capability, we must be mindful that we have to cater for fast, efficient, and cost effective assessment practices within SMEs to examine cloud capabilities. This is concerned with understanding the "business value" of cloud initiatives. Therefore, one may structure the main IT functions within the CSCAF to comprise four macro analytical views (Fig. 12.11):

- *Innovate*—identifying the processes and aligning capabilities with service opportunity
- *Collaborate*—examining and mapping the process and information exchanges
- *Cost*—determining the contributory value of the process
- *Compare*—benchmarking against existing cloud providers/users

Each of these macro capabilities will examine the value of the cloud capability maturity and examine its status within the maturity curve (on a 1–5 scale adopted from CMMI).

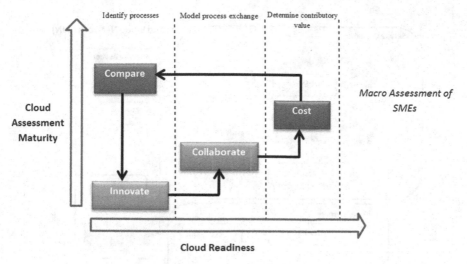

Fig. 12.11 SME Cloud Assessment model

From Fig. 12.11, the author establishes the macro view of the CSCAF which assesses organisational readiness and identifies the cloud capabilities. The model offers organisations the opportunity to identify the contributory value of providing or availing of service capabilities, thus offering a capability brokerage service (illustrated in Fig. 12.12). The "matching service" will assess cloud provider capabilities with customer service requirements. From a service provider's perspective, one can assess how companies develop new services and analyse their service functionality as part of the assessment process. The author is interested in identifying the contributory value of service interactions and exchanges as a result of various cloud capabilities. Cloud applications can drive the value of business through various business process exchanges of cloud capabilities and resources. Therefore, monitoring the exchange of service assets becomes a critical activity within the CSCAF. This research will also explore the visualisation of service brokerage through network analysis techniques to add greater transparency on value co-creation, for example, organisational network analysis (see [37, 38]). The author refers to this as the Cloud Value Network (CVN).

Figure 12.12 illustrates the overall context of the CSCAF. It examines the CVN from a number of functional perspectives including the service consumer, brokerage service, cloud provider, and the service auditor. These functions may be described as follows:

- *Service consumer*—identifies their service requirements and the value they wish to generate from their request of cloud capabilities and competences
- *Brokerage service*— examines service requirements and provides a matching service based on a Cloud Value Index tool

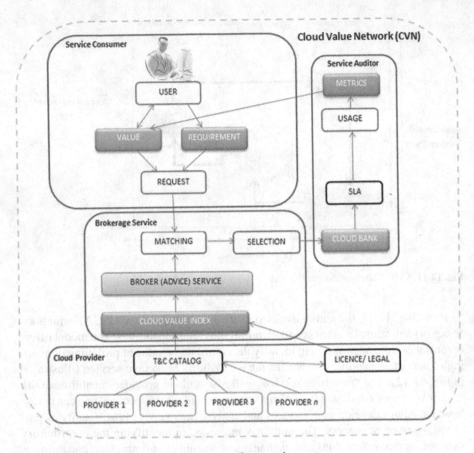

Fig. 12.12 Cloud service capability assessment framework

- *Cloud provider*—enlists their cloud capabilities and metrics to support a service catalogue of service capabilities. These metrics are referenced and matched with user requirements
- *Service auditor*—provides a governance service to monitor QoS and service requirements which supports the establishment of service value metrics. This also provides a reporting mechanism to support managers' decision-making tasks in their adoption/provision of cloud capabilities

These processes support our ability to establish the CSCAF through the cloud value index for service capabilities. Initially, the author examine the characteristics which are often associated with SME cloud services and provide an easily adopted framework solution which supports managers' decisions on cloud evaluations. The research will adopt a colour code system to support managers' ability to quickly visualise "goodness" and areas which warrant some concern through a "traffic light" system (i.e., a green, amber, and red colour scheme). Each characteristic is then referenced with their capabilities through the cloud life-cycle and feeds back into our cloud value index for more in-depth analysis.

12.6.1 Supporting CSCAF Analysis

The CSCAF offers a simplified analytical approach toward the assessment of cloud capabilities at various managerial levels in the cloud provision models (i.e., BPaaS, SaaS, PaaS, and IaaS). The contributory value of a CSCAF analysis highlights where issues exist in the cloud operations. Although there is no "one size fits all" approach to cloud service provision, there are certain criteria which must be met in delivering cloud solutions. This chapter encapsulates this in what is described as "cloud capabilities" which demonstrates CSPs' strengths and weaknesses in specific services.

12.7 Assessing Cloud Capabilities

The CSCAF affords managers the opportunity to assess the organisational capabilities through a number of processes illustrated in Fig. 12.6. This section examines these processes with particular attention on the matching and filtering process to align service capabilities with opportunities to support cloud readiness.

12.7.1 Matching Process

As cloud capabilities become an organisational asset, our attention can move toward the collection of CSP capability libraries where services interoperate through cloud services to become plug-in capabilities. Matching service requirements with CSP capabilities becomes a useful evolutionary step. Sourcing cloud solutions challenges our traditional understanding of acquiring on-site tangible solutions. The cloud demands a lot of trust and confidence in meeting expectations and responsibilities, thus placing immense importance on matching and managing cloud capabilities through trusted assessment practices. Therefore, one must consider a number of key factors, including establishing trust through legal guidance from improved methods associated with the following factors:

- Responsibility
  - For CSP suppliers
  - For CSP customers
- Quality
  - QoS
  - Quality of experience (QoE)
- SLAs
- Compliance
- Security
  - Access control
  - Data storage

- – Data in transit
- – Non-disclosure agreement
- Policy
  - – Data storage
  - – Data protection provisions
- Availability
  - – Offer backup and restore services
- Accountability and liability
  - – Service provider or reseller
  - – Own data centres or rely on a third party
  - – Direct management of third party management
  - – Data protection
- Compatibility of technology
  - – Compatible with current specifications
  - – Barriers for future CSP
- Professional recognition
  - – Cloud certification, trust standards, and reliability standards

The matching process examines the various capabilities associated with CSPs and examines the competence and policies which are employed to secure a quality service (QoS and QoE). When various matches are identified, a filtering process begins to align the cloud strategy with various capabilities on offer.

12.7.1.1 Universal Description Discovery and Integration

The UDDI project, developed in 2000, is directed at establishing publishing standards for Web services. UDDI supports an extensible mark-up language (XML)-based platform-dependent framework which describes, discovers, and integrates business processes. This is particularly apt within cloud computing as services are provided through various digital channels. Discovering service transactions across a cloud ecosystem is a complex task when organisations try to assess service requirements. UDDI is one approach which manages the distributed business data through a global registry of services. This manages the business and development of publishing and locating service information. This may be categorised into three information UDDI registry pages:

- *White pages*—basic organisational identification and contact information to discover a service
- *Yellow pages*—information about categorising a service
- *Green pages*—technical details which describes the behaviour and location of specific services

Thus, UDDI provides several key initiatives for various service stakeholders to describe, discover, and integrate services. There is considerable value of this approach within cloud computing context to support the importation and exportation of specific service capabilities. The UDDI registry host can support our development of a

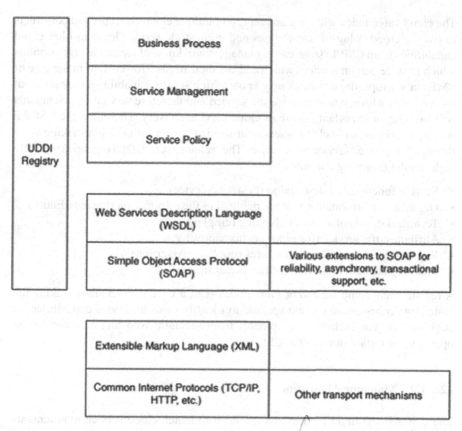

Fig. 12.13 Conceptual relationship between UDDI and other protocols in the Web services stack [51]

cloud value index within the CSCAF to establish a cloud capability matching criteria. Thus, CSPs can list capabilities on a UDDI cloud registry (i.e., the CCR) and define their service applications which are integrated by simple object access protocol (SOAP). The UDDI extends other industry standards, which include HTTP, XML, XML Schema (XSD), SOAP, and Web service description language (WSDL). The relationship between UDDI and other standards is illustrated in Fig. 12.13.

The UDDI interface may be described as the contact which the service provider commits itself to a promise to implement through a Web service. The language used to describe the interface is supported through the technical model or "tModel". A tModel is a form of meta-data and represents an interface which an organisation is going to develop and register. The tModel is a data structure which represents an XML Web services type in UDDI registry. Therefore, the tModel has two key functions; to tag a service capability and to abstract the key functionalities associated with the service capability. The author proposes that each CSP will register their service capabilities with UDDI through a defined list of service types, i.e., a service catalogue. This will allow cloud capabilities to become searchable and retrievable through the CSCAF.

The cloud value index will store and represent unique cloud concepts and constructs to (re)use cloud "plug-in" capabilities and orchestrate service logic to filter cloud capabilities from CSP. In some cases, managers will know of reputable organisations which provide certain services which address their needs. However, as in the case of SMEs or startups, organisations may know which service capabilities they need but have no idea who is best to provide the service and therefore service trust standards will become an important feature of cloud service delivery. Therefore, the CSCAF will be a more feasible cloud assessment service to support decision-making tasks through categorised service information. The framework of UDDI registries typically includes the following attributes:

- Service functionality description (busienssService)
- Organisation information that are publishing the information (businessEntity)
- Technical details of a service (bindingTemplate)
- Attributes of a service (for example, taxonomy)
- Registry entities relational structures (publisherAssertion)
- Tracking changes to service entities (subscription)

A registry may comprise one or more nodes (i.e., a UDDI server) thus making the matching process more context specific to identify suitable service capabilities. In addition, one can include developments from semantic Web literature and linked open data to further develop the CSCAF.

12.7.1.2   Matching Algorithm

The CSCAF algorithm is based on the need to match cloud service requirements with provider capabilities. The outputs from the matching process are also ranked based on user reviews to improve the efficiency of cloud capability matching (see Fig. 12.14).

The match must consist of the CSP reported (and committed to) output and the customer experience output. The degree of success will ultimately depend on suitability of the match detected and the relations between the service concepts using ontological information. The matching engine can draw an inference between the capability inputs and outputs of the service requests on the basis of ontology's within the CCR. For example, consider the following simple scenario. An SME is considering the possibility of outsourcing its IT security capability and allow them to concentrate on their core business process selling books online. An example of their decision process to examine the quality of a service provider is illustrated in Fig. 12.15. This provides an overview of their consideration to outsource their security capability for the online book store.

Through the use of the CSCAF, the service matching and filtering process will support the customer in seeking available cloud services and support their decision-making process.

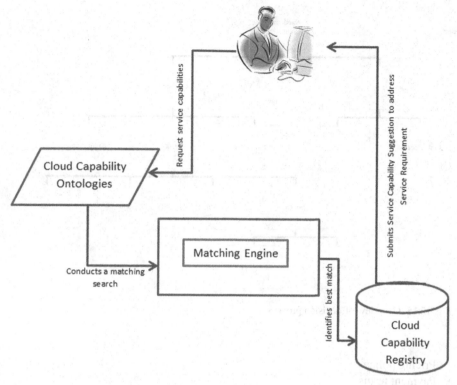

Fig. 12.14 CSCAF matching process

12.7.2 *Filtering Process*

The third phase of the selection process consists of filtering capabilities. The filtering process is used to determine which CSP meets the operational needs. Although an organisation may retrieve a number of cloud capability providers, managers must examine whether the service meets their needs and will have to filter the WSDL file to investigate the service inputs and outputs through referenced service tModel data structures. Thus, the service profile indicates the service functionality (i.e., cloud capabilities, reputation and trust standards) which customers might avail off. Therefore, we must record the critical data associated with service capabilities, such as defining the actor, record information about the service provider, and determine the functional attributes (e.g., QoS rating) of the service capability. We anticipate that the service capabilities will support the development of a CSR which catalogues the service functionalities to offer a flexible matching engine and ranking based on similarity of service requests. Short-listing CSPs may be based on the following criteria:

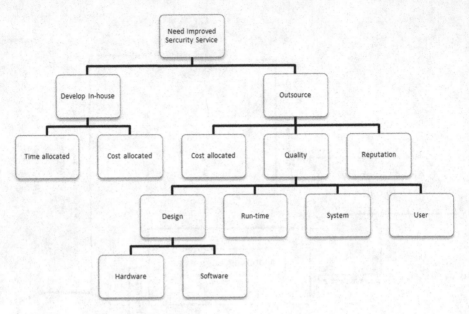

Fig. 12.15 Overview of decision process

- Pricing policy
- Payment terms
- Contract duration
- Termination options
  - Contract renewal and amendment
- Organisational profile
  - Geographical
  - Reputation (for example, QoS and/or QoE)
  - Trust
  - Technological migration
  - Cost implications (e.g., backups and recovery)
- Accountable for software licensing (especially IaaS and PaaS)
  - Data location
  - Data legislation adhere too (geographic)
  - Right to carry out an audit
  - SLA complaints procedure

From the aforementioned list, one can identify some of the key filtering decision criteria which may influence the consumption of CSP capabilities to support and align with their business strategy. This is particularly important for SMEs.

12.8   Aligning Requirements with Capabilities

Before entering into a service relationship, it is important that customers understand the operating processes and procedures to ensure proper controls and monitoring practices. The author examined SMI and ITSM to identify which capabilities and metrics are more appropriate for SMEs. This research also adds capabilities and metrics within the CSCAF (i.e., drill-down on service performance):

- *Scalable*
  - Ability to add or remove computing resources
  - Bandwidth, storage, and compute power, SLAs
- *Virtualized*
  - Information services
  - Servers, storage, and applications
- *On-demand*
  - Computer resources and applications
  - Allocated or removed within seconds at the request of the user
- *Internet powered*
  - Internet capacity
- *Multi-tenant capable*
  - Resources (e.g., network, storage, and compute power)
  - Shared among multiple enterprise clients, thereby lowering overall expense
  - Resource virtualization is used to enforce isolation and aid in security
- *Service level assured*
  - The CSP ensures a specific guaranteed server uptime, server reboot, network performance, security control, and time-to-response to the customer, with agreed upon service provider penalties if those SLA guarantees are not met.
- *Usage priced*
  - No up-front cost to the user
  - Per-use basis for bandwidth, storage, and CPU

While the aforesaid list captures the main concerns listed throughout literature for SMEs, the author examines how this applies to develop greater analytical ability to support decision-making processes. The development of the CSCAF assessment process (Fig. 12.16) shed some light on this. This is the first phase of the assessment agenda and there are plans to develop an online assessment tool which will allow SMEs to access the assessment process and report on their cloud readiness, capabilities and ultimately, the opportunities which exist to address business concerns.

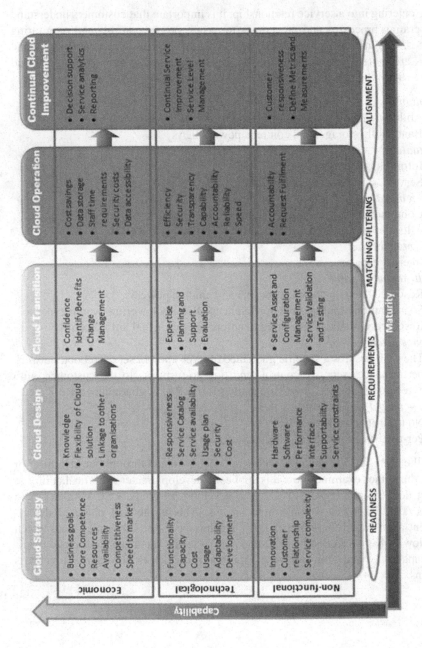

Fig. 12.16 CSCAF Assessment process

The objective of the CSCAF (Fig. 12.16) is to develop a much larger cloud analytics standard. The CSCAF is categorised into three main domains—economic, technological, and non-functional which adopt both a qualitative and quantitative analytical lens. These categories are applied to the five service lifecycle stages which accommodates for readiness, requirements, matching/filtering, and alignment. In short, these measures examine how one can:

- Improve customer service
- Increase revenues
- Cut operational costs
- Build trust standards
- Transfer knowledge of work activities
- Build measurement goals and processes
- Instill improved measurement techniques
- Encourage process ownership in developing/implementing improvements
- Communicate the measurement goals
- Establish link between activities, organisation goals, and the customer

Having assessed the various cloud capabilities, the assessment focuses on presenting the results with regards the cloud service lifecycle in terms of process readiness.

- *Strategy readiness (SR)*—focuses on how the cloud will align with the organisational strategy while understanding the general demands to benefit from the promise of the cloud
- *Design readiness (DR)*—balancing service requirements with service capabilities
- *Transition readiness (TR)*—moving the service into operation through service provisions
- *Operation readiness (OR)*—examining effective and efficient service operations to (re)align the cloud strategy
- *Continuous improvement readiness (CIR)*: monitoring the governance and CSFs (metrics and KPIs) to report on service capabilities throughout the cloud lifecycle

We can model the organisational position through a snapshot where CSPs and users may view their readiness toward solutions (see Fig. 12.17). The model represents a conceptual view of service capabilities and customer experience. Figure 12.17 offers an exemplary solution toward reporting cloud capabilities to SME managers. Each phase in the cloud lifecycle is scored (out of 5) to indicate it readiness to offer/avail of cloud solutions (0 = not ready; 5 = ready).

Figure 12.17 provides a snapshot on how we anticipate reporting CSCAF to decision-makers presenting an easily applied and acted upon assessment process. This provides a scoring overview of how CSP may assess their business environment and examine cloud readiness.

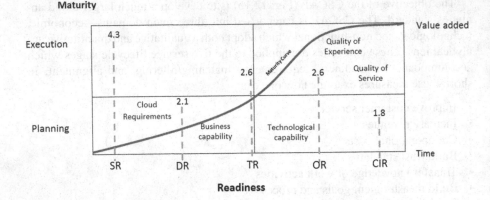

Fig. 12.17 Example of reporting through CSCAF

12.9 Future Work

This chapter discusses the initial steps to establishing the CSCAF. There are many other challenges ahead. For example, Garg et al. [40] identifies some of the main challenges which we will also address, includes:

- Leveraging the full potential of cloud environments
- Identifying requirements and characteristics of service client against cloud providers
- Decision-making regarding providers ability to provide QoS requirements
- Examining various performance levels and reporting mechanisms
- Identifying pricing strategies
- Examining issues around cloud reliability
- Enhancing cloud security technologies and policies

While we cater for these issues in the CSCAF (see Fig. 12.16), we reverse the logic of these being issues and suggest that cloud providers ought to promote their capabilities through publically available capability assessments, allowing clients to best match organisational capabilities with their requirements. This promotes the concept of "plug-in capabilities". From this research perspective there was a challenge facing cloud computing on how to assess cloud capabilities within SMEs. Firstly, this research surveyed the literature to identify the key characteristics of cloud services and cloud providers. The work carried out by Iosup et al. [53, 54] examines the performance of task applications within various cloud initiatives. They also examine tools to monitor and analyse cloud performance throughout the literature. Their work supports this quest to establish the CSCAF and provide a more personalised and indeed accurate approach to cloud readiness and cloud service improvement through:

- Customer-driven approach
- Business value- centric approach

Fig. 12.18 CSCAF components

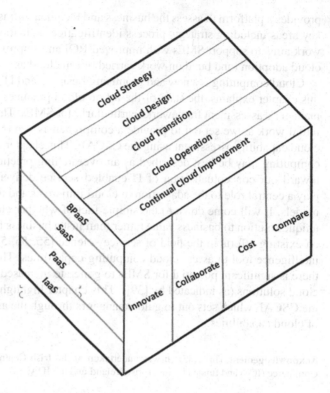

- Market sensitive resource managements
- Change recommendation

These tasks all form part of our future plans for the CSCAF. In addition, the author has identified the need to incorporate other leading standards, such as business process management notation (BPMN). This will add to the richness the CSCAF since BPMN does not support the visualisation of modelling organisational strategy through assessment tools or specific business rules. There are significant opportunities to address this gap and support industry on both an assessment and modelling of end-to-end process within the CSCAF. It will also promote a shared understanding and reuse of cloud capability improvement and optimisation.

12.10   Discussion and Conclusion

This chapter offers a discussion on the development of the CSCAF. It highlights the need to examine the cloud lifecycle from a number of viewpoints as illustrated in Fig. 12.18.

The CSCAF comprises several key components which allow us to view cloud assessments and readiness from a novel perspective. By incorporating this model, it provides a platform to assess the business and technical infrastructure in a number of key areas including strategy, process identification, valuation, and alignment. This work aims to support SMEs with improved ROI and improved business models for cloud adoption (and build on work carried out in cloud assessment [39].

Cloud computing is a new and promising business and IT paradigm. However, as this chapter explains, the state-of-the-art on cloud practices has limited support for manager's assessment frameworks particularly for SMEs. This chapter discusses our initial work as we set out to provide a comprehensive and practical framework for cloud capability assessment using the CSCAF. This chapter demonstrates that cloud computing may be best described as an overarching practice with many solutions toward our conceptualisation of IT-enabled service delivery. Cloud requirements play a central role to the adaptation of cloud initiatives and the deployment of cloud models. It will come down to the simple fact of whether cloud computing offers a unique solution to business value rather than just a business fad. The work will build on existing efforts in the field of service science [55, 56, 57] to deliver a business intelligence tool to assess cloud computing capabilities. The author advocates that there is significant potential for SMEs to generate increased business value through cloud solutions (as indicated by [39]). This chapter highlights the need to introduce the CSCAF which sets out to guide managers through the assessment and selection of cloud capabilities.

Acknowledgement This research was undertaken at the Irish Centre of Cloud Computing and Commerce (IC4) and funded by Enterprise Ireland and the IDA.

References

1. Cisco CloudWatch Report (2012) Summer 2012. cisco.com/cisco/web/UK/assets/cisco_cloudwatch_2012_2606.pdf. Accessed 20 Nov 2013
2. Normann R (2001) Reframing business: when the map changes the landscape. Wiley, Chichester
3. Fitzsimmons JA, Fitzsimmons MJ (2004) Service management-operations, strategy, and information technology, 4th edn, international edn. McGraw-Hill, Irwin
4. Spohrer J, Maglio PP, Bailey J, Gruhl D (2007) Steps toward a science of service systems. IEEE Comput 40(1):71–77
5. Chesbrough H (2011) Bringing open innovation to services. MIT Sloan Manage Rev 52(2):85–90
6. Orand B (2010) The unofficial ITIL® v3 foundations course in a book. ITILYaBrady Publisher, Richmond
7. Sharif AM (2010) It's written in the cloud: the hype and promise of cloud computing. J Enterp Inf Manage 23(2):131–134
8. Armbrust M, Fox A, Griffith R, Joseph A, Katz R, Konwinski A, Lee G, Patterson D, Rabkin A, Stoica I, Zaharia M (2009) Above the clouds: a Berkeley view of cloud computing. Technical report no. UCB/EECS-2009-28, University of California at Berkley, USA. Feb 10, 2009
9. National Institute of Standards and Technology (NIST). http://csrc.nist.gov/groups/SNS/cloud-computing/cloud-def-v15.doc. Accessed 20 Nov 2013

10. Gartner (2011) Predicts 2012: four forces combine to transform the IT landscape. http://www.gartner.com/resources/228700/228739/predicts_2012_four_forces_co_228739. pdf. Accessed 20 Nov 2013
11. Cohen H (2012) Cloud computing still faces obstacles to adoption. Eweek, January 17th, http://www.eweek.com/c/a/Data-Storage/Cloud-Computing-Still-Faces-Obstacles-to-Adoption-761567/. Accessed 20 Nov 2013
12. Buyya R, Yeo CS, Venugopal S (2008) Market-oriented cloud computing: vision, hype, and reality for delivering IT services as computing utilities. Proceedings of the 10th IEEE international conference on high performance computing and communications
13. Gillett FE (2008) Future view: the new tech ecosystems of cloud, cloud services, and cloud computing for vendor strategy professionals. Forrester Research, Inc. August 28th
14. Cearley DW (2010) Cloud computing-key initiative overview. Gartner Inc. http://www.gartner.com/it/initiatives/pdf/KeyInitiativeOverview_CloudComputing.pdf. Accessed 20 Nov 2013
15. Wang L, von Laszewski G, Kunze M, Tao J (2008) Cloud computing: a perspective study. Proceedings of the grid computing environments (GCE) workshop, November
16. EC Expert Report (2010) The future of cloud computing-opportunities for European cloud computing beyond 2010. http://cordis.europa.eu/fp7/ict/ssai/docs/cloud-report-final.pdf. Accessed 20 Nov 2013
17. Zeithaml VA, Parasuraman A, Berry LL (1990) Delivering quality service: balancing customer perceptions and expectations. Free Press, New York
18. Kleinrock L (2005). A vision for the internet. ST J Res 2(1):4–5
19. Carr N (2008) Big switch: rewiring the world, from Edison to Google. Norton, New York
20. Friedman TL (2006) The world is flat. Penguin Books, New York
21. Hofmann P, Woods D (2010) Cloud computing: the limits of public clouds for business applications. IEEE Internet Comput 14(6):90–93
22. Reynolds E, Bess C (2009) Clearing up the cloud: adoption strategies for cloud computing. Cut IT J June/July:14–20
23. Milne (2010) IT value transformation road map vision, value, and virtualization, VMWare report, IT Process Institute
24. Clarke R (2010) Computing clouds on the horizon? Benefits and risks from the users perspective, 23rd Bled eConference, Slovenia
25. Weinman J (2008) 10 laws of cloudonomics. http://gigaom.com/2008/09/07/the-10-laws-of-cloudonomics/. Accessed 20 Nov 2013
26. Tapscott D, Caston A (1993) Paradigm shift: the new promise of information technology. McGraw-Hill, New York
27. Dwivedi YK, Mustafee N (2010) It's unwritten in the cloud: the technology enablers for realising the promise of cloud computing. J Enter Inf Manage 23(6):673–679
28. Mooney J, Gurbaxani V, Kraemer K (1995) A process oriented framework for assessing the business value of information technology. In proceedings of the 16th international conference on information systems, Amsterdam, pp 17–27
29. Aalst WMP van der (2010) Configurable services in the cloud: supporting variability while enabling cross-organizational process mining. In international conference on cooperative information systems (CoopIS 2010), vol 6426 of lecture notes in computer science, pp 8–25. Springer-Verlag
30. Open Group (2009) Risk taxonomy. http://pubs.opengroup.org/onlinepubs/9699919899/toc.pdf. Accessed 20 Nov 2013
31. Fiegler A, Dumke RR (2011) Growth- and entropy-based SOA measurement-vision and approach in a large scale environment. 2011 joint conference of the 21st international workshop on software measurement and the 6th international conference on software process and product measurement
32. Raines G (2009) Cloud computing and SOA. The MITRE corporation. www.mitre.org/work/tech_papers/tech_papers_09/09_0743/09_0743.pdf. Accessed 20 Nov 2013
33. Mettler T (2009) A design science research perspective on maturity models in information systems, Universität St. Gallen, St. Gallen, Switzerland, Technical Report BE IWI/HNE/03, 2009

34. Gefen D, Zviran M, Elman N (2006) What can be learned from CMMi failures? Commun Assoc Inf Syst 17(1):36
35. Humphrey WS (2005) Foreword. In M Bush and D Dunaway, CMMI® Assessments-motivating positive change (Sei Series in Software Engineering). Addison-Wesley Professional
36. Brooks P (2006) Metrics for IT service management. Van Haren Publishing, Zaltbommel
37. Orand B (2010) The unofficial ITIL® v3 foundations course in a book. ITILYaBrady Publisher, Richmond
38. Luftman J (2003) Assessing IT/business alignment. Inf Strategy 20(1):33–38
39. Carroll N, Helfert M, Lynn T (2013) A contingency model for assessing cloud composite capabilities, the 3rd international conference on cloud computing and services science (CLOSER 2013), Aachen, Germany
40. Garg SK, Versteeg S, Buyya R (2011) SMICloud: a framework for comparing and ranking cloud services, fourth IEEE international conference on utility and cloud computing
41. Sycara K, Lu J, Klusch M, Widoff S (1999) Dynamic service matchmaking among agents in open information environments. ACM SIGMOD record (Special issue on semantic interoperability in global information systems), 28, 1, pp 47–53
42. Paolucci M, Kawmura T, Payne T, Sycara K (2002) Semantic matching of web services capabilities. Proceedings of the international semantic web conference (ISWC), pp 333–347
43. Control Objectives for Information and Related Technology (COBIT) framework. http://www.isaca.org/Knowledge-Center/cobit/Pages/Overview.aspx. Accessed 20 Nov 2013
44. Lainhart JW (2001) An IT assurance framework for the future. Ohio CPA J 60(1): 19–23
45. Cloud Commons Consortium (2010) 'Cloud commons', Miscellaneous
46. Klems M, Nimis J, Tai S (2009) Do clouds compute? A framework for estimating the value of cloud computing. Designing e-business systems. Markets, services, and networks, lecture notes in business information processing, vol 22, p 110
47. Cloud Service Measurement Initiative Consortium (CSMIC). http://csmic.org/about-csmic/. Accessed 20 Nov 2013
48. Capability Maturity Model Integration. http://www.sei.cmu.edu/cmmi/. Accessed 20 Nov 2013
49. Persse JR (2006). Process improvement essentials. O'Reilly Media Inc, Sebastopol
50. Humphrey WS (1989) Managing the software process, reading, reading. Addison Wesley, Massachusetts
51. Universal Description, Discovery and Integration (UDDI). http://uddi.xml.org. Accessed 20 Nov 2013
52. ITIL Service Lifecycle. http://www.itil-officialsite.com/. Accessed 20 Nov 2013
53. Iosup A, Yigitbasi N, Epema D (2011a) On the performance variability of production cloud services. Proceedings of IEEE/ACM international symposium on cluster, cloud, and grid computing, CA, USA
54. Iosup A, Ostermann S, Yigitbasi N, Prodan R, Fahringer T, Epema D (2011b) Performance analysis of cloud computing services for many-tasks scientific computing. IEEE Trans Parallel Distrib Syst 22(6):931–945
55. Carroll N (2012) Service science: an empirical study on the socio-technical dynamics of public sector service network innovation, PhD Thesis, University of Limerick
56. Carroll N, Whelan E, Richardson I (2010) Applying social network analysis to discover service innovation within agile service networks. J Serv Sci 2(4):225–244
57. Carroll N, Richardson I, Whelan E (2012) Service science: exploring complex agile service networks through organisational network analysis'. Chap. 8 In: X Wang, N Ali, I Ramos, R Vidgen (ed) Agile and lean service-oriented development: foundations theory and practice. pp 156–172. IGI Publishing

Part V
Applications in Education and Other Scenarios

Chapter 13
Cloud Computing Within Higher Education: Applying Knowledge as a Service (KaaS)

Alexandros Chrysikos and Rupert Ward

Abstract The advent of cloud computing in recent years has sparked interest from various institutions, organisations and users who wish to take advantage of its features. Cloud computing provides on-demand computer resources as a service, enabling flexible information technology (IT) usage via scalability and a cost efficient (pay-per-use) approach. As well as traditional cloud computing services (software, platform and infrastructure as services), there is an emerging concept which integrates knowledge organisations and knowledge management. The Knowledge as a service (KaaS) is delivered via knowledge markets within a cloud environment. In this article, the authors present and analyse the KaaS concept together with its advantages and disadvantages. Furthermore, after an analysis of eLearning environments in the UK higher education institutions (HEIs), the potential KaaS benefits in the UK HEIs are also presented, demonstrating how KaaS conceptual models from industry could be used in the UK HEIs. The underlying theory behind KaaS is also discussed, with the conclusion highlighting potential opportunities and benefits that KaaS can provide to the UK HEIs.

Keywords Cloud services · eLearning environments · Higher education institutions · Knowledge as a service · Knowledge management · Knowledge organisation · Universities · Virtual learning environments

13.1 Introduction

Higher education (HE) is characterised by the tension between the quality of provision and the drive to provide affordable HE to more and more people [1]. IT has an increasing role in supporting cost reduction, quality improvement, and through this, educational sustainability [2].

A. Chrysikos (✉) · R. Ward
School of Computing, University of Huddersfield, Huddersfield, UK
e-mail: Alexandros.Chrysikos@hud.ac.uk

R. Ward
e-mail: R.R.Ward@hud.ac.uk

Z. Mahmood (ed.), *Continued Rise of the Cloud,* Computer Communications and Networks, DOI 10.1007/978-1-4471-6452-4_13,
© Springer-Verlag London 2014

Since the computer network development boom, at the end of the last millennium, technology use has become increasingly mainstream. The HE is no exception to this change but there has been limited consideration to date of the role of cloud services within HE. The HE industry is rather a special industry [3], providing knowledge-based products which are sensitive to both reputational and social variation. Technology is becoming increasingly important as a method of differentiating both the products and associated services provided by HEIs. Furthermore, due to the development of web technologies, such as Web 2.0 and cloud computing, HEIs use of technology, and the technology itself are constantly changing [4]. This new environment, therefore, includes a new generation of eLearning ecosystems, including virtual learning environments (VLEs), which need to be able to run a wide variety of applications, support multiple hardware devices and provide data storage in the cloud [5]. At the same time, there are also rapid changes in both technological infrastructure and software applications. In this constantly changing environment replacing existing fixed infrastructure and applications with a more responsive and updateable cloud-based solution therefore provides significant potential gains for institutions.

The KaaS is an emerging concept which integrates knowledge organisation, knowledge markets and knowledge management [6]. The KaaS is a system that provides content-based information, knowledge and data as organisational outputs providing answers to queries, enabling facilitation and providing advice for students and staff [6]. These outputs are meant to satisfy a user or a person's individual needs.

To understand KaaS's potential use in the UK HEIs, an analysis of KaaS's current status, its relationship with cloud computing, and how its conceptual models operate is required. Before doing this though, we need to first define KaaS.

13.2 Defining Knowledge as a Service (KaaS)

Drucker [7] states that "knowledge has become the central resource and knowledge has to be challenged, increased constantly and improved or it vanishes" [4, 5]. Knowledge is not only a resource which is there for mining but also an active service. Knowledge services are essential infrastructure and key components of the knowledge society [8], which can be implemented as an IT-enabled process that organises knowledge and transforms it into real value [8]. As a result, it helps improve knowledge worker productivity, increase the human capital, build Communities of Practice (CoPs) and bridge knowledge divides. In addition, it promotes learning in organisations which enables stable innovation and sustainable economic growth in the knowledge society [8].

As has been previously stated, the cloud computing service models are software as a service (SaaS), platform as a service (PaaS) and infrastructure as a service (IaaS). The KaaS is a corresponding service to these models. The KaaS is a new concept in the education field and was first introduced in Japan in 2009 [9].

It is a new research field, and with the rapid development of cloud computing and knowledge management, knowledge service has been integrated as a service that

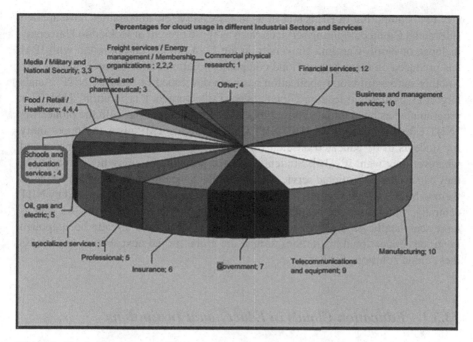

Fig. 13.1 Cloud computing usage [12]

combines knowledge resources [9, 10]. The outcome of such a service is that users can exchange and share knowledge.

13.3 Cloud Computing Within Higher Education Institutions

Cloud computing offers both services and virtualisation, often via outsourcing, reducing the cost of equipment installation and on-going IT administration [11]. Gartner's survey results [12] show that cloud computing is being used mainly in business and finance sectors rather than education (see Fig. 13.1); however, it also shows that proportionally there is significant potential growth for cloud computing within HE.

Examples of this potential can be seen in recent initiatives involving both educational institutions and private companies. In the EDUCASE Conference of 2009, Bernard Golden, CEO of consulting company HyperStratus, stated that HE IT organisations should perform application triage as well as finding low-cost places to transfer low-value software [13]. Golden also identified that cloud computing was an excellent technology to be used to transfer low-value software applications [13]. The HE IT services no longer has the luxury to provide universal coverage. Instead of offering inadequate applications to everyone, reduced resources should be prioritised and transferred to the most needed areas [13].

Cloud computing in HE is still in its infancy. Very few universities have applied substantial Cloud computing services, such as those present at Hokkaido University in Japan or North Carolina University in the USA, where co-operation with IBM has produced an open-source cloud computing solution called cloud.com [14, 15]. Another successful cloud application has been developed in India by NIIT "Asia's largest IT trainer and leading Global Talent Development Corporation" [16]. This programme has been initiated through GNIIT cloud computing, with the pioneering "NIIT Cloud Campus TM" [16]. NIIT Cloud Campus TM "gives the opportunity for students to be educated on their own terms, at their own place, whenever and wherever they want it" [16]. Students have the potential to enjoy high mobility as they can access educational services via a mobile device or netbook which connects them to NIIT's Cloud Campus TM network. All these services are managed by NIIT centrally, which uses the benefits of cloud computing technology [16]. As well as large scale applications, other cloud education services have already been applied in various educational institutions around the globe. In the next section we discuss these cloud solutions further.

13.3.1   Education Clouds in Educational Institutions

Educational institutions around the world already provide online and cloud education services. The most significant amongst them are outlined as follows:

13.3.1.1   Educational Services Available Online

Some educational services available online are as follows:

- **Intel AppUp Center (www.appup.com):** It provides a resource centre and catalogue for cloud-based mobile services. This site can also serve as a model for how an education services catalogue could be created for the development and distribution of education cloud services.
- **iTunes University (www.apple.com/education/itunes-u):** This site is a large-scale distribution system for lectures, language lessons, films, labs, audio books, tours, etc.
- **Skool.com (www.skoool.com):** The site offers a number of learning objects freely available for use via the Internet, as well as a set of toolkits for open-ended learning.
- **Educational Elements (www.intel.com/education/elements):** These are professional development services, which feature a set of online, self-paced courses that focus on helping teachers, become proficient with project-based learning, student collaboration and twenty-first century skills development. These courses can be integrated along with others and made available though an education cloud [17].

13.3.1.2 Education Cloud Examples and Resources

Some education cloud examples and resources are discussed as follows:

- **Intel Clarkstown Central School District:** The Clarkstown Central School District uses Google Apps to coordinate curricula and resources within schools and across the district. Innovative uses of the calendar, shared documents and shared sites make it easy for teachers to follow district curriculum plans, keep up with school-related events, and create and share curriculum resources.
- **Laboratory for Continuous Mathematical Education, St. Petersburg, Russia:** This project is supported by *HP Innovations in Education grant*. It connects students with scientific researchers, giving them an opportunity to experience professional research practices while also building their own technical skills. The students work with researchers from both scientific and industrial professions.
- **Columbia Secondary School**: A partnership between the New York City Department of Education, Columbia University, and the Columbia Secondary School has led to the deployment of cloud-based systems including a custom content management system and *Google Apps*. The students are using these cloud applications to do research and to collaborate in new ways.
- **Eagle County School District**: The Eagle County School District in Colorado is implementing a cloud computing system that will make tools for email, word processing, presentations and calendaring accessible to everyone in the district.
- **Cloud-computing infrastructure and technology for education (CITE)**: This project, from MIT's climate modeling initiative, looks at ways to use cloud computing resources to perform scientific research, both in university labs and in K-12 classrooms.
- **TeacherTube** : This cloud-based video service is modeled after YouTube but is designed specifically for teachers, schools and homeschoolers. It offers a wide range of educational videos on a variety of topics [17].

As can be seen from the limited online educational services and the education clouds listed above, there is still very limited use of the cloud within HEIs. This is something to be excepted as the current period can be seen as the rise of the cloud. The focus of the next section is to present a review of the most important cloud computing advancements developed by the UK government agencies, councils and education institutions during the last 2 years, when the UK HE agencies have decided to promote new technology trends.

13.4 Cloud Computing in the UK Higher Education Institutions

Technology use changes the educational experience, and the costs involved in maintaining facilities and providing up-to-date systems can be challenging [18]. Approaches, such as cloud computing offer the sector new opportunities to maintain quality and manage costs.

So far, within the UK HE sector, the most important influence in promoting cloud computing has been the Higher Education Funding Council for England (HEFCE). HEFCE funds colleges and universities in England through a programme of investments and services to deliver efficiencies via shared services in cloud computing applications and infrastructure [19].

Another funding programme for cloud computing promotion has been offered by the University Modernisation Fund (UMF). The UMF, which is also administered by HEFCE, supports "the development of sector-based cloud computing facility" providing benefits through a range of innovative resources [18, 19], including more comprehensive suites of applications, environment and support management, and simple data storage in secure off site servers. Cloud computing may also offer significant cost benefits for institutions when strategic decisions regarding information communications technology (ICT) provision are made and choices of outsourced and managed in-house solutions are considered [18, 19].

In February 2011, HEFCE and the Joint Information Systems Committee (JISC) announced a £12.5 million fund to support the delivery of cloud-based services for UK research and education [18]. The Joint Academic Network (JANET) is delivering "the national brokerage in order to aid in the procurement of the cloud computing services by delivering a national commission" [19]. Eduserv, a non-profit body dedicated to work with HE and government, is providing the Cloud Infrastructure Pilot [18, 19]. There are also partners (universities) aiding this effort including Kent, Exeter, Oxford, De Montfort, Sunderland, Leicester, Southampton and Edinburgh [19].

Apart from solutions brokered through government agencies, there are also solutions being provided by the commercial sector. Microsoft and Google continue to provide services and applications (i.e. data storage, e-mail, Google Docs, Office 365) which can be used for educational purposes [18]. The competition between these two companies has enabled HEIs to benefit from the development of off-site email services free of charge [20]. The University of Westminster provides an example of the benefits that can be delivered to an institution when it saved £1 million by moving services to the Cloud, cutting its expenditure on software upgrades and new hardware [18, 19]. They also benefitted from reduced time spent on user and systems support, with a lower than expected number of support calls to their cloud provider [18, 19]. JISC Director of Service Relationships, David Utting, has stated that "cloud computing services have the potential to bring high efficiencies to higher education institutions" [19]. He also stated that he recognises "the need to demonstrate to the users the security and robustness of working in an education and research cloud" [19] and that there were a number of problems with data stored in Public Clouds "which is why JISC is working with JANET (UK) in order to provide a private higher education cloud to ensure that universities can have secure data" [19].

In 2102, Curtis and Cartwright published a cost analysis of cloud computing research on behalf of JISC and the Engineering and Physical Sciences Research Council (EPSRC). The result was a report targeting anyone in the HE community with a particular interest in cloud computing. The report included a review of cloud computing for researchers, information for research computing managers and for

HEIs who provide access to cloud computing services for their researchers, as well as information regarding funding bodies that award relevant grants [21]. In 2013, JISC signed a new strategic alliance with JANET and Microsoft. The new arrangements offer improved access to applications and infrastructure services like research projects, websites and VLEs [22].

The private connection of these networks reduces data transfer over the publicly used internet [22] and enables a high bandwidth connection which will benefit over 18 million students and staff via Microsoft Windows Azure. Paul Watson, Professor of Computing Science at Newcastle University, comments:

"Cloud computing has the potential to revolutionise research by offering vast compute resources on-demand. At Newcastle University, we already have over £20M of research projects that are supported by the cloud. However, one of the major barriers holding back further cloud adoption is the time it takes to transfer large datasets from the lab to the cloud for analysis. This new link between JANET and the Azure Cloud removes this barrier, and will allow a far greater range of research projects to fully exploit the benefits of cloud computing" [22].

As negotiated by JANET, an extra benefit that occurs from the alliance agreement is that the UK HEIs can benefit from standard terms and conditions on Microsoft's cloud-based Office 365 suite [22]. Goldsmiths, for example, have benefitted from this agreement as one of a select group of institutions responsible for enabling the alliance, and as an early adopter of the technology. Haddadeh (2013), Director of IT Services at Goldsmiths stated that "The work on Office 365 will save the sector considerable time and money in legal due diligence and speed up adoption of Office 365. We're really pleased with the roll-out at Goldsmiths and our staff and students are already enjoying using the new system. I'm looking forward to the benefits the strategic alliance can bring" [22]. The strategic alliance demonstrates the desire and commitment of UK education and research institutes to adopt cloud technology, "complementing our world class fibre network with Microsoft's leading technologies to support the sector" as stated by Dan Perry, Director of Product and Marketing at JANET [22].

As cloud computing develops within the UK HEIs its potential benefits, and those of KaaS, must be clearly understood if the UK HEIs are to benefit fully from its implementation. It is therefore useful at this point to review these benefits.

13.4.1   Cloud Computing Benefits for the UK HE Institutions

Cloud computing technology can offer the UK HEIs benefits and opportunities including:

- Low IT costs
- High bandwidth connection
- An effective way to scale technology requirements
- High performance, efficiency and access to a wide range of shared resources
- An innovative environment of scalable services [18, 23]

The UK HEIs can lower IT costs from centralising server provision and gaining from the resulting economies of scale. High bandwidth can be achieved from dedicated private network connections reducing network traffic. Effective scalability can be provided through dynamic (on-demand) provisioning of resources on a self-service (real-time) basis. An innovative environment of scalable services is offered to the users by the provider. High performance and efficiency can be achieved through the use of JANET, the private network that connects the networks of the UK HEIs and reduces data transfer over the publicly used internet.

The area where cloud computing technology could benefit the UK HEIs the most is eLearning. The UK HEIs already use eLearning services through VLEs. A cloud computing service can maximise the VLE's capabilities through KaaS. The structure and organisation of the VLEs currently used by the UK HEIs can critically affect the potential use of KaaS. Thus, before the KaaS capabilities are presented, a brief review of current VLEs and there links to cloud computing has to be presented.

13.5   Cloud Computing and VLEs

Over the last 10 years the Internet has changed from a static environment to a dynamic one, with the environment now offering greater opportunities for users to run software applications, create online services and share information [24]. The cloud computing environment enables the development of new eLearning generation ecosystems which can run a wide range of applications while at the same time storing data in the cloud [25].

VLEs which are currently applied by most of the UK HEIs do not follow these new technological trends [26, 27]. According to a survey conducted by Weller for the Institute of Education Technology, 86 % of respondents from the UK HEIs reported the presence of a VLE in their institution [26, 27], with examples of VLEs including Blackboard, Moodle, Sakai, WebCT, SharePoint, University, etc. [28]. However, the most important part of the survey was the issues that arose from this use, which included the following criticisms:

- No strong pedagogy
- Content confused
- No clear combination of high quality and average tools
- Support only a teacher–classroom model
- No meeting the needs of each different course area
- No support to high level of interoperability [26, 27]

The UK HEIs eLearning requirements are constantly changing and therefore responsive systems which enable rapid improvement and development of eLearning solutions are necessary [24]. According to Dong et al., the new direction of eLearning is building and hosting the eEducational systems in the cloud [29]. Cloud computing technology also provides further advantages through dynamic scalability and the use of virtualised resources as a service via the Internet [25].

Cloud computing provides a variety of benefits to overcome the challenges related with traditional IT. Such challenges are the setup of accessible and reliable servers, networks, services, storage and applications [30]. The main benefits of cloud computing for eEducational systems include increased mobility for a global workforce [31, 32], reduced cost of setup and maintenance [33, 34], rapid elasticity with scalable infrastructure and IT department transformation where cloud technology focuses on innovation rather than on implementation and maintenance [30, 35]. Another important cloud computing benefit for eEducational systems is the reallocation of resources. As cloud computing improves technology setup, maintenance becomes the service provider's responsibility. As a result, an institution's IT staff can focus on developing innovative resources and solutions as well as providing better support to students and instructors. There are various areas in which more intensive help from IT staff can be beneficial to institutional instructors. Firstly, as institutional instructors move to more mobile and online instruction methods in their courses, IT staff can help them optimize the use of the available eEducational systems in order to increase efficiency and effectiveness of the delivered instructional process [30]. Secondly, as online instruction tends to become more personal via the extensive use of online conference tools, such as WebEx, Blackboard Collaborative, etc. instructors can benefit from intensive initial support in the technical aspects of integrating these tools into their teaching methods [30]. Thirdly, IT staff can help instructors to improve and develop technical skills by using Web 2.0 tools, such as wikis and blogs. In this way, IT staff can help instructors to effectively integrate these collaborative tools within their courses in order to improve both the student learning performance and experience [36, 37].

Fundamental changes are occurring in democratising the relationship between students and lecturers [38] and in providing more effective methods for students to access appropriate material, which is central to meeting student needs.

Recently, there has also been a significant growth and developments within the eLearning marketplace. Uden et al. state, what Cowley mentioned, that there is a set of contextual elements which should be considered in order to make eLearning more effective at facilitating learning in complex situations [39]. These elements are:

- Teach skills: Learners need to know how to use whatever learning system is available.
- Subject matter skills: Learners should have some prerequisite skills to benefit from the course.
- Environment: Learners need a certain environment (software, PCs, connection, etc.).
- Content: It must have interactive design.
- Support: There has to be a mechanism to support learners when run into problems.
- Instructor: He/she organises the schedule, tries to draw learners into discussion, is aware of learners' needs and involvement levels, and provides learners with necessary resources and additional learning material.
- Organisation: It focuses on time, learning and resources availability.
- Technology: It should have an effective role [39].

All the aforementioned elements are part of the eLearning ecosystem or ecology that is needed for the new generation of eLearning systems which means VLEs must become more advanced [40]. VLEs should remain comprehensive and capable of adapting to new tools and technologies, adapting to different learning styles, integrating new learning approaches and responding to changing learning conditions [41].

Some insights for developing cloud computing strategies for eEducational systems which are based on previous experience in distance learning, are presented in the following. The insights discussed here are not a set of instructions on how to adapt cloud computing, as it is unlikely that cloud computing can address all IT problems, but it can be seen as a solution to many problems [42]. Every institution that uses eEducational system will have to use its own diligence in order to determine if cloud computing benefits overcome the risks, based on its own unique institutional circumstances and environment. Infosys Corporation researchers suggest a series of steps for cloud adoption. These are assessment, validation, preparation and execution [43]. In addition, institutions which are determined to adopt cloud computing need to plan and follow a strategy based on their own unique needs. The following insights offer a good strategic guidance for eEducational administrators as they integrate cloud computing as part of IT strategy [30].

- **Evaluate and select cloud service providers using multiple criteria:** According to Thethi (2009), there are four criteria: geographic alignment, operational alignment, technology alignment and cloud platform maturity [43]. Even if, operational ability, cost and scalability are important when an institution chooses a cloud service provider, it also needs to evaluate the cloud compliance and privacy needs. Specifically, institutions should look for cloud service providers who can offer high-quality customer experience and cost-effective architecture [44]. Furthermore, Leong and Chamberlin (2010) propose weightings evaluation criteria and additional criteria that address eEducational needs [44].
- **Select the type of cloud solution that fits the structure of the institution's instructional activities:** For small institutions a straightforward adoption might be the public cloud because such institutions lack the necessary in-house IT technology and support [30]. On the other hand, large institutions which have already invested in their own IT infrastructure should consider maximizing existing assets through the deployment of a hybrid cloud. They could start with transferring the existing IT systems and applications in an internal private cloud [45]. Then, they can develop a small-scale exploratory cloud and conduct pilot testing. By the time IT staff have developed the necessary IT experience and skills, the institution can move further and deploy more private clouds, and finally deploy a hybrid cloud (in general, a hybrid approach brings together both private and public cloud). Furthermore, all the non-core IT applications should be outsourced to public clouds where possible [46], and overall an institution should focus initially on SaaS before moving to PaaS and IaaS. A gradual evolution of cloud services will give time for institutions to better understand the benefits of cloud computing for them.

- **Partner with other institutions using eEducational systems in the cloud:** A partnership with other institutions can offer the most benefits to both faculty and students. An eEducational learning community would allow online learning applications and resources to be shared across the whole distance learning community [30]. This also means that faculty and students from various institutions can have equal access to online learning and teaching resources. In addition, existing professional associations can take a leadership role and co-operate with their members in order to promote cloud adoption, develop evaluation criteria and standards, and ensure effective implementation [30]. Furthermore, they should develop information policies and agreements for eEducational learning and address important shared issues, such as security, copyright and privacy protection for financial and personal information as well as educational resources [30].
- **Use of a holistic approach :** In the marketplace, there is a variety of cloud service providers. Therefore, a careful evaluation is needed in order to compare the cloud service providers' capabilities. The main purpose of the evaluation is for an institution to choose the cloud service provider who can cover its specific requirements and needs [30]. Contract issues within cloud service providers can always be a potential problem. For instance, codifying the minimum levels and parameters for every element of the service and the remedies for failure to meet requirements. Another example is affirming ownership of an institution's data stored on the service provider's system and specifying the institution's right to get it back. Other issues can be specifying the institution's right and cost to continue or stop using the service; detailing the system security standards and infrastructure to be maintained by the service provider along with the institution's right to audit compliance [47]. Thus, eEducational systems administrators should apply a holistic approach when considering adoption of cloud computing. Careful planning, education of stakeholders and top management support are all necessary to identify the best cloud strategy.

13.5.1   Current Status of VLEs

In the past, the need for deeper integration with administrative systems in the UK HEIs led to the concept of the managed learning environment (MLE) [28]. Later on, the availability of new web-based tools and the requirement for higher personalisation gave rise to the concept of the personal learning environment (PLE). A debate ensued, where people entirely reconceptualised the learning environment notion [48]. During these phases, the VLE has remained a dominant force within the educational institutions, though there remains a tension regarding the roles of VLEs within the institutional community, particularly in regard to levels of customisation/personalisation for individuals and institutions, levels of open access and constraints related to network security [28].

Partly as a response to changes in technology, increased student input into university delivery and the strategic challenges facing HE, many UK HEIs continue to review their VLE provision alongside exploring possibilities for increased administrative integration and improved responsiveness to changing pedagogical requirements [28].

As VLEs are reviewed a question naturally arises. Could cloud computing better support the UK HEIs eLearning needs?

13.6   Benefits of Cloud Computing and KaaS for the UK HE

Cloud computing can offer the UK HEIs enhanced capabilities for eLearning services which are more agile and student focused than traditional VLE approaches. This can be achieved through KaaS, a cloud service approach to knowledge. Cloud computing enables the following:

- Permanence of data—there is no need for data transfer from one computer device to another when a new one is being bought. That means that users (students and staff) can create a repository of information that is saved and can be used as long as they want [39].
- Reductions in onsite data storage requirements—there is no need for back-up as everything is stored in the cloud.
- There is high processing power which can be compared to supercomputer level [25].
- There is improved engagement in teaching and learning [48].
- Better crash recovery., Data loss is not possible due to the fact that everything is stored in the cloud [24].
- Students and staff members have access to their files from any place as soon as they have internet access and a computer device (laptop, smartphone, desktop computer, PDA) [48].
- Students will have a richer and wider range of learning experience through ubiquitous computing [39].
- HEIs to provide a low cost solution for instructors, students and researchers [25];
- There is dynamic scalability on demand [49].

In addition, according to Wheeler and Waggener [50], cloud computing can offer educational institutions the following features:

- Centralised data storage: Applications and data are stored in the cloud; so, a new student or staff member can be connected fast and easy.
- Improved improbability: It is difficult for fraud people to steal sensitive data, such as results, examination questions, tests.
- Data access monitoring: It is easier as only one place should be supervised, not all university's computers.
- Virtualisation: Rapid replacement of a compromised cloud located server is possible without major damages or costs.

Such services are already widely used in the private sector. In 2006, Amazon extended its Amazon Web Service (AWS) in Amazon Elastic Compute Cloud (EC2) which allows users to use Amazon's processing power to run their own applications [25]. In 2008, Google released its Google App Engine which is a platform that users can develop and host their own applications on. In addition, IBM released the cloud burst—a self-contained, pre-packaged cloud that contains software, hardware, middleware and applications for faster deployment and application development [51]. The last example comes from Microsoft, which in January 2010 announced the Windows Azure platform. Azure is a "flexible cloud platform that lets users focus on solving educational problems, addressing students' needs and provides necessary web tools for education" [25].

All the cloud computing approaches discussed so far are offered to users through service models (SaaS, PaaS, IaaS, KaaS). The new service model KaaS brings together two important ideas, crowd sourcing and SaaS [52, 53]. The KaaS uses its ability to connect, on-demand, an information need with the correct information response [53]. The information sources, the information cloud, is delivered through the Internet and then delivered via SaaS, providing information rather than software functionality [52, 53].

The KaaS theoretically could be applied wherever knowledge works. An early adoption, though, could take place where knowledge rapidly changes and can easily be productised, such as IT system troubleshooting and configuration [52, 53]. In such an environment knowledge could be productised as helpdesk support, tailored software (software based on customer specifications) and training videos [53]. A natural marketplace is then created for providers and customers to exchange knowledge for cash in real time [52, 53]. As KaaS is a cloud computing service that embeds cloud computing technology features, but what are these features? The next section presents the features of cloud computing that add value to KaaS.

13.6.1 What Features Cloud Computing Adds to KaaS?

The KaaS is a cloud computing service that can enhance knowledge management in every organisation that operates knowledge. In addition, KaaS has the potential to enable organisational knowledge to be used and shared. The value of cloud computing for the UK HEIs is in embedding the KaaS cloud service. The most significant benefits for the UK HEIs include:

- Many experts can work on the same problem at the same time [52].
- Knowledge availability (Anywhere/Anytime): The users can take action whenever they need [53].
- Expert knowledge is gained, not just experts: Users are empowered with knowledge [53].
- Get what you need: The resources are not wasted sifting through unnecessary information [52].
- Pay for what you need: Money is not wasted on information that is not needed [52].

The KaaS offers benefits which are similar to, or influenced by, cloud technology. In other words, KaaS embeds cloud computing features and therefore can bring innovation faster and provide more targeted information for its users [54]. Users including students, university staff, government services and enterprise services can therefore apply organisational knowledge and knowledge management through KaaS, though this is not without its drawbacks. These drawbacks are the subject of the next section.

13.6.2   Potential Concerns of Using KaaS

As far as using KaaS applications in eLearning environments, there are a few concerns which need consideration. These are:

- Security issues must be dealt with. In particular, control access to the extracted knowledge and privacy protection in both knowledge extraction and knowledge utilisation (i.e. protect data privacy and privacy of queries of a knowledge consumer) [55]
- Knowledge breaching attacks, where an adversary may recover the knowledge underpinning a knowledge service. In cases like this, without an adequate protection against this attack KaaS would not take off, as service providers would fear for their return on investment [55]
- Quality control standards, for example the ability to limit the pool of cloud-based subject matter experts to only the most qualified [53]
- Accurate information extraction. In order to pull the correct knowledge from the cloud, packaged in the most appropriate container, the user must be able to extract it [53]

The KaaS must be based on a solid foundation in order for customers to invest in it. To understand how to develop effective and secure knowledge services, some conceptual models have been developed, and these are presented in the next section together with examples of existing conceptual models and trials of KaaS applications in organisations. Again examples come from industry as educational use is still in its infancy.

13.7   Conceptual Models and KaaS

The KaaS is not a single application but a collection of tools running in the cloud [54]. The following conceptual models are knowledge models that have been developed and tested in industry and involve embedding KaaS within organisations. There are no models yet that have been developed and tested in HEIs as KaaS has not been extensively applied in this sector yet.

The first conceptual model, from Hitachi, attempts to add KaaS to social infrastructure [56]. Hitachi focuses on three major technical issues, extraction of knowledge from large volumes of data, privacy protection and how to make use

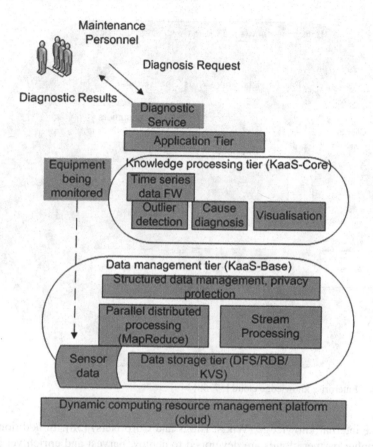

Fig. 13.2 Overview of maintenance diagnostic service [56]

of data that may contain personal information [56]. In this model KaaS is designed to operate with a wide range of data gathered from global positioning system (GPS), integrated circuit (IC) card, radio frequency identification (RFID) and other sources [56].

Figure 13.2 depicts an overview of Hitachi's Maintenance Diagnostic Service. The process shows the analysis algorithms for a KaaS platform which undertakes high speed data analysis of large amounts of sensed data [56]. The maintenance diagnostic service includes "pressure, fitting temperature and other sensors to the equipment to be maintained and analysing the status data collected by these sensors to detect outliers in the equipment" [56]. The target is to avoid downtime that is caused by unexpected faults and to reduce maintenance costs.

A second example comes from Delic and Riley [57] and involves an enterprise knowledge cloud. An abstracted business enterprise architecture is shown in Fig. 13.3.

This architecture interconnects business suppliers and partners to companies, consumers and customers. It then uses cloud technology in order to process, harvest

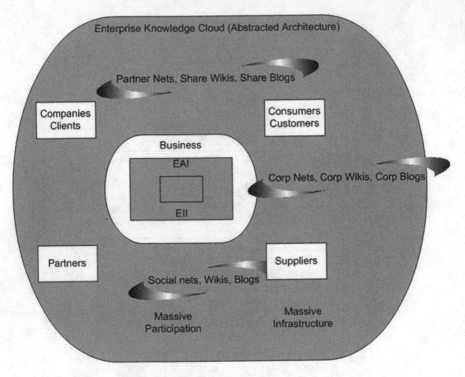

Fig. 13.3 Enterprise knowledge cloud [57, 58]

and use internal knowledge (Wikis, Blogs and Corp Nets) [58]. In addition, similar supplier/partner clouds are developed to deploy, harvest and enrich yet another knowledge cloud [58]. Every cloud in Fig. 13.3 is an autonomous entity capable of managing, collecting, warehousing and serving knowledge to its own group of users [58]. Nevertheless, even if these clouds are independent, they have to overlap, interconnect and share knowledge under certain safeguards and rules [58]. This ensures that consumers and customers will have access to relevant internal enterprise knowledge or supplier/partner knowledge via the enterprise [58].

The aforementioned examples of KaaS conceptual models show how KaaS can be implemented in knowledge systems. The potential applications of KaaS within knowledge services are many. KaaS can benefit consumers, enterprises and customer enterprises by enabling high speed data, large levels of data analysis, and enriched knowledge clouds with more efficient data managing and warehousing. These are important factors for modern knowledge economies to consider in order maintaining their competitive advantage. A practical example of KaaS application in HEIs is the use of KaaS to improve student retention and student performance. This can happen through knowledge and data sharing amongst an institution's departments. A more efficient data operation can lead to integrated services which can offer reliable data analysis. This can improve the quality of an institution's offering product, which is

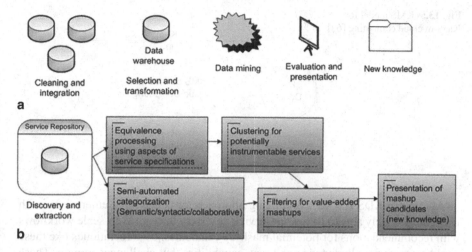

Fig. 13.4 (a) KDD phase (b) KDS phases [59]

knowledge, as well as improved student services. Improved student services can then lead to higher student satisfaction and as a result better student retention.

The next section focuses more on KaaS technology and deals with the underlying theory behind KaaS.

13.8   Underlying Theory Behind KaaS

The KaaS, as a new technology, has various approaches and methods that can be applied. Such approaches can lead to new capabilities, but at the same time can also lead to new challenges. The aim of this section is to provide a better understanding of the way KaaS functions.

Knowledge discovery in knowledge services is critical for all the service-oriented systems [59]. In services, such as KaaS, data integration and service mash-ups are very common and the tools used should be accurate and effective.

An approach suggested by M. Brain Blake [59] which can be applied to loud computing and in particular to KaaS, is knowledge discovery in services (KDS). The KDS is similar to knowledge discovery in databases (KDD). The KDD includes four phases which include cleaning and integration, selection and transformation, data mining and evaluation and presentation [60]. The KDS offers similar benefits to KDD, but also introduces new issues [59]. The KDS follows similar processes namely: discovery, equivalence processing, clustering, categorisation, filtering and presentation [59], however KDS's advantage comes from the more detailed specifications in the early phases of the process [59]. Figure 13.4 is a visual illustration of the knowledge discovery phases of KDD and KDS as suggested by M. Brain Blake.

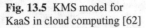
Fig. 13.5 KMS model for
KaaS in cloud computing [62]

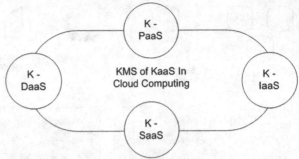

Automated KDS is a very promising approach for educational enterprises, with users immediately able to follow up service discovery through Web-scale workflows with recommendations for potential mash-up candidates [59]. Techniques like these could promote new knowledge and new capabilities, but challenges remain. These challenges are:

- Leveraging service specification structures: In KDS or KDD data integration is an important obstacle for automation. Even if, service specifications offer structure for interface descriptions, a service's underlying parts still demand correlation with other service parts [59]. Practically, semantic descriptions are absent from openly available Web services. A challenge is to leverage service specifications' structure and implicit semantics to aid in determining equivalences among messages across disparate services [59].
- Leveraging human interactions: Human actors (users) continuously adopt social networking environments like Twitter and Facebook. Users tag elements, services and blogs within these environments. Those user-made tags could help on predictions when categories of services are likely to add value on a specific set of users [59].
- Developing common situational awareness presentation environments: The connective data which integrates services into mash-ups are correlated with time, user identification and location. There are many cases where a particular mash-up leverages multiple dimensions [61]. A common visual environment would aid in standardising service development environments. Stakeholders will be interested in created services that are compatible for integration from their inception [61].

Knowledge organisation and knowledge management are also parts that integrate with the emerging concept of KaaS. Another knowledge management system/model, suggested by Eri et al. (2010), is the interconnection of knowledge management system (KMS) components within a cloud computing environment [62]. In the context of KMS and cloud computing environments, any knowledge which is provided by the community of practice (CoP) is indicated by "K (Knowledge)". For example, K-SaaS stands for Knowledge of SaaS. We have K-PaaS, K-IaaS and K-DaaS (data storage), respectively [62]. The overall model of KMS aiding KaaS through a cloud computing CoP is shown in Fig. 13.5.

Table 13.1 Five layer
framework for knowledge
cloud service [63]

Context layer
Knowledge service layer
Knowledge resource layer
Knowledge organisation layer
Knowledge support layer

A final conceptual model for KaaS relevant to the current work is provided by Ju and Shen [63]. The KaaS is an organisational process that contains the organisation and collection of knowledge resources and knowledge delivery services [63]. In general, it covers a lifecycle from knowledge generation to dissemination. High quality service (HQS) is dependent on the design of value-added services and knowledge resource quality [63]. For these reasons Ju and Shen propose a five-layer framework for the development of a KaaS platform which is suitable for offering a knowledge cloud (see Table 13.1).

The knowledge support layer, as the most important layer, is supported by bodies of knowledge (BOKs), involving related domains and standards (industry and international), and providing a scientific guide for knowledge resource collections (books, papers, reports, multimedia, etc.) [63]. Another interesting suggestion from Ju and Shen is the need for a dedicated team of professionals under the name of "Professional Knowledge Service Workers" (PKSW) tasked with supporting the knowledge services [63]. These "workers" would have specific domain expertise and general service knowledge and would be tasked with collecting, discovering, organising, updating and disseminating knowledge services [63]. Furthermore, they should provide knowledge services for other knowledge "workers".

Using this model, KaaS knowledge should be distributed through different domain repositories and should be deployed from separate locations via cloud connections [64]. Resource knowledge can then still be virtualised as a centralised knowledge repository with easy access [64]. The public platform also provides each domain with a visual interface, via a tag cloud, helping improve resource location [64].

The KaaS cloud technology together with its underlying theory and conceptual models, point to service-centric knowledge environments being at the centre of the next generation of internet opportunities, enabling new methods for knowledge discovery and distribution. These service-based capabilities will open up new relationships and inter-organisational workflows not only for industry but also in HE. Before finishing this chapter, it is, therefore, useful to look forward to the potential benefits of this technology within HE and to consider the likely implications.

13.9 Opportunities and Benefits of KaaS for the UK HE

There are five key elements which are essential for a successful education transformation. These are policy, curriculum and assessment, research and evaluation, professional development and ICT [17].

The proliferation of affordable internet connectivity, computers and rich educational content has led to a global phenomenon in which communication technology and information are used to transform education [17, 65]. Cloud computing technology and KaaS are now playing a key role in these changes. Making ICT easier to integrate into educational delivery and more affordable to implement, will enable education to be further transformed, and through KaaS students will be able to develop new skills to meet the evolving needs of the knowledge society.

The opportunities offered by KaaS in HE are not just in service improvement but also in cost reductions and hence they can potentially lead to an expansion of provision to the benefit of more students. Educational transformation can provide opportunities and advantages to anyone who can access it [17, 54, 66]. As an example to illustrate this point, Portugal has recently undertaken a 2 year nationwide educational transformation which has amongst other benefits provided significant economic savings, with an additional 2.26 billion Euros added to Portugal's economy and computers now available for every student in the country. It has also through its digital education initiative created 1,500 new jobs [17, 54, 66]. Cloud computing and KaaS initiatives are starting to be developed within the UK HEIs and promise similar opportunities both for saving money and enhancing provision, creating more jobs via centralised services, scalability, mobile accessibility and being environmentally sustainable.

Cloud computing and KaaS could also offer educational opportunities within the UK HEIs including enhanced national academic rankings, improved student performance, higher graduation rates and attainment [54, 66]. The opportunities and benefits of using KaaS for improving national competitiveness and productivity should not be underestimated, with new jobs, innovation and the cultivation of entrepreneurship clear benefits from more effective technology use [54, 65, 66]. The future possibilities for both the UK and its HEIs are significant, and strategic investment and development are clearly required. It is only to be hoped that leaders respond quickly enough to this changing environment—heading for the cloud rather than having their heads in the clouds.

13.10   Conclusion and Further Opportunities

Seventy-five percent of the economic activities in advanced countries are generated in service industries, where knowledge is the primary resource [57]. Knowledge is important because it brings innovation and as a result innovation brings progress.

The effective use of knowledge in the UK HEIs can help stimulate students' interests and creativity and this in turn can lead to innovation. VLEs have made a good start in enabling information sharing and knowledge exchange amongst students, researchers and staff members of the UK HEIs. Cloud computing technology with KaaS and its unique features and functionalities offer the next big step which is almost total system integration and collaboration. Inevitably, information and knowledge sharing will happen, with KaaS being a tool to achieve this.

Observing industry's efforts in using KaaS applications, the UK HEIs could take many useful ideas for similar KaaS applications in the HE sector. It must not be forgotten that enterprises and the UK HEIs are in close cooperation through research programs and often have common objectives, with both seeking innovation and the creation of knowledge.

The KaaS can provide cloud-based knowledge repositories. Such repositories could be available for private cloud users or to the public via subscriptions [54]. For the UK HEIs, further research is required on cloud-based educational models exploring how knowledge can be shared and distributed, via network-centred universities, through KaaS [65].

Using KaaS provides the opportunity for the UK HEIs to gain a short term strategic advantage, gaining in both efficiency and effectiveness. Close relationships between universities and commercial enterprises is an important factor within this. Universities could introduce a knowledge service platform in order to promote themselves, introducing rich content expertise and knowledge. On the other hand, by collaborating on technology with universities, companies may be able to gain a competitive edge in technological knowledge [67, 68].

The KaaS can increase competition amongst HEIs through its benefits. It can offer increased consumer behavior, improve student retention and upgrade the HEIs product. Students will feel they get the value of the money they spend in order to get educated.

In conclusion, we are still in the early stages of cloud computing adoption in both industry and the UK HEIs. The KaaS is still relatively undeveloped and any solutions will need thorough testing for both efficiency and effectiveness. The agreement between the UK HEIs and Microsoft signals the start of the age of cloud computing within HE and more cloud services will follow, as will KaaS. It is therefore important that further research is conducted into the use of KaaS in the UK HEIs so that its application can be better understood, and its potential benefits fully realised.

Acknowledgements The authors would like to thank the University of Huddersfield for providing the facilities to carry out this study.

References

1. Alexander B et al (2008) Social networking in higher education. In: Katz RN (ed) The tower and the cloud: higher education in the age of cloud computing. EDUCASE, Boulder
2. Vanquero LM (2011) EduCloud: PaaS versus IaaS cloud usage for an advance computer science course. IEEE 54(4):590–598
3. Wang B, Xing HY (2011) The application of cloud computing in education informatization. IEEE, international conference on computer science and service
4. Ouf S, Nasr M, Helmy Y (2011) An enhanced eLearning ecosystem based on an integration between cloud computing and Web 2.0. IEEE, 2011
5. Helmy Y, Ouf S, Nasr M (2011) An enhanced eLearning ecosystem based on an integration between cloud computing and Web 2.0. IEEE, 2011

6. Eri ZD, Abdullah R, Talib AM (2010) A model of knowledge management system for facilitating knowledge as a service (KaaS) is cloud computing environment. IEEE, 2010
7. Drucker PF (2010) The Drucker lectures. McGraw Hill, New York
8. Ju D, Shen B (2011) On building knowledge cloud. IEEE, 2011
9. Fan F, Lei F, Wu J (2010) The integration of cloud computing and the instruction. IEEE, 2011
10. Wu KD (2009) Japan operators' cloud computing commercial overall arrangement, vol 22. Communication World, China, p 31
11. Open Grid Forum (2009) Cloud storage for cloud computing. Storage networking industry association. http://www.snia.org/cloud/CloudStorageForCloudComputing.pdf. Accessed 25 May 2013
12. Gartner (2009) Cloud computing inquiries at Gartner. http://blogs.gartner.com/thomas_bittman/bittman/2009/10/29/cloud-computing-inquiries-atgartner. Accessed 24 May 2013
13. Golden B (2009) What cloud computing can do for higher education? CIO. http://www.cio.com/article/510798/What_Cloud_Computing_Can_Do_for_Higher_Education. Accessed 20 May 2013
14. Moothoor J, Bhatt VA (2010) A cloud computing solution in universities, IBM. http://www.ibm.com/developerworks/webservices/library/ws-vcl/index.html?ca=drs-. Accessed 20 May 2013
15. Calif C (2011) Hokkaido University builds Japan's largest academic cloud using Cloud.com. http://cloud.com/hokkaido-university-builds-japan%E2%80%99s-largest-academic-cloud-using-cloudcom. Accessed 20 May 2013
16. Business Standard (2011) NIIT offer's India's first cloud campus. http://www.business-standard.com/india/news/niit-offers-indias-first-cloud-campus/439061/. Accessed 20 May 2013
17. Fogel R (2010) The education cloud: delivering education as a service. White Paper, BergLib
18. Universities UK (2011) Efficiency and effectiveness in higher education: a report by the Universities UK Efficiency and Modernisation Task Group. Publications and Documents, September 2011
19. JISC (2011) Cloud services for education and research—projects and partners announced. http://www.jisc.ac.uk/news/stories/2011/06/cloudservices.aspx. Accessed 18 May 2013
20. Clark M, Ferrell G, Hopkins P (2011) Study of early adopters of shared services and cloud computing within higher and further education Newcastle-upon-Tyne. Report produced by HE Associates Ltd., p 68
21. Hawtin R, Hammond M, Gillam L, Curtis G (2012) Cost analysis of cloud computing for research. Document and Publications, EPSRC and JISC. http://www.jisc.ac.uk/media/documents/programmes/. Accessed 13 May 2012
22. JISC (2013) Over 18 million students and staff to benefit from faster, more secure cloud-computing. http://www.jisc.ac.uk/news/over-18-million-students-and-staff-to-benefit-from-faster-more-secure-cloud-computing-21-may. Accessed 12 June 2013
23. Katz R, Goldstein P, Yanosky R (2009) Cloud computing in higher education. EDUCAUSE, NITLE Summit
24. Pocatilu PF, Alecu et al (2010) Measuring the efficiency of cloud computing for eLearning systems. Romania/January 2010
25. Ouf S, Nasr M, Helmy Y (2011) An enhanced eLearning ecosystem based on an integration between cloud computing and Web 2.0. IEEE
26. Weller M (2006) VLE 2.0 and future directions in learning environments. Institute of Educational Technology. The Open University, Milton Keynes
27. Pole R, Hole S, Jones K, Williams J, Toole AM (2010) eDiscovery learning: an evaluation of Web 2.0 technology to enhance learning. HE Academy, ICS, 2010
28. MacNeil S, Kraan W (2010) Distributed learning environments. JISC Cetis, 2010
29. Dong B, Zheng Q et al (2009) An eLearning ecosystem based on cloud computing infrastructure. The ninth IEEE international conference on advanced learning technologies. China. IEEEXplore

30. He W, Cernusca D, Abdous M (2011) Exploring cloud computing for distance learning. Online J Distance Learn Adm. University of West Georgia, Distance Education Center, vol XIV, Fall 2011
31. Armbrust M, Fox A, Griffith R, Joseph A, Katz R, Konwinski A, Lee G, Patterson D, Rabkin A, Stoica I, Zaharia M (2010) A view of cloud computing: clearing the clouds away from the true potential and obstacles posed by this computing capability. Commun ACM 53(4):50–58
32. Dong B, Zheng Q, Yang J, Li H, Qiao M (2009) An e-learning ecosystem based on cloud computing infrastructure. Proceeds in 9th IEEE international conference on advanced learning technologies, ICALT. Riga, Latvia, July 15–17, pp 125–127
33. Jaeger PT, Lin J, Grimes J (2008) Cloud computing and information policy: computing in a policy cloud? J Inf Technol Politi 5(3):269–283
34. Rittinghouse J, Ransome J (2009) Cloud computing: implementation, management, and security. CRC Press, US
35. Dong J, Han J, Liu J, Xu H (2010) The shallow analysis of the enlightenment of cloud computing to distance education. International Conference on E-Health Networking, Digital Ecosystems and Technologies (EDT), 2010, pp 301–303
36. Trentin G (2009) Using a wiki to evaluate individual contribution to a collaborative learning project. J Comp Assist Learn 25(1):43–55
37. Cole M (2009) Using wiki technology to support student engagement: lessons from the trenches. Comput Educ 52:141–146
38. Alshahrani S, Ward R (2013) Student's views on using WEB2.0 (social web) to interact with their lectures, Digital Library. http://library.iated.org/view/ALSHAHRANI2013-STUhttp://library.iated.org/view/ALSHAHRANI2013STU. Accessed 26 June 2013
39. Uden L, Wangsa IT et al (2007) The future of eLearning: eLearning ecosystem. The inaugural IEEE international conference on digital ecosystems and technologies, IEEE DEST, IEEEXplore
40. Jax K (2007) Can we define ecosystems? On the confusion between definition and description of ecological concepts. 2 October, 2007
41. Gutl C, Chang V (2008) The use of Web2.0 technologies and services to support eLearning ecosystem to develop more effective Learning Environments. The ninth IEEE international conference on advance learning technologies, IEEEXplore, 2008
42. Blanton S, Schiller C (2010) Is there safety in the cloud? EDUCAUSE Quarterly 33(2). http://www.educause.edu/EDUCAUSE+Quarterly/EDUCAUSEQuarterlyMagazineVolum/Is ThereSafetyintheCloud/206543
43. Thethi JP (2009) Realizing the value proposition of cloud computing: CIO's enterprise IT strategy for cloud. http://www.infosys.com/cloud-computing/white-papers/Documents/realizing-value-proposition.pdf. Accessed 9 Sep 2013
44. Leong L, Chamberlin T (2010) Magic quadrant for cloud infrastructure as a service and web hosting. Research Note, Gartner Group. http://c1776742.cdn.cloudfiles rackspacecloud.com/downloads/pdfs/GartnerMagicQuadrant.pdf. Accessed 9 Sep 2013
45. Li H, Sedayao J, Hahn-Steichen J, Jimison E, Spence C, Chahal S (2009) Developing an enterprise cloud computing strategy. Intel White Paper. http://premierit.intel.com/docs/DOC–5578
46. Motahari-Nezhad HR, Stephenson B, Singhal S (2009) Outsourcing business to cloud computing services: opportunities and challenges. Technical Report HPL-2009-23. January 2009
47. Trappler TJ (2010) If it's in the cloud, get it on paper: cloud computing contract issues. EDUCAUSE Quarterly, 33(2). http://www.educause.edu/EDUCAUSE+Quarterly/ EDUCAUSEQuarterlyMagazineVolum/IfItsintheCloudGetItonPaperClo/206532
48. Al-Zoune M, El-Soud SA, Wyne MF (2010) Cloud computing based eLearning system. Int J Distance Educ Technol (IJDET) 8(2):1–14
49. Ercan Y (2010) Effective use of cloud computing in educational institutions. Procedia social and behavioural sciences. Science Direct, 2010

50. Wheeler B, Waggener S (2009) Above campus services: shaping the promise of cloud computing for higher education. November/December, 2009
51. Bein D W (2008) The impact of cloud computing in WEB2.0. USA, August 2008
52. Kisker H (2009) The rise of the collaborative cloud. The forester blog for vendor strategy professional, 2009
53. CumulusIQ (2009) Knowledge as a service. October, 116 Research Drive, 122, 2009
54. Tsui E, Cheong KF, Sabettzadeh F (2010) Cloud-based personal knowledge management as a service (PKMaaS). IEEE, 2010
55. Xu S, Zhang W (2005) Knowledge as a service and knowledge breaching, IEEE, 2005
56. Ueda R, Sato Y, Mori M, Nakamura K, Sagawa N (2010) KaaS knowledge platform facilitating innovation in social infrastructure. Hitachi Review 59(5):2010
57. Tsui E (2011) Knowledge management research centre. Repository of Hong Kong Polytechnic University (HKPoLyY), 2011
58. Delic KA, Riley JA (2009) Enterprise knowledge clouds: nest generation KM systems? Jeffs Publications, Rileys, 2009
59. Brain Blake M (2009) Knowledge discovery in services. IEEE Press, 2009
60. Han J, Kamber M (2001) Data mining: concepts and techniques. Morgan Kaufmann, 2001
61. Blake MB, Nowlan MF (2008) Predicting service mashup candidates using enhanced syntactical message management. Proceedings of international conference on services computing (SCC 08), IEEE Press, pp 229–236
62. Darleena Eri Z et al (2010) A model of knowledge management system for facilitating knowledge as a service (KaaS) in cloud computing environment. IEEE Press, 2010
63. Ju D, Shen B (2011) On building knowledge cloud. IEEE Press, 2011
64. Ju D, Shen B (2010) A design framework for public knowledge service platform. Proceedings for KaaS 2010. American Scholars Press, 2010
65. Yuru W, Xinfang L, Xianchen Z (2010) Cloud computing and its application to construction of web-based learning environment. International conference on computer application and system modeling (ICCASM 2010)
66. Intel (2010) The economic benefits of strategic ICT spending. White Paper. Accessed 16 June 2013
67. Qingsong S, Yinan S (2011) Evaluation research on the university knowledge service facing to enterprises. ICII, IEEE, 2011
68. Gans JS, Stern S (2003) The product market and the market for ideas: commercialization strategies for technology entrepreneurs. Res Pol 32:333–350

Chapter 14
Cloud Computing Environment for e-Learning Services for Students with Disabilities

Aleksandar Milić, Konstantin Simić and Miloš Milutinović

Abstract This chapter discusses design of cloud computing environments for e-learning services and applications for students with disabilities. The main idea is to expand the corpus of e-learning services adjusted for students with disabilities. The rationale is that e-educational systems are becoming more complex and educational institutions need a new solution for deploying e-learning services. The cloud computing environment gives a new perspective to educational process in terms of usage of educational applications, software, and system for e-education. Regardless of the rapid development of information and communication technologies, there is a low level of inclusion of students with disabilities into the education process. Therefore, in this chapter the authors present a model of cloud computing environment for providing e-learning services developed with respect to the needs of students with disabilities. The model includes a variety of services, applications and components integrated into the e-learning Web portal. These services provide numerous features: a choice of different types of teaching materials, an integration of interactive voice response system within the learning management system, a mobile messaging service, etc. As a proof of the concept, a number of components of the model were implemented for students with disabilities within the Laboratory for e-business, Faculty of Organizational Sciences, University of Belgrade. Results and our impressions are presented.

Keywords Cloud computing · E-learning services · E-learning · Students with disabilities · E-education · Disability

A. Milić (✉) · K. Simić · M. Milutinović
Faculty of Organizational Sciences, University of Belgrade,
Jove Ilića 154, Belgrade, Serbia
e-mail: milic@elab.rs

K. Simić
e-mail: kosta@elab.rs

M. Milutinović
e-mail: milosm@elab.rs

Z. Mahmood (ed.), *Continued Rise of the Cloud,* Computer Communications
and Networks, DOI 10.1007/978-1-4471-6452-4_14,
© Springer-Verlag London 2014

14.1   Introduction

The ability to provide access to services and information 24 h a day, seven days a week, is an emerging force today. Nowadays, higher education institutions are turning attention and resources to provide information and services on-line, and to use technology for improvement of the educational process. As a result, the e-educational system is revolutionized. In this new age, a good e-educational system is an accessible e-educational system. A good e-educational system needs to have an immediate access to pertinent information.

Further, information and communication technology (ICT) changes the educational systems and their possibilities, thereby enabling an educational process to be offered in way that responds to students' needs and demands. The ICT is a tremendously valuable tool for encouraging the development, inclusion, and participation of collectives traditionally excluded from several areas of social and cultural life. This feature has enabled higher education institutions to include groups of students with disability to participate in the general curriculum and to successfully achieve academic success. According to the World Health Organization (WHO), a disability is "any restriction or lack (resulting from any impairment) of ability to perform an activity in the manner or within the range considered normal for a human being."

A very important topic nowadays is the issue of designing new educational services and adjusting current educational services to suit the needs of a disabled student. While the amount and type of accessible information increases, learning environments, which offer the same content to all participants, and the same navigational options, cannot satisfy the demands [1]. The problem is that the learning material does not take into consideration the students' personal learning needs [2, 3]. Because of the learning environments' limitations, there is a need for a transition from Web-based learning environments, which are developed with a motto, such as "One size fits all", to an adaptive Web-based learning [1, 4, 5].

With a huge growth in the number of users, services, education contents, and resources, e-learning systems become more and more large-scale. One of the basic problems in developing the environment for an e-education system is how to provide scalability and reliability of educational applications and services. One of the possible solutions is infrastructure based on the cloud computing concept.

This chapter discusses one possible approach to providing e-education services for a student with disabilities. The developed model is based on the cloud computing infrastructure. The model includes all services necessary for the inclusion of students with disabilities. The rest of the chapter is organized as follows: in the second section, a theoretical background of cloud computing and implemented e-education services for people with disabilities is given; the third section describes the different approaches for delivering e-learning services through cloud computing; in Sect. 14.4 a model for the usage of e-learning services for students with disabilities through cloud computing is proposed. Section 14.5 gives details on the realization of the proposed model within the e-learning system of the Laboratory for e-business at the University of Belgrade. The next Sect. 14.6 discusses benefits from the developed cloud computing services that students with disabilities can achieve. Finally, concluding remarks are given.

14.2   Theoretical Background

14.2.1   E-Learning and Cloud Computing

The majority of educational institutions own a computer centre which is designed and built specifically for their own use. The efficiency of the existing resources represents a problem. The capacity of computer centre gradually becomes inadequate to meet the demands of scientific research and educational activities, while at the same time it becomes expensive to maintain. In each semester students mostly require the most modern hardware with specific software requirements for their laboratory exercises and practical projects. Therefore, a low utilization of available resources requires a different approach to the implementation of infrastructure systems for e-learning.

The best solution that information technologies could provide to users at higher education institutions and to their computer centers is the development of an information technology (IT) infrastructure model based on the cloud computing concept. The concept of cloud computing is a business model and technology platform, which is the result of evolution and convergence of many seemingly independent computing trends. The cloud computing infrastructure for educational institutions allows for an efficient usage of the existing resources and gives a new perspective to scalability and reliability of educational applications, software, and a system for e-education. The cloud computing concept and its characteristics can help higher education institutions improve productivity and enhance hardware and software resource management which are necessary to provide e-education features, scientific and research activities, and student projects [6].

The IT infrastructure of a higher education institution is a set of hardware, software, computer network, associated facilities meant to provide modern services and network resources, the Internet connection and communication with other scientific research and higher education institutions, to promote scientific research and educational processes. A majority of resources in the e-learning system are deployed and assigned for some specific tasks or services, and physical machines are usually stacked simply and exclusively. With the growth of resources, the utilization of these resources becomes another problem. During the education process a large amount of teaching material is generated, which further aggravates the available resources. One of the biggest problems in the implementation of IT infrastructure is a competitive access to shared resources in the higher education institution.

14.2.2   People with Disabilities

Developing learning environments and systems which provide education while satisfying the individual differences, such as learning styles, learning preferences, interests, etc. can be very beneficial. These environments/systems utilize different solutions, such as various teaching strategies to lessen the specific learning disability

[7]. People with disabilities face many difficulties in their everyday lives, depending on the type of their disability. They are frequently the subjects of discrimination. Students with disabilities often have problems related to accessibility of teaching materials. Adequate categorization of people with disabilities can be used to prevent this discrimination of people with disabilities.

When the literature is reviewed, it can be seen that classifications of specific learning disabilities are expressed differently by different researchers. The most frequently used classifications of computer learning disability include visual impairments, hearing impairments, motor impairments, and cognitive impairments. Opposing these classifications, some specialists [8, 9] claim that specific learning disabilities can vary from one child affected to another, and such disability can be observed in a couple of areas and in some children, which cannot be classified. These disabilities are briefly introduced in the following:

Visual Impairments The visual impairments include:

- Total blindness: People who are totally blind cannot see at all; therefore, when accessing the Internet or using computerized equipment, these individuals typically rely on screen reader devices.
- Low vision: People with low vision can see images; however, they cannot see most images clearly.
- Color blindness: People with color blindness have difficulty in perceiving certain colors and/or combinations of colors. These individuals may, however, have no difficulty seeing black and white images or varying shades of grey [10].

Hearing Impairments Hearing impairment disabilities vary in type and severity. People who have a hearing impairment may have a diminished ability to hear certain frequencies (pitches), or they may have difficulty hearing at all frequency levels.

Motor Impairments Some learners with motor impairment disabilities may have limited use of their hands; others may not be able to use their hands at all. Conditions that may lead to a motor impairment disability include arthritis, amputation, birth defects, cerebral palsy, essential tremor, loss or damage of limbs, muscular dystrophy, multiple sclerosis, spina bifida, spinal cord injury, neurological conditions, paralysis, and Parkinson's disease. Hudson [11] maintains that individuals who have motor impairment disabilities commonly experience difficulties accessing computer keyboards and mice; therefore, they often rely on special assistive technologies in order to interact with a computer.

Cognitive Impairments Cognitive impairments involve a wide variation of memory, perception, problem-solving, and conceptualizing challenges. Cognitive impairments are often attributed to conditions, such as autism, brain injury, cerebral palsy, epilepsy, mental retardation, or neurological impairment [12]. Cognitive impairments can also include developmental disabilities, pervasive developmental disorders, Rett syndrome, and William's syndrome [13].

Students with learning disabilities constitute the largest group of students with disabilities at the college level. Some authors [14] suggested the need for new educational materials to develop students' thinking ability, increase their motivation, and assess their learning. Carnine [15] and Ellis [16] advocate focusing teaching strategies and instructional materials for all students on developing higher order thinking processes. Rieth and Polsgrove [17] discuss three models for creating a curriculum for students with learning disabilities. Their goals include enabling students to better process information, improving their coping and problem-solving skills, developing their interpersonal skills, and enabling them to establish social support networks. Classroom simulations promote all four of these goals and could be effectively utilized in any of the three models discussed [18].

14.3 Approaches to Delivering e-Learning Services to Students with Disabilities

To bring services to people with disabilities, there are two commonly utilized approaches. The first approach involves the utilization of an assistive technology. The second approach involves the utilization of a design principle referred to as the universal design.

14.3.1 Universal Design

The term "universal design" was coined in the 1970s as an architectural concept for making facilities accessible to all persons without the help of special assistance or devices. Since that time the universal design concept has been adopted by many additional fields including the computer industry, telecommunications, and information systems [19]. Universal design can be defined as the theory and practice pertaining to design, development, and implementation of communication, information, and technology products and services that are equally accessible to individuals who are disabled.

The Universal design for learning (UDL) is a research-based model for curricular design. The model ensures participation in the higher education institution program for all students, including those with disabilities. The UDL offers options for how educational resource is presented, how students respond or demonstrate their knowledge and skills, and how students are engaged in learning. The UDL implementation provides the opportunity for all students to access, participate in, and progress in the higher education institution curriculum by reducing barriers to instruction.

The UDL addresses three learning networks within a broadly defined concept of curriculum that includes goals, materials, methods, and assessment [20]. According to the following three UDL principles, each area of the curriculum should provide multiple, varied, and flexible options for representation, expression, and engagement:

- Principle 1: It provides multiple means of representation (recognition network). Present information and content in different ways.
- Principle 2: It provides multiple means of action and expression (strategic network) and differentiates the ways in which students can express what they know.
- Principle 3: It provides multiple means of engagement (affective network) and stimulates interest and motivation for learning.

Section 508 Standards [21] defines assistive technologies as "any item, piece of equipment, or system, whether acquired commercially, modified, or customized, that is commonly used to increase, maintain, or improve functional capabilities of individuals with disabilities."

14.3.2 Assistive Technology

In the context of Web accessibility assistive technologies include various hardware and software solutions that improve the life quality of the people with motor and hearing impairments and those with sensory and mental disabilities. Some examples are electronic aids, such as special keyboards, alternative commands, and auxiliary means for communication, such as ergonomic aids and specific software. These modern technical aids and adapted software enable persons with disabilities to be independent and to communicate.

Assistive technologies can be classified into the following groups:

Aids for Blind Persons These are:

- Voice program that includes two components: screen reader and speech synthesizer. Screen reader transforms users' actions and screen content into text, while synthesizer transforms text into voice. One of the most used readers worldwide is job access with speech (JAWS).
- Braille display is a monitor for blind persons that presents text in Braille letters.
- Braille keyboards can replace standard keyboards. They contain the same keys as those on the typewriter for blind persons: Braille typewriter, and some other additional keys for navigation.

Aids for Weak-Eyed Persons These are:

- Software for enlarging content on the screen with or without voice commands
- Keyboards with big letters for the weak-eyed
- Special keyboards, adaptable keyboards, mini keyboards, keyboards with enlarged keys, etc.
- Special mice, mice with adapted shape, etc.
- Touch screens

Web accessibility should be perceivable, operable, understandable, and robust. If any of the principles are not taken into account, some users will not be enabled to access the content.

- Perceivable means that all information and components on a page have to be notable and accessible in the way the user would like. Non-textual content, such as images, audio, and video content, have to be visible, i.e., the user can see them in a proper way. For instance, for those who cannot hear, the content should be readable; for those who cannot see, the content should be available using some other non-visual media.
- Operable means that link both navigation elements and user interface elements are designed in the way that is useful for all users, i.e., they should be operable. Each element on the page has to be available via the keyboard. Users should be given enough time to read and explore the content, except in the case of real time operations, such as taking tests and auctions. Users should be provided with adequate support when they explore the Web page content, search for information, and determine position within site.
- The principle of understandability could be explained as a principle that provides a clear and understandable content presentation. The content has to be readable and predictable, i.e., Web pages work in the common way (opening pages in new tab or window, etc.). Further, support for users should be ensured. For instance, when the user fills a form, the system should notify the user whether some field has been omitted, which field it is and give more explanations related to the proper filling of the form.
- Robustness is a concept that implies a high level of compatibility between pages and user agents, including auxiliary technologies. All the elements should have a start and the last tag, have to be nested according to specification and must not contain double attributes.

14.4 A Model of Cloud Infrastructure for E-Learning

Cloud computing refers to providing and using computational resources via the Internet [22]. It enables an access to technology in the form of services available on demand. Cloud computing is an area of computing that refers to providing users with highly scalable IT capacities as services via the Internet [23]. It is an abstract, scalable and controlled computer infrastructure that hosts applications and services for end users. Services and data coexist in shared and dynamically scaled set of resources [24].

Applying cloud computing in higher education institutions improves efficiency of the existing resources usage, as well as reliability and scalability of software tools and applications for e-education. Given the fact that most of resources are strictly allocated to applications, physical machines are used for application, or particular tasks that are to be executed on that particular machine. If a system becomes busy and overloaded, problem of scalability will be solved by adding new physical resources. Introducing new resources implies a significant increase in costs. Given this fact, it is necessary to find some other way of solving the problem of scalability and usage of resources. Simultaneous access to common resources is one of the most important problems in using the IT infrastructure. Cloud computing can bring a new value to an e-education system, because educational services can be delivered in a reliable and efficient way.

Basic components of the faculty e-education model are:

- Services for e-education (identity management system, e-mail, learning management system, document management system, customer relationship management, portal services, etc.)
- Software components—modular object oriented developmental learning environment (Moodle), OpenNebula, open lightweight directory access protocol (LDAP), Apache, MySql, etc.
- Network and hardware infrastructure
- Users (students, non-teaching staff, etc.)

14.4.1 Network Infrastructure

Before developing the model of a cloud computing infrastructure it is necessary to build a network infrastructure that is suitable for e-learning. Network infrastructure is mandated to provide information, communication services, and the Internet connection for teachers, students, and external partners. Network infrastructure has to provide a basis for the implementation of the e-education and scientific research of high availability, scalability and reliability. In addition to services for employees and students, the system must provide support for collaboration with partners and external partners in distributed research teams. The primary tasks network infrastructure has to meet are flexibility of the information system and a high level of security. Further, the infrastructure should enable quick, easy, and inexpensive installation of new hardware systems and software using the concepts of cloud computing.

Part of the network infrastructure should be implemented as a common network infrastructure. The other part of the network infrastructure should be a virtual network infrastructure in the private cloud.

All users of the service can be classified into the following categories:

- Employees have the highest level of administrative rights and privileges of all services.
- Associates have a smaller set of privileges.
- Students have access to the set of student services.

For the design and implementation of the computer network hierarchical model is used. This model is based on the principles of hierarchy and modularity. By applying this model complex network is divided into layers, defining the specific functions of each layer. The conceptual computer network architecture is shown in Fig. 14.1.

The core layer is the backbone of the network and at the same time the most critical place in the network. It provides connectivity between the distribution layer devices, and therefore high availability and redundancy are very important. Since this layer aggregates the traffic from all the devices of the distribution layer devices

Fig. 14.1 Conceptual logic
networks scheme

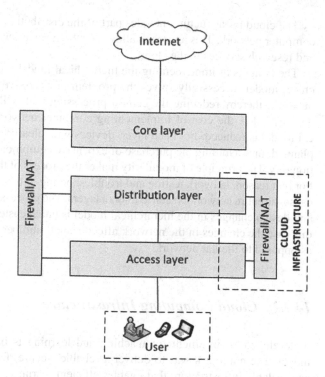

implemented at the central layer (routers and switches), it must support high data rates with low latency. On this layer, the security issue is of great importance. Processing large amounts of data, as well as connections to the Internet require the implementation of high-performance devices on this layer.

The distribution layer is the interface between the core and access layers. The role of this layer is to provide aggregation of data from the access layer before forwarding these data to the core layer. The distribution layer controls the flow of traffic using the policy and defining broadcast domains, which can be achieved by implementing routers or virtual local area networks (VLAN). On this layer, there are high-performance devices. In order to achieve a high degree of availability, redundant devices are implemented. Part of the distribution layer is implemented as a virtual network infrastructure in the cloud.

The access layer is the interface to end users and also represents the connection of user devices with the rest of the network. In addition to user devices (computers, printers, IP phones, etc.) at this layer the routers, switches, hubs, and wireless access point may also be included. The main task of this layer is connecting to a network and access control in order to define which devices have access rights and the right of communication over the network.

The firewall/network address translation (NAT) is a software or hardware part of network infrastructure that controls the incoming and outgoing network traffic. The main task of this part of the network is to control packets based on a defined set of rules. The NAT is the process of modification of IP addresses in the IPv4 header when passing through the routing device.

The cloud infrastructure includes part of the distribution and access layers of the computer network. This approach allows for the further development of educational and research services in the cloud.

The benefits of implementing the hierarchical model are numerous. The hierarchical model successfully solves the problem of excessive broadcast traffic on the network, thereby reducing the central processing unit (CPU) load of the network devices. Also, the cost of implementing computer network based on a hierarchical model is reduced. For each layer, devices with clearly defined functionality are planned, thus avoiding the purchase of expensive equipment with superfluous functionality. The principle of modularity makes the process of the system design simple. For that reason, network testing and troubleshooting in the network is simplified because the entire network is seen as a set of layers. The process of network maintenance and design changes in the hierarchical model is much easier to implement, since in this case the changes in the network affect a small number of devices and services, as opposed to the flat network.

14.4.2 Cloud Computing Infrastructure

A developed environment for teaching and learning is based on a private cloud model. The main task was to deliver a reliable, secure, fault-tolerant, sustainable, and scalable infrastructure that enables efficient learning. A logical architecture of the implemented cloud computing infrastructure is shown in Fig. 14.2.

Network services have to provide more flexibility of the IT infrastructure while at the same time preserving a safe network environment. The limitations encountered in the implementation of network services include a heterogeneous network environment, the security access and links between different identities, multiple passwords, and a user account life cycle. Overcoming these constraints in the development of network services puts the focus on the entire process of managing digital identities.

The process of managing the information on the digital identity of entities in order to control access to resources is commonly referred to as *identity management*. In order to define a good structure of the directory for identity management, it is necessary to define the user roles and privileges in the system. Every user within the model has a set of defined privileges in a specific sub-environment, in a specific context and for a specific service. The main problem of integration in a heterogeneous environment is to provide a unique method for identification and authentication of system users.

Numerous research works have proved that security, digital identity, and access management are essential for a successful deployment of infrastructure for e-learning [25, 26, 27]. For this set of tasks, the LDAP is chosen as a directory service. Users use the same credentials to access different services. Depending on users' roles and needs, specific cloud services are provided through an appropriate deployment model:

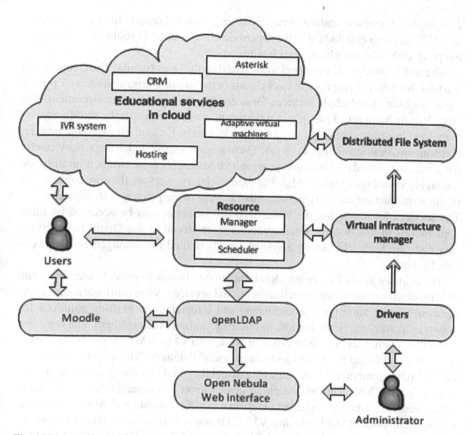

Fig. 14.2 Logical architecture of cloud computing infrastructure

- Software as a service (SaaS)—is provided mainly to teachers and students. These services include the software necessary for the realization of e-learning (e.g., Moodle, communication tools, etc.) and specific solutions necessary for the realization of the teaching process (e.g., interactive voice response; IVR system).
- Platform as a service (PaaS)—is provided to teachers and students who need to teach and learn subjects that include using software tools that cannot be distributed to every student (e.g., students do not own the required hardware).
- Infrastructure as a service (IaaS)—is managed by administrators and can be offered to a university's departments for developing their own virtual laboratories.

There are several open source packages that take a holistic approach and integrate all of the necessary functionality into a single package (virtualization, management, interfaces, and security). When added to a network of servers and storage, these packages produce flexible cloud computing and storage infrastructures (IaaS). The OpenNebula is issued under the Apache license. It supports private cloud construction, as well as the idea of hybrid clouds. A hybrid cloud permits combining a private cloud infrastructure with a public cloud infrastructure (such as Amazon) to enable even higher degrees of scaling. After analyzing different reports found in the literature [28], one can conclude that the OpenNubula is a suitable solution to deploying the private cloud of an educational institution.

The architecture of the private cloud is based on the OpenNebula. The OpenNebula is a tool that enables on-premise IaaS clouds in the existing infrastructures. A private cloud uses the OpenNebula services for accessing the virtualized environment. The OpenNebula has a set of pluggable modules to interact with specific middleware of the Cloud infrastructure (e.g., virtualization hypervisor, cloud services, file transfer mechanisms, or information services). These adaptors are called drivers. Services for the access to a virtual environment provide an interface for monitoring, migrating and managing virtual machines (VMs). The OpenNebula drivers are the core components of the infrastructure and only the administrators have the privileges to manage them. The services for managing the virtualized infrastructure can be accessed by other applications in the system. User credentials are stored in the OpenLDAP. Every user can save their VMs using a system for distributed file management, Network File System.

The primary goal of a private cloud implementation is to provide users with run of virtualized infrastructure, environment, and services. Virtual infrastructure management system automates, coordinates, and integrates the existing solutions for networking, storage, virtualization, monitoring, and user management. The key components of the model enable an efficient work with VMs. VMs are put on the image repository and could be moved and run on users' demands. The system component for VM management enables achieving scalability and reliability of implemented services on the VM. The private cloud layer (driver) that enables access by using virtualized infrastructure includes: (1) Virtual machine manager (VMM) driver used for creation, control, and tracking VM (2)Transfer drivers used for transmission, replication, removing and creating VM images (3) Information driver that controls and tracks machines and other hardware performances.

Security is one of the big concerns in this model. The main goal that security should fulfill is creating a highly available system and a secure environment. The physical security that makes the system resistant to attacks created at the VM, requires a strict separation between the physical environment and the VM. The only access point to virtual environment is delegated to the VM that is connected to a physical network interface. By using a firewall, the system is protected from unauthorized access to virtual networks and to the system itself. The firewall disables communication between VMs in configured virtual networks. During the VM exploitation failovers could occur, thus the work of the whole system could be threatened. In order to quickly recover the system, requirement for distributed file system (DSF) is necessary. The DSF possesses a defined fault tolerant, realized through data replication on different physical machines.

14.4.3   Services for E-Education

A key part of the described model is the Moodle LMS learning management system as the aggregator and integrator of all components and services. The Moodle LMS provides services for collaboration and communication which do not meet all the requirements of student needs. The LMS is built as a VM within the private cloud that is managed through the administrative part of the OpenNebula interface. This VM has certain hardware resources and can be expanded during the work or moved by introducing a new, more powerful machine. Students access the portal and resources only within the educational research resource pool. Logging into the portal enables the use of student services. All access rights for e-education services are written in LDAP. Students and employees can use an interactive voice response machine and receive an SMS notification about courses they are subscribed to. The model enables students to exercise developing and managing VM for hosting, thus they can get practical knowledge from different areas.

Further, in order that the students should try out all the advanced techniques and technologies it is necessary to ensure the use of different operating systems, development platforms, software tools, database management tools, Web servers, browsers, etc. Therefore, using a developed cloud computing infrastructure each student accesses a VM that hosts a required image. After the closure of work, the student's results can be saved for further work or analysis. The advantage of this approach is that the student needs only an Internet connection for work and a complete hardware and software necessary to successfully master the matter are provided at a higher education institution.

14.4.4 Network Performance Monitoring System

The primary task of the network performance monitoring system is to oversee and monitor the parameters of network devices and services. Considering the structure and characteristics of the network infrastructure, it was decided to implement network monitoring using the simple network management protocol (SNMP). [29]. For network devices, it is necessary to monitor the network traffic on interfaces and the CPU usage. For servers and VMs, it is necessary to monitor the following parameters:

- Traffic on interfaces
- Processor availability
- Memory consumption
- Number of processes
- Number of logged users

In order to monitor the network parameters, in the computer network of the laboratory for e-business Cacti application was implemented. Cacti application is installed in a VM on a server with a CentOS 6.4 operating system. The access to the application is made via the Web interface.

The main task of the Cacti application is to monitor the parameters of network devices and servers (Fig. 14.3). The SNMP protocol is mainly used for collecting data from network devices (routers, switches, etc). For security reasons, the SNMP access should be limited to the management station, which is implemented by access lists.

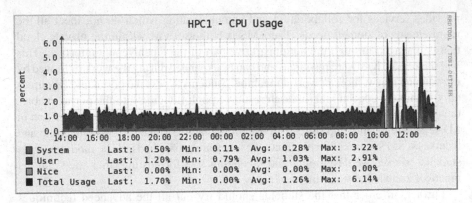

Fig. 14.3 CPU usage on one of the servers

14.5 Implementation of Application Services in E-Education

According to numerous research works, the Moodle is one of LMSs with the largest number of functionalities and services [30, 31]. The Moodle is flexible for implementing new components and integration with other systems and technologies.

The laboratory for e-business, at the Faculty of Organizational Sciences, organizes its courses at all levels of study, using a blended learning concept [32]. More than 900 students have access to more than 100 online courses, created within the e-learning system management Moodle LMS. The Moodle is an open-source system for managing teaching and learning via the Web. It is widely used by many universities and instructors. In the scope of the Moodle courses, we use a lot of additional software and applications.

Problems arise when a large number of students simultaneously access the system (taking tests, uploading or downloading large amounts of data, setting homework, etc.). At these moments, the server load is near the maximum and then it is necessary to provide the scalability and reliability. In order to overcome these problems and improve the system performances, the Department for e-business has implemented a cloud computing infrastructure described in the previous section. The infrastructure includes 160 CPU with more than 4TB of memory. The implemented infrastructure based on cloud computing enabled an efficient and scalable work of teachers and students.

According to the four principles of Web accessibility and according to the proposed model, some adjustments were introduced in scope of the laboratory for e-business, Faculty of Organizational Sciences, Belgrade. These adjustments include an adaptation of current services and teaching materials, as well as customization of design of the e-learning Web portal. This e-learning system is realized by using the Moodle learning management system. Customizing the portal to students with visual impairments is performed in several ways. Each non-text element is described in detail and also students are able to change the theme of the portal (font, colors, element layout, etc.). In Fig. 14.4, an example is given of the image which has additional descriptions and can make materials more accessible to students who are blind by providing

Fig. 14.4 Image with additional descriptions

Fig. 14.5 Choosing between
different text sizes

meaningful alternate or long descriptions (alt tags) for each non-text element on the page. Alt tags are a descriptive text that shows up when a mouse-arrow hovers over a non-text element. Screen-reading devices are able to read these image descriptions to students.

Students are able to choose between four available different Web portal themes. They are also able to choose one of two available text sizes for each theme. Used themes are customized for people with low vision and color blindness. In Fig. 14.5, an example of choosing between different text sizes is shown.

In addition to customizing the design of the current e-learning portal, the system is extended with a new IVR service. The infrastructure for this system is shown in Fig. 14.6. This service helps students with visual and motor impairments. A student with special needs chooses whether he/she wants to take a normal or accessible test and whether he/she has visual or motor problem(s). These data are saved into the Moodle database, as well as the phone number which the student will use for accessing the system. While taking the test, the student is being identified by comparing the phone number which is used for accessing the system with the phone number stored in the database. The system checks if the student has the privilege for accessing the test and if it is the case, the student can start the test. For a student with visual problems, the voice synthesizer reads the questions. Students answer the questions by pressing the appropriate keypad key. All questions are previously prepared and there are four available answers. Only one answer is a correct one.

Our IVR solution [33] can also be used by students with motor impairment and by everyone, as well. Students with motor impairment may have a difficult time

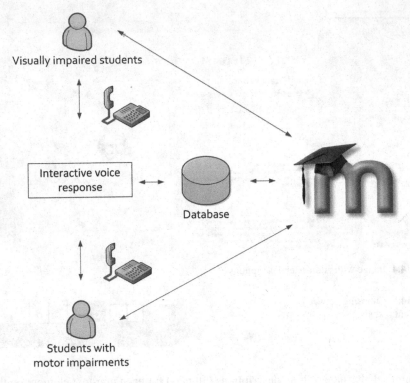

Fig. 14.6 Infrastructure of an IVR system for e-learning

interfacing with their computer. Therefore, the IVR in their case has a long timeout of 30 s per question. The IVR also has a built-in basic speech recognition mechanism. All questions have four available responses. The student chooses only one response. Response can be given by pressing the appropriate key or by saying the response. The speech recognition mechanism is simple because the system distinguishes only four words (one, two, three, and four). If the student does not respond in the scheduled time interval, all skipped or unanswered questions will be read again and the student will have another chance to answer them. After finishing the test, the result is read to the student by the IVR system and it is stored in the Moodle database. The number of accessing the test by a single student can be limited.

The proposed model is appropriate because it allows a high-level scalability and reliability for e-learning services. Numerous researchers show [34, 35, 36] that in a dynamic environment, such as learning environment, cloud computing represents a most convenient approach in developing infrastructure. The main reason why there is no quantitative result or analysis of the presented model is the number of students with disabilities on our courses. Each year there are only a few students with some impairment but nevertheless some trends can be noticed. Students with disabilities choose examinations and courses which are realized on the described platform. Furthermore, they participated in improving the platform through practical work on their final examination.

There are a few problems which are identified. Our IVR solution for the speech recognition engine shows some malfunctioning. Speech recognitions systems behave well when it comes to the English words. For languages for which the speech recognition system is not especially developed some problems occurred.

14.6 Conclusion

In this chapter we discussed new possibilities and solutions in the area of cloud computing. We used cloud computing in order to improve the development of the IT infrastructure of a higher education institution. Cloud computing allows for a seamless integration of all the components necessary for learning activities. A private cloud was developed on the existing IT infrastructure. The main goal was to emphasize the advantages and constraints of applying cloud computing in education. A successful realization of teaching and learning processes requires the use of various applications and services.

This research introduced a model of e-learning services developed with respect to needs of students with disabilities. The key advantage of the suggested approach is that it is designed to use the existing resources of an educational institution to provide an integrated and high performance environment for teaching and learning of students with disabilities. The model includes various applications and components integrated into the e-learning system. As a proof of the concept, a few components of the model were implemented for students with disabilities within the laboratory for e-business, the Faculty of Organizational Sciences, University of Belgrade.

The study presented in this chapter demonstrates a measurable improvement of the system for e-learning for students with disabilities by introducing cloud services and integrating them with the Moodle Learning Management System. The results of the research showed that students achieved good results when studying in the e-learning environment improved with cloud computing technologies.

Future research directions include the establishment of an inter-institutional initiative for building a prototype of cloud computing infrastructure that can be shared, and organized for educational, scientific, and research purposes as well as for developing a virtualization platform that can deploy different VMs on the fly on students' requests.

References

1. Brusilovsky P (2001) Adaptive hypermedia. Int J User Model User-Adapt Interact 11(1/2): 87–110
2. Brusilovsky P, Eklund J (1998) A study of user model based link annotation in educational hypermedia. J Univers Comput Sci 4(4):429–448
3. Hollink V, Someren MV, Wielinga BJ (2007) Discovering stages in web navigation for problem-oriented navigation support. User Model User-Adapt Interact 17:183–214 (Springer Netherlands)

4. Brown E, Cristea A, Stewart C, Brailsford T (2005) Patterns in authoring of adaptive educational hypermedia: a taxonomy of learning styles. Educ Technol Soc 8(3):77–90
5. Brusilovsky P, Peylo C (eds) (2003) Adaptive and intelligent web-based educational systems. Int J Artif Intell Educ 13(2–4):159–172 (Special Issue on Adaptive and Intelligent Web-based Educational Systems)
6. Caron E, Desprez F, Loureiro D, Muresan A (2009) Cloud computing resource management through a grid middleware: a case study with DIET and Eucalyptus. In: Proceedings of Cloud 2009 IEEE international conference on cloud computing, IEEE Computer Society, Los Alamitos, pp 151–154
7. Polat E, Adiguzel T, Akgun OE (2012) Adaptive web-assisted learning system for students with specific learning disabilities: a needs analysis study. Educ Sci Theory Pract Spec Issue (Autumn) 12(4):3243–3258
8. Clark DB, Uhry JK (1995) Dyslexia: theory and practice of remedial instruction, 2nd edn. York, Baltimore
9. Myers PI, Hammill D (1976) Methods for learning disorders, 2nd edn. Wiley, New York
10. Paciello MG (2000) Web accessibility for people with disabilities. Publishers Group West, Berkeley
11. Hudson L (2002) A new age of accessibility. Library J 48:19–21
12. Rowland C (2004) Cognitive disabilities part 2: conceptualizing design considerations. http://www.webaim.org/techniques/articles/conceptualize/?templatetype=3. Accessed 1 July 2013
13. Seeman L (2002) Inclusion of cognitive disabilities in the web accessibility movement. In: Proceedings of the 11th international World Wide Web Conference, Honolulu, Hawaii
14. Resnick LB, Klopfer LE (1989) Toward the thinking curriculum: an overview. In: Resnick LB, Klopfer LE (eds) Toward the thinking curriculum: current cognitive research. Association for Supervision and Curriculum Development, Pittsburgh, pp 1–18
15. Carnine D (1991) Curricular interventions for teaching higher order thinking to all students: introduction to special series. J Learn Disabil 24:261–269
16. Ellis ES (1993) Integrative strategy instruction: a potential model for teaching content area subjects to adolescents with learning disabilities. J Learn Disabil 26:358–383
17. Rieth HJ, Polsgrove L (1994) Curriculum and instructional issues in teaching secondary students with learning disabilities. Learn Disabil Res Pract 9(2):118–126
18. Miksch KL (2003) Universal instructional design in a legal studies classroom, curriculum transformation and disability: implementing universal design in higher education (Higbee JL (ed)), University of Minnesota, Minneapolis, MN
19. Tobias J (2003) Universal design: is it really about design? Information technology and disabilities. http://people.rit.edu/easi/itd/itdv09n2/tobias.htm. Accessed 1 Sept 2012
20. Hitchcock CG, Meyer A, Rose D, Jackson R (2005) Equal access, participation, and progress in the general education curriculum. In: Rose D, Meyer A, Hitchcock C (eds) The universally designed classroom: accessible curriculum and digital technologies. Harvard Education Press, Cambridge, pp 37–68
21. United States Access Board (2000) Electronic and Information Technology Accessibility Standards. http://www.access-board.gov/guidelines-and-standards/communications-and-it/about-the-section-508-standards/section-508-standards. Accessed 12 May 2014
22. Sultan N (2010) Cloud computing for education: a new dawn? Int J Inf Manage 30(2):101–182
23. Srinivasa RV, Nageswara R, Kumari K (2009) Cloud computing: an overview. J Theor Appl Inf Technol 9(1):71–76
24. Jin H, Ibrahim S, Bell T, Gao W, Huang D, Wu S (2010) Cloud types and services. In: Furht B, Escalante A (eds) Handbook of cloud computing. Springer, New York
25. Zhang Y, Chen J-L (2010) Universal identity management model based on anonymous credentials. In: IEEE international conference on services computing, Miami, Florida, pp 305–312
26. Zhang Y, Chen J-L (2011) A delegation solution for universal identity management in SOA. IEEE Trans Serv Comput 4(1):70–81

27. Hayes B (2008) Cloud computing. Commun ACM 51(7):9–11
28. Wen X, Gu G, Li Q, Gao Y, Zhang X (May 2012) Comparison of open-source cloud management platforms: OpenStack and OpenNebula. In: 2012 9th international conference on fuzzy systems and knowledge discovery (FSKD), Sichuan, China, IEEE Computer Society, Los Alamitos pp 2457–2461
29. Ren XF, Zheng G (2013) Distributed network performance test and analyses based on SNMP protocol. Zhongguo Ceshi/China Measurement Test 39(1):105–109
30. Graf S, Kinshuk (2008) Analysing the behaviour of students in learning management systems with respect to learning styles. In: Wallace M, Angelides M, Mylonas P (eds) Advanced in semantic media adaptation and personalization. Springer series on studies in computational intelligence, vol 93. Springer, Berlin, pp 53–74
31. Graf S, Kinshuk, Liu T (2009) Supporting teachers in identifying students' learning styles in learning management systems: an automatic student modelling approach. J Edu Technol Soc 12(4):3–14
32. Despotovic-Zrakić M, Markovic A, Bogdanovic Z, Barac D, Krco S (2012) Providing adaptivity in Moodle LMS courses. Edu Technol Soc J 15(1):326–338
33. Grujic DD, Milic AR, Dadic JV, Despotovic-Zrakic MS (November 2012) Application of IVR in e-learning system. In: 20th telecommunications forum (TELFOR), 2012, IEEE, pp 1472–1475
34. Despotović-Zrakić M, Simić K, Labus A, Milić A, Jovanić B (2013) Scaffolding environment for adaptive e-learning through cloud computing. Edu Technol Soc 16(3):301–314
35. Dreher P, Vouk M (2012) Utilizing open source cloud computing environments to provide cost effective support for university education and research. In: Chao L (ed) Cloud computing for teaching and learning: strategies for design and implementation. Information Science Reference, Hershey, pp 32–49
36. Fernández A, Peralta D, Herrera F, Benítez JM (January 2012) An overview of e-learning in cloud computing. In: Workshop on learning technology for education in cloud (LTEC'12), Springer, Berlin, pp 35–46

Chapter 15
Application Scenarios Suitable for Deployment in Cloud Environments

Rahul Bandopadhyaya and Vinay Rangaraju Nagavara

Abstract Cloud computing is currently one of the most talked about emerging technologies which is continually becoming stabler and more reputable. Consumers are now aware of the type of applications that are best suited for the cloud-computing infrastructure. For example, Web-based applications or Web-based services are the best candidates to be moved to the cloud. At a very high level, we can easily make a decision for the application's fitness to cloud infrastructure, based on its implementation type, that is if it is Web-based then it is suitable; if desktop-based then it may not be. However, it would be useful if it is possible to have a mechanism to determine which specific kind of application scenarios will best leverage the cloud infrastructure to meet its requirements. The aim of this chapter is to put forward ten such specific application scenarios which would be suitable to be moved to cloud environments or which could be further developed to be ultimately deployed in cloud infrastructure. The chapter also provides justification for such migration. The primary focus would be to help the decision maker to quickly come to a conclusion; that is, given a particular application scenario, whether the application should be moved or further developed for cloud-computing infrastructure. By application scenarios, what are depicted here are the different business requirements which may be developed and presented as working modules, for example, online polling system, Web analytics component, data replication system, etc. The chapter does not aim to teach how to code using different cloud infrastructure provided building blocks, but to present ideas to best leverage these cloud-based building blocks, to overcome certain limitations and constraints in different types of applications.

Keywords Availability · Azure · Data management · Data replication · Event processing · Grid computing · Healthcare · Parallel computing · Reliability · ROI · Scalability · Service bus · Subscription system · Telematics · Web analytics

R. Bandopadhyaya (✉) · V. R. Nagavara
InfosysLabs, Infosys Limited, Electronics City, Hosur Road, Bangalore,
Karnataka 560100, India
e-mail: rahul_bandopadhyaya@infosys.com

V. R. Nagavara
e-mail: vinay_r@infosys.com

Z. Mahmood (ed.), *Continued Rise of the Cloud,* Computer Communications
and Networks, DOI 10.1007/978-1-4471-6452-4_15,
© Springer-Verlag London 2014

15.1 Introduction

In this chapter, we explore a number of different scenarios, captured from different domains like retail, electorate polling, medical, agriculture, etc. We explain how widely and vastly cloud may be leveraged, and we will also see that its scope is not just confined to one or a few fields of life. We will discuss how, with some intelligent decision making, cloud computing may be used in more or less every sector of the society.

In these scenarios, specific real-life problems are depicted. We then attempt to explain how, witfully using information technology (IT) and cloud computing any inherent problems can be addressed and accordingly eradicated. Some of these scenarios have already been explored and are currently being used by different entrepreneurs. The others, for which we may not find today a real-time implementation, may still have potential and will be certainly explored in the near future.

In all the different scenarios that are being identified in the subsequent sections of the chapter, we have made references to Windows Azure provided building blocks. The purposes of these references are to present the scenarios in a more realistic manner. Any similar building blocks from any other cloud-computing infrastructure provider like Amazon, Salesforce, etc. may also be leveraged to achieve the similar benefit.

So, let us quickly have a brief look at the different application scenarios which will be considered in detail in the subsequent sections.

15.1.1 Telematics—To Collect Data from Mobile Devices

Telematics is a process of collecting data from different mobile devices, analyzing the collected data and then sharing the pattern(s) and/or intelligent meaning of the data. We will explain in detail here how using cloud building blocks we may favourably achieve the capabilities of Telematics.

15.1.2 Web Analytics for Online Websites

Web analytics is a very useful tool in the world of Web applications to understand the behaviour and need of the target audience. Here we will see how cloud building blocks could be leveraged to achieve this.

15.1.3 Online Examinations and Results

Nowadays many examinations and competitions for admission to renowned colleges and organizations are being changed from subjective mode (i.e. descriptive-type answering mode) to objective mode (i.e. choice-based answering mode). This change in methodology favours the online administration of these examinations. And accordingly, it makes the evaluation process more accurate as well as faster. We will learn here why cloud infrastructure should be used for these types of application.

15.1.4 Publication–Subscription System

Publication–subscription is a kind of system where a user/client (i.e. the subscriber) of a service (i.e. the publisher) needs to get some kind of alert/message from the service as and when some specific kind of event occurs (at the service side). For example, the news service provider. This section will tell the benefit of using cloud infrastructure in such system.

15.1.5 Application Data Back-Up/Replication

Application data management is equally important like the application management. Here, we will discuss why cloud infrastructure should be used for very commonly occurring data management operations, such as: (1) data back-up and (2) data replication.

15.1.6 Polling in Democracies

In democracies, elections involve an electorate of hundreds of millions. There is enormous expenditure associated with the election process which uses millions of electronic voting machines (EVMs). An equally whopping sum is spent on the process of counting the votes. This section will explain why cloud building blocks should be used in those scenarios.

15.1.7 Agricultural Data Analysis

Agriculture plays an important role in the development of a country. For a few countries the major source of income is agriculture and hence it plays a substantial role in growth of those countries. Losses in agriculture due to irrational decisions of the farmer, poor infrastructure and non-scientific methodologies cause food losses. We will learn that cloud could be best used to address these issues.

15.1.8 Application with Predictable and Unpredictable Varying Loads

Here, we will talk about some common scenarios with fluctuating and huge network loads and we will also discuss why cloud is the best hosting environment for such applications.

15.1.9 Health Care

Many countries face the challenge of providing quality medical care in rural areas and even in remote parts of urban areas. Distant regions in any country face problems in the training and appointment of doctors, inadequate infrastructure, lack of financial resources as well as issues like reputed doctors/surgeons disliking living in rural settings. In this context, providing quality medical care to people in remote areas becomes a challenge. We will see here how cloud could be leveraged to address these challenges.

15.1.10 Cloud Empowered Small and Start-Up Enterprises

Efficient expenditures, efficient resource management and quick response times are critical for small start-ups to grow their businesses. Start-ups face challenges in giving out their online services in terms of procuring high-end servers for robustness, reliability and availability. We will discuss here how cloud blocks should be used to handle this challenge.

15.1.11 Telematics—To Collect Data from Mobile Devices

Today, one can hardly think of any daily routine without mobile phones. These mobile phones are getting smarter and more intelligent with the introduction of various outstanding technologies. The capabilities of the mobile phone are not just limited to making and receiving calls—it also helps in storing and collecting intelligent data like the user's geological location; searching for habits like favourite restaurant, favourite food; etc. And with data like these, there are technologies, which using artificial intelligence can help in some important decision making. Telematics is also one such technology.

Telematics [1] is a process of collecting data from different mobile devices, analyzing the collected data and then sharing the pattern(s) and/or intelligent meaning of the data, refer to Fig. 15.1. It is one of those processes which use a lot of computation and storage resources:

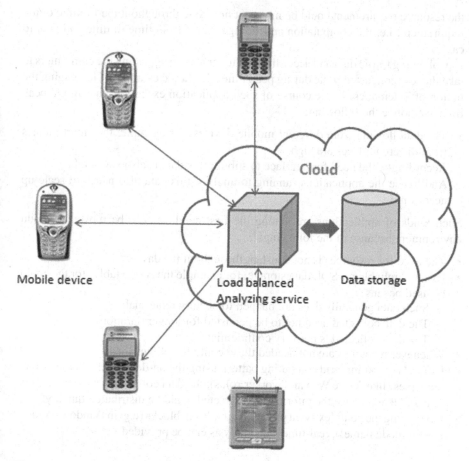

Fig. 15.1 Telematics to collect data from mobile devices

- For storing the collected data
- For analyzing the data and arriving to an intelligent meaning or pattern
- And lastly but equally important for the flow of data from the mobile devices used for collecting the data to the data-analyzing process and again the flow of the so-formed pattern or intelligence of the data to the intended party or agents.

In this scenario, the resource requirement is not constant, i.e. during peak time the flow of data will be more and hence the computation needed to analyze the data will be also more. Similarly, depending upon the type of data to be collected, the occurrence of the peak time will change, that is it may not only come every day but may occur weekly or monthly. Say for instance, we are collecting data related to the road traffic. The peak time may occur every day and in fact more than once in a day but if we are collecting data related to the amount of rainfall from different regions, then the peak time may occur once in a month or even after longer time gap. So the resource requirement could be more but not same throughout the lifetime of the requirement, i.e. the computation and storage varies from time to time and case to case.

Collecting traffic data and accordingly after analysis suggesting the commuters to take the less congested route during peak time is a classic example of leveraging the notion of Telematics. In the course of such application execution, during the peak time, we notice the following:

- The data flowing from different mobile devices, for example, the smart phones from different places are high.
- Accordingly, the need for interface to submit this data is also very high.
- And hence the applications running to analyze this data also needs to scale up accordingly.

Such kinds of applications are among the best candidates to be moved to cloud environment because of the following:

- The need for resources is not constant throughout the day.
- Fast and reliable no-SQL data storage, for example the Azure table storage could be used because:
  - Such data generally does not happen to be very relational.
  - The data collected need not to be persisted for longer duration.
  - The data collected is not very confidential.
- Whenever resources are not needed these could be relinquished.
- Parallel computing/grid computing pattern using the on-demand available virtual machines (like Azure Web and worker roles), the data collected can be processed in parallel and hence the information extracted could be distributed quickly.
- Leveraging the complex event processing building blocks (e.g. in Windows Azure, Austin (code name)), real-time data analysis can be provided.

15.2   Web Analytics for Websites

It is very important for an administrator of a website (for example, an online retail store, video portal, etc.) to understand the need of the target audience. For instances, in an online retail store, it is important to understand what kinds of product are more searched, etc. This information helps the application owner to make the necessary changes and take decisions to best suit the audience and hence make the most from the application.

Web analytics is a useful tool in the world of Web applications to understand the behaviour and needs of the target audience [2]. For instance, consider the scenario of a video portal which provides the hosting environment for different videos under different categories. Using Web analytics, the application administrator may fairly understand:

- Which types of video are most watched, that is the categories under which videos are more liked.

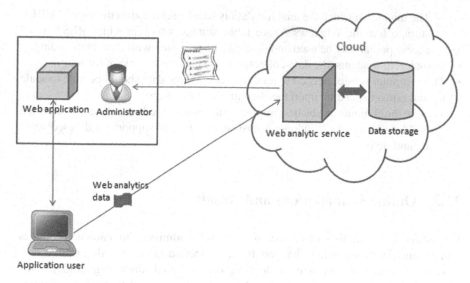

Fig. 15.2 Web-analytics for online websites

- The trends being followed while watching, e.g. whether the users are watching the full video or doing fast forward, etc.
- Any specific kind of search done most by user on the portal, etc.

And, on the basis of the aforesaid findings, the Web application and its content may be modified to best suit the need of audience.

Let us look at Web analytics implementation on a very high level (refer to Fig. 15.2); for collecting analytic data in the Web application for all the intended kind of events like button click, etc., client side scripts are added to send the intended data to the remote analytics service. Generally, the scripts make some GET or POST service call (preferably asynchronous) with intended information similar to the following:

http://some-web-analytic-service.com/<client_identifier>/data?param1=value1&param2=value2 ....etc

where, client_identifier identifies the Web application in question, the $param(n) = value(n)$ depicts the different analytics data collected for the Web application to be analyzed.

At the Web analytics service side, such data is collected and analysis report is provided on demand. This kind of analytics services and their back end data store could be moved to cloud because:

- The analytics data for an application/client is very huge and random for each and every intended client side event.
  - For the persistence of such kind of data, a no-SQL data store is most suitable, as the kind of data collected will generally vary from application to application and storage like Windows Azure table storage could be best leveraged.

- The manner in which the analytic data is sent (refer the aforementioned URL), storage like the Windows Azure table storage which provides REST-based access points may be used and data can be persisted with minimum coding.
- In such requirements, the data collected also need not to be kept for long.
- The computer service needed to analyze such a huge data should be able to scale up and down depending upon the Web application usages.
  - Here the compute can be best implemented using cloud infrastructure provided building block like Windows Azure worker role to support need based scale up and down.

15.3   Online Examinations and Results

Nowadays many examinations and competitions for admission to renowned colleges and organizations are being changed from subjective mode (i.e. descriptive-type answering mode) to objective mode (i.e. choice-based answering mode). This change in methodology favours the online administration of these examinations. And accordingly, it makes the evaluation process more accurate as well as faster.

The application used to conduct the examination needs to be accessible only during a specific time span and this need could be generally once or twice in a year, that is generally for a very small duration. Moreover to support the online examinations like the entrance test for engineering or management studies, where the number of aspirants appearing from across the country and even across the globe counts to many hundreds of thousands, the hardware/infrastructure needed is very high. And these results in a huge investment which will be used only for a small duration, consequently the return on investment (ROI) is not that impressive.

Similar is the concern in the support of online results of some general elections or examinations; here also the application and its supporting infrastructure are needed only for a small duration. These kinds of applications could very well be moved to cloud infrastructure because (also refer to Fig. 15.3):

- The infrastructure needed to support such application is required for a very small duration and that too it should be capable enough to support the maximum possible user load.
  - Cloud computing building block like the Azure Web roles could be leveraged so that the infrastructure could be easily created as well as scaled up to support the maximum possible user load.
  - The cost of ownership is also low as now one needs to pay for the infrastructure only for the duration it is used.
- The data to support the examination is not required to be accessible for long durations.
- During off-season, after proper data back-up, unnecessary computation and storage instances can be relinquished.

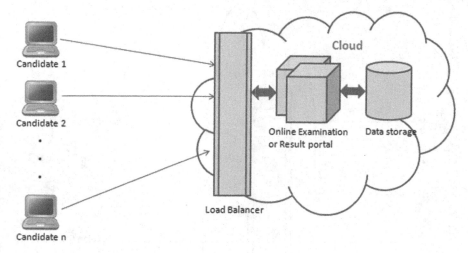

Fig. 15.3 Online examinations and online results

15.4   Publication–Subscription System

Publication–subscription [3] is a type of system where a user/client (i.e. the sub-scriber) of a service (i.e. the publisher) needs to get some kind of alert/message from the service as and when some kind of event occurs at the service side. For example, the news service provider. To implement such system, we have two options:

- *Approach 1*: The client keeps polling the service for the latest event or message after some fixed duration.
    - In this type of implementation, due to the continuation polling, the communi-cation bandwidth may get blocked.
    - If the client is some kind of mobile device, then the process to do continuous polling leads to more battery usage, that is, the battery life will be hampered.
- *Approach 2*: The service takes the responsibility to the send the alert/message to the intended clients whenever any event occurs.
    - In this type of implementation, the client, while subscribing to a service, pro-vides a call-back for itself. And whenever any event occurs on the service side, the service uses this call-back to intimate the client.
    - This generally leads to the opening of many ports for call-back in the client device. That is, for each different kind of service subscription, one call back is provided and hence one port is opened. And the client keeps listening to these ports for incoming messages. If the client is some kind of mobile device then opening and listening of ports, which needs some kind of computation, also leads to excess battery usage.

However, given the pros and cons of the aforesaid two options, the second option is more widely accepted. Refer to Fig. 15.4. For the implementation of the second

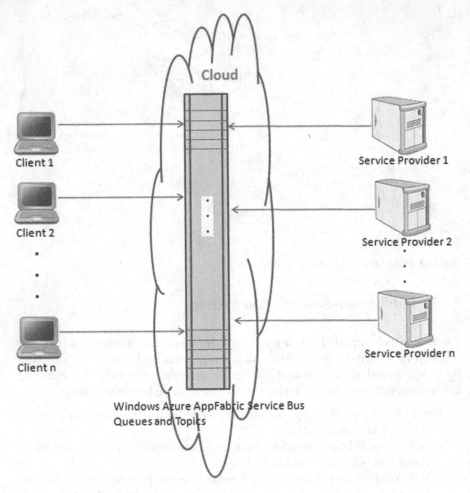

Fig. 15.4 Publication–subscription system

option and to overcome its cons, the purpose of providing call back can be outsourced to an external system:

- The interested client for services subscribe to a single end point, e.g. to one external system. And hence provide one call back that leads to opening and listening on a single port.
- The external system on behalf of the interested clients subscribes to one or more services.
- The external system, using some multiplexing mechanism, sends the intended messages from all the subscribed services to the client through the single port.
- Thus, the need for providing many call-backs and hence the need for opening many ports is outsourced to the external system.

Data Backup

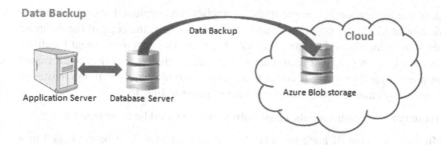

Data Replication

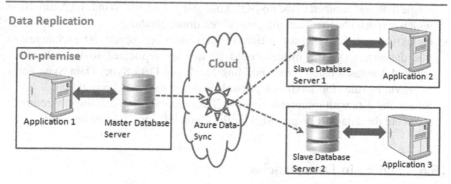

Fig. 15.5 Application data back-up/data replication

Examples of such external systems include Windows Push Notification Services (WPNS), Apple Push Notification Service (APNS), etc. Having mentioned the importance of implementing an external system, cloud infrastructure provided application blocks could be leveraged to implement such system:

- For instance, the Windows Azure AppFabric Service Bus Brokered Messaging could be used.
- Publish/subscribe mechanism provided by Windows Azure Service Bus Brokered Messaging (in the form of queues and topics) may be used to create disconnected client-server communication between many publishers and many subscribers.
- Scalability of the service provider is achieved by supporting load balancing among one and more publisher and subscriber.

15.5 Application Data Back-Up and Replication

Application data management is equally important like the application management. In this context, some commonly occurring data management operations are:

- Back-up of data, for example old transaction records [4]: For instance, for online retail portals the old transaction data may mount to the factor of tera-byte and peta-byte and keeping the back-up of such a amount of huge data is as costly [5] as keeping the current data. Refer to Fig. 15.5.

- Database replication [4]: Sometimes for applications deployed in distributed environment like partly on-premise and partly off-premise, the copy of the database needs to be maintained in more than one location. The data in different locations also has to be in sync, for example one database is master (say, the one situated on-premise) and the other needs to be synchronized frequently with the master as soon as any changes are done to the master. Refer to Fig. 15.5.

For these types of requirements, cloud infrastructure could be leveraged to:

- Minimize the cost of back-up: The data to be backed up can be packaged in a single blob and dumped in the no-SQL kind of database like Windows Azure Blob which is much cheaper than the general relational database.
- Quickly automate synchronization of the database copies: The changes in one database, e.g. the master could be quickly replicated to the other distributed databases using Azure building block like Data-Sync. Data-Sync helps in providing rules for maximum possible and best data synchronization.
- Secure the data with minimum cost [6]: The required setup and the environment to secure the data will be provided by the cloud infrastructure on demand.

15.6 Polling in Democracies

In democracies, the elections involve an electorate of hundreds of millions. There is enormous expenditure associated with the election process which uses millions of electronic voting machines (EVMs). An equally whopping sum is spent on the process of counting the votes [7].

To thwart rackets and scams during elections, the ballot paper voting mechanism is rapidly being replaced by EVMs. Once the voting has ended and until the day of poll results, the EVMs are warehoused under heavy security.

The counting process uses a lot of manual assembling and disassembling of EVMs with computers to calculate the number of votes cast. EVMs themselves form storage resources until the counting day. The addition of votes from various EVMs, at times, can be done manually too. This involves a lot of manpower in terms of persons who count and also the persons who observe the process. This laborious process also introduces delay in the announcement of results.

Internet-enabled EVMs can be of enormous advantage here. Refer to Fig. 15.6. These devices will read the voting pattern and relay the data to a cloud-based application which is controlled and monitored by the election commissioner. This application can also provide real-time voting patterns across the country and the results can be announced as soon as the last vote is cast. This scenario is one of the candidates to be moved to cloud because:

- Elections happen once in a while; hence, the compute power can be shifted to cloud.
  - Azure roles may be leveraged for implementing the compute part. And once the election is over, the non-required roles (like those used for data collection from EVM) can be decommissioned after proper data back-up.

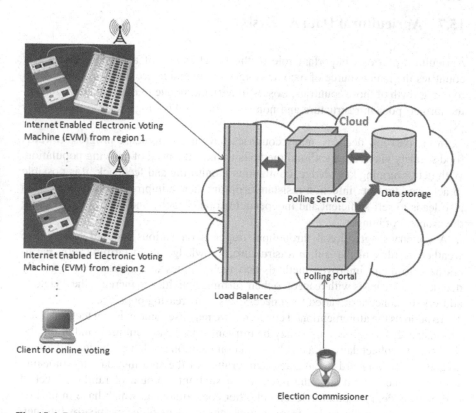

Fig. 15.6 Polling in democracies

- Once the voting is done in any region, the data in the EVM can be synchronized to the cloud storage and local EVM data can be erased completely.
  - The need for EVM to be stored and protected for a longer period of time can be avoided and these can be reused in other booths as soon as the last vote is cast and data is uploaded to cloud.
  - The data collected need not to be persisted for long duration on EVMs due to limited number days of battery capacity.
- Since the back-end application having the responsibility of analyzing the data from EVMs and declaring the result is a cloud-based application/service, this can be leveraged to implement on-line polling application. Thus citizens who do not have manual access to the nearest polling booth, may use this online application and cast their vote.
- EVMs increase the efficiency of the electorate system with real-time monitoring of the voting patterns.

15.7 Agricultural Data Analysis

Agriculture plays an important role in the development of a country. For a few countries the major source of income is agriculture and hence it plays a substantial role in growth of those countries. Losses in agriculture due to irrational decisions of the farmer, poor infrastructure and non-scientific methodologies cause food losses [8].

In the past few decades, many countries have made immense progress towards food security via new agricultural methods to meet the need of growing population. With better farming knowledge, continuous monitoring and feedback, it is possible to achieve bug free, infection resistant crop and hence improve productivity. This also leads to self-sufficient and independent food capacity and result in alleviating the problem of hunger.

A country's agricultural throughput depends on various internal factors like weather, fertility of the soil, infrastructure, knowledge about farming, etc. Farmers have to adopt improved methods and technologies in agriculture to logically decide on daily basis with respect to their farming activities to increase their yield to address the concern of varied food necessities of increasing populace.

To address the aforementioned concerns, we may use some existing technologies. For instance, a wireless sensor may be implanted in the agricultural land at regular distances to collect daily data on chemical composition and hence the fertility of the soil. It will also record the average temperature of the area in a day, the moisture content in the air and soil, the intensity of sunlight, amount of rainfall, level of carbon dioxide, precipitation level and other contextual data which have impact on agricultural output. These data from various sensors are recorded in a nearby Internet-enabled device, which will in turn talk to a cloud-based application and push all this data. An agricultural scientist who has the access to such data can view the summary of this data on daily basis in a particular region/county/state/country and can advise the farmer on how to proceed with his farming in the future. The scientists, farmers and government officials collaboratively may use this data to analyze for possible problem and accordingly suggest the corresponding corrective measures to handle it better. Refer to Fig. 15.7.

By adopting cloud infrastructure for this scenario:

- We can leverage no-SQL (non-RDBMS-based) storage because the data collected may not follow any specific schema.
- The data collected is not very sensitive and can be used for general research purposes, e.g. by university students.
- Data can be made easily and cheaply accessible over the Internet so that anybody can voluntarily analyze it and suggest some better resolution in case there is any problem faced by agriculturists in any particular region.
- Since these types of implementation are not for commercial use, the lesser the investment, the better it is. Hence, it is beneficiary to leverage the less expensive cloud-based infrastructure like Azure Web roles instead of traditional hosting environment.

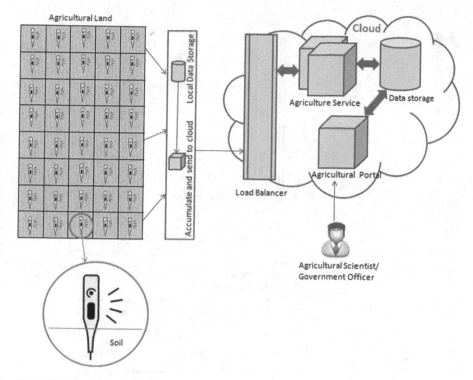

Fig. 15.7 Agricultural data analysis

15.8 Applications with Predictable and Unpredictable Varying Loads

Some common scenarios of hugely fluctuating network loads are:

- Cases like that of news websites—the news websites may experience huge loads during breaking news or any news which is of national/international importance.
- Cases like that of retail website—during holidays offers which results in the busiest online shopping days of the year.

News websites belong to unpredictable load category. High-impact news, which is highly unpredictable, generates lots of user load. Also, usually in the morning the number of users accessing the news websites will be much greater compared to news readers at night time.

On the other hand, a retail online store will also experience drastic difference in user loads especially very high during festive seasons and holidays. Traditionally, at the beginning of the Christmas shopping season, most retailers experience extremely high user access on their websites when they offer promotional sales to kick off the shopping season. This is an example where one can predict increase in user loads at different times of the year. Due to this heavy surge of user access during these times

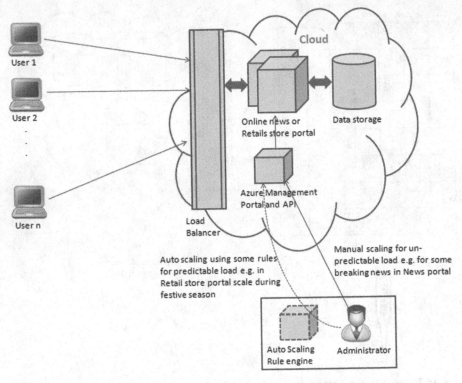

Fig. 15.8 Application with predictable and unpredictable varying loads

of the year, the server hosting these sites should be capable of handling the varying loads. Commissioning of new servers during peak load time and decommissioning extra servers when the user load is low, is a costly operation and time consuming in a traditional deployment.

Cloud-based building blocks may be leveraged to develop such websites:

- For unpredictable user load like those in the news website, the website administrator may quickly increase/decrease the website instances like those possible for Azure roles using the Azure management portal. Refer to Fig. 15.8.
- For predictable user loads like retail websites, auto scaling rules may be provided. For instance in case of Azure role, using Azure management API one may write rules to automatically change/restrict the instance counts for any specific timeframe in a year. Refer to Fig. 15.8.

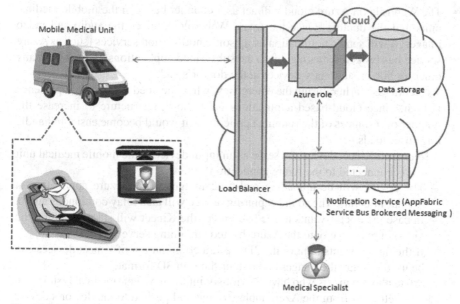

Fig. 15.9 Health care

15.9   Health Care

Many countries face the challenge of providing quality medical care in rural areas and even in remote parts of urban areas. Distant regions in any country face problems in the training and appointment of doctors, inadequate infrastructure, lack of financial resources as well as issues like reputed doctors/surgeons disliking living in rural settings. In this context, providing quality medical care to people in remote areas becomes a challenge [9, 10]. To address this challenge, a possible solution may be an Internet-enabled mobile healthcare unit which interacts with cloud-based applications, which acts as a two way communication channel between the patients and doctors. Refer to Fig. 15.9.

Mobile healthcare units can also have surgery facilities through which a patient can be treated/operated by a doctor remotely. With these mobile units the physical presence of the doctor/surgeon is not needed at places where the patient is located. With this the patients can afford world class treatments/prescriptions/consultations in the proximity of their residential locations.

These units help the patients to have multiple opinions with various doctors around the world in an affordable manner. A major advantage of mobile healthcare units is during wartime to treat the soldiers in the battlefield and to cater to victims of natural disaster-affected areas which need numerous mobile units and hence increased user load.

Such an implementation may be considered to be moved to cloud as:

- The Web role on Azure cloud will act as a channel between the mobile medical units and the doctors. Once the Azure Web role receives the audio and video images, it will send a notification using some notification services (such as Azure service bus brokered messaging) to the subscribed applications on phones or any other mobile or stationary devices at the doctor's end.
- As mentioned earlier during the emergency, when the need for such tele-presence is high, since cloud-based applications have the infrastructure to increase the number of instances of the running application, it would become easier to handle huge user loads.
- A Microsoft Kinect device can serve as an input device at the mobile medical unit which is connected to the Azure application.
  - The device will be uploading real-time images to the Azure application at regular intervals. The sound capturing device will also relay continuous audio.
  - In case the doctor wants to see live video, the Kinect will start streaming the video in real-time onto the Azure-hosted streaming server.
  - If the doctor wants to have the 3D view, a combination of Kinect devices can be used to relay the images and render them in 3D format.
- The data about patients who have previously interacted, their medical history can also be retrieved from the Azure table storage and pushed to the doctor's device and the doctor can instantly be aware of the patient's health history.

15.10   Cloud Empowered Small and Start-Up Enterprises

Efficient expenditures, efficient resource management and quick response times are critical for small start-ups to grow their businesses. Start-ups face challenges in giving out their online services in terms of procuring high-end boxes for robustness, reliability and availability [11]. IT infrastructure acts as a huge barrier for entry into a market which is a convincing viewpoint for start-up ventures determined on trading their goods or services at the earliest possible time and also to compete with the existing big players in the market sharing the same business domain.

Moving their online services to cloud-based infrastructure can be an effective solution for these problems (refer to Fig. 15.10). Using cloud and following a few steps, start-ups can avail computing power depending on user load. With cloud computing there is no prerequisite for purchasing operating system and hardware licences and also there is no need to domestically manage the IT department. This results in the reduction of management costs of hardware and also online operating costs. Also, start-ups have to pay only for what they use which reduces their investments and get freed of issues like delays in hardware procurement.

The key benefits for small and start-up enterprises to move to the cloud-based environment are:

- Initial investment is less and charged as per usage.
- Quickly move to market by rapid deployment of services.
- No dependency on location and hardware devices.

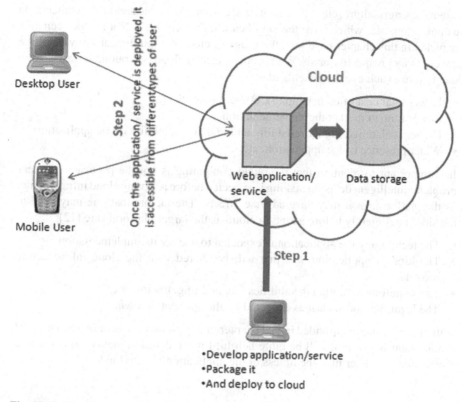

Fig. 15.10 Cloud empowered small and start-up enterprises

- Scalable infrastructure based on the load.
- Manageability becomes easier as the infrastructure is maintained by cloud providers.

15.11 Conclusion

The aforementioned application scenarios are identified from the day-to-day real-life examples. We tried to pin point and explain the problems/constraints currently prevailing in such distributed applications and how such problems/constraints could be best addressed using cloud computing infrastructures.

The types of applications best suited for cloud computing infrastructure are not limited to the aforesaid list and, here, we tried to identify just the ten suitable scenarios from the potential real-time implementations.

The intention of this chapter was also to put forward the vast and wide scope of the cloud computing. With some careful comprehension and important decision making, the benefit of cloud computing can be leveraged in many areas like health care, telematics, agriculture, etc. These include areas apart from the areas like retail, online examination, etc. which have the significant influence of IT. Not all the scenarios depicted in this chapter have seen the usage of cloud computing currently but these are certainly prospective areas. With proper usage of cloud computing infrastructure, one is sure to achieve the benefits like:

- Lower total cost of ownership (TCO) but higher ROI.
- Lower time to market the implementation.
- Higher scalability, higher reliability and higher availability of the application
- Wider presence of the application, etc.

It is important to mention that the cloud computing is not the panacaea of every problem; intelligent decision making is expected before adopting cloud infrastructure as the platform, or it may have adverse effects. The factors that one may need to consider intelligently before adopting cloud as the target platforms are [12]:

- The technology the application is expected to use for its implementation
- The kind of application data that will be shared with the cloud infrastructure provider
- The requirement around the abilities like auditing, tracing, etc.
- The legalities and securities expected by the application owner

With the information provided in this chapter, if any similar application scenario and requirement is given, it will be quite helpful for the decision makers to come to a conclusion and determine the fitness of the application in the cloud.

References

1. Gartner, Telematics (nd) http://www.gartner.com/it-glossary/telematics. Accessed 24 Oct 2013
2. Open Web Analytics (nd) http://www.openwebanalytics.com/. Accessed 24 Oct 2013
3. Mackenzie N (2011) Windows Azure AppFabric service bus brokered messaging, convective. http://convective.wordpress.com/2011/09/21/windows-azure-appfabric-service-bus-brokered-messaging/. Accessed 7 Mar 2013
4. Twinstrata (nd) Connect Veeam Backup & Replication to Cloud Storage. http://www.twinstrata.com/CloudArray-Veeam-Backup-Replication. Accessed 7 Mar 2013
5. SearchDataBackup (nd) Cloud backup (online backup). http://searchdatabackup.techtarget.com/definition/cloud-backup. Accessed 23 Oct 2013
6. Ruggiero P, Heckathorn MA (2012) Data backup options. http://www.us-cert.gov/sites/default/files/publications/data_backup_options.pdf. Accessed 10 Oct 2013
7. Election Commission of India (nd) FAQs—electronic voting machines (EVMs). http://eci.nic.in/eci_main1/evm.aspx. Accessed 7 Mar 2013
8. Food and Agriculture Organization of the United Nations (nd) The phenomenal growth of China and India. http://www.fao.org/docrep/009/ag087e/AG087E05.htm. Accessed 7 Mar 2013
9. Express Healthcare (nd) Cloud Computing in Healthcare. http://healthcare.financialexpress.com/201109/itathealthcare04.shtml. Accessed 23 Oct 2013
10. Cisco (nd) Cloud Computing for Healthcare. http://www.cisco.com/web/strategy/healthcare/cloud_healthcare.html. Accessed 23 Oct 2013
11. Nirix (nd) Small Business Cloud. http://www.nirix.com/business-cloud/small-business-cloud/. Accessed 24 Oct 2013
12. Morgan L, Lero C, Kieran, National University of Ireland Galway (2013) Factors affecting the adoption of cloud computing: an exploratory study. http://www.staff.science.uu.nl/Vlaan107/ecis/files/ECIS20130-710-paper.pdf. Accessed 12 Oct 2013

ERRATUM to Chapter 12

Noel Carroll, Markus Helfert and Theo Lynn

Z. Mahmood (ed.), *Continued Rise of the Cloud*, Computer Communications and Network DOI 10.1007/978-1-4471-6452-4_12, pp 289–336, © Springer-Verlag London 2014

DOI 10.1007/978-1-4471-6452-4_16

This chapter was originally published as *Towards the Development of a Cloud Service Capability Assessment Framework* by Noel Carroll. At the request of Noel Carroll, Markus Helfert and Theo Lynn have been added as co-authors of the chapter.

Z. Mahmood (ed.), *Continued Rise of the Cloud,* Computer Communications and Networks, DOI 10.1007/978-1-4471-6452-4_16,
© Springer-Verlag London 2014

Index

Z. Mahmood (ed.), *Continued Rise of the Cloud,* Computer Communications and Networks, DOI 10.1007/978-1-4471-6452-4,
© Springer-Verlag London 2014

Printed in the United States
By Bookmasters